ROCKVILLE CAMPUS LIBRARY

WITHDRAWN FROM LIBRARY

CHELSEA HOUSE PUBLISHERS

Modern Critical Views

HENRY ADAMS
EDWARD ALBEE
A. R. AMMONS
MATTHEW ARNOLD
JOHN ASHBERY
W. H. AUDEN
JANE AUSTEN
JAMES BALDWIN
CHARLES BAUDELAIRE
SAMUEL BECKETT
SAUL BELLOW
THE BIBLE
ELIZABETH BISHOP
WILLIAM BLAKE
JORGE LUIS BORGES
ELIZABETH BOWEN
BERTOLT BRECHT
THE BRONTËS
ROBERT BROWNING
ANTHONY BURGESS
GEORGE GORDON, LORD BYRON
THOMAS CARLYLE
LEWIS CARROLL
WILLA CATHER
CERVANTES
GEOFFREY CHAUCER
KATE CHOPIN
SAMUEL TAYLOR COLERIDGE
JOSEPH CONRAD
CONTEMPORARY POETS
HART CRANE
STEPHEN CRANE
DANTE
CHARLES DICKENS
EMILY DICKINSON
JOHN DONNE & THE
  17th-CENTURY POETS
ELIZABETHAN DRAMATISTS
THEODORE DREISER
JOHN DRYDEN
GEORGE ELIOT
T. S. ELIOT
RALPH ELLISON
RALPH WALDO EMERSON
WILLIAM FAULKNER
HENRY FIELDING
F. SCOTT FITZGERALD
GUSTAVE FLAUBERT
E. M. FORSTER
SIGMUND FREUD
ROBERT FROST

ROBERT GRAVES
GRAHAM GREENE
THOMAS HARDY
NATHANIEL HAWTHORNE
WILLIAM HAZLITT
SEAMUS HEANEY
ERNEST HEMINGWAY
GEOFFREY HILL
FRIEDRICH HÖLDERLIN
HOMER
GERARD MANLEY HOPKINS
WILLIAM DEAN HOWELLS
ZORA NEALE HURSTON
HENRY JAMES
SAMUEL JOHNSON
BEN JONSON
JAMES JOYCE
FRANZ KAFKA
JOHN KEATS
RUDYARD KIPLING
D. H. LAWRENCE
JOHN LE CARRÉ
URSULA K. LE GUIN
DORIS LESSING
SINCLAIR LEWIS
ROBERT LOWELL
NORMAN MAILER
BERNARD MALAMUD
THOMAS MANN
CHRISTOPHER MARLOWE
CARSON MCCULLERS
HERMAN MELVILLE
JAMES MERRILL
ARTHUR MILLER
JOHN MILTON
EUGENIO MONTALE
MARIANNE MOORE
IRIS MURDOCH
VLADIMIR NABOKOV
JOYCE CAROL OATES
SEAN O'CASEY
FLANNERY O'CONNOR
EUGENE O'NEILL
GEORGE ORWELL
CYNTHIA OZICK
WALTER PATER
WALKER PERCY
HAROLD PINTER
PLATO
EDGAR ALLAN POE

POETS OF SENSIBILITY &
  THE SUBLIME
ALEXANDER POPE
KATHERINE ANNE PORTER
EZRA POUND
PRE-RAPHAELITE POETS
MARCEL PROUST
THOMAS PYNCHON
ARTHUR RIMBAUD
THEODORE ROETHKE
PHILIP ROTH
JOHN RUSKIN
J. D. SALINGER
GERSHOM SCHOLEM
WILLIAM SHAKESPEARE (3 vols.)
  HISTORIES & POEMS
  COMEDIES
  TRAGEDIES
GEORGE BERNARD SHAW
MARY WOLLSTONECRAFT SHELLEY
PERCY BYSSHE SHELLEY
EDMUND SPENSER
GERTRUDE STEIN
JOHN STEINBECK
LAURENCE STERNE
WALLACE STEVENS
TOM STOPPARD
JONATHAN SWIFT
ALFRED LORD TENNYSON
WILLIAM MAKEPEACE THACKERAY
HENRY DAVID THOREAU
LEO TOLSTOI
ANTHONY TROLLOPE
MARK TWAIN
JOHN UPDIKE
GORE VIDAL
VIRGIL
ROBERT PENN WARREN
EVELYN WAUGH
EUDORA WELTY
NATHANAEL WEST
EDITH WHARTON
WALT WHITMAN
OSCAR WILDE
TENNESSEE WILLIAMS
WILLIAM CARLOS WILLIAMS
THOMAS WOLFE
VIRGINIA WOOLF
WILLIAM WORDSWORTH
RICHARD WRIGHT
WILLIAM BUTLER YEATS

Further titles in preparation.

Modern Critical Views

JAMES JOYCE

Modern Critical Views

JAMES JOYCE

Edited with an introduction by

Harold Bloom

Sterling Professor of the Humanities
Yale University

1986
CHELSEA HOUSE PUBLISHERS
New York
New Haven   Philadelphia

PROJECT EDITORS: Emily Bestler, James Uebbing
ASSOCIATE EDITOR: Maria Behan
EDITORIAL COORDINATOR: Karyn Gullen Browne
EDITORIAL STAFF: Perry King, Bert Yaeger
DESIGN: Susan Lusk

Cover illustration by Frank Steiner

Copyright © 1986 by Chelsea House Publishers, a division of Chelsea House
Educational Communications, Inc.

Introduction copyright © 1986 by Harold Bloom

All rights reserved. No part of this publication may be reproduced or transmitted, in any
form or by any means, without the written permission of the publisher.

Printed and bound in the United States of America

Library of Congress Cataloging in Publication Data

James Joyce.
     (Modern critical views)
     Bibliography: p.
     Includes index.
     Summary: Nineteen critical essays on the Irish writer
and his works.
     1. Joyce, James, 1882–1941—Criticism and interpretation
—Addresses, essays, lectures. [1. Joyce, James,
1882–1941—Criticism and interpretation—Addresses,
essays, lectures. 2. English literature—Irish authors
—History and criticism—Addresses, essays, lectures]
I. Bloom, Harold. II. Series.
PR6019.09Z6335   1986   823'.912   85–25553
ISBN 0–87754–625–8

Chelsea House Publishers
Harold Steinberg, Chairman and Publisher
Susan Lusk, Vice President
A Division of Chelsea House Educational Communications, Inc.
133 Christopher Street, New York, NY 10014

Contents

Editor's Note

This book gathers together a representative selection of the best criticism available on the writings of James Joyce, arranged in chronological order of publication. The emphasis is on recent criticism, though I have begun the volume with Samuel Beckett's excursus on Dante, Bruno, Vico and Joyce, which was the splendor of *Our Exagimination Round his Factification for Incamination of Work in Progress* (1929). This is preceded by my "Introduction," a Bloomian excursus upon the Jewishness of Bloom and upon Joyce's agon with Shakespeare. Beckett's secret burden is Joyce's agon with the great Italians, and in some sense I find that the unintentional burden of S. L. Goldberg's meditation upon Joyce and Homer.

Richard Ellmann, Joyce's biographer and definitive scholar, prefers to see Joyce as a lord of eminent domain, beyond agon and anxious only to incorporate as many influences as he possibly can. The first of Ellmann's two pieces in this volume gives us Bloom as Shelleyan Prometheus, courageously defying the Citizen in the "Cyclops" episode. It is followed here by the novelist Anthony Burgess, with his unmatched description of "the Dublin sound" of Joyce's language. Harry Levin's ruminations upon the manuscript version of *Ulysses* are succeeded by Ellmann's second analysis, this time of those elements in Joyce's consciousness that conducted incessant guerrilla warfare against the institutions of Ireland, the Roman Catholic Church in particular. Hugh Kenner, pope of the alternative tradition to that of Ellmann in Joyce studies, wittily reads Molly as a returned Muse who is beyond mere objectivity.

A new movement in Joyce studies, much influenced by current modes of criticism, is represented by many of the subsequent essays. Jennifer Schiffer Levine's analysis of originality and repetition in *Finnegans Wake* and *Ulysses* emphasizes the reader's work in the process of continually reformulated speculations. Deborah Pope, considering Stephen's versions of heaven and hell in the *Portrait*, sees them as creative misreadings of one another. In an intricate tracing of the relation between literary ancestors or paternal figures and Joyce's obsessive themes of paternity, Mary T. Reynolds illuminates the complex stance that Joyce takes up toward Dante. With Karen Lawrence's account of the "Eumaeus" episode in *Ulysses*, we are shown how deliberate a defense Joyce made of his language against his own aesthetic heritage, and ultimately against all prior language.

The varieties of critical reading augment in diversity with the movement to Roland McHugh's admirable plain speaking about the experience that *Finnegans Wake* offers persistent common readers. This is counterbalanced by two notable Marxist critiques, with Fredric Jameson's placement of *Ulysses* in history, and an economical reading of Joyce's one drama, *Exiles*, by Raymond Williams. An attempt to counter male psychological criticism of Molly Bloom's concluding interior monologue is carried through with equal economy by Gabriele Schwab.

Francis Warner's judicial overview of Joyce's verse is followed by the late Sir William Empson's defense of Joyce's "intentions" in *Ulysses*, in a polemic aimed at the school of Kenner. A distinguished instance of a belated school, "Post-Structuralist Joyce," is provided by Daniel Ferrer's deconstructionist reverie upon the "Circe" episode. This book ends in a way fitting to Joyce, with a circular return to beginnings in *Dubliners*, perhaps the finest single volume of short stories in the English language. Patrick Parrinder's comprehensive survey demonstrates again how permanently Joyce recorded a crucial part not only of the moral history of his country, but of the literary culture of the West.

Introduction

I

It is an odd sensation to begin writing an introduction to a volume of Joyce criticism on June 16, 1985, particularly if one's name is Bloom. Poldy is, as Joyce intended, the most *complete* figure in modern fiction, if not indeed in all Western fiction, and so it is appropriate that he have a saint's day in the literary calendar: Bloomsday. He is, thankfully, no saint, but a mild, gentle sinner; in short, a good man. So good a man is he that even the critic Hugh Kenner, who in his earlier commentary saw Poldy as an instance of modern depravity, an Eliotic Jew as it were, in 1980 could call Joyce's hero "fit to live in Ireland without malice, without violence, without hate." How many are fit to live, in fact or fiction, in Ireland or America, without malice, without violence, without hate? Kenner, no sentimentalist, now finds in Poldy what the reader must find: a better person than oneself.

Richard Ellmann, Joyce's biographer, shrewdly says of Poldy that "he is not afraid that he will compromise his selfhood." Currently fashionable criticism, calling itself "Post-Structuralist Joyce," oddly assimilates Joyce to Barthes, Lacan, Derrida; producing a Poldy without a self, another floating signifier. But Joyce's Poldy, as Ellmann insists, is heroic and imaginative; his mimetic force allies him to the Wife of Bath, Falstaff and Sancho Panza, and like them his presence is overwhelming. Joyce's precursors were Dante and Shakespeare, and Poldy has a comprehensiveness and immediacy worthy of his ancestry. It is good to remember that, after Dante and Shakespeare, Joyce cared most for Wordsworth and Shelley among the poets. Wordsworth's heroic naturalism and Shelley's visionary skepticism find their way into Poldy also.

How Jewish is Poldy? Here I must dissent a touch from Ellmann, who says that when Poldy confronts the Citizen, he states an ethical view "more Christian than Judaic." Poldy has been unbelieving Jew, Protestant and Catholic, but his ethical affirmations are normative Jewish, as Joyce seems to have known better than Ellmann does. When Poldy gazes upon existence, he finds it good. The commonplace needs no hallowing for Poldy. Frank Budgen, taking the hint from Joyce, emphasizes how much older

Poldy seems than all the other inhabitants of Joyce's visionary Dublin. We do not think of Poldy as being thirty-eight, prematurely middle-aged, but rather as living in what the Hebrew Bible called *olam:* time without boundaries. Presumably, that is partly why Joyce chose to make his Ulysses Jewish rather than Greek. Unlike a modern Greek, Poldy is in surprising continuity with a lineage of which he has little overt knowledge. How different would the book have been if Joyce had centered on a Greek living in Dublin? The aura of exile would not be there. Joyce, the Dubliner in exile, tasting his own stoic version of a Dantesque bitterness, found in Poldy as wandering Jew what now seems his inevitable surrogate. Poldy, not Stephen, is Joyce's true image.

Yet Poldy is certainly more like Homer's Ulysses than like the Yahwist's Jacob. We see Poldy surviving the Cyclops, but not wrestling with one among the Elohim in order to win a new name for himself. Truly Jewgreek, Poldy has forsworn the Covenant, even if he cannot escape from having been chosen. Joyce, too, has abandoned the Church, but cannot escape the intellectual discipline of the Jesuits. Poldy's sense of election is a little more mysterious, or perhaps it is Joyce's sense of his hero's election that is the true mystery of the book. At the end of the Cyclops episode, Joyce evidently felt the necessity of distancing himself from Poldy, if only because literary irony fails when confronted by the heroic pathos of a creation that defies even Joyce's control.

> —Are you talking about the new Jersusalem? says the citizen.
> —I'm talking about injustice, says Bloom.
> —Right, says John Wyse. Stand up to it then with force like men.

But that is of course not Poldy's way. No interpolated sarcasm, however dramatically wrought, is able to modify the dignity of Poldy's rejoinder:

> —But it's no use, says he. Force, hatred, history, all that. That's not life for men and women, insult and hatred. And everybody knows that it's the very opposite of that that is really life.
> —What, says Alf.
> —Love, says Bloom. I mean the opposite of hatred.

Twelve delirious pages of hyperbole and phantasmagoria follow, detailing the forced exit of the noble Poldy from the pub, and ending in a grand send-up indeed:

> When, lo, there came about them all a great brightness and they beheld the chariot wherein He stood ascend to heaven. And they beheld Him in the chariot, clothed upon in the glory of the brightness, having raiment

as of the sun, fair as the moon and terrible that for awe they durst not look upon Him. And there came a voice out of heaven, calling: *Elijah! Elijah!* And he answered with a main cry: *Abba! Adonai!* And they beheld Him even Him, ben Bloom Elijah, amid clouds of angels ascend to the glory of the brightness at an angle of forty-five degrees over Donohoe's in Little Green Street like a shot off a shovel.

It is all in the juxtaposition of "ben Bloom Elijah" and "like a shot off a shovel," at once a majestic deflation and a complex apotropaic gesture on Joyce's own part. Like Falstaff and Sancho Panza, Poldy runs off with the book, and Joyce's strenuous ironies, dwarfing the wit of nearly all other authors, essentially are so many reaction-formations against his love for (and identity with) his extraordinary hero. Homer's Ulysses may be as complete as Poldy, but you wouldn't want to be in one boat with him (you would drown, he would survive). Poldy would comfort you in every sorrow, even as he empathizes so movingly with the pangs of women in childbirth.

Joyce was not Flaubert, who at once was Madame Bovary and yet was wholly detached from her, at least in aesthetic stance. But how do you maintain a fixed stance toward Poldy? Falstaff is the monarch of wit, and Sancho Panza the Pope of innocent cunning. Poldy's strength, as Joyce evidently intended, is in his completeness. "The complete man" is necessarily a trope, but for what? On one side, for range of affect, like Tennyson's Ulysses, Poldy is a part of all that he has met. His curiosity, his susceptibility, his compassion, his potential interest—these are infinite. On another side, for cognitive activity, Poldy, unlike Stephen, is certainly not brilliant, and yet he has a never-resting mind, as Ulysses must have. He can be said to have a Shakespearean mind, though he resembles no one in Shakespeare (a comparison of Poldy and Shylock is instructive). Poldy is neither Hamlet nor Falstaff, but perhaps he is Shakespeare, or Shakespeare reborn as James Joyce, even as Stephen is the younger Dante reincarnated as Joyce. We can think of Poldy as Horatio to Stephen's Hamlet, since Horatio represents us, the audience, and we represent Shakespeare. Poldy is our representative, and it is Joyce's greatest triumph that increasingly we represent him, as we always have and will represent Shakespeare.

Post-Structuralist Joyce never wearies of reminding us that Poldy is a trope, but it is truer to say that we are tropes for Poldy, who as a superminesis of essential nature is beyond us. I may never recover from a walk through a German park with a dear friend who is the most distinguished of post-Structuralists. When I remarked to him, in my innocent cunning, that Poldy was the most lovable person in Western fiction, I provoked him to the annoyed response that Poldy was not a person, but only language, and that Joyce, unlike myself, knew this very well. Joyce knew very well that Poldy was more than a person, but only in the sense that Poldy was a humane and humanized God, a God who had become truly a bereft father, anguishing for his lost Rudy. Poldy is not a person only if God is not a person, and the God of the Jews, for all his transcendental sublimities, is also very much a person and a personality, as befits his immanent sublimities. Surely the uniqueness of Yahweh, among all the rival godlings, is that Yahweh is complete. Yahweh is the complete God, even as Poldy is the complete man, and God, after all, like Poldy, is Jewish.

II

French post-Structuralism is of course only a belated modernism, since everything from abroad is absorbed so slowly in xenophobic Paris. French Hegel, French Freud, French Joyce are all after the event, as it were, just as French romanticism was a rather delayed phenomenon. French Joyce is about as close to the text of *Ulysses* and *Finnegans Wake* as Lacan is to the text of *Three Essays on the Theory of Sexuality* or Derrida to Hegel and Heidegger. Nor should they be, since cultural belatedness or Alexandrianism demands the remedy of misprision, or creative misreading. To say that "meaning" keeps its distance from Poldy is both to forget that Poldy is the Messiah (though which Messiah is not clear) and that one name (Kabbalistic) for Yahweh is "language." The difference between Joyce and French Joyce is that Joyce tropes God as language and the belated Parisians (and their agents) trope the Demiurge as language, which is to say that Joyce, heroic naturalist, was not a Gnostic and Lacan was (perhaps unknowingly).

As a knowing Gnostic, I lament the loss of Joycean heroic naturalism and of Poldy's natural heroism. Let them deconstruct Don Quixote; the results will be as sorrowful. Literary criticism is a mode which teaches us not only to read Poldy as Sancho Panza and Stephen as the Don, but more amiably takes us back to Cervantes, to read Sancho as Poldy. By a Borgesian blessing in the art of mistaken attribution, we then will learn to read not only *Hamlet* and the *Inferno* as written by Joyce, but *Don Quixote* as well, with the divine Sancho as an Irish Jew!

Joyce necessarily is closer to Shakespeare than to Cervantes, and Joyce's obsession with *Hamlet* is crucial in *Ulysses*. His famous reading of Hamlet, as expounded by Stephen, can be regarded as a subtle coming-to-terms with Shakespeare as his most imposing literary father in the English language. Ellmann, certainly the most reliable of all Joyce scholars, insisted that Joyce "exhibits none of that anxiety of influence which has been attributed to modern writers. . . . If Joyce had any anxiety, it was over not incorporating influences enough." This matter is perhaps more dialectical than Ellmann realized. Not Dante, but Shakespeare is Joyce's Virgil, as Ellmann also notes, and just as Dante's poetic voice matures even as Virgil fades out of the *Commedia,* so Shakespeare had to fade out of *Ulysses* even as Joyce's voice matured.

In Stephen's theory, Shakespeare is the dead king, rather than the young Hamlet, who becomes the type of the Romantic artist, Stephen himself. Shakespeare, like the ghost, has been betrayed, except than Anne Hathaway went Gertrude one better, and cuckolded the Bard with both his brothers. This sexual defeat has been intensified by Shakespeare's loss of the dark lady of the sonnets, and to his best friend, a kind of third brother. Shakespeare's revenge is to resurrect his own dead son, Hamnet, who enters the play as Prince Hamlet, with the purpose of vindicating his father's honor. Such a resurrected son appears to be free of the Oedipal ambivalences, and in Joyce's view does not lust after Gertrude or feel any jealousy, however repressed, for the dead father. So Stephen and Poldy, as two aspects of Shakespeare/Joyce, during the "Circe" episode gaze into a mirror and behold a transformed Shakespeare, beardless and frozen-faced ("rigid in facial paralysis"). I do not interpret this either as the view that Poldy and Stephen "amount only to a paralytic travesty of a Shakespeare" (W. M. Schutte) or that "Joyce warns us that he is working with near-identities, not perfect ones" (Ellmann). Rather, I take it as a sign of influence-anxiety, as the precursor Shakespeare mocking the ephebe Joyce: "Be like me, but you presume in attempting to be too much like me. You are merely a beardless version, rigid in facial paralysis, lacking my potency and my ease of countenance."

The obscene Buck Mulligan, Joyce's black beast, weakly misreads *Hamlet* as masturbation and Poldy as a pederast. Joyce himself, through Stephen, strongly misreads *Hamlet* as the cuckold's revenge, a play presumably likelier to have been written by Poldy than by Stephen. In a stronger misreading still, I would suggest that Joyce rewrites *Hamlet* so as to destroy the element in the play that most menaces him, which is the very different, uncannily disinterested Hamlet of Act V. Stephen quotes the subtle Sabellian heresy that the Father was Himself His Own Son. But what we may call the even subtler Shakespearean heresy (which is also Freudian) holds rather that the Son was Himself His Own Father. This is the Hamlet of Act V, who refers to his dead father only once, and then only as the king.

Joyce's Hamlet has no Oedipus complex. Shakespeare's Hamlet may have had one, but it passes away in the interval between Acts IV and V.

Stephen as the Prince does not convince me; Poldy as the ghost of the dead king, and so as Shakespeare/Joyce, is rather more troublesome. One wishes the ghost could be exorcised, leaving us with the fine trinity of Shakespeare/Poldy/Joyce, with Poldy as the transitional figure reconciling forerunner and latecomer, a sort of Messiah perhaps. Shakespeare is the original Testament or old aesthetic Law, while Joyce is the belated Testament or new aesthetic dispensation. Poldy is the inter-Testamentary figure, apocryphal and apocalyptic, and yet overwhelmingly a representation of life in the here and now. Joyce went on to write *Finnegans Wake*, the only legitimate rival to Proust's vast novel in the Western literature of our time. More than the difficulties, both real and imaginary, of the *Wake* have kept Joyce's common readers centered upon *Ulysses*. Earwicker is a giant hieroglyph; Poldy is a person, complete and loving, self-reliant, larger and more evocative even than his book.

SAMUEL BECKETT

Dante... Bruno. Vico.. Joyce

The danger is in the neatness of iden-
tifications. The conception of Philosophy and Philology as a pair of nigger
minstrels out of the Teatro dei Piccoli is soothing, like the contemplation
of a carefully folded ham-sandwich. Giambattista Vico himself could not
resist the attractiveness of such coincidence of gesture. He insisted on
complete identification between the philosophical abstraction and the empirical illustration, thereby annulling the absolutism of each conception—
hoisting the real unjustifiably clear of its dimensional limits, temporalising
that which is extratemporal. And now here am I, with my handful of
abstractions, among which notably: a mountain, the coincidence of contraries, the inevitability of cyclic evolution, a system of Poetics, and the
prospect of self-extension in the world of Mr. Joyce's *Work in Progress*.
There is the temptation to treat every concept like "a bass dropt neck fust
in till a bung crate," and make a really tidy job of it. Unfortunately such
an exactitude of application would imply distortion in one of two directions.
Must we wring the neck of a certain system in order to stuff it into a
contemporary pigeon-hole, or modify the dimensions of that pigeon-hole
for the satisfaction of the analogymongers? Literary criticism is not book-
keeping.

Giambattista Vico was a practical roundheaded Neapolitan. It
pleases Croce to consider him as a mystic, essentially speculative, *"disdeg-
noso dell' empirismo."* It is a surprising interpretation, seeing that more than
three-fifths of his *Scienza Nuova* is concerned with empirical investigation.

From *James Joyce/Finnegans Wake: A Symposium. Our Exagimination Round His Factification
for Incamination of Work in Progress.* Copyright © 1929 by Sylvia Beach. New Directions
Books.

Croce opposes him to the reformative materialistic school of Ugo Grozio, and absolves him from the utilitarian preoccupations of Hobbes, Spinoza, Locke, Bayle and Machiavelli. All this cannot be swallowed without protest. Vico defines Providence as: *"una mente spesso diversa ed alle volte tutta contraria e sempre superiore ad essi fini particolari che essi uomini si avevano propositi; dei quali fini ristretti fatti mezzi per servire a fini più ampi, gli ha sempre adoperati per conservare l'umana generazione in questa terra."* What could be more definitely utilitarianism? His treatment of the origin and functions of poetry, language and myth, as will appear later, is as far removed from the mystical as it is possible to imagine. For our immediate purpose, however, it matters little whether we consider him as a mystic or as a scientific investigator; but there are no two ways about considering him as an *innovator*. His division of the development of human society into three ages: Theocratic, Heroic, Human (civilized), with a corresponding classification of language: Hicroglyphic (sacred), Metaphorical (poetic), Philosophical (capable of abstraction and generalisation), was by no means new, although it must have appeared so to his contemporaries. He derived this convenient classification from the Egyptians, via Herodotus. At the same time it is impossible to deny the originality with which he applied and developed its implications. His exposition of the ineluctable circular progression of Society was completely new, although the germ of it was contained in Giordano Bruno's treatment of identified contraries. But it is in Book 2, described by himself as *"tutto il corpo . . . la chiave maestra . . . dell opera"* that appears the unqualified originality of his mind; here he evolved a theory of the origins of poetry and language, the significance of myth, and the nature of barbaric civilization that must have appeared nothing less than an impertinent outrage against tradition. These two aspects of Vico have their reverberations, their reapplications—without, however, receiving the faintest explicit illustration—in *Work in Progress*.

It is first necessary to condense the thesis of Vico, the scientific historian. In the beginning was the thunder: the thunder set free Religion, in its most objective and unphilosophical form—idolatrous animism: Religion produced Society, and the first social men were the cave-dwellers, taking refuge from a passionate Nature: this primitive family life receives its first impulse towards development from the arrival of terrified vagabonds: admitted, they are the first slaves: growing stronger, they exact agrarian concessions, and a despotism has evolved into a primitive feudalism: the cave becomes a city, and the feudal system a democracy: then an anarchy: this is corrected by a return to monarchy: the last stage is a tendency towards interdestruction: the nations are dispersed, and the Phoenix of

Society arises out of their ashes. To this six-termed social progression corresponds a six-termed progression of human motives: necessity, utility,
convenience, pleasure, luxury, abuse of luxury: and their incarnate manifestations: Polyphemus, Achilles, Caesar and Alexander, Tiberius, Cali-
gula and Nero. At this point Vico applies Bruno—though he takes very
good care not to say so—and proceeds from rather arbitrary data to philosophical abstraction. There is no difference, says Bruno between the smallest possible chord and the smallest possible arc, no difference between the
infinite circle and the straight line. The maxima and minima particular
contraries are one and indifferent. Minimal heat equals minimal cold.
Consequently transmutations are circular. The principle (minimum) of one
contrary takes its movement from the principle (maximum) of another.
Therefore not only do the minima coincide with the minima, the maxima
with the maxima, but the minima with the maxima in the succession of
transmutations. Maximal speed is a state of rest. The maximum of corruption and the minimum of generation are identical: in principle, corruption
is generation. And all things are ultimately identified with God, the universal monad, Monad of monads. From these considerations Vico evolved
a Science and Philosophy of History. It may be an amusing exercise to take
an historical figure, such as Scipio, and label him No. 3; it is of no ultimate
importance. What is of ultimate importance is the recognition that the
passage from Scipio to Caesar is as inevitable as the passage from Caesar
to Tiberius, since the flowers of corruption in Scipio and Caesar are the
seeds of vitality in Caesar and Tiberius. Thus we have the spectacle of a
human progression that depends for its movement on individuals, and which
at the same time is independent of individuals in virtue of what appears to
be a preordained cyclicism. It follows that History is neither to be considered
as a formless structure, due exclusively to the achievements of individual
agents, nor as possessing reality apart from and independent of them, accomplished behind their backs in spite of them, the work of some superior
force, variously known as Fate, Chance, Fortune, God. Both these views,
the materialistic and the transcendental, Vico rejects in favour of the
rational. Individuality is the concretion of universality, and every individual
action is at the same time superindividual. The individual and the universal
cannot be considered as distinct from each other. History, then, is not the
result of Fate or Chance—in both cases the individual would be separated
from his product—but the result of a Necessity that is not Fate, of a Liberty
that is not Chance (compare Dante's "yoke of liberty"). This force he called
Divine Providence, with his tongue, one feels, very much in his cheek.
And it is to this Providence that we must trace the three institutions

common to every society: Church, Marriage, Burial. This is not Bossuet's Providence, transcendental and miraculous, but immanent and the stuff itself of human life, working by natural means. Humanity is its work in itself. God acts on her, but by means of her. Humanity is divine, but no man is divine. This social and historical classification is clearly adapted by Mr. Joyce as a structural convenience—or inconvenience. His position is in no way a philosophical one. It is the detached attitude of Stephen Dedalus in *Portrait of the Artist,* who describes Epictetus to the Master of Studies as "an old gentleman who said that the soul is very like a bucketful of water." The lamp is more important than the lamp-lighter. By structural I do not only mean a bold outward division, a bare skeleton for the housing of material. I mean the endless substantial variations on these three beats, and interior intertwining of these three themes into a decoration of arabesques—decoration and more than decoration. Part 1 is a mass of past shadow, corresponding therefore to Vico's first human institution, Religion, or to his Theocratic age, or simply to an abstraction—Birth. Part 2 is the lovegame of the children, corresponding to the second institution, Marriage, or to the Heroic age, or to an abstraction—Maturity. Part 3 is passed in sleep, corresponding to the third institution, Burial, or to the Human age, or to an abstraction—Corruption. Part 4 is the day beginning again, and corresponds to Vico's Providence, or to the transition from the Human to the Theocratic, or to an abstraction—Generation. Mr. Joyce does not take birth for granted, as Vico seems to have done. So much for the dry bones. The consciousness that there is a great deal of the unborn infant in the lifeless octogenarian, and a great deal of both in the man at the apogee of his life's curve, removes all the stiff interexclusiveness that is often the danger in neat construction. Corruption is not excluded from Part 1 nor maturity from Part 3. The four "lovedroyd curdinals" are presented on the same plane—"his element curdinal numen and his enement curdinal marrying and his epulent curdinal weisswasch and his eminent curdinal Kay o' Kay!" There are numerous references to Vico's four human institutions—Providence counting as one! "A good clap, a fore wedding, a bad wake, tell hell's well": "their weatherings and their marryings and their buryings and their natural selections": "the lightning look, the birding cry, awe from the grave, everflowing on our times": "by four hands of forethought the first babe of reconcilement is laid in its last cradle of hume sweet hume."

Apart from this emphasis on the tangible conveniences common to Humanity, we find frequent expressions of Vico's insistence on the inevitable character of every progression—or retrogression: "The Vico road goes round and round to meet where terms begin. Still onappealed to by the cycles and onappalled by the recoursers, we feel all serene, never you fret, as regards our dutyful cask. . . . [B]efore there was a man at all in Ireland there was a lord at Lucan. We only wish everyone was as sure of anything in this watery world as we are of everything in the newlywet fellow that is bound to follow. . . ." "The efferfreshpainted livy in beautific repose upon the silence of the dead from Pharoph the next first down to ramescheckles the last bust thing." "In fact, under the close eyes of the inspectors the traits featuring the chiaroscuro coalesce, their contrarieties eliminated, in one stable somebody similarly as by the providential warring of heartshaker with housebreaker and of dramdrinker against freethinker our social something bowls along bumpily, experiencing a jolting series of prearranged disappointments, down the long lane of (it's as semper as oxhousehumper) generations, more generations and still more generations"—this last a case of Mr. Joyce's rare subjectivism. In a word, here is all humanity circling with fatal monotony about the Providential fulcrum—"the convoy wheeling encirculing abound the gigantig's lifetree." Enough has been said, or at least enough has been suggested, to show how Vico is substantially present in the Work in Progress. Passing to the Vico of the Poetics we hope to establish an even more striking, if less direct, relationship.

Vico rejected the three popular interpretations of the poetic spirit, which considered poetry as either an ingenious popular expression of philosophical conceptions, or an amusing social diversion, or an exact science within the reach of everyone in possession of the recipe. Poetry, he says, was born of curiosity, daughter of ignorance. The first men had to create matter by the force of their imagination, and "poet" means "creator." Poetry was the first operation of the human mind, and without it thought could not exist. Barbarians, incapable of analysis and abstraction, must use their fantasy to explain what their reason cannot comprehend. Before articulation comes song; before abstract terms, metaphors. The figurative character of the oldest poetry must be regarded, not as sophisticated confectionery, but as evidence of a poverty-stricken vocabulary and of a disability to achieve abstraction. Poetry is essentially the antithesis of Metaphysics: Metaphysics purge the mind of the senses and cultivate the disembodiment of the spiritual; Poetry is all passion and feeling and animates the inanimate, Metaphysics are most perfect when most concerned with universals; Poetry, when most concerned with particulars. Poets are the sense, philosophers the intelligence of humanity. Considering the Scholastics' axiom: "*nientee nell'intelleto che prima non sia nel senso"* it follows that poetry is a prime condition of philosophy and civilization. The primitive animistic movement was a manifestation of the *"forma poetica dello spirito."*

His treatment of the origin of language proceeds along similar lines. Here again he rejected the materialistic and transcendental views: the one declaring that language was nothing but a polite and conventional symbolism; the other, in desperation, describing it as a gift from the Gods. As before, Vico is the rationalist, aware of the natural and inevitable growth of language. In its first dumb form, language was gesture. If a man wanted to say "sea," he pointed to the sea. With the spread of animism this gesture was replaced by the word: "Neptune." He directs our attention to the fact that every need of life, natural, moral and economic, has its verbal expression in one or other of the 30,000 Greek divinities. This is Homer's "language of the Gods." Its evolution through poetry to a highly civilized vehicle, rich in abstract and technical terms, was as little fortuitous as the evolution of society itself. Words have their progressions as well as social phases. "Forest-cabin-village-city-academy" is one rough progression. Another: "mountain-plain-riverbank." And every word expands with psychological inevitability. Take the Latin word: "Lex."

1.	Lex	=	Crop of acorns.
2.	Ilex	=	Tree that produces acorns.
3.	Legere	=	To gather.
4.	Aquilex	=	He that gathers the waters.
5.	Lex	=	Gathering together of peoples, public assembly.
6.	Lex	=	Law.
7.	Legere	=	To gather together letters into a word, to read.

The root of any word whatsoever can be traced back to some pre-lingual symbol. This early inability to abstract the general from the particular produced the Type-names. It is the child's mind over again. The child extends the names of the first familiar objects to other strange objects in which he is conscious of some analogy. The first men, unable to conceive the abstract idea of "poet" or "herd", named every hero after the first hero, every poet after the first poet. Recognizing this custom of designating a number of individuals by the names of their prototypes, we can explain various classical and mythological mysteries. Hermes is the prototype of the Egyptian inventor: so for Romulus, the great law-giver, and Hercules, the Greek hero: so for Homer. Thus Vico asserts the spontaneity of language and denies the dualism of poetry and language. Similarly, poetry is the foundation of writing. When language consisted of gesture, the spoken and the written were identical. Hieroglyphics, or sacred language, as he calls it, were not the invention of philosophers for the mysterious expression of profound thought, but the common necessity of primitive peoples. Convenience only begins to assert itself at a far more advanced stage of civilization, in the form of alphabetism. Here Vico, implicitly at least, distinguishes between writing and direct expression. In such direct expression, form and content are inseparable. Examples are the medals of the Middle Ages, which bore no inscription and were a mute testimony to the feebleness of conventional alphabetic writing: and the flags of our own day. As with Poetry and Language, so with Myth. Myth, according to Vico, is neither an allegorical expression of general philosophical axioms (Conti, Bacon), nor a derivative from particular peoples, as for instance the Hebrews or Egyptians, nor yet the work of isolated poets, but an historical statement of fact, of actual contemporary phenomena, actual in the sense that they were created out of necessity by primitive minds, and firmly believed. Allegory implies a threefold intellectual operation: the construction of a message of general significance, the preparation of a fabulous form, and an exercise of considerable technical difficulty in uniting the two, an operation totally beyond the reach of the primitive mind. Moreover, if we consider the myth as being essentially allegorical, we are not obliged to accept the form in which it is cast as a statement of fact. But we know that the actual creators of these myths gave full credence to their face-value. Jove was no symbol: he was terribly real. It was precisely their superficial metaphorical character that made them intelligible to people incapable of receiving anything more abstract than the plain record of objectivity.

Such is a painful exposition of Vico's dynamic treatment of Language, Poetry and Myth. He may still appear as a mystic to some: if so, a mystic that rejects the transcendental in every shape and form as a factor in human development, and whose Providence is not divine enough to do without the cooperation of Humanity.

On turning to the *Work in Progress* we find that the mirror is not so convex. Here is direct expression—pages and pages of it. And if you don't understand it, Ladies and Gentlemen, it is because you are too decadent to receive it. You are not satisfied unless form is so strictly divorced from content that you can comprehend the one almost without bothering to read the other. This rapid skimming and absorption of the scant cream of sense is made possible by what I may call a continuous process of copious intellectual salivation. The form that is an arbitrary and independent phenomenon can fulfil no higher function than that of stimulus for a tertiary or quartary conditioned reflex of dribbling comprehension. When Miss Rebecca West clears her desk for a sorrowful deprecation of the Narcisstic element in Mr. Joyce by the purchase of 3 hats, one feels that she might very well wear her bib at all her intellectual banquets, or alternatively, assert a more noteworthy control over her salivary glands than is possible for Monsieur Pavlorom's unfortunate dogs. The title of this book is a good example of a form carrying a strict inner determination. It should be proof against the usual volley of cerebral sniggers: and it may suggest to some a dozen incredulous Joshuas prowling around the Queen's Hall, springing their tuning-forks lightly against finger-nails that have not yet been refined out of existence. Mr. Joyce has a word to say to you on the subject: "Yet to concentrate solely on the literal sense or even the psychological content of any document to the sore neglect of the enveloping facts themselves circumstantiating it is just as harmful; etc." And another: "Who in his hearts doubts either that the facts of feminine clothiering are there all the time or that the feminine fiction, stranger than the facts, is there also at the same time, only a little to the rere? Or that one may be separated from the other? Or that both may be contemplated simultaneously? Or that each may be taken up in turn and considered apart from the other?"

Here form *is* content, content *is* form. You complain that this stuff is not written in English. It is not written at all. It is not to be read—or rather it is not only to be read. It is to be looked at and listened to. His writing is not *about* something; *it is that something itself.* (A fact that has been grasped by an eminent English novelist and historian whose work is in complete opposition to Mr. Joyce's). When the sense is sleep, the words go to sleep. (See the end of *Anna Livial.*) When the sense is dancing, the words dance. Take the passage at the end of Shaun's pastoral: "To stirr up love's young fizz I tilt with this bridle's cup champagne, dimming douce from her peepair of hideseeks tight squeezed on my snowybreasted and while my pearlies in their sparkling wisdom are nippling her bubblets I swear (and let you swear) by the bumper round of my poor old snaggletooth's solidbowel I ne'er will prove I'm untrue to (theare!) you liking so long as my hole looks. Down." The language is drunk. The very words are tilted and effervescent. How can we qualify this general esthetic vigilance without which we cannot hope to snare the sense which is for ever rising to the surface of the form and becoming the form itself? St. Augustine puts us on the track of a word with his *"intendere"*; Dante has: *"Donne ch'avete intelletto d'amore,"* and *"Voi che, intendendo, il terzo ciel movete"*; but his *"intendere"* suggests a strictly intellectual operation. When an Italian says to-day *"Ho inteso,"* he means something between *"Ho udito"* and *"Ho capito,"* a sensuous untidy art of intellection. Perhaps "apprehension" is the most satisfactory English word. Stephen says to Lynch: "Temporal or spatial, the esthetic image is first luminously apprehended as selfbounded and selfcontained upon the immeasurable background of space or time which is not it. . . . You apprehend its wholeness." There is one point to make clear: the Beauty of *Work in Progress* is not presented in space alone, since its adequate apprehension depends as much on its visibility as on its audibility. There is a temporal as well as a spatial unity to be apprehended. Substitute "and" for "or" in the quotation, and it becomes obvious why it is as inadequate to speak of "reading" *Work in Progress* as it would be extravagant to speak of "apprehending" the work of the late Mr. Nat Gould. Mr. Joyce has desophisticated language. And it is worth while remarking that no language is so sophisticated as English. It is abstracted to death. Take the word "doubt": it gives us hardly any sensuous suggestion of hesitancy, of the necessity for choice, of static irresolution. Whereas the German "Zweifel" does, and, in lesser degree, the Italian "dubitare." Mr. Joyce recognises how inadequate "doubt" is to express a state of extreme uncertainty, and replaces it by "in twosome twiminds." Nor is he by any means the first to recognize the importance of treating words as something more than mere polite symbols. Shakespeare uses fat, greasy words to express corruption: "Duller shouldst thou be than the fat weed that rots itself in death on Lethe wharf." We hear the ooze squelching all through Dickens's description of the Thames in *Great Expectations*. This writing that you find so obscure is a quintessential extraction of language and painting and gesture, with all the inevitable clarity of the old inarticulaton. Here is the savage economy of hieroglyphics. Here words are not the polite contortions of 20th century printer's ink. They are alive. They elbow their way on to the page, and glow and blaze and fade and disappear. "Brawn is my name and broad is my nature and I've breit on my brow and all's right with every feature and I'll brune this bird or Brown Bess's bung's gone bandy." This is Brawn blowing with a light gust through the trees or Brawn passing with the sunset. Because the wind in the trees means as little to you as the evening prospect from the Piazzale Michelangiolo—though you accept them both because your non-acceptance would be of no significance, this little adventure of Brawn means nothing to you—and you do not accept it, even though here also your non-acceptance is of no significance. H. C. Earwigger, too, is not content to be mentioned like a shilling-shocker villain, and then dropped until the exigencies of the narrative require that he be again referred to. He continues to suggest himself for a couple of pages, by means of repeated permutations on his "normative letters," as if to say: "This is all about me, H. C. Earwigger: don't forget this is all about me!" This inner elemental vitality and corruption of expression imparts a furious restlessness to the form, which is admirably suited to the purgatorial aspect of the work. There is an endless verbal germination, maturation, putrefaction, the cyclic dynamism of the intermediate. This reduction of various expressive media to their primitive economic directness, and the fusion of these primal essences into an assimilated medium for the exteriorisation of thought, is pure Vico, and Vico, applied to the problem of style. But Vico is reflected more explicitly than by a distillation of disparate poetic ingredients into a synthetical syrup. We notice that there is little or no attempt at subjectivism or abstraction, no attempt at metaphysical generalisation. We are presented with a statement of the particular. It is the old myth: the girl on the dirt track, the two washerwomen on the banks of the river. And there is considerable animism: the mountain "abhearing," the river puffing her old doudheen. (See the beautiful passage beginning: "First she let her hair fall and down it flussed.") We have Type-names: Isolde—any beautiful girl: Earwigger—Guinness's Brewery, the Wellington monument, the Phoenix Park, anything that occupies an extremely comfortable position between the two stools. Anna Livia herself, mother of Dublin, but no more the only mother than Zoroaster was the only oriental stargazer. "Teems of times and happy returns. The same anew. Ordovico or viricordo. Anna was, Livia is, Plurabelle's to be. Northmen's thing made Southfolk's place, but how-multyplurators made eachone in person." Basta! Vico and Bruno are here, and more substantially than would appear from this swift survey of the question. For the benefit of those who enjoy a parenthetical sneer, we would draw attention to the fact that when Mr. Joyce's early pamphlet *The Day of Rabblement* appeared, the local philosophers were thrown into a state of some bewilderment by a reference in the first line to "The Nolan." They finally succeeded in identifying this mysterious individual with one of the obscurer ancient Irish kings. In the present work he appears frequently as "Browne & Nolan," the name of a very remarkable Dublin Bookseller and Stationer.

To justify our title, we must move North. *"Sovra'l bel fiume d' Arno alla gran villa."* Between *"colui per lo cuiverso—il meonio cantor non è più solo"* and the *"still to-day insufficiently malestimated notesnatcher, Shem the Penman,"* there exists considerable circumstantial similarity. They both saw how worn out and threadbare was the conventional language of cunning literary artificers, both rejected an approximation to a universal language. If English is not yet so definitely a polite necessity as Latin was in the Middle Ages, at least one is justified in declaring that its position in relation to other European languages is to a great extent that of mediaeval Latin to the Italian dialects. Dante did not adopt the vulgar out of any kind of local jingoism nor out of any determination to assert the superiority of Tuscan to all its rivals as a form of spoken Italian. On reading his *De Vulgari Eloquentia* we are struck by his complete freedom from civic intolerance. He attacks the world's Portadownians: *"Nam quicumque tamobseenae rationis est, ut locum suae nationis delitosissimmcredat esse sub sole, huiceliam proe eunctis propriam volgare licetur, idest maternam locutionem. Nos autem, cui mundus est patria . . . etc."* When he comes to examine the dialects he finds Tuscan *"turpissimum . . . fere omnes Tusei in suo iurpiloguio obtusi . . . non restat in dubio quin aliud sit vulgare quod quaerimus quam quod attingit populus Tuscanorum."* His conclusion is that the corruption common to all the dialects makes it impossible to select one rather than another as an adequate literary form, and that he who would write in the vulgar must assemble the purest elements from each dialect and construct a synthetic language that would at least possess more than a circumscribed local interest: which is precisely what he did. He did not write in Florentine any more than in Neapolitan. He wrote a vulgar that *could* have been spoken by an ideal Italian who had assimilated what was best in all the dialects of his country, but which in fact was certainly not spoken nor ever had been. Which disposes of the capital objection that might be made against this attractive parallel between Dante and Mr. Joyce in the question of language, i.e. that at least Dante wrote what was being spoken in the streets of his own town, whereas no creature in heaven or earth ever spoke the language of *Work in Progress.* It is reasonable to admit that an international phenomenon might be capable of speaking it, just as in 1300 none but an interregional phenomenon could have spoken the language of the Divine Comedy. We are inclined to forget that Dante's literary public was Latin, that the form of his Poem was to be judged by Latin eyes and ears, by a Latin Esthetic intolerant of innovation, and which could handly fail to be irritated by the substitution of *"Nel mezzo del cammin di nostra vita"* with its "barbarous" directness for the suave elegance of: *"Ultima regna canam, fluido contermina mundo,"* just as English eyes and ears prefer: "Smoking his favourite pipe in the sacred presence of ladies" to: "Rauking his flavourite turfco in the smukking precincts of lydias." Boccaccio did not jeer at the *"piedi sozzi"* of the peacock that Signora Alighieri dreamed about.

I find two well made caps in the *Convivio*, one to fit the collective noodle of the monodialectical arcadians whose fury is precipitated by a failure to discover "innocefree" in the Concise Oxford Dictionary and who qualify as the "ravings of a Bedlamite" the formal structure raised by Mr. Joyce after years of patient and inspired labour: *"Questi sono da chiamare pecore e non uomini; chè se una pecora si gittasse da una ripa di mille passi, tutte l'altre le andrebbono dietro; se una pecora per alcuna cagione al passare d'una strada salia, tutte le altre saltano, eziando nulla veggendo da saltare. E io ne vidi già molte in un pozzo saltare, per una che dentro vi salto, forse credendo di saltare un muno.* " And the other for Mr. Joyce, biologist in words: *Questo* (formal innovation) *sarà luce nuova, sole nuovo, il quale sorgerà ore l'usaio tramonterà e darà luce a coloro che sono in tenebre e in oscurità per lo usato sole che a loro non luce.* And, lest he should pull it down over his eyes and laugh behind the peak, I translate *"in tenebre e in oscurità"* by "bored to extinction." (Dante makes a curous mistake speaking of the origin of language, when he rejects the authority of Genesis that Eve was the first to speak, when she addressed the Serpent. His incredulity is amusing *"inconvenienter pulatur tam egregium humani generis actum, vel prius quam a viro, foemina profluisse."* But before Eve was born, "the animals were given names by Adam," the man who "first said goo to a goose." Moreover it is explicitly stated that the choice of names was left entirely to Adam, so that there is not the slightest Biblical authority for the conception of language as a direct gift of God, any more than there is any intellectual authority for conceiving that we are indebted for the "Concert" to the individual who used to buy paint for Giorgione).

We know very little about the immediate reception accorded to Dante's mighty vindication of the "vulgar," but we can form our own opinions when, two centuries later, we find Castiglione splitting more than a few hairs concerning the respective advantages of Latin and Italian, and Poliziano writing the dullest of dull Latin Elegies to justify his existence as the author of *Orfeo* and the *Stanze*. We may also compare, if we think it worth while, the storm of ecclesiastical abuse raised by Mr. Joyce's work, and the treatment that the Divine Comedy must certainly have received from the same source. His Contemporary Holiness might have swallowed the crucifixion of *"lo sommo Giove"* and all it stood for, but he could scarcely have looked with favour on the spectacle of three of his immediate predecessors plunged head-foremost in the fiery stone of Malebolge, nor yet the identification of the Papacy in the mystical procession of Terrestial Paradise with a *"puttana sciolta."* The *De Monarchia* was burnt publicly under Pope Giovanni XXII at the instigation of Cardinal Beltrando and the bones of its author would have suffered the same fate but for the interference of an influential man of letters, Pino della Tosa. Another point of comparison is the preoccupation with the significance of numbers. The death of Beatrice inspired nothing less than a highly complicated poem dealing with the importance of the number 3 in her life. Dante never ceased to be obsessed by this number. Thus the Poem is divided into three Can-tiche, each composed of 33 Canti, and written in terza rima. Why, Mr. Joyce seems to say, should there be four legs to a table, and four to a horse, and four seasons and four Gospels and four Provinces in Ireland? Why twelve Tables of the Law, and twelve Apostles and twelve months and twelve Napoleonic marshals and twelve men in Florence called Ottolenghi? Why should the Armistice be celebrated at the eleventh hour of the elev-enth day of the eleventh month? He cannot tell you because he is not God Almighty, but in a thousand years he will tell you, and in the meantime must be content to know why horses have not five legs, nor three. He is conscious that things with a common numerical characteristic tend towards a very significant interrelationship. This preoccupation is freely translated in his present work: see the "Question and Answer" chapter, and the Four speaking through the child's brain. They are the four winds as much as the four Provinces, and the four Episcopal Sees as much as either.

A last word about the Purgatories. Dante's is conical and conse-quently implies culmination. Mr. Joyce's is spherical and excludes culmi-nation. In the one there is an ascent from real vegetation—Ante-Purgatory, to ideal vegetation—Terrestial Paradise: in the other there is no ascent and no ideal vegetation. In the one, absolute progression and a guaranteed consummation: in the other, flux—progression or retrogression, and an apparent consummation. In the one movement is unidirectional, and a step forward represents a net advance: in the other movement is non-directional—or multi-directional, and a step forward is, by definition, a step back. Dante's Terrestial Paradise is the carriage entrance to a Paradise that is not terrestial: Mr. Joyce's Terrestial Paradise is the tradesmen's entrance on to the sea-shore. Sin is an impediment to movement up the cone, and a condition of movement round the sphere. In what sense, then, is Mr. Joyce's work purgatorial? In the absolute absence of the Absolute. Hell is the static lifelessness of unrelieved viciousness. Paradise the static lifelessness of unrelieved immaculation. Purgatory a flood of movement and vitality released by the conjunction of these two elements. There is a continuous purgatorial process at work, in the sense that the vicious circle of humanity is being achieved, and this achievement depends on the re-current predomination of one of two broad qualities. No resistance, no eruption, and it is only in Hell and Paradise that there are no eruptions, that there can be none, need be none. On this earth that is Purgatory, Vice and Virtue—which you may take to mean any pair of large contrary human factors—must in turn be purged down to spirits of rebelliousness.

Then the dominant crust of the Vicious or Virtuous sets, resistance is provided, the explosion duly takes place and the machine proceeds. And no more than this; neither prize nor penalty; simply a series of stimulants to enable the kitten to catch its tail. And the partially purgatorial agent? The partially purged.

S. L. GOLDBERG

Homer and the Nightmare of History

At the beginning, Stephen's crisis is portrayed in terms of his rejection of Mulligan, or rather of the image of him Mulligan wishes to impose. Against Mulligan's easy compromise with the material values he affects to despise, and his possessiveness and aesthetic provinciality—both of which are neatly exemplified in *his* naming of the tower in which they live the *omphalos*—Stephen opposes his scorn in return, a scrupulous evasion of commitment, and a contemptuous compliance with Mulligan's desire for the key to the Martello tower. When Mulligan (and the peasant milk-woman whose respect for him identifies the nature of his power) usurp what Stephen regards as his place, he is ready to go. The key is, of course, a symbol of his attachment to a centre; he is willing enough to give it up when he feels the centre (home and country) usurped, but he goes with the burden of bitterness. And as Wyndham Lewis and Mr. Kenner have pointed out, his emotional attitudes do seem rather theatrical. In this first chapter, he gives the impression of posturing—an impression only the more heightened by the contrast with his more private attitudes as they are revealed in the third chapter ("Proteus"): the rigid and somewhat operatic posture largely dissolves once we see him from the inside. Here, in "Telemachus," he is presenting an image of himself to the world; but he is presenting it in deliberate opposition to those Mulligan and others wish him to adopt. His own image may be false and immature; theirs, he

From *The Classical Temper: A Study of James Joyce's "Ulysses."* Copyright © 1961 by S. L. Goldberg. Barnes and Nobel Books, and Chatto and Windus, Ltd.

feels, would involve a fundamental lie to his true nature and vocation. "To discover the mode of life or of art whereby [his] spirit could express itself in unfettered freedom": his own youthful image, inadequate as it is already beginning to appear to him, at least offers a negative ideal, and he uses it as a shield. If he cannot be much more positive, he does know what he does not want.

The waves of his personal crisis spread wider than the immediate struggle with Mulligan, however. For one thing, he is entangled with a kinetic remorse, a sense of guilt arising from his rejection of Roman Catholicism and the fear that his rejection may have contributed to his mother's death. This, it must be said, is an aspect of his character that does seem wholly theatrical, an unpleasant combination of self-accusation, self-pity and pride. He can evidently see through the current "romantic" and pretentious twaddle about Ireland, as his speculations about the milk-woman suggest. But although he savours that sentimentality with a dry irony, it is in fact very like many of his own thoughts about his mother:

> In a dream, silently, she had come to him, her wasted body within its loose graveclothes giving off an odour of wax and rosewood, her breath bent over him with mute secret words, a faint odour of wetted ashes.
> Her glazing eyes, staring out of death, to shake and bend my soul. On me alone. The ghostcandle to light her agony. Ghostly light on the tortured face. Her hoarse loud breath rattling in horror, while all prayed on their knees. Her eyes on me to strike me down. *Liliata rutilantium te confessorum turma circumdet; iubilantium te virginum chorus excipiat.*

Yet it is worth noticing that, even despite the self-pity, the unfortunately Gothic horrors, and the overelaborate cadences (which it is hard to be quite sure whether to ascribe to Stephen or to Joyce), the passage does conclude with an instinctive, and significantly direct, cry for freedom and life:

> Ghoul! Chewer of corpses!
> No, mother.
> Let me be and let me live.

It is hardly a conscious critical response, an appeal to ideals positively held; Stephen is too divided for that. It is still a kinetic reaction, but it is very much in the right direction.

Similarly with the other false images of himself: he regards them, as he had regarded them in the *Portrait*, as nets to be avoided. The Englishman, Haines, comments,

—After all, I should think you are able to free yourself. You are your own master, it seems to me.

    —I am the servant of two masters, Stephen said, an English and an Italian. . . .

    —And a third, Stephen said, there is who wants me for odd jobs.

As Haines replies, "It seems history is to blame." To Stephen the past does seem almost overwhelmingly determinant. He sees tradition not as a lib-erating force but (with a more intimate knowledge of some traditions than has every *laudator temporis acti*) as constricting and deadening. Yet again, although his freedom seems little more than the minimum of mere escape, he is shown groping towards something more. Carefully placed beside this conversation with Haines is a passage about a man drowned in the bay, which reinforces the point already implicit in Stephen's rejection of possible masters. Throughout *Ulysses* the sea appears as a symbol of the chaotic flux of experience, the element; drowning is defeat, submergence, the death of the spirit in the overwhelming flood of kinetic appetencies. Stephen fears death by water. The drowned man objectifies his fear of suffocation, his need to rise above the waves, to swim in the element—in other words, to achieve a free *stasis* of spirit by understanding and accepting himself, his predicament, and his necessities. He must, as he clearly realizes, launch out. When the chapter ends, he is literally homeless. We do not know where he is going, nor does he.

    The second chapter explores the historical aspects of his situation further. It begins by crystallizing our feeling, and Stephen's too, about his "victory" over Mulligan and his other potential masters: it is not enough, not decisive, indeed Pyrrhic. And the main theme of the chapter is Ste-phen's hostility to, and fear of, the past. Time seems to him only to repeat itself in "the same room and hour, the same widsom. . . . Three nooses round me here," or in the repeated experience of the Jews:

Time surely would scatter all. A hoard heaped by the roadside: plundered and passing on. Their eyes knew the years of wandering and, patient, knew the dishonours of their flesh.

    —Who has not? Stephen said.

In short, "history was a tale like any other too often heard." The individual seems helplessly bound to the pattern; the "dear might of Him that walked the waves" does not exist for Stephen. He can see as little in the present as he can see in Elizabethan England—"an age of exhausted whoredom groping for its god." The ages, as John Eglinton puts it, seem only to "succeed one another" without change or hope. So conceived, history must seem a nightmare.

—History, Stephen said, is a nightmare from which I am trying to awake.
　　From the playfield the boys raised a shout. A whirring whistle: goal.
What if that nightmare gave you a back kick?
　　—The ways of the Creator are not our ways, Mr. Deasy said. All history moves towards one great goal, the manifestation of God.
　　Stephen jerked his thumb towards the window, saying:
　　—That is God.
　　Hooray! Ay! Whrrwhee!
　　—What? Mr. Deasy asked.
　　—A shout in the street, Stephen answered, shrugging his shoulders.

Stephen cannot accept that history moves to any supernatural end outside itself. If God exists, He manifests Himself here and now, in all life however pointless or trivial it may seem. History is not like a detective story; there are no comforting revelations to follow. When Stephen uses teleological arguments himself later on, he does so only analogously for another and very different conclusion.

　　His obsessive fear of the past is partly balanced, however, by a different strain of thought about history. If past events limit the present and the future, they also, as acts of will, liberate possibilities into the world of fact. Stephen ponders this dual aspect of history in Aristotelian terms:

> Had Pyrrhus not fallen by a beldam's hand in Argos or Julius Caesar not been killed to death. They are not to be thought away. Time has branded them and fettered they are lodged in the room of the infinite possibilities they have ousted. But can those have been possible seeing that they never were? Or was that only possible which came to pass? Weave, weaver of the wind.

And during the schoolboys' reading of *Lycidas*, the grounds of hope occur to him: time is not only a burden, it is also a means to the fruition and fulfilment of the soul in action. As he tells himself a little later, he could, if he willed it, break free of his present nooses—and in fact he does. History involves more than the ossification of life; it is also dynamic:

> It must be a movement then, an actuality of the possible as possible. Aristotle's phrase formed itself within the gabbled verses and floated out into the studious silence of the library of Sainte Geneviève where he had read, sheltered from the sin of Paris, night by night. By his elbow a delicate Siamese conned a handbook of strategy. Fed and feeding brains about me: under glowlamps, impaled, with faintly beating feelers: and in my mind's darkness a sloth of the underworld, reluctant, shy of brightness, shifting her dragon scaly folds. Thought is the thought of thought. Tran-

quil brightness. The soul is in a manner all that is: the soul is the form of forms. Tranquillity sudden, vast, candescent: form of forms.

The relevance of this (even the Siamese student) to his moral problems as an artist, his desire to mature and freely and creatively to act, requires no emphasis. Mr. Deasy's ambiguous wisdom confirms the implications of Stephen's drift: "to learn one must be humble. But life is the great teacher." For Stephen's situation, that cliché is the wisdom of Nestor.

"Proteus" develops these implications still further, both in Stephen's reflections about them and in the dramatic presentation of the way his reflections themselves progress. Joyce's writing here has often been praised for its sensitive delicacy, but it is not always realized how much more it is than that, how finely and firmly the chapter is organized as a poetic, dramatic unit. Generally speaking, the chapter explores the Protean transformations of matter in time—matter, as we should expect from Stephen's aesthetic theory, both as object, the "ineluctable modality of the visible and audible," apprehensible only in the condition of flux, and as subject, Stephen himself. In the one aspect, Stephen is seeking the principles of change and the underlying substance of sensory experience; in the other, he is seeking his self among its temporal manifestations. Consequently, he seems narcissistic, self-conscious, *lisant au livre de lui meme* like Hamlet. Yet, although he is still egocentric and still in uneasy kinetic relationship to his environment and himself, he exhibits in this chapter more of the incipient irony he had displayed at the end of the *Portrait,* a dawning capacity to stand off from himself and critcize what he sees, and concomitantly, to observe external reality with a certain detachment. His potentiality of growth is perhaps here most clearly visible. The humourless and priggish aesthete appears much less certain about his poses; he has after all, we discover, some sense of the ridiculous and some glimmerings of maturer values. "Proteus," in fact, is the crucial chapter for our conception of him. Without it, his other appearances in the book would hardly convince us of his solidity or interest as a protagonist; as it is, they are all enriched and qualified by his presentation here.

The setting on the seashore has an obvious metaphorical significance. Stephen speculates at the edge of life about the meanings in, and beyond, the immediate sensible world—his material as an artist. Bloom, who finds himself on the same shore in the evening, can make nothing of it:

All these rocks with lines and scars and letters. O, those transparent! Besides they don't know. What is the meaning of that other world. I called you naughty boy because I do not like.

> [He draws with a stick: I. AM. A.]
> No room. Let it go.
> Mr. Bloom effaced the letters with his slow boot. Hopeless thing
> sand.
> Nothing grows in it. All fades. . . .

But Stephen has the intellectual and imaginative capacity to read the "signatures of all things," to penetrate the diaphanous sensible world and the ineluctable *nacheinander* and *nebeneinander* placed before the individual consciousness, the world that is "there all the time without you: and ever shall be, world without end."

His thoughts turn to the permanent patterns of change—in particular, to the pattern of the life-cycle within which the individual's destiny is played out. He scorns theosophical hocus-pocus about the navelcord, but he acknowledges the common bond of continuity it represents. For him—and for Bloom, too—womankind represents the permanent force and pattern of biological history: birth, copulation, family and death. Indeed, when we recall the figure of Molly Bloom, it is true to say that this is one of the constant symbolic values of the book as a whole. Women do not figure in it as people but as biological symbols. And the polarity some of Joyce's critics have observed between Stephen ("intellectual life") and Molly ("biological life") already exists in Stephen's own point of view— especially in the rather abstractly "deep" speculations about Woman in which both he and Bloom sometimes indulge.

The first transformation of "matter" lies in the changing substance of Stephen's thoughts from the life-cycle in general towards his family and its particular life, and equally in his rejection of their "paralysis": "Houses of decay, mine, his and all. . . . Come out of them, Stephen. Beauty is not there." His father, as he says to Bloom later, is "all too Irish," and his criticism here includes the whole "hundred-headed rabble of the cathedral close," the general state of Ireland.

Swift provides the link to the second transformation—Stephen's "temptation" to enter the priesthood, or, more generally, to achieve and exercise magical powers; and, correspondingly, in "subjective" terms, his rejection of the possibility in both its religious and aesthetic aspects:

> Cousin Stephen, you will never be a saint. . . . You were awfully holy, weren't you? . . . On the top of the Howth tram alone crying to the rain: *naked women!* What about that, eh?
> What about what? What else were they invented for?
> . . . You bowed to yourself in the mirror, stepping forward to applaud earnestly, striking fact. . . . No-one saw: tell no-one. Books you

were going to write with letters for titles. . . . Remember your epiphanies
on green oval leaves, deeply deep. . . . Someone was to read them there
after a few thousand years, a mahamanvantara. Pico della Mirandola like.
Ay, very like a whale. When one reads these strange pages of one long
gone one feels that one is at one with one who once. . . .

The sharp juxtaposition of this mystico-Symbolist nonsense with the "grainy
sand" in the following line adds Joyce's endorsement to Stephen's self-
criticism; clearly, we are not invited to take the aesthetic attitude Stephen
parodies very seriously. Nor, for that matter, are we Stephen's third transformation, which begins with the sight of a "maze of dark cunning nets."
He himself punctures the attitude of the *esprit libre* he had adopted on his
flight to Paris: "My latin quarter hat. God, we simply must dress the character."

With his latest transformation—failed missionary to Europe, be-
draggled Icarus—he is naturally less detached and less critical. He recognizes
his failure, but the recognition is qualified by his sense of undefeated pride:

> His feet marched in sudden proud rhythm over the sand furrows, along
> by the boulders of the south wall. He stared at them proudly, piled stone
> mammoth skulls. Gold light on sea, on sand, on boulders. The sun is
> there, the slender trees, the lemon houses.

Despite the earlier *debâcle*, Paris still represents something of value to him,
though he also recognizes the meaning for himself in Kevin Egan, exiled
revolutionary in Paris, forgotten, remembering Sion. But all his retrospec-
tion leads him finally to a crucial decision which involves a crucial perception:

> He has the key. I will not sleep there when this night comes. . . . Take
> all, keep all. My soul walks with me, form of forms.

The decision to leave again is more than a recognition that he has been
forced out; it is based on a firmer knowledge of what his nature positively
seeks—the discovery of itself in a deeper experience of ordinary life.

His self-identification with the introspectively heroic Hamlet is the
last transformation of matter portrayed. The significance of the parallel is
mainly suggested and dramatically qualified by Stephen's theory in "Scylla
and Charybdis," but it is also partly qualified (and naturally it can only be
partly) by his own self-critical reflections here. The significant point emerges
from his fear of attack by a dog on the beach: "Respect his liberty. You
will not be master of others or their slave." He rejects all violence. The
nightmare of history is within him—

> Famine, plague and slaughters. Their blood is in me, their lusts my waves.
> I moved among them on the frozen Liffey, that I, a changeling, among
> the spluttering resin fires. I spoke to no-one: none to me.

As he says at the end of "Circe," it is *within* that he must kill the king and
the priest, symbols of spiritual tyranny and slavery. His means to freedom
are still silence, exile, and cunning—the evasion of action and violence—
but they also seem like cowardice. He wonders if he too is not another
"pretender": he fears drowning, he is not a strong swimmer; he hates water;
life may well overwhelm him. In short, ironic self-scrutiny has begun to
temper his will.

His reflections now turn reflectively upon themselves. He identifies
himself with the sniffing dog, "tatters," "poor dogsbody," fox who has buried
his mother under a hollybush; he sees himself "vulturing the dead," "looking
for something lost in a past life"—

> Dogskull, dogsniff, eyes on the ground, moves to one great goal.

His search for the self beneath the protean flux of life concludes with such
partial knowledge as he is capable of discovering and with a recognition of
the nature of his search. The future can be only prefigured: in a symbolic
dream ("That man led me, spoke. I was not afraid"); in his adolescent
longing for contact with the female tides of life; in his continual effort
to find his self in reality yet avoid the sterility of solipsism, to grasp
the significance of the sensible world, where subject and object unite by
"parallax":

> Hold hard. Coloured on a flat: yes, that's right. Flat I see, then think
> distance, near, far, flat I see, east, back. Ah, see now. Falls back suddenly,
> frozen in stereoscope. Click does the trick.

The scribbled note for his poem is part of the action of the chapter, a
transformation that transcends all those that precede it, an emblem of the
"great goal" of his process of self-scrutiny, a symbol in little of *Ulysses* itself.
History, understood, moves towards the goal of art, but art is itself a symbol
of the wider spiritual life it ideally embodies. The phrase from Yeats that
Stephen quotes—"and no more turn aside and brood"—signalizes his progress to a precarious *stasis*, or at least to a less kinetic frame of mind, in
which he tries to express the sound and unending movement of water, his
sense of the life into which he must plunge. That his present *stasis* is
precariously unstable is implicit in the way he tries to accept his fear and
the necessary rôle of death in life; the language reflects an intention, an
effort, more than achieved assurance:

God becomes man becomes fish becomes barnacle goose becomes feather-bed mountain. Dead breaths I living breathe, tread dead dust, devour a urinous offal from all dead. Hauled stark over the gunwale he breathes upward the stench of his green grave, his leprous nosehold snoring to the sun.

A seachange this, brown eyes saltblue. . . . Just you give it a fair trial. . . .

. . . Evening will find itself.

. . . Yes, evening will find itself in me, without me. All days make their end. . . .

This is a passage less important for the symbolic relationships it suggests (father—sea—life, urine—death, etc.) than for the dramatic significance of its tone. Stephen's trust in the future is no mere involuntary drifting with the stream. As the rest of the chapter has established, he has some appreciation of the direction he must take and of the importance of growing towards it as well as simply willing it. His attitude still remains tentative, largely a passive, but watchful, waiting. In order to crystallize its positive value, Joyce must direct us outside Stephen's consciousness, and this he does with the "objectively" rendered episode of the ship at the very end of the chapter. Revealed to Stephen's significantly "rere regardant" gaze, her sails "brailed up on the crosstrees, homing, upstream, silently moving, a silent ship." With the final hint that he too is silently moving homeward, Stephen is dismissed, and the stage is set for Bloom. . . .

. . . Unlike Stephen, Bloom is not much aware of his own individual character, nor is he concerned with establishing any special relationship between himself and "life." He *is* alive. Of course, as we have seen, we cannot take him as fully alive, an unqualified hero, but his common humanity does represent that "life" against which Stephen is placed.

Bloom engages with everyday life at many points—that is the primary and obvious significance of the Odyssean parallel: he is an "allround-man." More important, however, is the way in which he engages—the sense in which his completeness is a sign of moral vitality and his consciousness the expression of a man truly, if not ideally, alive. For all his comparative unselfconsciousness he is not unreflective; for all his absorption in everyday matters, he is far from completely absorbed by them. His active consciousness is the clearest basis of his moral stature and his dramatic significance; he is a modern Odysseus, expressing himself less in outward action than in inward awareness. Much of his pathos, much of the dramatic irony, derives from this limitation of his capacity for physical action, but neither this, nor the limitations of his intelligence and sensibility, destroy his fundamental dignity. This dignity, however, lies ultimately in his unselfconscious being, in what he *is* unknown to himself, which it is one of Joyce's prime intentions to reveal to us in "Circe" and "Ithaca." The most important difference between Bloom and Stephen is that while Stephen aspires to a special dignity of his own as an artist, he has not achieved it, where Bloom does possess his dignity, and all the more securely because he is never for one moment aware that he does—or that he possesses heroic dimensions.

His first appearance places him in careful *contrast* to Stephen. The first fact we learn about him is his liking for the inner organs of beasts and fowls: "most of all he liked grilled mutton kidneys which gave to his palate a fine tang of faintly scented urine." We recall Stephen's reflection on the previous page, at the end of "Proteus": "dead breaths I living breathe, tread dead dust, devour a urinous offal from all dead." Where Stephen can slip free of the dead hand of the past and accept the necessity of death only fitfully and with difficulty, Bloom accepts death easily and transforms it into life. One need not solemnly trace the symbolism of offal and urine through the whole book—though it is important to remember that Stephen and Bloom urinate together before they part—in order to perceive this major difference between the attitude of the two men to the dead past. But so far this is not a realized difference, only the symbol of one dramatically established in the acts and consciousness of Bloom as the action proceeds.

In "Calypso," where Bloom's racial and familial relationships are first outlined, his awareness of them is inevitably his awareness of time. He considers a prospectus for recultivating Palestine; his mind turns to a sudden vision of the Holy Land as barren, exhausted, dead: "Grey horror seared his flesh. . . . Cold oils slid along his veins, chilling his blood: age crusting him with a salt cloak. Well, I am here now." From the horror of the past he turns to the living flesh of the present: "to smell the gentle smoke of tea, fume of the pan, sizzling butter. Be near her ample bedwarmed flesh. Yes, yes." This does not represent the whole of his attitude to the past, of course, but already it is clear that he does not agonize in the matter of Stephen. Even when he is immediately reminded that the ample bed-warmed flesh is waiting for Blazes Boylan, and the thought of the future chills him like the thought of the dead Promised Land, he does not remain fixed in his pain. His mind constantly shifts between past, present and future. The little discussion about "metempsychosis" establishes one of the verbal symbols of this movement: they say we have forgotten the lives we are supposed to have lived in the past, Bloom tells Molly; "some say they remember their past lives." Bloom himself forgets and remembers as a human being active in the present. If he recalls his ghosts, he salutes them and passes on. Where Stephen fights and struggles and has suicidal impulses, Bloom wears the past, and hence the present, more easily. At the end of "Hades," after he has faced the shadow of death, his thoughts "turn aside and no more brood": "Back to the world again. Enough of this place. . . . Plenty to see and hear and feel yet. Feel live warm beings near you. Let them sleep in their maggoty beds. They are not going to get me this innings. Warm beds: warm fullblooded life." He recognizes the savagery of life, the necessity even of killing ("Eat or be eaten. Kill! Kill!"), but, unlike Stephen, he can accept this without the knowledge corrupting the springs of action. He moves on always, rejecting the false *stasis* of imprisoning frustration: "Life those chaps out there must have, stuck in the same spot. Irish Lights board. Penance for their sins." To Bloom, life presents itself as an inescapable activity, the moral exigencies of which control the influence of the past as much as the influence of the past controls them.

Like Stephen, he recognizes the general patterns that circumscribe the life of the individual, though his awareness has a very different tone: "It's the blood sinking in the earth gives new life. Same idea those jews they said killed the christian boy. Every man his price." He preserves the same tone in his reflections about himself too:

> June that was too I wooed. The year returns. History repeats itself. . . . Life, love, voyage round your own little world. And now? . . .
> All quiet on Howth now. The distant hills seem. Where we. The rhododendrons. I am a fool perhaps. He gets the plums and I the plum-stones. Where I come in. All that old hill has seen. Names change: that's all. Lovers: yum yum.
> . . . She kissed me. My youth. Never again. Only once it comes. Or hers. Take the train there tomorrow. No. Returning not the same. . . . The new I want. Nothing new under the sun. . . . Think your escaping and run into yourself. Longest way round is the shortest way home. . . . All changed. Forgotten. The young are old. . . .

Bloom's pathos here arises from his helpless recognition of ineluctability; it is the helplessness of humanity itself. As the contrasting echoes of Stephen's parable of the plums and of his speculations about the actualization of the self in experience suggest, Bloom's recognition is an experiential one, not a merely theoretical acceptance like Stephen's. For him, the life-cycle, the biological limits of the individual's experience, are a felt part of his actual life. He accepts the universe not because he has found any intellectual formula into which he can fit it, but for the more compelling reason that he simply has to. Inasmuch as he does so, moreover, he represents one of the values Joyce expresses in the work. Bloom's simple awareness of these natural patterns is not offered as stupidity or moral surrender, but as a kind of unthinking wisdom. Thus, when Bloom hears of Mrs. Purefoy's difficult lying-in, "his heavy pitying gaze absorbed her news. His tongue clacked in compassion. Dth! Dth!"—the suggestion of the life-cycle is Joyce's as much as, if not more than, Bloom's. Or again, when Bloom actually visits the hospital and hears of the death of a friend, he stands silent "in wanhope," whereupon the narrative comments in general terms on the inevitability of death. Even though Joyce makes no unqualified endorsement of Bloom, he does in this endorse his characteristic attitude. So that when Bloom's attitude to time and Stephen's are finally juxtaposed in "Ithaca," we should recognize the sense in which the former's is a criticism of the latter's. Standing beneath the stars and ready to part, they hear, as Bloom had heard among his thoughts of Dignam's death in the morning, the bells of St. George's church striking the passage of time:

What echoes of that sound were by both and each heard?

By Stephen, an echo of his unpurged remorse:

Liliata rutilantium. Turma circumdet.
Iubilantium te virginum. Chorus excipiat.

By Bloom, an echo of death, and yet also an incipient turn from it:

Heigho, heigho,
Heigho, heigho.

His attitude can be easily mistaken for a completely passive resignation. In fact, it is something rather different, an *active* resignation, so to speak. Certainly, Bloom does not do obvious battle with his world, though we should remember that he has lost one job "for giving lip" and stands up to the Citizen where no one else does. He does occasionally surrender to a sentimental and uselessly nostalgic acceptance of things as they are—his daughter, Milly, usually provokes this reaction: "A soft qualm, regret, flowed down his backbone, increasing. Will happen, yes. Prevent. Useless: can't move . . ." He submits without overt protest or resistance to the petty indignities that mark his social exclusion. On the other hand, his important acceptances are made with an awareness of the complexities: they are not easy resignations by any means. His proposals to Stephen for future meetings—meetings that William Empson has argued are to be regarded as having really taken place and to be the real point of the book— are the product of his deep and pathetic desire for friendship. The proposals are, in fact, accepted by Stephen. Bloom, however, knows more than to take the arrangement at face-value:

What rendered problematic for Bloom the realisation of these mutually selfexcluding propositions?

The irreparability of the past: once at a performance of Albert Hengler's circus . . . an intuitive particoloured clown . . . had publicly declared that he (Bloom) was his (the clown's) papa. The imprevidibility of the future: once in the summer of 1898 he (Bloom) had marked a florin . . . for possible, circuitous or direct, return.

Was the clown Bloom's son?

No.

Had Bloom's coin returned?

Never.

In short, if Bloom accepts the past as it has been and life as it is, it is not because he does not also desire them otherwise.

Probably the most important illustration of his whole general attitude is provided by his feelings about Molly's adultery. These change, or rather crystallize, during the course of the book, and in fact this crystallization is one of the central threads of the action. Bloom's first reactions are distress and emotional flight; when he sees Boylan in the street, for example, he meets the insupportable by escaping into the Museum, turning to the refuge of "cold statues" and "the Greek architecture." When he does allow his mind to dwell on the situation, it is with a certain self-pity and nostalgia: "Me. And me now." Later on, the art of song in the "Sirens" chapter induces another mood, more reflective, more detached, in which he is able to generalize his situation:

> Thou lost one. All songs on that theme. Yet more Bloom stretched his string. Cruel it seems. Let people get fond of each other: lure them on. Then tear asunder. . . . Human life. . . .
> Yet too much happy bores. He stretched more, more. Are you not happy in your? Twang. It snapped.

His personal isolation is heavily emphasized in this chapter, of course, but it is an isolation which is partly an active movement of his mind towards a fuller understanding of his past and present situation (that the chapter is focused upon an *art*, and that Bloom's capacity to comprehend his situation is as limited as the elasticity of his string, are equally significant). But understanding of a sort he does achieve:

> I too, last my race. Milly young student. Well, my fault perhaps. No son. Rudy. Too late now. Or if not? If still?
> He bore no hate.
> Hate. Love. Those are names. Rudy. Soon I am old.

By evening ("Nausicaa"), he has begun to see Molly's behaviour in an even wider context as only one more illustration of the laws of attraction, of a universal natural process. And his reconciliation to her proposed tour with Boylan is significantly juxtaposed with his charitable thoughts about the Citizen who had abused and assaulted him. His mood is not quite a surrender to mere amoral natural processes; it includes a positive charity, a compassionate realization of the common human lot. The mocking sound of the cuckoo that concludes the chapter seems cheap, almost irrelevant, by comparison; its irony leaves his substance untouched. Still further, in "Circe" and "Eumaeus," he comes to recognize that his own sexual failure has a good deal to do with Molly's infidelity. Gradually he moves from *kinesis* to "a silent contemplation," which is summed up in "Ithaca":

> With what antagonistic sentiments were his subsequent reflections affected?
> Envy, jealousy, abnegation, equanimity.

Envy of Boylan, jealousy of Molly, abnegation for complicated motives, and equanimity because, finally, Molly's act is "more than inevitable, irreparable."

> Why more abnegation than jealousy, less envy than equanimity?
> From outrage (matrimony) to outrage (adultery) there arose nought but outrage (copulation) yet the matrimonial violator of the matrimonially violated had not been outraged by the adulterous violator of the adulterously violated. . . .

> By what reflections did he, a conscious reactor against the void of incertitude, justify to himself his sentiments?
> [The naturalness of the attraction and the act]: the futility of triumph or protest of vindication: the inanity of extolled virtue: the lethargy of nescient matter: the apathy of the stars.

The equanimity results in a final satisfaction in the warmth and beauty of Molly's female "mute immutable mature animality"—the eternally given, but never to be possessed, richness of the flesh.

> The visible signs of antesatisfaction?
> An approximate erection: a solicitous adversion: a gradual elevation: a tentative revelation: a silent contemplation.
> Then?
> He kissed the plump mellow yellow smellow melons of her rump, on each plump melonous hemisphere, in their mellow yellow furrow, with obscure prolonged provocative melonsmellonous osculation.
> The visible signs of postsatisfaction?
> A silent contemplation: a tentative velation: a gradual abasement: a solicitous aversion: a proximate erection.

That Bloom's silent contemplative *stasis* is followed by a kind of *kinesis* (characteristically weak and ambiguous, we might notice) marks the difference between the continuing process of life and the fixity of art. If Bloom's slaying of the suitors by a victory over himself seems paltry or despicable by contrast with Ulysses' more conclusive methods, we must not therefore suppose that Joyce is being simply ironical at Bloom's expense. He rarely supports his characters in postures of moral violence; his notion of true moral activity is less overtly militant. Bloom kills his enemies, as Stephen hopes to do, within, and they are not Molly's suitors so much as his own inner frustrating imbalance of envy, jealousy and excessive abnegation. He wins a temporary equanimity, but clearly no final victory. Life, Joyce implies, is not art; there is nothing concluded, no absolute command possible.

Bloom's comparative freedom from guilt, remorse, nostalgia, jealousy, egotistic assertion and other nightmares of history is to be contrasted with Stephen's bondage. Similarly, his curiosity and openness to experience, unlike Stephen's search for "life," express a desire to place the past at the disposal of the future. Where Stephen is a novice, incapable as yet of using the past and so in search of a spiritual father, Bloom is oppressed by the complementary frustration that, as the last of his race, he has no one to whom he can hand on his spiritual gift.

The problem haunts him all through the book, emerging perhaps most explicitly as he sits with the young men in the hospital ("Oxen of the Sun") where he has been drawn by his compassion for Mrs. Purefoy and kept by his half-conscious attraction to Stephen. After a passage in which Mulligan mocks Stephen's divine analogies ("the black panther was himself the ghost of his own father"), Bloom, contemplating the label on a bottle of Bass, passes to the "incorruptible eon of the gods." "What is the age of the soul of man?" Bloom relives his own youth—"he is young Leopold, as in a retrospective arrangement, a mirror within a mirror (hey, presto!), he beholdeth himself." But the mirror clouds; "now he is himself paternal and these about him might be his sons. Who can say? The wise father knows his own child." His intense regret that he has not fathered a living man-child, his unwilled frustration, reflects mirror-wise the deliberate contraception that forms the abstract theme of the chapter:

No, Leopold! Name and memory solace thee not. That youthful illusion of thy strength was taken from thee and in vain. No son of thy loins is by thee. There is none now to be for Leopold, what Leopold was for Rudolph.

For Bloom, as his "soul is wafted over regions of cycles of cycles of generations that have lived," the past is barren, "Agendath is a waste land,"

horrible and damned. But womankind, "link between nations and generations . . . sacred life-giver," still remains, with her potentialities for the
future—"And, lo, wonder of metempsychosis, it is she, the everlasting
bride, harbinger of the daystar, the bride, ever virgin. It is she, Martha,
thou lost one, Millicent, the young, the dear, the radiant."

Bloom cannot understand, any more than Stephen, what he can
offer the younger man. It is certainly not his good advice, nor anything he
could formulate consciously; the essence of his gift is that he is unconscious
of it—it is what he represents and is. Partly, of course, he is Stephen's
possible "material" as an artist, the City against which Stephen reacts and
which is therefore the necessary subject of his self-reflective art. More,
however, he represents a relationship to the history of his own people that
is analogous to Stephen's and yet unlike it. It is part of Bloom's relevance
that, like Stephen, he also embodies a racial tradition (which is also a
spiritual tradition), even though it is consciously present to him only in
fragments. His "defective mnemotechnic" links him with attitudes and
patterns of life that he unwittingly re-experiences in his own circumstances.
They are not Jewish in the narrowest sense; they have a wider reference,
which emerges in "Circe," and to Bloom himself Christ is a symbol both
of his values and the mixed tradition whence they derive: "Well, his uncle
was a jew, says he. Your God was a jew. Christ was a jew like me." The
racial parallel with Stephen is explicitly drawn in "Ithaca": both inherit a
long and rich tradition, both are conscious only of fragments of it. Yet the
contrast between the two men is equally explicit and equally important.
Where Stephen consciously (and uneasily) rejects, Bloom accepts. Once,
earlier, Bloom had impatiently criticized his father's beliefs and practices;
now, they appear to him "not more rational than they had then appeared,
not less rational than other beliefs and practices now appeared." As we
shall see, this detachment is by no means the whole of Bloom's attitude,
for much else in it is, as it should be, quite unconscious; his significance,
nevertheless, is as an example, parallel to but contrasting with Stephen's
case, of an involuntary involvement, an involuntary exile, but a real if
unemphatic freedom.

Such contrasts between Bloom and Stephen would have little point
without the relationship that lies at the centre of the whole book: they are
here, as always, complementary counterparts, "fundamental and dominant," actuality and potentiality. The father-son theme is one metaphor
for this; the theory about Shakespeare another; the figure of Christ, in
whom are expressed the dichotomies of crucified citizen (Man) and crucified
artist (God), of action and passion, of involvement and freedom, is yet a
third. By its different aspects, the symbol of Christ links the diverse facts

of the situation Joyce explores, but the meaning of Joyce's *symbol* lies in the facts it orders. Unless the values it relates and expresses are themselves realized, imaginatively established as denotations, the symbol remains empty and inert. Stephen cannot be portrayed as the suffering and crucified Artist redeeming the world; in the very terms of the book, he lacks the freedom, the love, and the capacity, and has only the desire to become an artist and the uneasy realization of what is involved. For the most part, he rejects. He is Christ as the "black panther," and the very incompleteness of his state provokes the metaphor of Lucifer. Stephen as Christ often passes over into Stephen as Satan: it is a sign of his immaturity that he is ready to adopt either rôle at any time. He is not quite *der Geist, der stets verneint* of course; it is rather that his affirmations seem only velleities, or at best unachieved intentions. Bloom, therefore, must carry the heavier burden of significance—be not merely passive but active, not merely involved but free, not merely representative of, but crucified by, his world, the scapegoat and redeemer, and tied all the while by close analogy and parallel with Stephen, so that the reader may perceive what Stephen must learn to perceive: the values Bloom represents and the deep similarity between the two of them. Bloom's ambiguous position, his example, his love, his freedom, if only he could understand them, are what Stephen must come to. For the parallels between the two men are fundamental: Bloom's exclusion from society reflects Stephen's spiritual exile from it (a situation neatly portrayed early in the book when they are both at the newspaper office). Each is an alien in the life of Dublin. They are both isolated by "parallax," each in his personal world, and only a full spiritual outgoing—or its symbol, art—can alleviate their condition. They both reject violence and the senseless agitations of the mob as incompatible with the freedom and order they seek. They are both keyless, citizen and artist, yet both "born adventurers" and committed to the essential isolation of their individuality. They both have personal courage, one in his pride, the other in his humility. Both strive to awake from the nightmare of history, though Stephen cannot yet realize what values he seeks, and Bloom cannot express what he means. But his attempts are the justification for the Christ metaphor—his positive courage in "Cyclops," for example, but more especially his unalienated integrity in "Circe." The most important structural parallel between the two protagonists, in fact, is that between Stephen's self-examination of the past, which is conducted consciously, and Bloom's, which is necessarily much less conscious; between "Proteus" and "Circe." The connections between these two chapters, with all that is implied by those connections, is what really establishes the metaphor of paternity.

RICHARD ELLMANN

Bloom Unbound

In the "Cyclops" episode, the tampering with the surface of events is effected by means of a pair of narrators. The episode must have been difficult to write—how compose anything beyond the "Sirens?"—but Joyce manages to bring it off. Probably this episode profits from the famous scene in *Madame Bovary* where Emma and Rodolphe exchange tender sentiments about love while the judges of the cattle fair call out the prizes for pigs. Flaubert grants nature a straightforwardness against the false sentimentality of Emma and Rodolphe. Joyce in the "Cyclops" episode disproves sentimentality and swinishness both. He had already worked with inflation and deflation in the "Aeolus" episode, where Stephen's parable undercut Dublin's oratory. But that was a benign deflation; there is another kind of deflation, a malign one, which is inspired by meanness rather than by honesty. One of the two narrators of "Cyclops"—the one who carries the burden of the narrative—is a man of this kind, a man never named, but privately identified by Joyce with Thersites, the meanest-spirited man in the Greek host at Troy. It is Thersites who declares in Shakespeare's *Troilus and Cressida*, "Lechery, lechery; still, wars and lechery." His is a savage temperament, bent upon reduction. Joyce makes his Thersites a collector of bad and doubtful debts, an occupation which opens to him the worst secrets about everybody. That there might be a better side is inadmissible. A sponger and backbiter, he has no better side himself. He expresses more patently than Mulligan or Boylan the spirit of denial; sexless himself, he happily denies sexuality (as well as decency) to others. Much of what he claims to know is false, as his evident relish

From *Ulysses on the Liffey*. Copyright © 1972 by Richard Ellmann. Oxford University Press.

in every malicious tidbit implies. What he sees he sees vividly but he has a blind eye.

Joyce lets Thersites lead off: "I was just passing the time of day with old Troy of the D.M.P. at the corner of Arbour hill there and be damned but a bloody sweep came along and he near drove his gear into my eye." Here, as Gilbert indicates, is the first of the multitudinous references to putting out eyes which punctuate this episode, and allude to Odysseus' blinding of the Cyclops with a sharpened stick. But what is equally pointed is Thersites' obsequiousness towards the D.M.P., the Dublin Mounted Police. He is a coward before authority, frightened by any breach of the law, and Joyce reminds us of this at the end by having Thersites say that the Citizen, had he succeeded in hitting Bloom with the biscuit tin, would have been lagged for assault and battery and Joe Hynes for aiding and abetting him. Thersites pretends to be an outlaw, but no one minds more sheepishly than he the tables of the law.

As counterpart to Thersites Joyce established a second narrator, whose interruptions are sometimes a bit dull. They are not for that reason less necessary. Thersites initiates, the other narrator seconds in a different mode. What Thersites puts baldly, the second narrator figleaves overs. Joyce speaks of the technique of this episode as gigantism, no doubt thinking of the size of the Cyclops, but it is actually a give and take between belittlement and magnification. Thersites is all bile, his counterpart all oil. One is myopic, the other presbyopic. Thersites can take fairly innocent acts and make them out to be vile, his counterpart takes vile acts and makes them part of a frothy blancmange. In the Linati schema, Joyce indicates that Galatea plays a part in this episode, and it must be she, out of Handel's *Acis and Galatea*, who is wooed by Polyphemus the Cyclops but is unyielding there, as here, to his point of view. She trips while he lumbers. Perhaps also, since Joyce identifies the first narrator with Thersites, he has another narrator in mind, of an opposite disposition. His identity may be surmised: he strongly resembles Dr. Pangloss, in that he glosses over what Thersites regards as the worst of all possible worlds and makes of it the best. In this triad of chapters where the presence of Hume begins to be felt, he is joined by another eighteenth-century philosopher, "that moderate man Voltaire."

Besides the Cyclopeans Thersites and Pangloss, whose different eyefuls make double vision the dialectic of the episode, another Cyclopean, the Citizen, is introduced. The Citizen reflects the intensities of the first two in that, as a chauvinist, everything Irish is good, everything un-Irish is vile. Yet Joyce notes that the Cyclopeans were not only inimical to foreigners, but also unfriendly to each other. The Citizen is flagwaver and xenophobe, but he is also sponger and braggart, and, as Thersites attests, is not so Irish as he pretends, since he has broken the patriotic code by buying up the holding of an evicted tenant.

Joyce was delighted with the theme of the Cyclops. One-eyeism required the two one-eyed narrators and the one-eyed Citizen. In one way or another all the characters except Bloom are monocular. But Joyce was also pleased that Odysseus, asked his name by the Cyclops, replied *"Outis"* (a pun on his real name) or "No one," as if disdaining any identity; then, to compensate, when he and his men are almost safe away from the wrathful, blinded Cyclops, the hero cried out to him his full name, including its other half, Zeus (in Joyce's etymology). With this hint of his enemy's whereabouts and true identity, the Cyclops threw the rock which almost cut short these epical adventures. Joyce could easily see that in the "Cyclops" episode he must have Bloom, nominally a Christian, avow himself to be a Jew, and do so at the expense of prudence. He must also have Thersites know that Bloom's father had changed his name by deedpoll from Virag to Bloom.

To emphasize his theme Joyce frolics a good deal with namelessness and with names, with identity and mistaken identity. Among the details with which he thickens the major elements, little Alf Bergan imagines he has seen Paddy Dignam—or, as Doran half misnames him, *Willy* Dignam— still alive. The Citizen is never named, and Bloom in large stretches of the chapter, especially beginning and end, is referred to without being named. A dark horse has won the race, and Bloom is called "a bloody dark horse himself." The Citizen, because of his purchase of the evicted tenant's holding, is only half the man he seems. Bloom is temporarily blinded in not knowing what has stirred up the Citizen and the rest against him. But there is in fact a steady attack upon Bloom from all directions; he is not Bloom but Virag; he is not a man; he takes to his bed at times like a menstruant woman; he is no Irishman but what Thersites calls a Jerusalem cuckoo; he is no patriot, the Citizen insists; he is no husband, being a cuckold; no father (his child must be a bastard); worst of all, from Thersites' point of view, he is no treater. These are all aspects of Odysseus as *outis*, attempts to make him embody no-ness.

As a result of the hostility to Jews which Thersites manifests from the first page of his narrative, and of Bloom's assertion of himself in argument, as well as of the resentment at Bloom's supposed winnings on the race, he is placed in physical danger for the first time in the day. The Citizen's physical attack with the biscuit tin is the culmination of a series of lesser attacks. In "Scylla and Charybdis," Shakespeare suffered the indignities of love; here in the "Cyclops," Bloom must suffer the indignities of hatred. Thersites cannot abide Bloom or anything about him, his appearance, his speech, his vocabulary, his fund of information, his refusal to drink, his generosity to the widow Dignam. Joyce presents Bloom here as his worst enemy sees him. Not that Thersites is altogether disrespectful; as Joyce indicated to Frank Budgen, there is a sneaking admiration for Bloom's conversance with all subjects. Thersites is himself almost tongue-tied, his only remarks to the company being about drink.

Yet it is here that Bloom must show himself to be, on a minuscule stage, a true hero. Joyce was alive to the danger of falling into a little propaganda, in the way that he thought Tolstoy's "Master and Man" had done. Up to now Bloom has confronted hostile forces chiefly in his mind. Now he must meet them directly. He must be allowed to state an ethical view which is superior to that of the people around him. It is more Christian than Judaic, more Platonic than Aristotelian: Joyce selected what he needed. But it must not be sentimental. Bloom has said that Ireland is his nation, but he adds. "And I belong to a race too . . . that is hated and persecuted. Also now. This very moment. This very instant." The Citizen accuses him of Zionist daydreams, "Are you talking about the new Jerusalem?" "I'm talking about injustice," Bloom replies. John Wyse Power advises, "Stand up to it then with force like men." This rebuke leads Bloom to his culmination, "But it's no use. . . . Force, hatred, history, all that. That's not life for men and women, insult and hatred. And everybody knows that it's the very opposite of that that is really life." "What?" asks Alf Bergan. "Love . . . I mean the opposite of hatred. I must go now." To urge men to love, and then to speak of his own departure, connects Bloom for a moment to Christ. More naturalistically, with this position Bloom shows himself to be a two-eyed man; he counters directly the various exponents of single vision, the Citizen's chauvinism, Thersites' hatred, Pangloss's illusion.

In the Linati schema Joyce indicates that the cast of characters in this episode includes another interloper, Prometheus. Prometheus is a stranger addition to the cast than Galatea. It is likely that Joyce has in mind not the Prometheus of Aeschylus but of Shelley, whom he ranked (along with Shakespeare and Wordsworth) as one of the three great poets in English. Shelley's Prometheus is unbound when he retracts his curse against Jehovah, "I wish no living thing to suffer pain." He abjures as Bloom does the use of force, and Demogorgon is thereby enabled to announce as Bloom does the reign of love, which "folds over the world its healing wings."

> To defy Power, which seems omnipotent;
> To love, and bear. . . .
> This, like thy glory, Titan, is to be
> Good, great and joyous, beautiful and free;
> This is alone Life, Joy, Empire, and Victory.

It is love which saves from what Blake called "Single vision and Newton's sleep," and imparts double vision, perspective.

Perspective is itself parodied at the end of the episode when its two historians, Thersites and Pangloss, each having stared from his own eye in magnificent disregard of the other, combine their dictions with a sudden click: "And they beheld Him even Him, ben Bloom Elijah, amid clouds of angels ascend to the glory of the brightness at an angle of fortyfive degrees over Donohoe's in Little Green Street like a shot off a shovel!" In terms of the book's argument, this apotheosis flouts space just as the "Sirens" episode flouted time and its musical articulation. "Am I walking into eternity along Sandymount strand?" Stephen asks in "Proteus" and Bloom is propelled towards eternity now. Since the apotheosis is a comic one, it at once exalts Bloom and recalls him to purely human proportions.

Bloom's upholding of love against "force, hatred, history, all that," dovetails with Stephen's earlier statement that "history is a nightmare from which I am trying to awake." To both of them history presents itself as monolithic and glowering the encrustations of time ready to encompass the present and future. The Citizen meets the ferocity of history with an equal ferocity. Bloom meets it with a certain kindness, a certain humour (not touched on by Shelley's Demogorgon), a certain refusal to be taken in. Against the false dialectic of Thersites and Pangloss—the impulse to wrinkle and the impulse to smooth over, to belittle and to bloat, Bloom asserts a monistic decency. His defence of love, more Christian than the Christians', rouses the Cyclops's anger, but more, it awakens the whole book towards its fourth level of meaning, the anagogic one, in which "Love's bitter mystery" is to triumph. Stephen's theory of art has prescribed for it the act of love, but it is Bloom who must disclose what love is.

ANTHONY BURGESS

The Dublin Sound

In *A Portrait of the Artist as a Young Man*, the undergraduate Stephen Dedalus engages in a conversation on aesthetics with the Dean of Studies, an English Jesuit, "humble follower in the wake of clamorous conversions" (was Joyce, incidentally, already thinking of the title and subject-matter of his last book?). The Dean leads the conversation towards the "useful arts" and, talking of the art of filling a lamp with oil, uses the term "funnel," which Stephen has not met in that context: his word is "tundish," which the Dean does not know at all. (Like many dialect terms in Anglo-Irish, it is of respectable Middle English ancestry.) Stephen feels "a smart of dejection that the man to whom he was speaking was a countryman of Ben Johnson," and says to himself: "The language in which we are speaking is his before it is mine." This is sentimental and self-pitying, not easily forgivable even in an undergraduate, and to erect a sense of alienation on a single pair of words is perhaps going too far.

From a lexical point of view there are hardly any differences between Stephen's English and that of the Dean of Studies. Stephen, like the characters in Swift's *Polite Conversations*, will ask for tea or washing water to be "filled out"; he will eat a crubeen (a pig's or sheep's foot) and, in Cork, a drisheen or black pudding. He will refer to oxters rather than armpits and know that "plain" in Buck Mulligan's "Ballad of Joking Jesus" means beer (*locus classicus* in Flann O'Brien's *At Swim-Two-Birds*: "Do you know what it is I am going to tell you? A pint of plain is your only man.") But we need no special dictionary to read Joyce's plainer works. If, in

From *Joysprick*. Copyright © 1973 by Anthony Burgess. André Deutsch Ltd.

Finnegans Wake, the Gaelic element is large, this is because Gaelic is a foreign language with a special claim on Joyce's attention, since ancient Ireland coexists in the book with various kinds of modern Ireland, but the Gaelic lexicon that has already been compiled out of *Finnegans Wake* is no bigger than the German one. The Italian one (which has probably already been completed) must be the biggest of all. The works of William Faulkner and J. D. Salinger are foreign compared with *Ulysses:* Stephen and the Dean of Studies meet on everything but funnels and tundishes.

But the continuation of Stephen's dejected musing brings us to the real point about Anglo-Irish linguistic differences:

> . . . How different are the words *home, Christ, ale, master* on his lips and on mine! I cannot speak or write these words without unrest of spirit. His language, so familiar and so foreign, will always be for me an acquired speech. I have not made or accepted its words. My voice holds them at bay. My soul frets in the shadow of his language.

An American Joyce scholar recently saw in those four words "powerful symbols of dispossession," but one may reasonably ask what dispossession has to do with ale. What make Stephen's soul fret are the simple differences between his own pronunciation of the words and that of the Dean of Studies. He feels the inferiority of a provincial in the presence of a metropolitan or ruling-class accent: his case is little different from that of a Lancastrian or Northumbrian in the days when public-school English had power to frighten and humble. But Stephen feels the weight of three kinds of authority in the Dean's speech—the ruling class, the Imperial power, the international Church. His own accent is not merely provincial, it is also that of a subject people.

Let us consider the sounds they use respectively in these four key-words. The Dean has a diphthong in *home*—/oʊ/ or /əʊ/, while Stephen has a long open vowel —/ɔ:/. The diphthong of Stephen's *Christ* approaches /ʌɪ/ while the Dean's is a patrician /əɪ/, Stephen has, for *ale*, a high tense vowel followed by a clear l—/e:l/— while the Dean has a diphthong with a dark l—/eɪɫ/. The Dean's *master* has a back vowel and a final schwa—/ma:stə/; Stephen's has a front vowel and ends with a retroflex r—/mæstɹ/. Stephen, or Joyce, has cunningly chosen words that demonstrate very well the main phonic differences between the speech-systems of the English and Irish capitals.

Ironically, it is Stephen's own inherited Dublin speech that is nearer to the tongue of Ben Jonson than the Dean's Received Pronunciation (RP). Those admirers of Joyce who place him close to Shakespeare are unassailable in one respect: the English on which Joyce was reared, and out of which he contrived a literature even more idiosyncratic than Shakespeare's, had and still has many of the phonetic features of the language of Elizabethan London. What are thought of as essentially Anglo-Irish versions of the vowel in *tea, sea* and *beat* and the diphthong in *my, eye, fight* are close enough to the regular usages of Shakespeare. Falstaff puns on *reasons* and *raisins;* as late as Alexander Pope *line* is a rhyme for *join.* To be accurate about Dublin English, one must say that it fossilises most of the features of Pope's English, eighteenth-century English, and that this English still had many of the features of Elizabethan English. Joyce has to meet Swift and Sterne and Addison before he meets Shakespeare.

This is probably not the place to discuss the Great Vowel Shift which helped to turn the English of Henry V into that of our own day. It is enough to say that, in the mediaeval period of English, the *i* of *shine* had the value it still has in the Romance languages —/i:/—and the *ou* of *mouse* (a spelling introduced by the Normans to replace the more reasonable Anglo-Saxon *mūs*) meant what it still means to the French—/u:/. These vowels, being long, became increasingly unsteady (the tongue, like any other muscular organ, does not like to hold the same rigid position for too long a time), and they wavered themselves into the state of diphthongs. *Shine,* in RP, now has a firm /aɪ/, while *mouse* has a solid /aʊ/. But for a lengthy period both diphthongs, while their second element recalled quite clearly the parent vowel, though now in a shorter and slacker form, kept the first element in a vague central region. Shakespeare probably said /ʃəɪn/ and /məʊs/. A diphthong with a first element further back in the mouth than /ə/ was also acceptable—something like /ʌɪ/ or /ʏɪ/ for *shine* and /ʌʊ/ or /ʏʊ/ for *mouse*—and these, which we associate with Queen Anne and Swift and the *Spectator*, are still to be heard in Japanese and German Dublin.

When words like *shine* and *eye* and *I* and *my* jumped out of that /i:/ slot which is the front upper region of the mouth, words containing a double e—*meet, beet, queen* and so on—forgot that their vowel was a Continental /e:/ whose length was symbolised in the orthographic doubling, and rose to fill the high gap, giving the pronunciation in /i:/ that we share with the Elizabethans and the Augustans. On the rung below the ee-words were the ea-words—*meat, beat, quean* (meaning prostitute) and the rest. The second element of the digraph had been a signal to make a low e—/ɛ/, but now the low e became a high one, filling the empty slot. Words like *lady* and *make,* which in Chaucer's time had a Continental a—as in *chatte* or *acqua* —now rose to take over the discarded /ɛ:/. This general rising has continued, front and back, so that *meat* and *beat* have risen to the limit, giving us awkward homophones (the awkwardness is spectacularly to be observed in *queen* and *quean*, but the latter has dropped out of general use). *Make* rose to become /meɪk/ and was then dipthongised into /mɛɪk/. The modern Dublin situation has resisted those awkward homophones but has accepted, for the most part, the placing of words like *name* and *cream* in the same vocalic slot. The whole story of changing English pronunciation is a long one. The above partial summary is merely meant to show that the demotic speech of Dublin, and other parts of Ireland, has remained close to the standards which were accepted as cultivated and aristocratic in the days of the great Dean of St. Patrick's.

At its lower social levels, the English of Joyce's town continues to resist the influence of British RP and to combine with eighteenth-century English vowels and diphthongs consonants that show the influence of Erse. The Irish thetatismus which levels /θ/ and /ö/ under the dental /t/ and /d/ respectively (not alveolar, as in RP), the combination /tr/ in which the first element is so detalised as to lead some writers of Irish comedy to represent it as *thr* (as in *thrue* for *true*), the tendency to make affricates of medial and final /t/ and /d/—these seem to derive from consonantal usage in the native Celtic tongue, as does the clear l which is found in all positions in opposition to the RP darkening of l in final positions and before other consonants (RP *well* = /wɛl/; RP *built* = /bɪlt/). Educated Anglo-Irish speech retains the clear l but follows RP usage in respect of the other consonants, except that—as in all varieties of Irish English as well as American English and many British dialects—the letter r, in whatever position, is taken as a phonemic signal and not as a mere ghost or vowel-length sign. While speakers of RP pronounce *park* and *warm* as /paːk/ and /wəːm/ respectively, most Irishmen join Americans in pronouncing the written r as a retroflex consonant, or enunciating the preceding vowel with the tongue in a retroflex position.

Educated Irish speakers of English show willingness to come close to RP vocalic usage, though they are not always happy about the close diphthongs /eɪ/ and /oʊ/. We can be fairly sure, when reading *Ulysses*, that Joyce intends Mulligan to hail "our great sweet mother" as /öə siː/ and not /də seː/, though, when he refers to the time when "the French were on the sea," he has in mind the popular song "The Shan Van Vocht"—

> The French are on the sea,
> Says the Shan Van Vocht . . .
> They'll be here without delay,
> And the Orange will decay . . .

—and presumably adjusts his pronunciation accordingly. How Stephen Dedalus, in this phase of his postgraduate career, is meant to pronounce

English we cannot be sure. Mulligan refers to Stephen's "Oxford manner," which seems to imply an adjustment of his native phonemes to educated British usage, but we cannot easily accept that Stephen is now pronouncing *home* as /hoʊm/ or /hʊʊm/ or /həʊm/ and *master* as /maːstə/. To level *ee* and *ea* under the one vowel /iː/, to pronounce *might* as /maɪt/ and *join* as /dʒɔɪn/, while retaining other native vocalic and diphthongal usages, is the most an Irishman need do to qualify as an "educated" speaker.

Ulysses, which is a conspectus of so many things, may be taken as implying the whole spectrum of Dublin speech, and it would be amusing to sketch out a cline, with the speech of drabs and jarveys near the bottom and that of characters like J. J. O'Molloy and Professor MacHugh somewhere at the top. As it is, for the most part, far more enlightening to hear *Ulysses* read aloud (with the score on one's knee) than to peruse it silently, it is useful for the teacher of a Joyce course to have a rough repertory actor's notion of accent differentials. In the "Cyclops" chapter, where the narrative is entrusted to an anonymous low Dubliner, the idiom provides a clue to the accent:

> I was just passing the time of day with old Troy of the D.M.P. at the corner of Arbour Hill there and be damned but a bloody sweep came along and he near drove his gear into my eye. I turned around to let him have the weight of my tongue when who should I see dodging along Stony Batter only Joe Hynes.

Here "just" and "bloody" and "tongue" will probably have the vowel /ʊ/, whereas a more educated speaker would prefer, if not /ʌ/ (the RP vowel), at least /ʊ/. "My eye" will be /mɪj ʌɪ/, "around" something like /əˈræʊnd/, "Stony Batter" probably /stɔːnɪ bæteʳr/, the /t/ palatalised and affricated. The *ing* of "passing" and "dodging" will be pronounced as a syllabic /n/. Compare this with the way in which we may imagine Professor MacHugh, in the "Aeolus" episode, enunciating the following:

> —What was their civilisation? Vast, I allow: but vile. Cloacae: sewers. The Jews in the wilderness and on the mountaintop said: *It is meet to be here. Let us build an altar to Jehovah.* The Roman, like the Englishman who follows in his footsteps, brought to every new shore on which he set his foot (on our shore he never set it) only his cloacal obsession. He gazed about him in his toga and he said: *It is meet to be here. Let us construct a watercloset.*

The *wh* of "what" will be pronounced as an unvoiced semivowel /w/, whereas educated British usage would prefer /w/. The *a* of "civilisation" could be, instead of the RP /eɪ/, the vowel /eː/ or even one approaching /ɛː/. "Vast" would not be RP /vaːst/ but Elizabethan /væ.st/, but "vile" would conform with British usage except for the clear l (/vaɪl/, not /vaɪɫ/). The r in "sewers," "wilderness," "here," "alter" and "shore" would be pronounced as a weak retroflex consonant. The o-letter in "Jehovah," "Roman" and "toga" should be interpreted not as a diphthong (RP /oʊ/) but as the open sound /ɔ:/.

It is intriguing to consider how Leopold Bloom's speech would fit into the spectrum. His idiom, either in dialogue or interior monologue, is lacking in the broader Dublin features: it approaches the emancipated or "Londonised" language we associate with, say, Ignatius Gallaher the journalist (a character in the *Dubliners* story "A Little Cloud" who, in *Ulysses*, has become a newsman's myth). We may imagine Bloom—the "cultured allroundman" as Lenehan, in a moment of rare Dublin generosity, calls him—as possessing the ability to vary his speech according to the company, but as being totally incapable of sinking to the lowest demotic Dublinese. Certain actors playing the part of Bloom in radio adaptations of *Ulysses*, before the advent of the stage *Bloomsday* and the film *Ulysses*, both of which established Milo O'Shea as an authoritative interpreter of the role, attempted to give a "Jewish" quality to Bloom's speech. Whatever "Jewish" means, it can have no significance in terms of voice or accent. Jews using English as a second language may bring to it the usages of Yiddish or Ladino, but Bloom, though his father was Hungarian (and, according to the "Circe" episode, capable of English like "One night they bring you home drunk as dog after spend your good money"), is clearly a product of lower middle-class Dublin and its language is his. Stage "Jewishness" of the adenoidal variety would be totally out of place. We may take Bloom as a mediator, in speech as in other things, between his earthy wife Molly and the poetic Stephen.

Few readers have any doubts about the phonetic content of, say, Molly's final words:

> . . . and I thought well as well him as another and then I asked him with my eyes to ask again yes and then he asked me would I yes to say yes my mountain flower and first I put my arms around him yes and drew him down to me so he could feel my breasts all perfume yes and his heart was going like mad and yes I said yes I will Yes.

Joyce has established on her very first appearance that she has no education. "It must have fell down," she says, and "Tell us in plain words". But the implied lower-class Dublin speech does not fit in well with her declared background. Her father was a major in the Gibraltar garrison and her mother was Spanish. (I spent three years as a soldier in Gibraltar and find both her father's rank and his marriage implausible, but let that pass.) Molly would grow up speaking Andalusian Spanish (Joyce makes her approach it as though a Hugo grammar) and a kind of pseudo-patrician English imposed by her father's position in a closed and highly snobbish garrison society. Coming to Dublin as a young woman she would be unlikely to relinquish a sort of ruling-class accent and idiom. I think we have to remember that Joyce's shaping of his heroine's mind and speech owed more to the reality of his wife's perpetual presence than to the fictional imagination. Consider the following:

> Well I feel very knocked up to day you don't know what a thunderstorm is but if you went through one here you would not be worth much it was something dreadful it began last night about half past nine we were in the dining room with a few people and as it had been raining all day the people did not expect it and all of a sudden it came on lightening thunderbolts I thought it was our last I was almost stiff with fright for about twenty minutes then it poured and we went to bed about half past ten but I did not sleep then a hurricane began and lightening which lasted till halfpast five this morning . . .

That is not a discarded draft for "Penelope" but a letter from Nora Joyce.

It is no exaggeration to state that Joyce takes, among all the varieties of spoken English, only that of his own town seriously. When British English is heard in *Ulysses*, it is always in the form of a music-hall parody. In the "Cyclops" chapter "the stern provostmarshal, lieutenantcolonel Tomkin-Maxwell ffrenchmullan Tomlinson" murmurs to himself "in a faltering undertone": "God blimey if she aint a clinker, that there bleeding tart. Blimey it makes me kind of bleeding cry, straight it does, when I sees her cause I thinks of my old mashtub what's waiting for me down Limehouse way." In "Circe" the author Philip Beaufoy, on whose story "Matcham's Masterstroke" Bloom has innocently wiped his morning fundament, attacks this "particularly loathsome conduct" thus:

> You funny ass, you! You're too beastly awfully weird for words! I don't think you need over excessively disincommodate yourself in that regard . . . We are considerably out of pocket over this bally pressman johnny, this jackdaw of Rheims, who has not even been to a university . . . You ought to be ducked in the horsepond, you rotter!

American English is represented by a spirited parody of an evangelistic exhortation:

> Elijah is coming washed in the Blood of the Lamb. Come on, you wine-fizzling ginsizzling booseguzzling existences! Come on, you doggone, bull-necked, bettlebrowed, hogjowled, peanutbrained, weaseleyed fourflushers, false alarms and excess baggage. Come on, you triple extract of infamy!

> Alexander J. Christ Dowie, that's yanked to glory most half this planet from 'Frisco Beach to Vladivostok. The Deity ain't no nickel dime bumshow. I put it to you that he's on the square and a corking fine business proposition. He's the grandest thing yet and don't you forget it. Shout salvation in king Jesus. You'll need to rise precious early, you sinner there, if you want to diddle the Almighty God. Pflaaap! Not half. He's got a coughmixture with a punch in it for you, my friend, in his backpocket. Just you try it on.

Dublin English is apotheosised, in *Finnegans Wake,* to a universal language capable of absorbing all others. It is a remarkable prosodic achievement in that it can move from the lowest street colloquial to the sesquipedalian pedantic without transitional devices:

> He addle liddle phifie Annie ugged the little craythur. Wither hayre in honds tuck up your part inher. Oftwhile balbulous, mithre ahead, with goodly trowel in grasp and ivoroiled overalls which he habitacularly fondseed, like Haroun Childeric Eggeberth he would caligulate by multiplicables the alltitude and malltitude until he seesaw by neatlight of the liquor wheretwin 'twas born, his roundhead staple of other days to rise in undress maisonry upstanded (joygrantit!), a waalworth of a skyerscape of most eyeful hoyth entowerly, erigenating from next to nothing and celescalating the himals and all, heirarchitectitiptitoploftical, with a burning bush abob off its baubletop and with larrons o'toolers clittering up and tombles a' buckets clottering down.

But, of course, the seeds of this mad variety are already present in the real speech of Dublin, with its ability to encompass obscenity, seedy scraps of half-remembered learning, malapropism, the grandiloquent structures of oratory, euphony and balance for their own sake regardless of meaning. To take such a vehicle of social communication seriously is essentially not to take it seriously, since it has ludic elements in it which disappeared from British English. The book is based on the sound of Dublin English and it encompasses its entire orchestral spectrum. We may read the opening in the style of George Bernard Shaw—

> riverrun, past Eve and Adam's, from swerve of shore to bend of bay, brings us by a commodius vicus of recirculation back to Howth Castle and Environs

—and the ending in the style of any lachrymose old biddy in the snug—

> Bussoftlhee, mememormee! Till thousendsthee. Lps. The keys to. Given!
> A way a lone a last a loved a long the

—but, as the last word governs the first, we are in the same sentence and hence speaking with the same voice.

HARRY LEVIN

"Ulysses" in Manuscript

Almost unbelievably, it is now some fifty-odd years since the publication of *Ulysses* in 1922. That same year also witnessed the publication of *The Waste Land*, whose jubilee has lately been commemorated by a facsimile edition of its original manuscript. Nothing that has happened since to English prose or verse can be compared with the simultaneous impact of these two masterworks. In their turn, and after a probationary period of shock and incomprehension, they have been accorded a classic status among the artistic landmarks of our unclassical century. They have indeed been so canonized by criticism and scholarship that it has become hard for us to recapture a sense of the turmoil that engendered them. But now that we have printed access to the preliminary versions in each case, it becomes possible to follow the intricate processes whereby two of our greatest writers asserted their mastery. They could share certain attitudes and approaches, as Eliot pointed out when he hailed Joyce for containing his amorphous material within the ordered contours of rediscovered myth. It may be significant that neither was an Englishman; for each of them brought to the language a special dedication, as well as a special impatience with facile or flaccid styles. Yet they were widely divergent in native temperament as well as formal intention, and those divergences were mirrored in their respective methods of composition. Eliot's manuscript is twice the length of his poem; Joyce's is considerably shorter than his novel. Final redaction was largely a matter of cutting for Eliot, of amplification for Joyce.

The circumstances attending the present version ["Ulysses": A Facsimile of the Manuscript edited by Clive Driver] are well described by Mr.

From *Memories of the Moderns*. Copyright © 1975 by Harry Levin. New Directions Books.

Driver in his editorial introduction. This is—or sets out to be—the author's fair copy, though its increasing burden of afterthoughts, marginalia, inter-lineations, and corrections indicates that much of the text was still being drafted at first hand. Behind it looms the seven-year labor (closer to eight) of *"Treste-Zurich-Paris, 1914–1921"*: plans and notes and drafts extending through prior stages, thousands of descriptive details and associated ideas sorted out and recombined and interwoven into parallel streams of con-sciousness. Looking back toward those earlier endeavors, some of them recorded by notebooks in the Lockwood Library at the University of Buffalo, others in the outlines at the British Museum, we are bound to view the pages before us as the critical stage of a tremendous and complicated process of assemblage. But if we look ahead to the published version, we are bound to observe that the actual writing of the book went on continuously until it reached the printing press. Though the printers worked from typescript based in large part on this fair copy, the text would be corrected much further by the author, who supplied other texts for certain chapters pub-lished in periodicals and kept on adding and changing through as many as six or seven sets of page-proof. Joseph Prescott's unpublished Harvard dis-sertation, a careful study of the additions and changes in the galleys (*plac-ards*) now at the Houghton Library, bears the suggestive title, "James Joyce's *Ulysses* as a Work in Progress." Like Balzac, Joyce could not resist the compulsion to rewrite as he read proof, so that the definitive text would only be crystallized with the printer's last deadline.

These proofs afford an eloquent testimonial to the patience of the printer, Maurice Darantière, and the generosity of the publisher, Sylvia Beach. Thus, when at a momentary loss for the *mot juste*, Joyce could simply postpone it until the next proofreading. Into the library episode he inserted a line in which Malachi Mulligan parodies Synge: " 'Twas murmur we did for a gallus potion would rouse a friar, I'm thinking." Whereupon Joyce instructed the compositor in French to leave a space for six or seven additional words. Inspiration came to him succinctly with five words on the subsequent proof, catching both Synge's cadence and Mulligan's scur-rility: "and he limp with leching." In such a light as this it is understandable, though still rather awesome, that Joyce could send the body of his work to be set up before he wrote the concluding seven pages of Molly Bloom's soliloquy. He must have had that climax well in mind, but perhaps it was so climactic for him that he did not want others to see it except in print. (Two days before the date of printing, he was still writing it, as proof-sheets now at the University of Texas disclose.) Despite his failing eyesight, he cherished a Mallarméan feeling for the appearance of type upon a page.

Those headlines which intersperse the chapter located in a newspaper office were written afterward, and so were the opening paragraphs, as if in conformity with the journalistic procedures they illustrate. Moreover, Joyce transposed italics to Roman capitals, and experimented with the phrasing from proof to proof. "IN THE HEART OF THE METROPOLIS" was brought home by the adjective "HIBERNIAN," while "A STREET PROCESSION" became a more fastidious "CORTEGE."

Ulysses, in the Rosenbach Manuscript, is less interrupted by such devices as headlines, and it stands by itself except for Molly's peroration. To reread the story in Joyce's own hand is to enter his workshop; for, though it neatly subsumes the tangle of earlier recensions, it revises itself as it goes along and gathers codicils in the last two chapters. The peculiar slanting conformation of its margins seems to suggest a restless speeding-up as the lines move down, while the tendency to diminish in size—especially as contrasted with the twenty-one pages copied by Frank Budgen, or even with the larger and more regular holograph of *Stephen Hero* written nearly twenty years before—conveys a costive effect which readily submits itself to Freudian analysis. Joyce's handwriting anonymously submitted, has been analyzed by a student of graphology, Yvonne Skinner, who finds marked expressions of culture, intelligence, and sensitivity in his habits of penmanship. Mental energy, extreme self-consciousness, conscientiousness to the point of fussiness, powers of intense concentration and command of precise detail, musical if not mathematical talents, a rare combination of intuition and logic—these are traits that have imprinted themselves, according to Mrs. Skinner, along with impracticality, obstinacy, irritability, reticence, and occasional brusqueness. This can do no more than confirm what we already know from letters and memoirs, from Richard Ellmann's admirable biography, above all from our own unmediated impressions; but it marks a correlation that Joyce himself might have relished between his substance and his presentation.

There are some points where the manuscript carries more authority than the printed texts, which admitted and persisted in certain errata. Joyce went out of his way to specify that the first syllable of his hero's forename, as shouted and echoed in his first chapter should be spelled with twelve *e*'s: "Steeeeeeeeeeeephen!" Both the American and British editions have skimped on this long-drawn-out vocative. Both again have ignored a speech-prefix, thereby confusing the song of the moth with the voice of Mr. Bloom's grandfather. A more notable omission takes place at the end of the "Ithaca" chapter, in which the question "Where?" is supposed to be answered by a large period, cryptically symbolizing the world itself as it recedes into space.

Recognizing the danger of an oversight here, Joyce was explicit in his instructions to Darantière: "*La réponse à la dernière est un point.*" This is betokened by a small square in the first edition, and subsequently omitted as often as not. In general, since Joyce worked by accumulation, discarding little while amplifying and embroidering much, few passages appear in the manuscript that do not arrive at the final text in some form or other. An interesting exception crops up during Stephen's morning meditation, when he broods for a moment over "Wilde's love that dare not speak its name." The manuscript continues with four more words, which have been omitted from the book: "His arm: Cranly's arm." Stephen, recalling an early friendship signalized in *A Portrait of the Artist as a Young Man*, retrospectively hints that it may have had a homosexual tinge. Joyce evidently decided against that implication which was scarcely present when the phrase (in reverse) was introduced [elsewhere].

Stephen returns to youthful memories in eight lines later omitted from his Shakespearean discussion, where his mental comment includes a Latin definition of love from Saint Thomas Aquinas, who will be quoted elsewhere at all events. Those who are theologically inclined may ponder the significance of the marginal substitution on [the] page when Father Conmee is reading his breviary, wherein one of the displaced quotations seems to relate more directly than the substitute to the business of Bloomsday: "*Notus in Iudaea Deus. . . .*" Alterations of single words are often purely functional. A comparison of the contexts will show why "stretched" was altered to "inclined" or "procuress" to "bawd"; "ambled" was turned into "slunk" and "dog" into "beagle" with a clear gain in expressiveness. Joyce took particular pains to choose proper names that rang with an appropriate resonance. As a language teacher, he quite advisedly replaced Bué's by Chardenal's French primer. While he was revising his manuscript, he substituted Kino's for Hyam's as a brand-name for trousers. Minor personages were rechristened for local reasons when John Murray became Red Murray. The foreman Castell became Nannetti and the Honourable Mrs. Paget Butler became Mrs. Mervyn Talboys. Bloom's wife, singing in concerts under her maiden name, Madame Marion Tweedy, seems to have started her professional career as Madame Marie Meagher. Her manager and lover, the uncouth Boylan, is generally known by his nickname "Blazes"; but he had originally been baptized Edward, which was emended to Hugh E. in the latest proof.

Simplicity could never be anything more than a relative consideration with Joyce; but, insofar as the manuscript is simpler than its ultimate outgrowth, its story-line is more immediately graspable. Edmund Wilson argued that Joyce had overdone his verbal elaboration of *Finnegans Wake*, that it had proved more effective in the briefer and somewhat less highly wrought extracts published previously as *Work in Progress*. Yet, once a writer ventures so far afield, he transcends the usual norms, and the critic has no basis for imposing limits. There are likewise readers who prefer the more solidly naturalistic texture of *Stephen Hero* to the refined impressionism of the much-written *Portrait of the Artist*. But Joyce's master then had been Flaubert; and he was engaged in reproducing, on a more tentative scale, the efforts of documentation, arrangement, retrenchment, and distillation that had created *Madame Bovary*. Since his maturer aims were encyclopedic, his narrative techniques were—in his own coinage—"allincluding." Since nothing endemic to Dublin was alien to his panorama, there were always posterior touches of urban color to be worked in. The more he developed the minds of his characters, the greater the opportunities they opened up for reminiscence and coincidence, linking themselves with one another and with their environment. All the important connections had been established, and the basic synthesis achieved, by the time the manuscript was written out. But the habit of accretion would continue as long as the pages lay open to correction; as long as the snowball rolled, it would be augmented by fresh layers of observation and insight.

The specific differences that emerge from even the most casual collation of the Rosenbach facsimile with a standard edition of *Ulysses*, accordingly, are touchstones for Joyce's imagination in action. Every chapter, to be sure, presents a different problem, and—at least through the dramatic scenes that have been likened to Goethe's *Walpurgisnacht*—they tend to increase successively in length and complexity. All of them are meaningfully extended here and there, with new sidelights and unexpected linkages, as among the funeral guests in "Hades" or the assortment of pedestrians in "The Wandering Rocks" (it is convenient to make use of Joyce's Homeric terms as phantom chapter headings). Some episodes, the more technically experimental, had to be carefully elaborated and tightly composed from the outset, and have consequently been less reworked than the others: "The Sirens," to whose musical interplay he had already devoted five months, and "The Oxen of the Sun," where the evolution of English prose style is retraced by the obstetrical narration. Two other episodes, involving parody at a more limited and commonplace level, invited any number of addenda. The diction of "Nausicaa" is that of novelettes and advertisements in sentimental women's magazines, and Joyce could enhance the description of Gerty MacDowell by adding "that tired feeling" to the typescript and "blushing scientifically cured" to the proof. The parlance of

"Eumaeus" is a kind of masculine counterpart, the cliches of some long-winded pretender to what he would call *sang froid;* and Joyce took a grim pleasure in piling up such tired foreign phrases as *confrères hoi polloi,* and *tête-à-tête.*

Both in manner and subject, "The Cyclops" offered many opportunities for substantial interpolation. It is primarily a realistic monologue in a raffish Dublin idiom, with a good deal of barroom conversation; but its nationalistic and racial argument sets off a series of imaginary projections, both mythological and religious, with Ireland represented by its traditional heroes and the half-Jewish Bloom by the prophet Elijah. Joyce enlarged the easy flow of pub-talk by repeated extensions in the guise of epic catalogues or ecclesiastical litanies: a list of prominent clergymen, a roll-call of the saints, a survey of the natural beauties of Ireland, a fashionable wedding of the trees, a well-attended public execution. To an even greater degree, the section entitled "Ithaca" could be filled in and pieced out with lengthy inserts, since it had the segmented format of a catechism or set of examination questions and answers. Much of the supplementation is in an appended section of the manuscript, notably the sequence of parallels and contrasts between Bloom and Stephen. Still more would be interposed there in the way of material facts: the contents of the kitchen cupboard and of Bloom's desk, including the suicide note of his late father. The intimately personal strain, neutralized by statistical data and large abstractions, would blench before the chill of interplanetary distance. The *Verfremdungseffekt* of the farewell scene has been intensified in revision, when Bloom and Stephen hear the several echoes that have been haunting them all day: for Stephen his mother's funeral Mass, for Bloom the neighborhood church-bells.

"Penelope," the conclusion, is similar to the preceding "Ithaca," having been transcribed in a separate notebook where the opposite pages have ample room for the increment of marginalia, thus giving us the clearest enumeration of Joyce's second thoughts: e.g. the allusion to Rabelais. But, along with Molly's powerful valedictory, Joyce had many small particulars to add. His pun on Beerbohm Tree and Trilby's "barebum" adumbrates the sort of wordplay that would soon be engulfing him in *Finnegans Wake.* The keyword *yes* is enumerated more frequently in the definitive version, and the stress on continuity is strengthened by the elimination of introductory capitals and punctuation marks. Probably the focal chapter, certainly the longest, and the one most highly charged with emotions, however, is the expressionistic psychodrama of "Circe." What has gone before builds up to it; what comes later on subsides from it; hence we are not surprised that it should have become what it is by intensive reworking. This gave Bloom more chances to act out his fantasies, such as his elevation and condemnation in the role of Lord Mayor. A curious shift in the speech he makes just after that interlude modulates from "All is vanity" to "All insanity" conceivably because the message of Ecclesiastes would be cited and embroidered elsewhere. Stephen's epiphany, the apparition of his mother's ghost, had also to be heightened; and Joyce wrote in—on a page of the typescript subsequently presented by Miss Beach to Theodore Spencer—the most poignant touch, the echo of Mulligan's sneer: "She's beastly dead!"

The fuller treatment of Stephen's streetfight with Private Carr gets magnified to pageantlike proportions by the hallucinated stage directions involving King Edward VII, with characteristic gestures and responses from dozens of other figures among the audience who have wandered in from other parts of the story. The blow that lays Stephen low has been preceded by the reverberation from a black Mass—a reversal of the blasphemous chanting with which Mulligan began the book. This is spelled out more fully by spelling backward the name of God and a verse from the liturgy. Bloom rescues Stephen with the aid of the cheerful undertaker Corny Kelleher, who at various earlier moments has been heard to hum the amorous refrain: "With my tooraloom tooraloom. . . ." Therefore Joyce took care to write it in on the occasion of Kelleher's providential reappearance, and in the proofs it is used to orchestrate Kelleher's departure, when Bloom "assuralooms" him and he "reassuraloms" Bloom. What remains behind is the culminating epiphany, Bloom's vision, as he leans down over the prostrate Stephen, of his lost son Rudy. Here the manuscript contains the bare core of the human situation, to which it adds one bathetic detail, the white lambkin. The rich development came at a late stage in the proofs: the fragments of the Masonic oath with which Bloom swears himself to secrecy, the sentimentalized lineaments of the boy that might have been, had he lived to eleven instead of dying in infancy. And though the manuscript tells us that Rudy is reading, it is not until the proof that he "reads from right to left," apprising his wonderstruck father that the book he reads is in Hebrew.

Kelleher's "tooraloom" provides a minor instance of how Joyce associates themes, often musical or literary, with moods and characters. He found many new occasions for introducing and interweaving them while copying his work and preparing it for the press. Thus the theme of apocalypse ("shattered glass and toppling masonry") comes into its own in a stage direction for the midnight hallucination; but it first appears, and is slightly amended, as it flashes across Stephen's mind in the schoolroom, and it is interpolated among the musings of his morning stroll along the beach. *Agenbite of inwit,* the Middle English locution for remorse of conscience, has come to be regarded as a key to Stephen's character, above all to his relationship with his mother. Yet having been belatedly superimposed on the text, it is absent from the manuscript. *"Là ci darem la mano,"* the duet from *Don Giovanni,* is Bloom's byword for philandering. It is one of two numbers figuring in Molly's next concert program, the other being "Love's Old Sweet Song." One or the other runs through Bloom's mind all day, a latent reminder of Molly's affair with Boylan. Late at night, during Bloom's subsconscious encounter with an old flame, Mrs. Breen, she echoes the Anglo-Irish song: "the dear dead days beyond recall." The revised flirtation scene also echoes the repartee of the Mozart duet. Mozart makes a more problematic entrance into the manuscript on the verso of [one page] possibly an accidental intrusion in a hand which Mr. Driver has identified as that of Joyce's baritone son Giorgio, a transcription of the High Priest's *"In diesen heiligen Hallen"* from *Die Zauberflöte.* That bass aria has been referred to already under its Italian designation, *"Oui sdegno,"* just before Ben Dollard chooses to sing "The Croppy Boy." Why the Temple of the Sun should be invoked, when Bloom is entering a brothel, tempts speculation.

Trains of thematic association help to unify the heterogeneous subject matter after it has been set down and put together. A handbill announcing the modern Elijah, an American evangelist, has been crumpled up by Bloom and dropped into the Liffey. The chapter that chronicles the activities of numerous minor characters, "The Wandering Rocks," has three postscripts that trace this "skiff" as it floats out to sea, incidentally crossing the schooner that is to discharge W. B. Murphy, the nautical spokesman of "Eumaeus." Similarly, the five sandwich-men, advertising H. E. L. Y.'S, letter by letter, thread their way along the margin. In broaching sexual matters, then so delicate a concern and so much of an obstacle to free expression for Joyce's contemporaries, he became more explicitly candid as he rewrote. Because of Bloom's reluctance to name Boylan, the latter plays an elusive part in the interior monologue. Yet, as a billsticker by profession, he is identified with the observed announcement "POST NO BILLS," while the reconsidered context, by alluding to venereal disease, explains Bloom's secret fear: could his wife be infected through her adultery? The broken queries of the manuscript would scarcely be meaningful without the contextual gloss. The monosyllabic "Ow!" is somewhat better explained by "This wet is very unpleasant," and by the consequent realization that Bloom is feeling the aftereffects of his physical reaction to Gerty MacDowell's exhibitionism. The addendum, "Well the foreskin is not back," not only supplies another gloss; it reveals the ironic fact that the "half and half" Bloom, though victimized by antisemitism, has never been circumcized.

Afterstrokes round out the detailed portraiture, completing the intimacy of our acquaintance with the *dramatis personae*. We might have guessed that Bloom had trouble in throwing a ball at school, or that he once made timid advances to an indignant housemaid. But his underlying humanity emerges from humble acts and compassionate thoughts, as when he helps the blind piano-tuner across the street. In turning [the page], Joyce recopied and modified the operative sentence, bringing the two men close together physically through the sense of touch. On the margin he subjoined Bloom's psychological impulse: "Say something to him. Better not do the condescending. Something ordinary." Modification in the proof would lead to "a common remark" about the weather, and would indicate that this went characteristically unheeded. It is the proof once more that enables Bloom to probe his motivation in "The Lestrygonians," when he is meditating on his earlier happiness and the breakdown of his conjugal relations with Molly over the past ten years: "Could never like it again after Rudy." Molly herself makes no direct allusion to their dead child; note that her remembrance of having suckled him at her breast gets marginally shifted to their daughter Milly. Yet, in the course of her egocentric and sensual recollections, she does refer to "knitting that woollen thing"—an aftertouch which relies, for its emotional charge, on a cross-reference to an archaic paragraph in "The Oxen of the Sun," where Bloom recalls her grief over Rudy's death, and her pathetic hope that a little sweater she had knitted might lessen the rigors of winter burial.

The foregoing examples do no more than scratch the surface, though I hope they suggest the unique value and fascinating interest that this facsimile holds for those familiar with *Ulysses*. Most of my illustrations can be pursued much farther, and the practiced reader will have the pleasure of making his own discoveries, as he collates the manuscript with the book itself. He will be privileged to watch the artist at work, now smoothly copying from blotted and interlined drafts, now pausing to reconsider and retouch. Every word has entailed a complex decision. Some of those decisions are visible here in the author's correcting hand; others are to be inferred from the differences between the two redactions. We have become well aware of Joyce's achievement as an incomparable feat of literary organization, according with an elaborately preconceived design. Henceforth we can appreciate more concretely the last-minute insights, the more intuitive flashes of Joyce's artistry. Even Jung, a decade after its first appearance, characterized *Ulysses* as an enigma. To less percipient readers it seemed—as to the great majority of nonreaders—impenetrable. Yet during the last four decades the enigma has been so expounded, the novel has been so accepted, the style has been so scanned by so many admirers, that every phrase has come to seem inevitable. Stasis, the Joycean consummation, has indeed set in. Impressed by a classic, overwhelmed by a monument, we are likely to lose sight of all the problematic and dynamic elements that have gone into its composition. But Joyce had pledged his genius to demonstrating, as well as celebrating, the will to create.

It is something of a paradox that a novelist as committed as he was to the stylistic, esthetic, and formal aspects of his craft should have concentrated as intently on his private experience as he did. This he handled freely, though by no means romantically, since he had subjected it to naturalistic restraints. But his method controverts those critical purists who, in their devotion to the cult of form, would rule out the biographical background of a writer. A well-known formulation in the *Portrait of the Artist*, refining on an even better-known formula of Flaubert, emphasizes a transference from the lyric to the dramatic, from an artist's personality to the impersonality of art. The mean between them is the very act of artistic creation, to which we can bear witness through the document that has been reproduced herewith. It will catch the "fabulous artificer"—and how firmly the epithet is incised into the text—during those mellow hours when he has been putting the finishing touches upon his labyrinth. Not only will the spirit of Daedalus guide us through the maze; he will reveal some secrets of his creative artifice. On the relation of the myth to the novel, for instance: it seems clear that Joyce began by laying down the outline he had somewhat arbitrarily taken from Homer's *Odyssey*, and that he ranged more widely as he proceeded into the latterday welter of Dublin life. Having placed his mythical correspondences where they would serve as guidelines for the adventures of Bloom and Stephen, he consolidated and animated his picture of the society that would all too briefly interlink and ultimately isolate their lives.

Criticism has followed a parallel path, starting from the authorized commentary of Stuart Gilbert, which dwelled upon the Odyssean scheme as Joyce himself had imparted it, and gradually moving forward toward a broader comprehension of the more literal events of Bloomsday. It was in this connection that the term *exegesis*, hitherto reserved for interpretation of the Scriptures or hieratic books, came to be identified with the analytic reading of difficult secular literature—where it has more recently been reinforced by the adaptation of *hermeneutics*. Joyce, for whom esthetics was a lay religion, would have been pleased by the pious zeal of his exegetes, who have surrounded his works with Scholastic metaphrase and Talmudic conjecture. These are ironic reparations for all the neglect and obstruction and misunderstanding from which he had suffered until he was vindicated by the recognition of *Ulysses*. Once the ban of censorship was lifted, the volume moved quickly through the bookshops and libraries into the academic sphere of study and research. There it faces the hazards of over-reading. Joyce's intentions, though sometimes abstruse, were always concrete; his meanings, if recondite, would disclose themselves to perceptive scrutiny. As the mysteries have been unfolded, new interpreters have indulged in mystifications of their own. It is true that, besides the major precedent of Odysseus, Joyce alludes selectively to various other archetypes: Daedalus, Elijah, Don Giovanni, Jesus Christ. But it is either imposture or self-deception to argue, as one recent French commentator has done, that the twelve central chapters are respectively modeled on Suetonius' *Lives of the Caesars*.

Joyce's writing has a tough-minded objectivity which resists such subjective ingenuity and exposes farfetched pretentiousness. The task of his critics has been unduly complicated by their initial need to pave the way for appreciation with an emphasis on disclosure and decoding. As a consequence, we have tended to think about him rather too schematically, and to overlook the more immediate appeal that he can exert on so many other grounds. We have looked for keys, or else clung to vague analogies, rather than approaching him through his boundless particularity. This is understandable enough, since his searching curiosity, his passion for detail, and his exactitude in naming things are not easily blown up into arresting generalizations. Yet his distinguishing quality could be denoted by a favorite concept of his student days: *quiddity*, the whatness of anything or everything, that which makes it so uniquely itself. It was not for nothing that one of his poems got printed in Pound's anthology *Des Imagistes*, for he too professed the aim of the Imagists to behold and convey the object precisely. But he went beyond them in—the novelist's function—showing precisely how the existence of human beings is structured by objects. Whereas the poet could single out a perception and embody it in a poem, Joyce sought out those revealing juxtapositions which he termed epiphanies, and composed a novel by combining them *ad infinitum*. The manuscript of *Ulysses* is a quest for quiddities, a record of such perceptions as synthesized into a profoundly meaningful statement about the world. It is also a manual of style, which permits us line by line to participate in the struggles and share the triumphs.

RICHARD ELLMANN

The Consciousness of Joyce

In the first draft of "A Portrait of the Artist," which comes closer than any of his works to non-fictional autobiography, Joyce indicated that at one period in his development, he had been outspoken in his rebellion against institutions, specifically against the Church. "But that outburst over," he then writes, "it was urbanity in warfare." The term "urbanity" is misleading, it suggests indulgence and tolerance, and its relation to "warfare" is antithetical; a term less paradoxical would be "obliquity." This is the quality which shapes Joyce's treatment of institutions in all his works. It went with the distaste for didacticism, shared with Flaubert. Sometimes he is so oblique that he is believed in some quarters not to have been conducting warfare at all.

Apologists for his Catholicism have pointed out that he repudiates the Church in A Portrait only to the degree that it impinges upon his hero, and not absolutely. But that is merely to say that he keeps within the frame of his fiction; it does not reduce the authority of Stephen as a model. Joyce's attitude towards the State has also been misinterpreted, not least by Marxist critics. At the Congress of Writers in Kharkov in 1933, Karl Radek accused him of being a defender of bourgeois capitalism, and some non-Marxist critics, reading Ulysses the same way, have marvelled at what they take to be Joyce's complacency about the social order, or what Lionel Trilling has called his indifference to politics. Still, the author of Dubliners could scarcely be considered complacent, and the misconstrual arises from his indirectness. S. L. Goldberg has lamented that Joyce failed in Ulysses to display the evils of modern industrialism as D. H. Lawrence in Women in Love exposed the

From The Consciousness of Joyce. Copyright © 1977 by Richard Ellmann. Oxford University Press.

horrors of the coal mines. There would in fact be a difficulty in placing coal mines in an Irish setting. (Mr. Goldberg concedes this point.) Yet Joyce was not altogether at a loss because of the lack of heavy industry in his country. He used instead as his principal emblem of modern capitalism the newspaper, wasting the spirit with its peristent attacks upon the integrity of the word, narcotizing its readers with superficial facts, habituating them to secular and clerical authority. Even here Joyce's attack is oblique, but it is not indulgent, not tolerant, not indifferent. His obliquity was in the service of a point of view, an idea.

At the start of his career, he all but gave the idea a name. In the same draft, "A Portrait of the Artist," he concluded in a cryptic manner, "Already the messages of citizens were flashing along the wires of the world, already the generous idea had emerged from a thirty years' war in Germany and was directing the councils of the Latins." The generous idea was socialism, not particularized as to school; by the "thirty years' war in Germany" he may have meant the period after the Gotha agreement of 1875 when the socialist factions agreed to work together, and by the "councils of the Latins" he must have meant the socialist parties in the Latin countries. Not naming socialism except as "the generous idea" was probably part of that obliquity upon which he had set himself.

But at the close of this essay he makes another of his eloquent perorations: "To these multitudes, not as yet in the womb of humanity but surely engenderable there, he would give the word: Man and woman, out of you comes the nation that is to come, the lightening of your masses in travail, the competitive order is arrayed against itself, the aristocracies are supplanted, and amid the general paralysis of an insane society, the confederate will issues in action." The tone, if not the purport, is like that of other manifestoes, including the Communist one. He seems to agree with Marx that capitalism bears within itself its own destruction, and that aristocracies must go. The confederate will seems to mean the will of likeminded revolutionaries. Like W. H. Auden, Joyce conceives of the Just as sending out their messages across national boundaries, and imagines them as conspiratorially united, though he avoids those words, "confederate" being an oblique form of them.

His own function was that of a sentry sounding an alarm, in the name of what in *Stephen Hero* he called "a new humanity, active, unafraid and unashamed." As he said there,

> He wished to express his nature freely and fully for the benefit of a society which he would enrich and also for his own benefit, seeing that it was part of his life to do so. It was not part of his life to attempt an extensive

alteration of society but he felt the need to express himself such an urgent need, such a real need, that he was determined no conventions of a society, however plausibly mingling pity with its tyranny should be allowed to stand in his way, and though a taste for elegance and detail unfitted him for the part of a demagogue, from his general attitude he might have been supposed not unjustly an ally of the collectivist politicians, who are often very seriously upbraided by opponents who believe in Jehovahs, and decalogues and judgments with sacrificing the reality to an abstraction.

"Supposed not unjustly an ally of the collectivist politicians": the double negative may be oblique but its meaning is clear.

By the time Joyce rephrased this in the completed A *Portrait of the Artist as a Young Man,* it had become the question: "How could he hit their conscience or how cast his shadow over the imaginations of their daughters, before their squires begat upon them that they might breed a race less ignoble than their own?" To catch the conscience of the people in his book must be his motive. Literature is a revolutionary instrument, however roundabout it may move.

Ulysses is in fact, as I have intimated, Joyce's Trojan horse: a monument, but full of armed men; a comedy, but with teeth and claws. Stephen's insistence upon reconsidering time and space has another purpose besides the extolling of art's independence of these categories. It is political as well. For Stephen associates space with body and time with soul; the one is visible, the other invisible. He thereby relates them to the servitudes he has acknowledged in the first chapter of *Ulysses*: "I am the servant of two masters . . . and the holy Roman apostolic church." There is also a third, he says, who wants him for odd jobs—mother Ireland, herself the servant of a servant. The secular and spiritual powers, visible and invisible worlds, are equally extortionate. "Are not Religion and Politics the same thing?" asks Blake in *Jerusalem.* Stephen allies himself with another conviction of Blake, that "the king and the priest must be tied in a tether." Stanislaus reports in *My Brother's Keeper* that Joyce was fond of quoting this line before he left Dublin. As Blake said in his commentary on Dante, we must "go into the mind in which everyone is king and priest in his own house," and Yeats, in *Ideas of Good and Evil,* which Joyce had with him in Trieste, explained that "The phrase about the king and priest is a memory of the crown and mitre set upon Dante's head before he entered Paradise." The passage in Canto 27 of the *Purgatorio* (*"io te sopra te corono e mitrio"*) was then much in Joyce's mind, and he used it for symbolic effect as his predecessors had done. The priest lays claim to an eternity of time, as the king if he could would rule over infinite space; and against these forces, anthropomorphized in earthly authorities, Stephen and Bloom have to muster their own forces.

Ulysses provides a measure against which British State and Catholic Church can be evaluated, and Ireland as well, both in its patent collusion with these forces, and in the callousness which the desire for independence could evoke. If British tyranny was brutally materialistic, so was Irish fanaticism. Persecution, by Church or by State, whether of Jews or of artists, went with other forms of materialism, such as sexual cruelty and lovelessness. On the other side was an etherealism which included the diseased ideals of religion and patriotism, ideals without body and essences without form, antisexualism or love cheapened by sentimentality. The statues of Nelson and Moses, evoked in the newspaper episode, symbolize the two poles, while Parnell, whose image in the cabman's shelter seems equally false ("Dead he wasn't. Simply absconded somewhere"), is the local focus for political extravagance and violence.

What Joyce does is to bring pressure to bear at different points and with different degrees of intensity. It would have been possible for him to sharpen his pen by representing as ogres both Father Conmee, as a high functionary of the Church, and the Viceroy as the chief representative of the State. But he is careful not to do that. The Viceroy and Father Conmee, who traverse Dublin emblematically in the "Wandering Rocks" episode, are allowed to be personally inoffensive. Even the Cyclops, as Irish chauvinist, has a turn of phrase, though it's a wrong turn, and likes his dog, though it turns out to be somebody else's. Yet each is obliquely repudiated. Benevolent Father Conmee has no sense of the strength or value of the appetites he seeks to repress, nor of the rigidity of the Church which he serves so devotedly. But Bloom and Stephen, each in his own way, remark its sado-masochistic elements, and Stephen especially sees it as a nightmare preying upon the living. As for the Viceroy, Joyce represents him mildly enough as on his way to a charity benefit. The clatter and ringing of the viceregal carriage are grand. On the other hand, it is viceregal spies who report on the native populace to the Castle, and the viceregal soldiers who bully Stephen. Bloom, hearing the phrase, "Our lovely land," asks with a penitence which is emphasized, but he challenges the Citizen on the use of force, and has to endure the Citizen's attempt to use force against him. He challenges etherealism, too, in a small way by refusing to see a newspaper publisher as "the image of our Saviour," in a larger one by shrewdly anatomizing the rites of confession, communion, and extreme unction, by rejecting chastity, by repudiating the false idealization of both woman and of country.

Stephen is equally unwilling to accept the occupying authority, and he too has this for one of his targets. He savagely mocks both British glories and Irish chauvinism with his Parable of the Plums spat out upon Ireland's promised land from Nelson's pillar. Like Bloom, he repudiates the use of force to achieve independence, so will have nothing to do with Old Gummy Granny who offers him the glorious opportunity of dying in armed struggle for Ireland. After a booklong attack upon the etherealism of Dublin rhetoric, whether in the service of piety or patriotism, Stephen combats materialism when he tells Private Carr that he must kill the priest and king in his own mind, a political remark for which he is promptly knocked down.

The attack on space and time, then, is elaborately coordinated with an attack upon the visible and invisible authorities in Ireland. The attempt to destroy space and time through art becomes a similitude of the attempt to overcome State and Church through language, by rendering them ridiculous, by disclosing their secret natures, by flouting them directly and indirectly. Joyce's political awareness was based on considerable reading. His library in Trieste included especially books by socialists and anarchists. He had, for example, the first 173 Fabian tracts bound in one volume. Among other writers who interested him were notably the two anarchists, Kropotkin and Bakunin, and the social reformer, Proudhon.

Peter Kropotkin's pamphlet on *Anarchist Morality* denied any validity to the old dichotomy of egoism and altruism, on the ground that, willynilly, people's interests are mutual. Kropotkin might be borrowing from Joyce, rather than Joyce from Kropotkin, when he declares, "the condition of the maintenance of life is its expansion." Joyce read Proudhon's *Qu'est-ce que la propriété?* with equal attention. Proudhon defines slavery as murder and property as theft. His views appear to underlie the discussion in *Exiles* of robbery. Little Archie asks his father, Richard Rowan, whether there are robbers in Ireland as in Rome, and receives the reply, "There are poor people everywhere." Richard then goes on to ask, "Do you know what it is to give? . . . While you have a thing it can be taken from you. . . . But when you give it, you have given it. No robber can take it from you. . . . It will be yours always. That is to give." Richard in the play tries to apply this principle to love as well as to money. When Proudhon quotes an old definition of trade as the "art of buying for three francs what is worth six, and of selling for six what is worth three," he might be priming Stephen to reply to Mr. Deasy's attack on Jewish businessmen, "A merchant is one who buys cheap and sells dear, jew or gentile, is he not?" Proudhon's injunction, "Speak without hate or fear: say what you know," is also in the Joycean manner. "On then: dare it," Stephen tells himself. These radical reformers fascinated Joyce by the sweep and finality of their writings as well as by their subversiveness.

His principal political authority was, I think, Bakunin, whose *God and the State* (London: Freedom Press, 1910, translated by the anarchist Benjamin Tucker, himself one of Joyce's admirations) examined the relation between certain philosophical and political concepts in a way Joyce could put to use. Bakunin condemned on the one hand a brutal materialism, and on the other its seeming opposite, a lofty idealism; to both, he pointed out, *matter* was vile, a representation of "supreme nothingness." Joyce could take advantage of this hint by displaying the collusion between the brutal materialism of Buck Mulligan, his indifference to the consequences of his acts and words, and the mysticism of George Russell, for whom acts done in this world are merely lying semblances. Bakunin connects the materialism of the State with the idealism of the Church, and sees them both as united in the enslavement of humanity. "All religions are cruel, all founded on blood," he declares, and concludes that all religions "rest principally on the idea of sacrifice, that is, on the perpetual immolation of humanity to the insatiable vengeance of divinity." Bloom concurs: "God wants blood victim. Birth, hymen, martyr, war foundation of a building, sacrifice, kidney, burnt-offering, druid's altars." During the day both he and Stephen delineate the bloodthirstiness of Church and State, their cruelty and their urge to flatten out individual freedoms.

While Bloom's remarks, though a little muddled ("foundation of a building" does not fit in so well), are close to Bakunin's in their expression, Stephen is allowed by Joyce to put his own view more gnomically. So in Nighttown Stephen tells the soldier Carr, "You die for your country, suppose. But I say, let my country die for me. Up to the present it has done so. I don't want it to die." He is a little drunk, but he means that sacrifice can enslave as well as free. The purpose of nationalism is the expansion of life, not its abbreviation. Later Stephen remarks somewhat testily to Bloom, "You think I am important because I belong to the Faubourg Saint Patrice called Ireland for short. But I think Ireland is important because it belongs to me." The State is the instrument of its members, not their enslaver.

Notwithstanding such bursts of impatience, Stephen keeps in *Ulysses* as in *A Portrait* a basic loyalty to his country, and repudiates those who, as he shrewdly conjectures of Mulligan, will betray it. Whatever tendency Stephen has to wash his hands of Ireland, he cannot be anti-Irish for long. So at the end of *A Portrait*, having devoted one entry in his journal to mocking the Irish mentality, he comes to the conclusion, "Then into Nile mud with it!" But in his next entry he rebukes himself with the words, "Disapprove of this last phrase." In *Ulysses* he recognizes this kinship with even the grossest of his compatriots, "Their blood is in me, their lusts my waves." One of his most pro-Irish statements is unreported and has to be inferred from a remark which his music teacher makes in reply to something Stephen has just said. The teacher says in Italian, "I once had the same ideas when like you I was young. But then I became convinced that the world was a beast." What Stephen has just said, discreetly omitted by Joyce as too close to the knuckle, is that he intends to write for the benefit of his race; Artifoni's reply only shows that he has fallen into the idealist error of treating the world as vile.

Since they anatomize and deride Church and State alike, Bloom and Stephen might be supposed to be anarchists. Joyce has sometimes been linked to this point of view, too. He did maintain a lifelong interest in anarchism, and once, in a poem he wrote in Zurich, "Dooleysprudence," he expressed anarchist views in music hall terms:

Who is the funny fellow who declines to go to church
Since pope and priest and parson left the poor man in the lurch
And taught their flocks the only way to save all human souls
Was piercing human bodies through with dumdum bulletholes?
It's Mr Dooley,
Mr Dooley
The mildest man our country ever knew
'Who will release us
From Jingo Jesus'
Prays Mr Dooley-ooley-ooley-oo.

Who is the tranquil gentleman who won't salute the State
Or serve Nabuchodonesor or proletariat
But thinks that every son of man has quite enough to do
To paddle down the stream of life his personal canoe?
It's Mr Dooley,
Mr Dooley,
The wisest wight our country ever knew
'Poor Europe ambles
Like sheep to shambles'
Sighs Mr Dooley-ooley-ooley-oo.

Yet paddling his own canoe is not the policy of either Bloom or Stephen, nor, whatever his reticence in Switzerland and Paris about his politics, can it have been Joyce's. While neither Bloom nor Stephen offers a coherent programme of change, neither is satisfied with simply laying bare the in-adequacies of Irish spiritual and secular governors. Stephen is bent upon affirming, and needling his compatriots into affirming, the disused possibilities of life. He wants them to walk untrammelled by petrified dogmas. For Bloom what is truly life is love, possibly a crude term for his sense of mutuality of concern but at least a traditional one. As a young man he was a socialist, and annoyed Molly during their early acquaintance by informing her that Christ was the first socialist. The Church he finds bloodthristy and prone to make victims, the State the same. He has vague humanitarian goals. "From each according to his ability, to each according to his needs, and to everyone according to his deeds." On this plane Bloom appears ludicrous, and Bloomusalem is an appropriate emblem for his Utopian hopes of social regeneration. But clearly Joyce is here exaggerating to the point of absurdity Bloom's kindness and goodhearted civic feeling.

Bloom's politics do not stop here. If his ultimate goals are (like most people's) indistinct, he has an immediate one that he understands very well. For what it is we have to look at the final chapter. Since Molly Bloom is apolitical herself, her monologue is not the place we would expect to find political information. But she is distressfully aware that her husband has views. They are likely to get him into trouble, she feels. She mentions them, in fact she cannot help mentioning them both early and late in her monologue. Even during their courtship Bloom was for Home Rule and the Land League. She complains, "he was going about with some of them Sinner Fein lately or whatever they call themselves talking his usual trash and nonsense he says that little man he showed me without the neck is very intelligent the coming man Griffeth is he well he doesnt look it thats all I can say still it must have been him he knew there was a boycott. . . ." She is leery of her husband's losing his job with the *Freeman's Journal;* "well have him coming home with the sack soon out of the Freeman too like the rest on account of those Sinner Fein or the Freemasons then well see if the little man he showed me dribbling along in the wet all by himself round by Coadys Lane will give him much consolation that he says is so capable and sincerely Irish he is indeed judging by the sincerity of the trousers I saw on him. . . ." These references are insistent enough.

Joyce is sometimes said to have had no politics except regret for Parnell, yet he was not the man to worship the dead. For a long time now he had had his eye on a living leader, Arthur Griffith. Griffith, eleven years older than Joyce, had after some years of preliminary work founded in October 1902 the separatist organization which in 1905 was christened Sinn Féin (Ourselves Alone). (Molly Bloom anticipates by sixteen months the later name.) His principal coadjustor had been William Rooney, a patriotic poet, who had died in 1901 at the age of twenty-eight. In 1902 Griffith published Rooney's poems, and it fell to Joyce to review them for the Unionist *Daily Express* (for which Gabriel in "The Dead" also writes). The review attacked the poems first for being derivative, but more importantly, for being "full of tears and curses." "And yet he might have written well if he had not suffered from one of those big words which make us so unhappy." Griffith for answer quoted most of the review in an advertisement in his own newspaper, the *United Irishman,* and after "big words" added "[Patriotism]." It was a stroke Joyce could admire, even if aimed against himself.

He followed Griffith's subsequent activities closely, and in 1906 he made up his mind. A letter to his brother asserted flatly that a research speech in Dublin by Griffith had justified the existence of his newspaper. In this speech Griffith advocated the boycott of English goods that Molly mentions, and also an educational system, a national banking system and national civil service. He agreed with Bloom, and with Joyce, in not being a "physical force" man.

Although he refused to endorse the revival of the Irish language, Joyce was in other ways on the side of the separatist movement, and particularly of Griffith's programme. He thought that the time for parliamentary action, of the sort espoused by Parnell, was over, and that an economic boycott would have more hope of succeeding. Of course the fanaticism of the extreme Sinn Feiners did not attract him, and he satirizes it in the Citizen, whose battle cry, *Sinn Féin amhain* ("Ourselves Alone for ever"), serves as a stick to beat anyone he doesn't like. Stephen also speaks of the "archons of *Sinn Féin*" as giving Socrates his noggin of hemlock. But if Joyce did not like the extremist wing of the party, he approved Griffith's moderate programme.

He had personal and literary reasons as well for admiring Griffith. In 1911, when Joyce addressed a public letter to newspapers in Ireland about the suppression of *Dubliners,* most of the newspaper editors ignored it, only two published it, and of these two only Griffith risked libel action by publishing it in full. The next year, when Joyce was in Dublin, he asked and received Griffith's help for *Dubliners,* this time against the pseudo-nationalist machinations of an Irish publisher. From what he writes of his conversation with Griffith, he evidently won his help by insisting that his literary purpose was "the spiritual liberation of my country" (a phrase he used to Grant Richards on 20 May 1906)—*Dubliners* was not a summons to action, yet it exposed the shortcomings of Irish life under British rule. He also pointed out that he was the only Irishman on the Adriatic coast writing articles for Home Rule in Triestine newspapers. On this trip, too, he acquired two of Griffith's recent pamphlets on the Home Rule bill then under parliamentary debate.

In *Ulysses* Joyce was encouraged by Bloom's Hungarian origin to relate him to Griffith's programme. Martin Cunningham says Bloom gave Griffith the idea of the Hungarian system, that is, of a dual monarchy for

England and Ireland on the model of the Austro-Hungarian empire. For much of his life Griffith espoused it, but the Eastern Rising of 1916 made such a compromise impossible. Now total independence became his goal. He kept in the forefront of political activity, and in 1921 when the Irish Free State was in process of being created, he took a principal role. More to the point, for Joyce, was that on 8 January 1922 Arthur Griffith was elected first president of Ireland.

This was the moment when Joyce was completing *Ulysses*, a co-incidence he could not and did not resist. The references to Griffith in his final chapter are more than coincidence; Joyce wished to salute Griffith's at last successful efforts. Bloom is described as having once picked up Parnell's hat and handed it back to him, a homely gesture more attractive than rhetorical ones. Joyce offers Griffith, through the unwitting agency of Molly, a backhanded tribute, homely too. It was Griffith's programme, and not Parnell's, which had eventually won through. Ireland was achieving independence just as *Ulysses* was achieving publication. The political eman-cipation of Ireland had been accompanied by his old ally Griffith, and the emancipation of its conscience—Joyce's own lifetime work—was also ap-proaching culmination. Bloom's sometime socialism, and Joyce's sometime socialism and anarchism, are put behind in order to hail, in Joyce's own fashion, the new country and the political leader to whom he felt most closely allied.

Ultimately *Ulysses* too constituted a political act, in the oblique fashion that Joyce used to express himself. Its humour was not offhand but a means of comic exploration of the shortcomings of life in Ireland as lived under British and Catholic authorities. To those who lived meaninglessly in a brutal and consuming present, Joyce offered a world of accountability and did not shrink from calling it spiritual. To those who, nursed by locally distorted Catholic doctrines, spoke of spiritual realities as if they alone existed, he pointed to the realities of the body's life. Like Dante he felt empowered to confer mitre and crown, a new politics of mind and body. That *Ulysses* like the Free State could come to exist was a major blow against those who wished to envisage life in a narrower style than it spon-sored. The book summons into being a society capable of reading and enjoying it because capable of as frank and open an outlook on life as the book manifests. *Ulysses* creates new Irishmen to live in Arthur Griffith's new state.

For Joyce the creation of the Irish Free State was the culmination of his hopes. After 1922, the complexities that came with it interested him, and he followed them as he could from across the Channel. He mentions those who came after Griffith, De Valera in particular. The tergiversations of the Irish parties understandably did not arouse him to any strong partisanship. By this time, the political awareness demonstrated by his book made lesser manoeuvres redundant. On the other hand, the international situation pressed in upon him more and more. Joyce did not sign protests, and maintained his aloofness from all particular events except one, the Nazi butchery of the Jews. On this point—which was the touch-stone of politics in the 1930s—he did what he could, and by means of his intercession perhaps a dozen people were aided to escape from Germany. Such assistance meant more than many protests, and the idea of personal help pleased him best as his scepticism of institutions mounted.

Joyce's politics and aesthetics were one. For him the act of writing was also, and indissolubly, an act of liberating. His book examines the servitude of his countrymen to their masters in Church and State, and offers an ampler vision. While the criticism is severe, its aim is to unite rather than disunite. The central action of *Ulysses* is to bring together Stephen Dedalus and Leopold Bloom by displaying their underlying agree-ment on political views which the author thereby underwrites. The agree-ment is countersigned by Bloom's rescue of Stephen from army and police after the young man has mentally defied both Church and State. That the two men converge only partially does not diminish the exemplary value of their partial convergence. For a moment Bloom and Stephen, coming from the two ends of the alphabet, can become Blephen and Stoom.

So the pun on names is also a pun about existence, and the pun is Joyce's stock in trade beyond what is generally acknowledged. In a pun the component parts remain distinguishable, and yet there is a constant small excitement in their being yoked together so deftly and so improperly. An equivalence is at once asserted and questioned, sounds and senses in mutual trespass are both compared and contrasted. Puns are of different kinds, and their effect are also various, so that they make us laugh or wince, are random or substantive, conjure up lofty associations or vulgar ones. Words are expatriated and repatriated like Dubliners. Joyce exploited all these nuances, and the pun becomes the key to his work—a key both aesthetic and political, both linguistic and moral.

The pun extends beyond words. The same process goes on with people and incidents. A law of the Joycean universe is that every single thing is always on the verge of doubling with another. Doubling reaches a nightmare pitch in "Circe" when Bella becomes Bello, when Bloom doubles as Henry Flower and also as a woman, and when wallpaper and pictures assume human voices. But similar events occur throughout the book: Paddy

Dignam is dead; yet several people believe they have seen him or his ghost; that "the ghost walks" means that the paymaster on the newspaper is making his rounds, as well as that the majesty of buried Denmark walks the night along with the sepulchral wraith of Mary Dedalus. Bloom meets a sailor who calls himself Murphy but appears to be a mock Bloom, just as he meets M'Coy whose wife, like his own, is a soprano. In Molly Bloom's mind Mulvey on the Rock of Gibraltar doubles with Bloom on the Hill of Howth. The characters also tend to double with mythical archetypes, divine and human. The implications of the meeting of Bloom and Stephen, their connections with Ulysses and Telemachus, with King Hamlet and Prince Hamlet, with Shakespeare and Hamnet, are infinitely extensible. To the complaint that they do not fuse Joyce would doubtless have answered that the essence of the pun is not complete but incomplete juncture. To have them fuse would be to abolish the reason for their having been brought together. The parts of the pun keep their identities even while these are demonstrated to be less isolating than they appeared. And the resemblances between two men, and two sounds, are themselves made up of further resemblances to other people and other sounds.

That is why the word "metempsychosis" is mentioned so prominently in the first scene between Bloom and his wife. She wants to know what it means, and he endeavours not too successfully to explain it to her. The spirit of one word enters another, as the spirit of one situation, or of one being. The pun is metempsychosis. Whole areas of thought, as well as small knots of words, prove to be fluid rather than solid. In one of his letters, Joyce takes up a nine-word sentence in *Finnegans Wake* and finds seven meanings flowing through it:

L'Arcs en His Cieling Flee Chinx on the Flur.
1) God's in his heaven All's Right with the World
2) The rainbow is in the sky (arc-en-ciel) the Chinese (Chinks) live tranquilly on the Chinese meadowplane (China alone almost of the old continent[s] has no record of a Deluge. Flur in this sense is German. It suggests also Flut (flood) and Fluss (river) and could even be used poetically for the expanse of a waterflood. Flee = free
3) The ceiling of his m house is in ruins for you can see the birds flying and the floor is full of cracks which you had better avoid
4) There is merriment above (larks) why should there not be high jinks below stairs?
5) The electric lamps of the gin palace are lit and the boss Roderick Rex is standing free drinks to all on the "flure of the house"
6) He is a bit gone in the upper storey, poor jink. Let him lie as he is (Shem, Ham and Japhet)

7) The birds (doves and ravens) (of the jinnies is a cooin her hair and the jinnies is a ravin her hair) he saved escape from his waterhouse and leave the zooless patriark alone.

His explanations heap pun upon pun: Norah is a *patriark*, for example, but even more to the purpose is the way that nine words, in the process of evoking seven meanings, carry us from the flood to the rainbow, from China to Ireland, from God to man, from Browning to Bible, from activities to passivities, from acceptance to pity. Each pun in effect wreaks havoc with space and time, and with every form of settled complacency. Words are fractioned by ineptitude, yet the force that fractions also draws the world together. Near-misses of sound, sense, and finally, of form constitute the fabric of creation. Out of mala-propisms, spoonerisms, the world is born.

Punning offers then *countersense*, through which disparates are joined and concordants differentiated. Bloom momentarily appears to be a dentist of the same name, then is as promptly re-identified as a canvasser for advertisements. He becomes Elijah rising in his chariot to heaven, only to have it made clear that he is as little like Elijah as possible. As he listens to Simon Dedalus singing the role of Lionel in *Martha*, he is verbally united with performer and role as "Siopold." This series of doublings and undoublings—is one of which heroic and mockheroic are instances. It pervades Joyce's work as if it were a way in which the artist could imitate the duplexity of nature.

In *Ulysses* Joyce worked particularly with two kinds of countersense, which might be called the *undersense* and the *oversense*. The undersense is a current of sensation, often quite tangential, which keeps forcing its way to the surface of what is being thought. So Bloom, on the prowl for lunch, observes and considers many things; whatever he sees or ponders is flavoured by food. His momentary feeling of depression can find no metaphor except a gustatory one: "This is the very worst hour of the day . . . Hate this hour. Feel as if I had been eaten and spewed." Thinking unhappily of Boylan's cold-hearted womanizing, he sees the building he is passing as "cream curves of stone." At the cemetery the days of the month take on a mortuary tinge: "Every Friday buries a Thursday if you come to think of it." Joyce's method is to present the density of experience by concatenating incongruous sensations and thoughts. He comes close to the quick of the body as it is engaged in its secret transactions with the mind.

The second variety of countersense in Joyce is the *oversense*. Here concepts rather than sensations provide the atmosphere in which quite diverse material becomes enveloped. The first nine chapters of *Ulysses* concede validity to space and time, and the second nine chapters impugn that validity. The constructive Aristotle is allowed to posit a firm universe of distinct forms and selves, only to have this thrown into confusion by Humean scepticism, and only in the last chapters is stability recoverable, on altered terms. Joyce displays the oversense at work in segregating human behaviour into primarily spatial or primarily temporal activities. Space as oversense requires a geography lesson as time requires a history lesson; when space is in the ascendant, external actions occur, while when time is in the ascendant, the emphasis is on internal processes; space subsumes sculpture as time subsumes music. Such oversenses shape whole chapters of *Ulysses*. In *Finnegans Wake* the same pressures determine the characters of Shem and Shaun as they do of the Gracehoper and the Ondt:

> The Ondt was a weltall fellow, raumybult and abelboobied . . . He [the Gracehoper] had eaten all the whilepaper, swallowed the lustres, devoured forty flights of styearcases, chewed up all the mensas and seecles . . .

What is Joyce implying here? I think he is implying first that the system is closed and not open, that the number of human possibilities is limited and that, as we struggle for uniqueness, we discover that we are doing something not for the first time but for the millionth time. But if closed, the system is still fertile. The mind attempts, impartially, to multiply instances of itself in all possible slight variations. Simultaneities are everywhere. "Think you're escaping and run into your self," says Bloom, as if undoubling were necessarily doubling too.

With this recognition of universal intermingling Joyce attained his final unstated statement about life. Before him as before Whitman, stretched democratic vistas, and he could say that he contained multitudes. Yet he did not sentimentalize. What he had discovered was not that all forms were one form—a mystical conclusion—but rather that all forms proceed by incessant doublings and undoublings in which they remain enantiomorphous—that is, resembling each other but not superposable. Hierarchies disappear and the "aristocracies are supplanted," for all elements are common elements. The pun, verbal emblem of coincidence, agent of democracy and collectivist ideas, makes all the quirky particles of the world stick to each other by hook or crook. Such adhesiveness is unity or the closest to unity that can be envisaged.

HUGH KENNER

Joyce's Voices

If there was one thing of which James
Joyce was thoroughly convinced when he took up the story [of *Ulysses*],
with on his bookshelf a long work by a French scholar retracing Odysseus's
voyages through the Mediterranean, it was that whatever the *Odyssey* may
have been it was certainly not a "myth." It told of a man who lived and
fought and voyaged, a man not imagined by Homer but appropriated and
re-created by the imagination of Homer, much as Joyce himself proposed
to re-create a Dublin odd-jobs entrepreneur, reputedly of Jewish ancestry,
who went under the name of Mr. Hunter. Whatever we do not know about
Mr. Hunter we can be sure he was real. Joyce mentions his name in a letter
to his brother Stanislaus in a casual way that leaves no doubt he thought
Stannie would know who was meant. The mention occurs in the course
of a proposal to write a story called "Ulysses." Ulysses was real too.

So what had Homer done with the story? He had begun by asking
the Muse to help him, and not help him make the story up but help him
tell it. For his access to Homer, Joyce, with no classical Greek, is said to
have relied on fairly businesslike translations, Cowper's and Butler's, but
at least the first line of the Greek he carried in his memory: on one convivial
occasion he wrote it out to caption a sketch of Bloom. Its first four words
are *Andrah moi ennepe Mousa* [Tell me, Muse, of the man], naming in
sequence three persons: *andra*, the man, Odysseus; *moi*, the singer, Homer;
Mousa, the Muse, the authority. Homer's is the voice we first hear, but
what he tells us about that man the Muse must tell him. It is she who
knows, and he who words her knowledge; or does he simply voice her
words? A scholiast would be bold indeed who would venture to mark the

From *Joyce's Voices*. Copyright © 1978 by The Regents of the University of California.
University of California Press.

moment in the text at which Homer's narration is taken up by hers. He knows something of the story, but not enough to tell it unaided; is it the information he lacks, or the afflatus? Anyhow he knows the circumstances of the hero at the point where he directs the Muse to begin. Robert Fitzgerald catches the uncatchability of the transition:

> Begin when all the rest who left behind them
> headlong death in battle or at sea
> had long ago returned, while he alone still hungered
> for home and wife. Her ladyship Kalypso
> clung to him in her sea-hollowed caves—
> who craved him for her own. . . .

Where does Homer's prompting cease and the flow of the divine narrative commence? And does he ever wholly retire?

A more practical question is why the Muse is needed, and what her presence has to teach a modern writer. It depends which Homer we ask. Our most up-to-date Homer, Parry and Lord's "oral-formulaic" improvisor, may be disregarded since he was invented too late for Joyce to have heard of him (his answer would doubtless be that the Muse is the power who enables you to improvise several thousand hexameters on your feet at a go without getting stuck). The stained-glass Homer of Butcher and Lang commences "Tell me, Muse, of that man, so ready at need," because gentlemen inaugurate momentous things with prayer, but while Joyce sometimes felt like a Victorian engineer and compared work on *Finnegans Wake* to tunnelling through a mountain, he was unattracted by the role of Victorian gentleman. His Homer was such a workmanlike realist as Samuel Butler intuited (unencumbered, though, by Butler's coat-trailing about a Sicilian princess), and for such a Homer the use of a Muse is twofold. She can preside over elevations of style as they are needed; and she can share thematic knowledge with the author, who need no longer occupy that monocular "point of view" where Henry James was often so cramped.

For the occupant of a "point of view" is like a *voyeur* (how can he possibly have known?) while the events of the *Odyssey* are public property, in their main outlines known to everyone (like anything at all in Dublin). As Homer and the Muse and, yes, the audience all know the story of Odysseus, and the thing to be concentrated on is the texture of today's retelling, so all Dublin invariably knows who was just drinking with whom and what they quarrelled about, and many voices are free to address themselves to the work of elaboration, the most talented bearing the more intricate rhetorical burdens. Perhaps Joyce's sense of things was not as far from the oral formulaic as chronology might have led us to suppose.

He commences *Ulysses*, anyhow, as a sort of duet for two narrators, or perhaps a conspiracy between them. The doubleness he owes to Homer, and later his mischievous logical mind will have improvements to offer on what Homer suggests. At present, though, atop the Martello Tower, an ambiguously double narrator suffices: one voice perhaps better informed about stage-management, the other a more accomplished lyrical technician.

In the first episode, accordingly—wait, things are more complicated still. There is yet one more person present: a twentieth-century presence, the novel-reading reader, the creation of the books he has read already and now confronting one more new book. What the reader expects, in this first episode, controls much of what the first narrator can do. For the arts create their audiences who then control them, and as the Noh-goer was shaped by one kind of theater and Shakespeare's groundling by another kind, so the early twentieth-century novel-reader (by no means extinct today but greatly mutated) may be described as a complex of expectations and agreements-to-respond that has been shaped by Edwardian fiction, its contrivances, climaxes, "rattling good stories," above all by its unobtrusive novelese, the language Joseph Conrad and Ford Madox Hueffer steeled themselves daily not to write.

This language, not some unthinkable "objective" metalanguage, is what the first narrator of "Telemachus" employs as he moves characters about and reports their gestures. If we have difficulty noticing it, that is because certain narrative assumptions have changed little since 1904. To the inhabitant of a period the characterizing idiom of that period, whether in painting, in sculpture or in literature, is absolutely invisible. It took Conrad—a Pole, Joyce—a Dubliner, and Hueffer—who would rather have been writing in French—to detect Edwardian novelese accurately enough to avoid it, or (in Joyce's case) to use it deliberately before avoiding it deliberately.

It is by no means a contemptible idiom. It does not like "Nausicaa" novelese, strain after portentousness ("But who was Gerty?"). Its mannerisms, not easy to catalogue, include a certain fussiness about setting and decor (much "up" and "down" and "across"; much particularity of "jagged granite" and shafts of light meeting amid turning coalsmoke); a tendency toward longer speeches than later conventions would think plausible in casual dialogue; a predilection for eloquent dumbshow ("Stephen suffered him to pull out and hold up on show by its corner a dirty crumpled handkerchief"; and certain epithetic opulences we'll look at presently. The English novel's heritage from the English stage is appreciable here, though attenuated to a set of economical flourishes. It all suits "Telemachus," where everyone is acting: stage-Irishman, stage-Englishman, stage-poet.

So the style of "Telemachus," called in the famous schema "Narrative (young)," today gives off here and there an unmistakeable ring of Edwardian novelese. . . .

One voice then in this episode is moving characters about, and reporting their doings, in fluent unemphatic novelese, barely to be distinguished from a neutral idiom save by occasional "great searching eyes," an occasional "strong wellknit trunk" ("Laughter seized all his strong wellknit trunk"). Still it *is* an idiom however we characterize it: the voice of someone trying phrases to himself as he writes down a story. No "objective" style, Joyce is already hinting, can in truth be discovered to exist, no registration of so-many-things-almost-in-an-equal-number-of-words; an attempt to simulate one will itself be a style, a narrator's role.

And while the first voice attends to the chapter's housekeeping, a second narrative voice is uttering passages like the following:

> Woodshadows floated silently by through the morning peace from the stairhead seaward where he gazed. Inshore and farther out the mirror of water whitened, spurned by lightshod hurrying feet. White breast of the dim sea. The twining stresses, two by two. A hand plucking the harpstrings merging their twining chords. Wavewhite wedded words shivering on the dim tide.

Fulfilling one office of the Muse in periodically elevating the style, this second narrator has served an apprenticeship on *A Portrait of the Artist as a Young Man* and become a virtuoso of the Uncle Charles Principle: the narrative idiom bent by a person's proximity as a star defined by Einstein will bend passing light. The only person on the parapet now is Stephen. These thoughts of woodshadows floating are not Stephen's, not quite, but the sentences that brush them in absorb Stephen-words and Stephen-rhythms, moving us imperceptibly into Stephen's thoughts:

> A cloud began to cover the sun slowly, shadowing the bay in deeper green.
> It lay behind him, a bowl of bitter waters. Fergus' song: I sang it alone
> in the house, holding down the long dark chords.

Only if we catch the shift from third person to first are we assured that we have left the outside for the inside: are now in Stephen's mind, where "holding down the long dark chords" has a self-approving expressiveness. Inside Stephen's mind, where self-appreciation reigns, is a less blithe zone than the penumbra commanded by the dextrous second narrator, whose facility is Protean, whose responsibility is to the sensation reported rather than to the locked and cherished phrase, and whose deftness is seemingly incomparable. He and Stephen, with practice, are readily differentiated.

It is Stephen who hears the squeal of his ashplant's ferrule on the path as "My familiar, after me, calling Steeeeeeeeeeeephen," and it was on finicky Stephen's behalf that Joyce instructed the printer to put in 12 e's (except for the printer of the Rosenbach facsimile, no printer until this moment has ever obliged). It is the second narrator who manages such passing triumphs of narrative economy as the emergence of the elderly swimmer:

> An elderly man shot up near the spur of rock a blowing red face. He scrambled up by the stones, water glistening on his pate and on its garland of grey hair, water rilling over his chest and paunch and spilling jets out of his sagging black loincloth.

—how exact that twinned *rilling* and *spilling!*

This second narrator, vivid narrator, Muse, flaunts skills such as Stephen covets, hence a somewhat misleading likeness to Stephen's idiom. To perceive him clearly we must wait till Stephen is offstage and the only person present is Leopold Bloom. Then we shall recognize the virtuoso whose miracles of one-word *naming* we've already discussed, sharing narrative control with a less flamboyant craftsman whose Uncle Charles sensibilities respond to the pressure of Bloom's presence, and who takes us deftly in and out of Bloom's mind.

> Kidneys were on his mind as he moved about the kitchen softly, righting her breakfast things on the humpy tray. Gelid light and air were in the kitchen but out of doors gentle summer morning everywhere. Made him feel a bit peckish.

Here the two voices are just distinguishable. "Peckish," from the notation of Bloom's feelings, is a Bloom-word, but "gelid," responsible to the ambient light, is not. It is not even a word we should expect Bloom to know, any more than he would know words like *rhododaktylos*, which pertain to Homeric evocations of light. Joyce here offers the first signallings of what we've described as a technique for *separating* Bloom's thoughts from the narrative gestures.

These two narrators command different vocabularies and proceed according to different canons. At the outset their command is evenly matched, and the first three Bloom episodes, culminating in "Hades," exhibit an economical weaving of inner and outer, the brisk notations of Bloom's thought and the wonderfully compact narration glinting against one another. Thus when Bloom is in search of a secluded place to read his clandestine letter, we are told:

> With careful tread he passed over a hopscotch court with its forgotten pickeystone. Not a sinner. Near the timberyard a squatted child at marbles, alone, shooting the taw with a cunnythumb. A wise tabby, a blinking sphinx, watched from her warm sill. Pity to disturb them. Mohammed cut a piece out of his mantle not to wake her. Open it. And once I played marbles when I went to that old dame's school.

Here Bloom and narration receive equal time, equal emphasis. As we have come to expect, the textures are kept distinct: *pickeystone, squatted, taw, cunnythumb*—four unique words in two lines—and the elegantly enjambed construction "a wise tabby, a blinking sphinx," these are narrator's mannerisms; "Pity to disturb them" is unmistakeably Bloom's (and the uncertain referent of "them"—child or cat?—is James Joyce's). So it is in "Calypso," "Lotus Eaters," "Hades." . . .

After "Sirens" comes "Cyclops," and throughout "Cyclops" we hear nothing of Bloom's thoughts at all, only a few of his spoken words. Does this mean he is at last presented "objectively"? Not at all; for the second narrator has taken over completely, which is as though the Royal Mint had been commandeered by the Artful Dodger. Thoroughly bored with his assigned role as miniaturist of vivid descriptive bits, the second narrator is giving an expansive impersonation of a Dublin barfly, anonymous (like any narrator) and adrip with garrulous malice. "Old sheepsface," he calls Bloom, and "old lardyface," and other things more intricate and less complimentary. This barfly is the only *personified* narrator in the entire book, which is a way of saying that this episode alone is imparted through the cadence of speech, except when the impersonator, surpassing himself and perhaps remembering his caper with the headlines in "Aeolus," interrupts his own logorrhea with parodies, chiefly of newspaper clippings.

Having gotten this out of his system, our unbridled virtuoso next tries what he can do with a written idiom. Taking a quick glance at his assigned subject, three girls on the beach, he plunges in with the practiced fluency that guided a thousand Victorian pens:

> The summer evening had begun to fold the world in its mysterious embrace. Far away in the west the sun was setting and the last glow of all too fleeting day lingered lovingly on sea and strand, on the proud promontory of dear old Howth guarding as ever the waters of the bay, . . .

—everything, in short, going on as usual: Howth has not moved, nor the sun stayed in its course. He keeps this up for twenty pages, subjecting events as well as sensibilities to the coercions of this new style of his; so Bloom's watch proves to have stopped at the moment of Molly's adultery, just as it would have done were he a character in the kind of novel this style presupposes.

Suddenly the prime narrator—absent now for so long, perhaps at supper—snatches the pen and transcribes fifteen nearly unbroken pages of Bloom's interior monologue, the last long stretch of it we shall ever encounter. We are almost exactly at the midpoint of the book.

But the second narrator has by now grown in power like the Sorcerer's Apprentice. He retrieves the pen, and proceeds to demonstrate the interesting proposition that it was he who shaped the whole of English literature from earliest times until now. During his recapitulation of this chore ("The Oxen of the Sun") Bloom and Stephen are barely visible and wholly inaudible. Much as in the crucial chapter of Bloom's cuckolding we were almost continually distracted by tricksy imitations of musical effects, so now in the crucial chapter when after two near-misses—at the newspaper office, in the library—he and Stephen meet at last, we are debarred from scrutiny of either man's thoughts and prevented from hearing one word that is spoken by anybody, so enamored is the narrator of his system of stylistic impersonations. When late in the episode voices finally do break through, the first word is the name of a pub, spoken by Stephen; thereafter, assailed for five pages by nothing but voices, we can hardly make out whose they are or what they are saying. What is born in this birth-chapter, after forty paragraphs *in utero*, seems to be disembodied Speech, which promptly fills the universe with its yells.

And when, in the episode that follows, the longest by far in the book, typography assures us that we may expect ordered speeches at last—surely this is a play?—we find we are again being hoaxed, for we cannot be sure, reading speech after speech, what if anything was really said, what was only thought but not said, and what has been supplied by the second narrator as expressive substitute for words no one was obliging enough to speak or think.

So one way to describe the curious course of *Ulysses* from "Aeolus" to "Circe" is to plot the insolences of the second narrator, and it is easy to wish he would simply tell us what happened. . . .

"Some of my methods," Joyce later said, "are trivial; and some are quadrivial." At the very least, on the model of two-eyed men, reality exacted a doubling: in the earlier fictions, a double attitude, which *Ulysses* divides into a double narrator of whom one member has a repertory of impersonations. It seems evident after the event that nothing on the scale of *Ulysses* could have been written in the manner of *Dubliners* or the *Portrait*. About 1919, some five years into the work, Joyce was quite clear that it couldn't even be written in the manner in which he had started it. (Early drafts of "Cyclops," even, contain Bloom's interior monologue, and suggests an episode in the manner of, say, "Hades": a good flexible manner.) From the start he knew this at least, that the long book needed extensive effects of immediacy, inner as well as outer, to install us at once and apparently without mediation in the psychosensual reality of Dublin city and the vivid play of experiencing minds. Characters must have voices, spoken and un-spoken, but the office of distancing and differentiating had to be entrusted to an auxiliary narrative voice which could not be the voice of any character since no character beholds the book's entire action. For it is part of the book's theme that many unrelated actions are going on, linked by a grand design which can afford no comfort to any of the protagonists, conscious as they are of boredom and isolation.

So two schemes of narration were needed, an inner and an outer; we've seen how deliberately Joyce doubled the narrator's role in the very first episode, an episode he left pretty much alone when he went back and elaborated so many of the others. And the grand design needed to come together without some puppeteer-narrator seeming aware of it: some know-ing Thackeray to repack the puppets into the box, some Hardy to explain that the President of the Immortals had been having some sport. The grand design is a design of multiple misunderstandings; Bloom thinks for instance that Stephen is a Poet and Philosopher whom it is his own finest destiny to have brought home; Molly thinks she can look forward to a young lover, and also thinks she heard Bloom ask for an egg in bed. What a future all this points to!—especially since Stephen, so far as we can tell, has dis-appeared out of the universe. The book's way, bringing such themes to-gether, is not to assert the whimsical will of a President of the Immortals, but to clown through various systems of local presentation, all cohesive, hence Styles, and all wrong.

We should here reflect that wrongness and deception permeated the book back when its doings seemed under the control of the characters, long before a troublesome Stylist was usurping the foreground. The first usurper (Stephen says) was Mulligan; there were things he and Stephen weren't saying to each other; in particular, Stephen wasn't saying that he didn't plan to stay any longer, though "I will not sleep here tonight" was among his unvoiced thoughts. (Where will he sleep? And who'll buy Mulligan's drinks?) As for the Blooms, they evade each other like mad from the first encounter we witness.

—Who are the letters for?

He looked at them. Mullingar. Milly.

—A letter for me from Milly, he said carefully, and a card to you. And a letter for you.

He laid her card and letter on the twill bedspread near the curve of her knees.

—Do you want the blind up?

Letting the blind up by gentle tugs halfway his backward eye saw her glance at the letter and tuck it under her pillow.

"Carefully" is a word to note: Bloom's way of negotiating minefields. So is "for": she asks "Who are the letters for?" when she clearly means "from." And the letter addressed "Mrs. Marion" in a "bold hand" slides under the pillow. He knows this. She knows he knows it. Later:

A strip of torn envelope peeped from under the dimpled pillow. In the act of going he stayed to straighten the bedspread.

—Who was the letter from? he asked.

Bold hand. Marion.

—O, Boylan, she said. He's bringing the programme.

—What are you singing?

—La ci darem with J. C. Doyle, she said, and Love's Old Sweet Song.

This states the convention, that when Boylan comes what goes on will be musical. They both know differently. When that hour arrives, a gratuitousness of music will bewilder both Bloom and the reader. And at just about that hour, when divers styles commence to screen what is happening, Bloom commences on a sequence of doings he's evasive about with himself and will be downright untruthful about when he gets home to Molly (who has meanwhile been being downright unfaithful to him).

"Sirens" to "Circe," these episodes span events he will never discuss with her and about which he is less than frank with himself. They include: her adultery, his letter to Martha, his ignominious flight from Kiernan's pub, his onanism on the beach, his trip to Nighttown. And though nothing discreditable happened at the lying-in hospital he suppresses it also, because his presence there conflicts with an alternative version of the hours in question according to which (as he later sleepily informs the sleepy but suspicious Molly) he went to see Leah, supped with Stephen at Wynn's, and brought home a Stephen injured not by a soldier's blow outside Bella Cohen's but by "a falsely calculated movement in the course of a postcenal gymnastic display" (that's a part of his narrative one would wish to hear). And the episodes that prevarication screens from Molly are the same ones the second narrator's perversity imperfectly screens from us.

It is doubtful how far Molly is really deceived; for instance we are to learn that she has guessed about the correspondence with Martha, and also suspects that Poldy has been to Nighttown. But Homer's Ulysses was famous for lies, and communication between Joyce's Ulysses and his Penelope occurs chiefly around and under the words they speak. So one of the book's norms is the pack of lies by which husband and wife more or less keep in touch. The only words we can be sure have deceived Molly are ones Bloom will never remember speaking: "roc's auk's egg in the night of the bed, . . ." he muttered as he drifted down into sleep, and Molly misheard: "Yes because he never did a thing like that before as ask to get his breakfast in bed with a couple of eggs. . . ." Later she makes plans for daybreak marketing; "then I'll throw him up his eggs and tea in the moustache-cup"; and if she does Bloom will be mightily surprised. What brought *that* about? He will surely think she is penitent. Incipit, possibly, vita nuova, founded on a misheard mutter.

So deceiving Molly is part of the ritual for communicating with her, and deceiving Bloom a way of giving him messages ("I'm lonely, bored"). Deceiving the reader becomes, by a disconcerting extension, a way of establishing something about this book, about books, about life. . . .

The third and last part of *Ulysses*, the homecoming, is a coming home of narrative to the Muse. Its episodes are "Eumaeus," "Ithaca," "Penelope."

In "Ithaca" it is surely the "Tell me, Muse" formula that is generating, paragraph by paragraph, the entire chapter. One voice asks, the other imperturbably answers.

> How did they take leave, one of the other, in separation?
>   Standing perpendicular at the same door and on different sides of its base, the lines of their valedictory arms meeting at any point and forming any angle less than the sum of two right angles.
>   What sound accompanied the union of their tangent, the disunion of their (respectively) centrifugal and centripetal hands?
>   The sound of the peal of the hour of the night by the chime of the bells in the church of St. George.

The Muse answers tirelessly; she has geometry to impart, and metrical poetry, information about the characters' pasts and about their innermost thoughts; and she can deluge us with information we never thought to want, the acreage of the reservoirs of the Dublin waterworks or the output in candlepower of the gasflame on Bloom's kitchen range; she can rise also to a poetry of which we had not suspected the possibility, notably in the grave cadences which celebrate the domain of Odysseus, Water, for some 500 accurate ceremonious words, and conclude with "the noxiousness of its effluvia in lacustrine marshes, pestilential fens, faded flowerwater, stagnant pools in the waning moon."

And she is also androgynous Bloom, and the questioner is also Molly, the catechism dictated by the catechetical interrogation that has recently become a habit of Molly's and is barely sketched at the episode's close. So there are gaps, there are evasions, many. The very budget—Objectivity of Objectivities—is tampered with, to delete the sum left behind in the whorehouse. For though "objective" is what we generally hear "Ithaca" called, objective is exactly what it is not. It is incomplete and only inter-mittently straightforward, it is confined to no one's experience, it does not adhere except whimsically to a chronology of impressions—Gulliver in Lilliput by contrast told the plain truth—and it refuses restriction to the experiences of the senses. It encompasses even Bloom's Beatific Vision, life amid the eeltraps, lobsterpots, lawnmovers and lilactrees of Bloom Cottage, St. Leopold's, Flowerville.

> Could Bloom of 7 Eccles Street forsee Bloom of Flowerville?
>
> In loose allwool garments with Harris tweed cap, price 8/6, and useful garden boots with elastic gussets and wateringcan, planting aligned young firtrees, syringing, pruning, staking, sowing hayseed, trundling a weedladen wheelbarrow without excessive fatigue at sunset amid the scent of newmown hay, ameliorating the soil, multiplying wisdom, achieving longevity.

And his coat of arms will bear "the appropriate classical motto *(Semper paratus)*," the book's explicit acknowledgment of the epithet in the *Odyssey's* first line, *polytropos.*

This symbiosis by dialogue of author and Muse—one asking, one answering, the hero emerging, rotated, perfected, immobilized, apotheo-sized—is the point of classical balance: Bloom at home, fiction likewise come home to the place whence Objectivity's siren song once lured her away. Bloom not yet at home, we have the graceless "Eumaeus"; sprawling, architecturally defective alike in its plan and in the interstices of its sen-tences, as of Bloom himself, Museless, musing. Like *Gulliver's Travels,* incidentally, it grows curiously preoccupied with horses, and on its last page our old friend the Vivid Narrator, long mistaken by the vulgar for a connoisseur of excrement, supplies *Ulysses* with his last contribution, a few perfectly turned phrases that shine in the graceless syntax:

> The horse, having reached the end of his tether, so to speak, halted, and, *rearing high a proud feathering tail,* added his quota by letting fall on the floor, which the brush would soon brush up and polish *three smoking globes of turds. Slowly, three times, one after another, from a full crupper, he mired.*

Farewell, old virtuoso, that was done consummately.

Then "Ithaca," the ceremonious exchange between narrator and Muse, formal, the two sharing an idiom that they have under thorough command and that permits no voices to be heard but theirs. And finally

"Penelope": Muse without narrator, direct as "Eumaeus" is not, never elegantly varied but asprawl with a liquid formlessness of its own, to contrast
with the "Eumaeus" formlessness which is like a heap of magpie's gatherings.

"Penelope," unpunctuated, unnarrated—the only episode with not
one narrative interruption—would appear to show us how the Muse behaves
without Homer: a great feminine welling of lore and opinion and gossip
and feeling with (as Joyce himself said) neither beginning nor middle nor
end. "a quarter after what an unearthly hour I suppose they're just getting
up in China now combing out their pigtails for the day well soon have the
nuns ringing the angelus theyve nobody coming in to spoil their sleep
except an odd priest or two for his night office the alarmclock next door
at cockshout clattering the brains out of itself let me see if I can doze off
1 2 3 4 5 what kind of flowers are those they invented like the stars the
wallpaper in Lombard street was much nicer . . ."—it ends only when its
speaker falls asleep and may not end then.

This is a voice in the dark, cut off from sensory experience save for
bodily functions and the distant wail of a train: the voice of the pure
composing faculty, upwelling, all-knowing: she knows everything Bloom
thinks she doesn't, beginning with the contents of the drawer with the
erotic postcards in it and the fact of his correspondence with Martha Clif-
ford. "What sort of flowers are those they invented like the stars" indeed:
Bloom, who goes by the name of Henry Flower, has by now been assimilated
into the stars—"the heaventree hung with humid nightblue fruit"—and
the last surge of her monologue commences "I love flowers id love to have
the whole place swimming in roses."

Always, whatever she tells, she tells us of that man, *polytropos*,
"skilled in all ways of contriving." In her darkness the myths coalesce,
amid the coalescence of all particular things, and of all men into an epon-
ymous "him." And from the heart of the labyrinth where a Queen thanks
to Dedalus' contriving has coupled with a prize bull named Blazes, the voice
swells up of the eternal Ausonian Muse, readmitted to the domain of story-
telling from which Objectivity thought to banish her when it shut out myth
and rhetoric and supposed that the new heaven and the new earth could
be bought with particulate facts sequentially dispensed like copper coins.

JENNIFER SCHIFFER LEVINE

Originality and Repetition in "Finnegans Wake" and "Ulysses"

Most readers of *Ulysses*, and certainly of *Finnegans Wake*, seem to agree on one point at least: that the language in these texts is itself problematic and demands some special kind of response. In this essay I address the question of originality in literary language, trace its elaboration in *Finnegans Wake,* and show how the complex use of cliché in *Ulysses* involves us specifically in the play of origins and repetition. The movement of my argument suggests that the distinction between literary and ordinary language—between the original and the mass-produced or between "valuable" discourse and cliché—needs to be re-thought. This polemic, however, is too wide to be accommodated here and is left as an unspoken background to the discussion.

I should like to begin with some general notions in aesthetics and with a question about language. Man's first act, as Hegel defines it, was to give names to things and so, paradoxically, by this initial giving, to possess the world. This view of language subsumes a great deal of literary criticism (understandably so: it is an attractive rationale for our professional devotion to words). Not surprisingly then, the "real" plot in *A Portrait* has been seen as "a quest to find the defining unity, the composing harmony." And the answer, significantly, is to be found "in the labyrinth of language that

From *PMLA* 1, vol. 94 (January 1979). Copyright © 1979 by The Modern Language Association of America.

contains all human revelation . . . and to be found by the artist in naming the names." Language, thus seen by Dorothy Van Ghent, is a means of possession. But it is not, nor can it ever be, the direct expression of reality. It becomes, in turn, that by which we ourselves are possessed. In A *Portrait* this double edge of language has been noted. Hugh Kenner has written of Stephen's growing maturity as it is revealed in his attitude toward words: "It is [not] initially accurate to say that by naming things he acquires power over them; on the contrary, the names of things are already given, it is through their names that they have power over him." He goes on to image language as a Trojan horse "by which the universe gets into the mind" and against which the artist must remain on guard. By the very conditions of his birth, it would seem, Joyce was more likely to see into the deceitful power of words: the citizens of Anglo-Irish Dublin, like those of Svevo's Austro-Italian Trieste and Kafka's Germano-Czech Prague, were placed a priori at a distance from their own language. The scene in A *Portrait* between Stephen and the English-born dean of studies makes the dilemma clear. His teacher's accent—both upper-class and English—will not allow the young Dubliner to take the English words on his own tongue for granted. It is always a reminder of the "other" and of his otherness in relation to it. Perhaps this initial wariness of his own discourse forced on Joyce the painful but necessary truth that language is never "natural," that there is no inevitable relationship between the word and what it stands for. What is at issue is not just a feeling of foreignness within a particular language, but a putting into question of language itself. Once recognized, it places the speaker in a new, self-conscious relationship to all the systems of signs by which he constitutes himself and his world.

The difficulty of Joyce's language in *Ulysses* and *Finnegans Wake*—in effect, its un-naturalness—confronts readers and forces them into a certain relationship to the words. It is not just a case of trying harder, of making that Olympian effort to match Joyce's own effort in the writing. It is rather, a case of recognizing altered relationships between language and meaning, between the word as that which it refers to and the word as an element *within* a particular set of oppositions, within the particular structure that is language. The relationship between words and what they point to might now be seen as always already constrained by the organization of language itself, that is, by the relationships between words and words and between words and silence. Saussure's linguistic model, which is crucial to the work of Barthes, Derrida, and what has been called the *nouvelle critique*, argues specifically against "the nominalist view that words have meaning through standing as names for things." Pre-Saussurian linguistics assumes "that ready-made ideas exist before words" and "that the linking of a name and a thing is a very simple operation—an assumption that is anything but true."

Language cannot be understood merely as a name-giving system. It is not a mode of communicating a preexisting and already common experience. If it were so, then reading would be (as I. A. Richards and a whole tradition of Anglo-American criticism have implied) a process of *deciphering* language in order to pass right through it to the experience that it communicates. But if (as one critic of this view has argued) "language is grasped as a dominant articulation," "then the process of reading is the process of the interaction between the articulation of the text and the articulation of the reader." It is "this painful effort to read, in one and the same gesture, both oneself and the text before one's eyes." Ultimately, then, this reconsideration of language demands a more self-conscious, a more self-reflexive reader. For as long as words are thought of as tools by which we grasp reality—tools with no *necessary* distorting powers of their own, then we as readers are safe from speculations into our own relationship to language.

If words are never innocent or transparent, if they do not come "pure" to either reader or writer but are always part of a larger articulation, always used in some way, then a central problem must be that of origins— and if of origins, also of its corollary, originality. In our own culture these notions are part of a complex of ideas about art, value, and the relationship between the two. Briefly, they might be summarized as follows: that genius is an *individual* quality ("genius," "original," "eccentric," all somehow overlapping); that the artist is defined by his or her eccentricity, his or her transcendence of the group. (Thus the central distinction of literary language is that it is a consciously willed deviation from ordinary language.) It follows from all this that the work of art (as opposed to other kinds of objects) is characterized, and in turn given value, by the fact of an individual human consciousness (genius) at its source. Within the larger social and economic world in which works of art are bought and sold, this means that "the original" (as an actual object) assumes a greater cash value. Within the narrower and rather more rarefied contents of critical discourse the concept of "the original"—as the deviation from convention but also as the potential of a work to signal back to its shaping consciousness—is seen as a criterion of artistic value. Walter Benjamin has written that the aura, the authenticity (and, I would add, the originality) of the work of art links it to its ritual function. If we think of that function more specifically in its context of magic and religion as an attempt to make contact with a point of origins, to reconnect ourselves to a source of power and creation and to an original moment of full presence, critical reading may well be seen as a ritual act. I should specify here: the reference is to a particular tradition of critical reading that justifies itself ultimately as making contact with the great minds of the past and that hopes that—at some level—its own reading enacts more fully the conscious and unconscious intentions of the author. Fascinated with the process of creation, it identifies it only with the writer's work. I am concerned here not with the cruder notions of authorial intent but rather with a more diffuse and more powerful feeling that reading is a form of recreation: that readers lose themselves in, and are absorbed by, the author's language; that in the act of reading their only responsibility is to the individual consciousness behind the work. Recreation therefore signifies the double concept of re-creation/recreation: reenactment *and* relaxation. But this quest for the original tends to free the reader from that painful yet essential effort "to read, in one and the same gesture, both oneself and the text before one's eyes."

The modern period impinges on the notion of originality. Perhaps most clearly in the visual arts we can see, as Walter Benjamin has argued so brilliantly, that the developments in technology (and particularly in mass production) freed the work of art from its ritualistic function as a unique, original object that is built into a specific space and that signals to a specific making and turned it into a secular object free to move in time and space. The photograph and the print replace the fresco. Nevertheless, it could be pointed out that with literary works, unlike painting or sculpture, the idea that "the original" itself is essential to the full aesthetic experience does not really apply. On the contrary, the reproducibility of texts (so that each reader may have a personal copy and a private relationship to the words and to the pages) seems a natural—even a necessary— condition of reading. When Benjamin writes of the work of art in the age of mechanical reproduction and describes the shattering of the aura as the consequence of modern life, his description applies to what, at a certain level, has long been the reader's experience: "the technique of reproduction detaches the reproduced object from the domain of tradition. By making many reproductions it substitutes a plurality of copies for a unique existence. And in permitting the reproduction to meet the beholder or listener in his own particular situation, it reactivates the object reproduced. These two processes lead to a tremendous shattering of tradition." Within a literary context the age of mechanical reproduction, and the subsequent reconsideration of "the original" as an actual object, can be moved right back to the fifteenth century and Gutenberg's printing press. And yet the *idea* of "the original," the insistence on an individuality of language, remains a potent one for literature.

The more sensitive of Joyce's early readers, however antagonistic, were quick to notice something about his work's originality—or lack of it. Lawrence's comments are perhaps the best known. "My God," he wrote, "what a clumsy *olla putrida* James Joyce is! Nothing but old fags and cabbage-stumps of quotations . . . what old and hard-worked staleness, masquerading as the all-new!" So, too, Wyndham Lewis, for whom *Ulysses* was a "suffocating," "lifeless" "expanse of objects . . . the sewage of a Past twenty years old. . . ." And at the end "you feel that it is the very nightmare of the naturalistic method that you have been experiencing." If it is a nightmare, though, it is not necessarily a function of any one method. The horror of repetition, after all, is the nightmare of every writer, insofar as language is the record of what has already been said and written by other voices, other writers. T. S. Eliot, writing in *The Tyro* at the time of *Ulysses'* publication, was coincidentally providing a theoretical defense of Joyce's language. For him, the notion of writing as inevitable repetition was not an impulse toward death but, rather, a liberation of human discourse: "Whatever words a writer employs, he benefits by knowing . . . the *uses to which they have already been applied*. . . . The essential of tradition is in this; in getting as much as possible of the whole weight of the history of the language behind his word." This consciousness of language, however, is only a beginning. In *Finnegans Wake* we find a more radical and a more anxious investigation of origins and originality. Eliot's "tradition" implies, in a sense, that the uses of language are cumulative, that literature becomes progressively richer and more resonant. Perhaps it glances over the rather unflattering possibility that writing is a mode of copying—less an act of inclusion than of theft—and that the claim to "originality" is always suspect.

II

what do you think Vulgariano did but study with stolen fruit how cutely to copy all their various styles of signature so as one day to utter an epical forged cheque on the public for his own private profit. . . .

The question here—and the attack—are Shaun's. Jaundiced/Shaundiced they may be, but they represent a view of Shem, and of the writer, that reappears throughout *Finnegans Wake*. In the chapter on the lost letter and its recovery from the dung-heap, the author is referred to as "our copyist," and the potential meanings within "poorjoist" are no less suggestive. Joyce himself is in there somewhere and so is "perjurist," in turn supported (however ambiguously) by the literal "poor joist": a weak link in the whole network of lies. Is the "poorjoist" also a "prosodite": a prostitute of prose? According to Shaun, at least, that is a correct description of his brother the penman. The notion is taken up in the earlier chapter as well, for the letter is told "in universal, in polygluttural, in each auxiliary neutral idiom . . . a con's cubane, a pro's tutute . . . and anythongue athall." It is just the promiscuity of the language, the refusal of fixed or limited sources, that is so infuriating to Shaun. He calls Shem, as we have seen, "a thoroughpaste prosodite" and then, building himself up into a rage, "you . . . you . . . Europasianised Afferyank." The penman is here precisely one whose point of origins is multiple, all-embracing, even promiscuous—certainly one who is at home everywhere and nowhere at once.

The problem of origins is connected at several points to the notion of the writer as copyist and cheat. "Who can say," Shaun insists, "how many pseudostylic shamiana, how few or how many of the most venerated public impostures, how very many piously forged palimpsests slipped in the first place . . . from his pelagiarist pen?" Two notions of the author are superimposed here, and we are obliged to read the double image: Shem is both sham and shaman, plagiarist and Pelagian, conman and holy man. It may seem a strange juxtaposition, and yet the conception of the writer as quite legitimately a copy maker has a long and respectable history, invoked in the allusion to Pelagian, a monk of the early Christian era. Until writing became a common skill the scribe was one who in the main recorded what someone else had already said or made additional copies of what had already been written. The situation in the monasteries was analogous. The manuscripts so long and lovingly worked over were ultimately transcriptions—pious copies of the signature of God. He was the first cause and as such the only significant point of origin for language. Transcription was not theft: it was, rather, a recognition of our dependent and subordinate status. It is fair to say that the modern world no longer gives the holy sources total precedence. Instead, it places us at the center—makes us, in a sense, our own creators, and insists on the notion of originality. The old view of the writer as copier, always referring back to an earlier and more authoritative source, has been replaced by that of the writer as an original, whose ultimate value depends on a liberation from sources. And yet, as the lines from *Finnegans Wake* suggest, we may see writing as pious transcription or as deception and theft: total originality, given the shared nature of language, is impossible.

Throughout the *Wake* we are confronted with the dilemma of origins. "Where did thots come from?" Here the question is about thoughts and about Thot: God, and also about tots—where do children come from? Sexual experience, the fall from grace, the fall into knowledge: *Finnegans Wake* explores their interconnections. For language too the question is insistent. Adam's first act is to give things names: an act of possession but also a fall into limitation, a formalized recognition of our alienation. Words turn experience into the object of discourse, they place it at a distance, however much the intervening space may seem to be within man's control. Felt experience becomes something else in the moment it is verbalized.

What then are the possible relationships between language and experience, between language and a first act or a point of origin? Book I, Chapter iv of the *Wake* presents us with an interesting scenario: the story of a lost letter, a dunghill, and a little hen who scratches away till she recovers the manuscript from the mud and slime. The basic terms are these: on one hand—dirt, mud, chaos, formlessness; on the other—words and a meaning to be deciphered. One way of reading the section is through the problematic posed earlier in this discussion: the confrontation between experience and language, more specifically between the formlessness of experience and the formative, because patterned, powers of language. The most obvious relationship between the two would seem to be one of op-position. Thus the letter must be taken *out* of the dung-heap, cleaned up, held up to the light, before it can properly be read. And yet, can the letter ever be returned to the original moment of experience, before language intrudes, and to an original pristine state? Is it really possible to discriminate between the marks of the pen and the marks made by the mud of time and circumstances? It would seem that some kind of inexorable and irreversible change has indeed occurred. We cannot make a clear return to an original state, or even reproduce an earlier reading, but perhaps the mud and tea stains can help to answer the question of origin—the question asked as we begin the story: "Say . . . who in hallhagal wrote the durn thing anyhow?" The letter "has acquired accretions of terricious matter whilst loitering in the past . . . and, whether it be thumbprint, mademark or just a poor trait of the artless, its importance in establishing the identities in the writer complexus . . . will be best appreciated by never forgetting that both before and after the battle of the Boyne it was a habit not to sign letters always." At no time in history—or at least in Irish history—has the point of origins been made explicit. There are no precise signatures, only more or less accurate attempts at decoding a source. At the end we have to reconcile ourselves to reading the tea stains as well as the pen marks (as well as the claw holes made by previous readers: "the fourleaved shamrock or quadrifoil jab . . . perforations [made] by Dame Partlet on her dungheap."

Even though we cannot return to the actual point of origins we continue to be fascinated by it, to need to understand it, perhaps reenacting in this search a child's fascination with its own excrement and its own origins. Indeed, the polygluttural promiscuous language of the text seems to suggest such a connection. We have already seen how, as far as Shaun is concerned, Shem is no more than a conman. He goes on to describe how Vulgariano (Shem) or possibly the forged check (his writing) is dismissed by "Dustbin's United Scullerymaid's and Househelp's Sorority," and here the notion of writer and writing as a lump of dung—simultaneously fascinating and revolting—weaves in and out of the discourse. Shem is rejected by the Househelp's Sorority, who

> turned him down and assisted nature [in the best tradition of laxative advertisements?] by unitedly shoeing the source of annoyance out of the place altogether and . . . holding one another's gonk (for no-one . . . dared whiff the polecat at close range) and making some pointopointing remarks as they done so at the perfects of the Sniffey, your honour, aboon the lyow why a stunk, mister.

A stink, a skunk—either one or both—even before we reach this point we understand Shaun's innuendos. Vulgariano and his forged check have become a lump of dung to be kicked out of the way: horribly smelly but otherwise not really dangerous. The production of language and of human excrement is even more explicitly connected some pages on, in a seemingly intimidating Latin interlude. And yet we need not even pierce the alien surfaces to sense what it is about. Three parenthetical statements in English (notably straightforward English, as well) sketch in the story for us. Shem is creating ink—and ultimately words—out of his own piss and crap: "(highly prosy, crap in his hand, sorry!) . . . (did a piss, says he was dejected, asks to be exonerated) . . . (faked O'Ryan's, the indelible ink)."

Why the insistent link between verbal and anal productions? Is it any more than just a normal childish strategy of insult and attack—nothing yet in a child's experience seeming more insulting than still to be thought a baby, incapable of controlling one's own urges, marked as smelly and unclean? But other sections of *Finnegans Wake* take up the link. It is not to be discounted as an envious brother's "sour grapes." The letter-litter transformation (in turn adopted by the journal *A Wake Newslitter*) comes to mind. We might recall, too, how many of the chapters in *Ulysses* end in an ejaculation of some sort, as often as not excremental as phallic. In

Finnegans Wake the interconnectedness of human production is explored. "Where did thots come from?": a child's question about his own origins (where do tots come from?); about authority (where does Thot—god— come from?); about his own creativity (where do thoughts come from?). The questions have been posed earlier during the schoolroom lesson as well.

> All the world's in want and is writing a letters. . . . Ten men, ton men, pen men, pun men, wont to rise a ladder. And den men, dun men, fen men, fun men, hen men, hun men wend to raze a leader. . . . To be slipped on, to be slept by, to be conned to, to be kept up. And when you're done push the chain.

To write a letter . . . to rise a ladder . . . to raze a leader. . . . And when you're done push the chain. In the spaces between these phrases and the reader, and between these phrases and the rest of the text, a whole complex of possibilities is opened up, some of them touched on earlier in this discussion. Language is power, authority. To write a letter becomes "to rise a ladder." But it also involves sin and guilt, perhaps even original sin: "to raze a leader," to bring God down from his place on high and disobey him. How smooth the transformations of the phrases . . . the temptation is always there, implicit in the very sound of the words, to deny his authority, his privileged position as a final point of origin. And then, at the end, "when you're done push the chain." What does it mean, in this context of authority and guilt, to defecate and then to push the chain? The discovery of one's own productions as foul, vile, smelly, is surely a terrible moment in a child's life. To recognize in oneself a source for all that seems other to oneself is perhaps the beginning of guilt, certainly of alienation. It is not unlike the question of one's own identity and one's own origins. Where do tots come from? Where do *I* come from? Where does *that* (excrement, the other) come from? The points of origin are disturbingly close together. To make babies: to make excrement—with both there must be guilt, bringing more pain and suffering, more unpleasantness into the world. To be forced to recognize the other as other—another human being, a lump of dung—alien to oneself and perhaps even disgusting; but also to recognize the other as tied to oneself by the inexorable demands of one's own body: this is one of the paradoxes that *Finnegans Wake* asks us to explore.

We eat, digest, defecate. Our body wastes enter the earth and feed it so that we may once again eat, digest, defecate. The movement is circular but it is also progressive. Without it life would cease. So too with the children we produce: we are born, we breed, we die. Our children in turn repeat the process and their children after them. What looks like change is only, perhaps, recycling, and we are bound to a wheel of repetition. For the word too it is recycling, repetition, quotation. Words have always already been spoken; it is impossible to return to their points of origin, to deny all the uses they have already been put to. Ink out of one's body wastes: that is the image of *Finnegans Wake*. Total newness, total originality, is impossible, and so the writer's guilt becomes that of the thief and the conman. No wonder then that the letter smells like dung: it is recycled language, repeated discourse, sometimes even going to mold at the edges. Here is posed the writer's dilemma, just as it is the child's: to reconcile oneself to one's own limitation, to a point of origins that is simultaneously fascinating and repelling, to the complex relationships that both tie and divide one from one's own productions. Maturity brings a change: the horror of repetition, as of one's own excrement, is softened. Granted that the sources of words are outside one's control. That does not mean defeat for the writer, or an admission of impotence, but rather altered relations and new strategies of language.

Book II, Chapter ii, in which the children are having their lesson (a lesson that, not insignificantly, one critic has said is about "the nature of God," and another about "their mother's genital organs"), makes a formal point out of this problem of origins. It presents us with a number of visibly distinct discourses, one of which, straddling the bottom of each page, is entirely made up of footnotes. In the most obvious way, the academic pattern is easily recuperated through the schoolroom context of the scene. But there are other aspects of the footnote convention that bear examination here. Broadly speaking, the footnote has two functions: it provides that space within which the point of origins is given, in which quotations, allusions, and repetitions of all kinds are made explicit. It poses a clear hierarchy, too, between the major discourse and the discourses that surround it: those in the past, referred to now as sources; and those in a potential future, as yet only sketched in with a phrase or comment. The link between them is unambiguous (traceable from a precise point in the text to a particular footnote), and the relationship is always (by the simple fact of exclusion from the main text) a hierarchical one. These are the expectations we bring to bear on our reading of the chapter. They will provide a structure through which we try to make sense of particular words and phrases. Instead we find, from the first footnote on, that the hierarchies slide and crumble around us. We are given neither points of origin nor explanations but are plunged in medias res, it seems, into another discourse, which has no less significance (i.e., no less complex signifiers), and certainly no fewer mysteries waiting to be footnoted, than the central text to which it refers. The first footnote is a good example. Two new characters, "she" and "I," both unnamed—let alone a spate of blue canaries—are introduced in what *should* have been a pleasantly restful explanatory interlude. Similarly, too, [elsewhere], we are told to "halt for hearsake": a halt that is then footnoted at such length (almost the entire page) that by the end of the note the "halt" itself, and by implication the privileged status of the major discourse, have been, literally, written away.

There is to be no respite, it seems, from the polysemic and multi-directional logic of this text. The line reading from text to footnote and back again is not the clear straight line handed down by an a priori convention; it is, rather, a line that can be accurately traced only in the process of reading. It is no more to be taken for granted than is the denouement at the beginning of a story. The point is made quite visibly [in another footnote]. Instead of adding significant details to the text, the footnote . . . has had them all removed, even from itself. Nothing remains but a cryptic shell: "^{3}H' dk' fs' h'p'y." The connections have to be made, and placed, by the reader. The footnote itself will not deign to do so. Partly, of course, because of the difficulty of the whole chapter but also because of the mere look of the bottom of the page, all neatly numbered and arranged as though to say: 'Of course you will find an explanation here . . . ," the reader is constantly aware of missing connections. The negative space created, like the space between objects in a Cubist painting, becomes increasingly "there," solid. It is essentially the space between words and their points of origin—a space we have learned not to see or to keep within domesticable bounds by various means. One of these means is the footnote, which, at chosen moments, places the text in a precise and explicit relation to its sources. In *Finnegans Wake* nothing is made explicit. On the contrary, despite—or perhaps because of—such devices, everything is complicated. Even [another] exemplary-looking note . . . manages to make nonsense out of our expectations. It captures, ever so faithfully, the conventional phrasing of such citations: a perfect blend of country gentleman's pedantry, paternalism, nostalgia. "I have heard this word" the footnote tells us, "used by Martin Halpin, an old gardener from the Glens of Antrim who used to do odd jobs for my godfather, the Rev. B. B. Brophy of Swords." The only problem, and it is a problem, is that "this word" is the eminently straight-forward word "hole"—as little in need of its own footnote as any in the English language, unless, of course, as I think Joyce is considering here and throughout the *Wake*, *every* word makes a repetition, carries a past along with it, and as such invites the whole question of origins and originality. Conventional connections between word and source are deconstructed and rethought in *Finnegans Wake*. The text makes a joke of our expectation that origins (as, for instance, presented in a footnote) can ever be unself-consciously "given." Still, no matter how complicated the answer, how wobbly and ambiguous the line back to a source point, the question of origins has to be asked. It is as pressing it would seem for the writer as the larger question posed throughout the *Wake*: "Where did thots come from?"

But where does all this leave us as readers? The problem is surely part of our linguistic experience as well. It seems ironic that we become increasingly skeptical about the simple truth of origins (as given, for instance, in footnotes). And yet as readers we are continually relying on our knowledge and memory of an "original" to make sense of the text: we identify a meaning precisely because we can *re*-cognize, give a source to, a phrase that overlaps or underpins the language. Thus, we gladly fasten on the echoes of "for jollycomes smashing Holmes," or of "she could beth her bothom dolours he'd have a culious impression on the diminitive that chafes our ends." So much of this chapter (and indeed all of *Finnegans Wake*) is comprehensible, at least initially, because it is generated out of popular sayings, clichés, refrains . . . out of what has already been said and written, out of what is therefore hearable and readable.

The possibility that discourse is always in some sense quotation—that language, like food, repeats itself—is elaborately and wittily played on in *Finnegans Wake*. "Shem was a sham and a low sham and his lowness creeped out first via foodstuffs." His house is an assemblage of odds and ends—the fag ends of the world: spewed up food, excretions, repetitions, quotations from the earlier texts:

> The warped flooring of the lair and soundconducting walls thereof [the literary space, it seems, is not hermetically sealed but crisscrossed by language and speech] . . . were persianly literatured [again literature = litter] with . . . counterfeit franks [frankfurters/french francs], best intentions, curried [curry] notes, upset latten tinlacks [latin syntax in disarray: a tin of upset tin tacks] . . . painful digests [both a précis and a case of indigestion], magnifying *wine*glasses . . . once current puns [currant buns: spewed up food and language overlap], quashed quotatoes [mashed potatoes/quotations], messes of mottage [pottage/mottage: mot = word], unquestionable issue papers [tissue papers], seedy ejaculations [semen ejaculations, and the erotically remembered seed-cake in *Ulysses*] . . . spilt ink [ink = milk], blasphematory spits, stale shestnuts [stale chestnuts, clichés] . . . [now some pretty clear references to Joyce's earlier texts:] special sighs . . . ahs ohs ouis sis jas jos [James Joyce?] gias neys thaws sos, *yeses and yeses and yeses* . . . [and] all this *chambermade music*. . . .
> (italics and bracketed comments are mine)

If writing is largely quotation, then the notion of originality has to be rethought. Joyce, it would seem, was involved in such a reconsideration while writing *Finnegans Wake*. Eugene Jolas quotes him as saying that "Really it is not I who am writing this crazy book. It is you, and you, and you, and that man over there, and that girl at the next table." Obviously the balance between repetition and originality in the text is a complex one. As one critic has put it: "Although *Finnegans Wake* is thoroughly original . . . it may also be the most self-conciously unoriginal work in the language." It might be argued, of course, that Joyce had no option. The "pelagiarist pen" was forced on him by his eyesight, and he had to rely on his friends to do a great mass of reading for him. We do have the lovely story, however, of Joyce dictating a section of *Work in Progress* to Beckett, being interrupted by a knock at the door, and calling out: "Come in." Beckett, on his part, unaware of the shift in discourse, included it in his transcription, which, when read out, so delighted Joyce that he insisted it remain in the text. It seems strange to think of this multiple originality of the *Wake* and then remember the common attack on it: that it is only readable, ultimately, within its author's head. To a certain extent this is true of all texts so long as we measure our own reading against an authorial intention. But it is particularly ironic to give Joyce's reading such a privileged position when he himself was so willing to acknowledge, and even to welcome, the multiple sources of his work. Indeed, the notions of authenticity, of artist as conman and thief, are played on so insistently in *Finnegans Wake* that we cannot dismiss them as just a blind man's dilemma. If that were true, Joyce seems to be saying, we are all blind men: all interconnected to, and relying upon, one another—all perhaps stealing from one another—with every word we utter.

III

In the composition of *Ulysses* too the notion of writing as rewriting is insistent. It is even more obvious, possibly, than in the *Wake*, as in our reading we come across numerous word-forword transcriptions. A number of critics have traced Joyce's use of sources and pointed out the painstaking accuracy of his quotations. Even without that scholarly research, the reader would sense the aura of the real, its simultaneous precision and banality clinging to many phrases. The "quashed quotatoes" of *Finnegans Wake* are here carefully preserved, as far as possible, in their original state—at most steamed in their jackets. Even more important for my discussion is the nature of what has been so accurately transcribed: often the most banal, most stereotypic form of discourse, not so much the immortal lines from Homer as the clichés and repetitions of daily life. In this final section I trace briefly some of the ways in which *Ulysses* explores and illuminates the status of cliché. Belonging as it does to the larger self-reflexive discourse of the novel, it is more than the butt of Joyce's satire, for it shares in the whole process of deconstruction, exposing conventional responses, which characterizes the text.

With cliché we have the paradoxical situation of a discourse that is totally unoriginal and yet that—because we have already heard or said it ourselves—constantly reminds us of its origins. It is both the most natural (i.e., the easiest) form of discourse and the most unnatural, since it de-naturalizes language—making us conscious (self-conscious) of the act we have learned to take for granted: the first act of giving things names. This paradoxical situation, of course, characterizes cliché in the literary work, not in ordinary usage. For when we call something literature we have already put a frame around it, made a decision to read it with a certain kind of attention. Thus it is that whereas ordinarily the pat phrase may not call attention to itself, the clichés in *Ulysses* are significant *because* they are noticeable and, more particularly, recognizable.

Cliché is repeated discourse and we know it as such, as that which has already been said or written and which, in turn, is extremely easy to say again. But it plays on the question of origins and originality in a somewhat different way than would a quotation from the Bible or even a phrase from a popular song. Like them, it signals to itself as a repetition, dragging an original context along with it. The fact of origins is made clear. But unlike the biblical reference, the actual moment of origins is diffuse, promiscuous. Cliché is cliché because everybody had said it: it has become the used-up whore of discourse.

Playing on the notions of cliché as cheap and stolen goods, of its continual reappropriation/misappropriation, we have in "Circe" the perfect irony of Philip Beaufoy, cliché-monger extraordinary, accusing someone else—anyone else—of plagiarism. (We might note, too, the Freudian slips at the end, almost as though the clichés—by giving the conscious intellect a rest—were allowing the unconscious to surface: "he has cribbed some of my bestselling books, really gorgeous stuff . . . the love passage in which are beneath [above?] suspicion. The Beaufoy books of love and great possessions [passions?] . . . are a household word throughout the kingdom.") Cliché is theft, but it is a particularly stupid one, since the stolen goods are practically worthless. It offends, ultimately, on two counts, and both impinge on its originality: it is anything but new or original, and it lacks that aura of a volitional and unique consciousness as its source (the individual author as point of origins) that we both ascribe to and expect of literary (i.e., original) language.

In this sense the mere fact of the clichés in "Nausicaa" is as important in creating Gerty MacDowell's character as are their specific sources in advertising and pulp fiction. The impression we have throughout this section is of total passivity, not just the passivity imposed on nice young girls by a whole history of repressive sex roles but, on another level, of a radical inability or unwillingness to intervene in the *production* of discourse. There seems to be no central core to Gerty that can mediate the discourse. All is cliché, originating quite outside the character who utters it. Bloom too slides into stereotype, but there is always a tension, a resistance, between his own language and what he mechanically regurgitates. At one point in *Ulysses* he stands at the bookstand on O'Connell Bridge reading from *Sweets of Sin.* The clichés, like the promise of sensual pleasure, are tempting indeed. It would be easy to give in, to play the vanquished woman, to accept the alien discourse as the beautiful woman will accept the alien male, Raoul; and in fact Bloom begins to do so, overlapping the physical on the verbal surrender. But there is a counterinvasion by another discourse. The illusion of passionate but deodorized sex is broken: so too are the clichés it belongs to. They are not passively absorbed but entered into a complex kind of play with a far more personal and original set of images, which in turn do real violence—ultimately indeed annihilate them: "Feel! Press! Crushed! Sulphur dung of lions."

The general notion of cliché is that it is effortless, mechanical discourse—an image crystallized by Northrop Fry's description of an "automatic fluency, turning on a tap and letting a lot of platitudinous bumble emerge." It follows that (within a given culture) we all have access to the same tap, that for both writer and reader, speaker and audience, it is a mutual case of "just familiar words running along their own familiar tracks." If we think for a moment of the extent to which *Ulysses* is built up out of clichés, out of set phrases we already know and can easily recognize, then it ought to be a relatively easy text to read. And yet the reader's experience is often embarrassingly difficult. Somewhere along the way the "familiar tracks" have been sabotaged, and we find ourselves derailed, bumping along on a jolting series of prearranged disappointments. And since cliché, more than a more "literary" language, takes for granted a smooth and conflict-free relationship between language and experience, language and an audience, the discontinuity of its position in *Ulysses* makes the shock even more insistent. Bloom's discourse at the very end of "Nausicaa" is almost entirely made up of clichés or of words and phrases that we can recognize and that, in this sense at least, share the condition of cliché. As though to underline the point, the last words go on, mindlessly repeating themselves like a broken record stuck along an old familiar groove. But the total effect of the passage is no easy flow out of the metaphorical tap. The syntax has been chopped up, splitting clichés into their component words. While we recognize them as somehow belonging to self phrases and therefore potentially consumable, we are forced to deal with them on a word-for-word basis. And since the stereotype is a matter of structure, of a specific arrangement of words, the clichés of popular fiction are revitalized.

A great deal of the humor in *Ulysses* is generated out of this method. In "Eumaeus," for instance, during a long disquisition on Parnell and the related topics of marriage, love, adultery, and betrayal, all of which is more than generously studded with the "one current puns" and "quashed quotatoes" of repeated discourse, the story ends in a hilarious jumble of clichés. Rather like the children's game in which a body image is cooperatively built up out of individual bits—a man's head, perhaps, a giraffe's neck, a woman's torso, a frog's legs, and so on, all incongruous and yet ultimately somehow coherent (in that neck follows head, then upper torso, lower torso, etc.)—the final scene demands to be visualized in order to be appreciated. Parnell's supporters, we are told, "very effectually cooked his matrimonial goose, thereby heaping coals of fire on his head, much in the same way as the fabled ass's kick." For at least a moment we take the clichés literally, and, however subliminal, the visual impact is very funny indeed: a goose being cooked—perhaps with a wedding veil on—a sudden fire on some as yet unspecified person's head (probably the cook's, though possibly the goose's), and then to cap it all, an ass cavorting and kicking his way through the scene. When cliché functions *as* cliché the last thing we would feel obliged to do would be to take it literally or to consider any meaning other than the conventional one. But here the discourse is overloaded, the stereotypes too closely packed together, and we find ourselves reading the conventional phrases from a quite unconventional point of view. Instead of just recognizing them and "switching off" (as mechanical discourse they only expect a mechanical response), we are jolted wide awake by the discontinuity of the images.

Considering that clichés are always marked by an original context and therefore have a certain unavoidable rigidity, it seems inevitable that clashes of the sort we have just seen should occur when they are used in any quantity. (We might consider, too, as an extended example, the schizophrenic dialogue of "Circe" in which the clichés accumulate, signaling with great economy the fragmentation of the self in Nighttown.) In exploiting such clashes Joyce follows on a long comic and satirical tradition. What seems uniquely Joycean, however, is a more ambiguous series of

overlaps and discontinuities. Moments of real feeling in *Ulysses* are punc-
tuated, but not seriously threatened, by cliché. Instead, the already written
enters into a complex process of play, and of production, with "original"
discourse.

Bloom and Stephen sit together in the night shelter. The chapter
is "Eumaeus," notable—even in a text like *Ulysses*—for its "once current
puns." Indeed, it seems to be fueled by stereotype. Without access to it,
we feel, entire sentences would seize up and grind to a halt. And yet as
Bloom recounts his encounter with the citizen something quite unexpected
happens:

> —He took umbrage at something or other, that much-injured but on the
> whole eventempered person declared, I let slip. He called me a jew, and
> in a heated fashion, offensively. So I . . . told him his God, I mean
> Christ, was a jew too. . . . That was one for him. A soft answer turns
> away wrath. He hadn't a word to say for himself as everyone saw. Am I
> not right?
>
> He turned a long you are wrong gaze on Stephen of timorous dark
> pride at the soft impeachment, with a glance also of entreaty for he seemed
> to glean in a kind of a way that it wasn't all exactly . . .

Despite the individually banal phrases, the cumulative effect is neither
banal nor mechanical. The smooth, effortless rhythms of cliché have been
truncated, upsetting the ready-made meaning in their wake. In the second
paragraph the clichés of "soft porn" are wrenched out of their usual context
and transposed to a quite different structure of feeling in the man-to-man,
Stephen and Bloom relationship. There is, certainly, an element of comic
deflation here, but at the same time the original context underpins Bloom's
sexual and emotional vulnerability to the young man. Stephen is both to
be protected and to be feared. His virility makes him powerful: a potential
son but also a potential rival. In this moment we understand, precisely,
some of the *ambiguity* of the relationship between the two, and in a reversal
typical of *Ulysses*, we do so through a form of discourse that ordinarily
excludes just that element of experience—for cliché tends to suggest, not
least by its formal quality as a repetition, that nothing is so complicated
or uncertain that it cannot be *fully* accounted for with an old familiar
phrase.

Some pages later Bloom thinks over the quality of unexpectedness
that is so central to Stephen's character: "The queer suddenly things he
popped out with attracted the elder man. . . ." The conjunction of this in
itself original and "suddenly" phrase with the gray expanses of cliché by
which it is surrounded marks, in its turn, the element of shock, the queer

mixtures of fresh and stale discourse that keep the reader of *Ulysses* in such an unstable relationship to the text.

That instability is particularly marked in "Hades"—rather inevitably so if we consider how clichés attach themselves to central experiences like death. In this sense they function as ritual: a form of group bonding in which a structure of behavior is more important than its specific content. It is precisely its lack of originality that is a comfort, holding the unknown at bay. For our purposes at least, the interesting moments in the chapter are just those in which public and private discourses overlap. In Bloom's meditation on death there is a back-and-forth movement of language and of emotion, between a mechanical commonplace response and an original, slightly off-center detail: in the instability between the two we find ourselves, suddenly, quite moved.

> He looked down at the boots he had blacked and polished. She had outlived him, lost her husband. More dead for her than for me. [The string of clichés begins:] One must outlive the other. Wise men say. There are more women than men in the world. Condole with her. Your terrible loss. I hope you'll soon follow him. [This is original, to say the least. The solid ground of cliché collapses under us but is restored with the next sentence:] For Hindu widows only. [The language becomes barer; the references more personal:] She would marry another. Him? No. Yet who knows after? Widowhood not the thing since the old queen died. [And now a new string of clichés:] Drawn on a guncarriage. Victoria and Albert. Frogmore memorial mourning. But in the end [here we go again, sliding off the rails of one cliché right onto another: Grieving Queen becomes Plucky Little Widow:] she put a few violets in her bonnet. Vain in her heart of hearts. All for a shadow. Consort not even a king. Her son was the substance. Something new to hope for not like the past she wanted back, waiting. It never comes. One must go first: alone under the ground: and lie no more in her warm bed.
>
> (bracketed comments are mine)

Up to a certain point we can read this paragraph and maintain an amused detachment. As the bracketed interjections point out, it is largely an assemblage of secondhand discourse. There are surprises ("I hope you'll soon follow") and shifts of tone that make the ongoing reading more disturbing than it might be. But it is only at the end that the full force of the language hits us " . . . and lie no more in her warm bed": apart from the "blacked and polished" boots (and possibly the violets in the bonnet) this is the only physical detail in the paragraph. The unexpected sensuousness of the image is very powerful. It draws us in with an immediacy that makes it part of our own felt experience—it is no longer just a case of Hindu widows, grieving queens, or even of Bloom himself. More than that, the final sentence turns the conforting clichés of hope and resignation inside out. We are shifted away from the widow to the one who is dead, "alone under the ground," longing for life again and human warmth. Cliché is public discourse, it speaks for the living: that is one of its attractions. The dead are exiled and confined to silence. But suddenly here the discourse speaks for them, and we lose our safe position "on top" of the clichés. There is a dislocation as their recognizability and predictability, which had given us the illusion of control, momentarily break down. And so the form of our relationship to the phrases now enacts their more explicit "message," which is our precarious relationship to life itself.

Some pages later, again, Bloom's sensitivity to language, and to the experiences of life and death, is mediated through a string of clichés.

> Pray for the repose of the soul of. Does anybody really? Plant him and have done with him. Like down a coalshoot. [Hardly a conventional response—cliché's censorship has lifted:] Then lump them together to save time. All soul's day. Twentyseventh I'll be at his grave. [His father's memory: an individual response.] Ten shillings for the gardener. He keeps it free of weeds. Old man himself. Bent down double with his shears clipping. Near death's door. Who passed away. [We are starting to slide again . . .] Who departed this life. [In the very heart of automatic language—then a recognition:] As if they did it of their own accord. Got the shove, all of them. Who kicked the bucket.
>
> (bracketed comments are mine)

The interesting thing here is that Bloom himself—quite consciously—questions the stereotypes, pulls himself out of the easy flow ("Does anybody really?" "As if they did it of their own accord"), and then counters with another cliché ("Got the shove, all of them. Who kicked the bucket"). He himself, we feel, controls the disjunctions between the different systems of language. Some new possibility in cliché is being released. The phrases are indeed ready-made, repeated discourse—and yet if the metaphorical tap is being turned on we have a real sense of an active speaker being there to turn it off again, or at least to vary the flow. Bloom is not just a passive channel (as we feel Gerty MacDowell is) but is well aware of his own relationship to his discourse. He is consciously exploring the power of stereotype. Through phrases that have been repeated over and over again he shapes his own response to death. The violence—and the humor—of the final images are important. But so is the fact that they are not in themselves original. This does not make them meaningless or banal. On the contrary: meaning is always a function of its context, and, as we have seen, the special character of cliché is that it already carries with it a highly marked context. For us, the readers, therefore, the central experience is one of difference. We find ourselves involved in a kind of double-reading, reading the cliché both in the text and in the meta-text of memory. "Got the shove, all of them. Who kicked the bucket." Two contexts, or points of source, are pulling at the phrases here: an original one informed by a sardonic, even dismissive, humor (cliché as self-defense, a withdrawal from reality); and a new context of anger and pain in the allusion to Bloom's own father. The violence of the images marks a repressed violence in Bloom. Cliché now exposes vulnerability in the same moment that it rejects it. The truth of death—at least for Bloom—lies just in that space between absurdity and pain. His meditation is strung along a series of pat phrases and yet is very subtle in its final impact.

All language, of course, is to some extent determined by the previous uses to which it has been put. In the case of cliché, however, we might well think of it as overdetermined; so loaded, and so publicly loaded, with a previous context that in the process it has become much harder to manipulate. The problem it sets is very much like that of the "found object" for the painter. The point is *not* to deny the original meaning or context—that is, to use tin in such a way that it looks like wood, or a torn bit of paper like a detail of trompe l'oeil painting. A simple code of artistic honesty would have determined the use of wood, or of oils, to begin with. Rather, the intention must be to create a tension within the work between tin as tin and tin as an element on a canvas. The viewer/reader should remain conscious of, and even be pulled between, the two meanings. In words of *objet trouvé* collage, as in Joyce's *Ulysses* and *Finnegans Wake*, the transformation of the object (or of the discourse) from its meaning in the "real" world to its new meaning in the fiction is never a completed process. Rather, it is arrested just at that point where both contexts are still viable but where neither has displaced the other. At these moments the viewer/reader is truly involved in a work of progress, and the description may apply as much to the viewer/reader's own work as to that of the author's. For the potential significance of the collage/text is not realized unless the reader can bring the two contexts into play.

One of the advantages of sterotype is its reliability. As public discourse, already shared by both author and reader, it generates a whole set of shared expectations that can then be used in the production of meaning. As long as the expectations are fulfilled, the process seems "natural," and we will not be particularly aware of our own presence in the text. But in *Ulysses* the clichés are at a distance from both their original and their new contexts: expectations are undermined, denied rather than confirmed. At these moments of emptiness, when what should have happened has not happened, we each begin to see our own role in the work. In "Aeolus," as Professor MacHugh recalls the debate on the Irish language, we quickly recognize the dramatic clichés and prepare ourselves to see "the patriot-roused - from - his-deathbed-to-give-a-final-speech-and-bring-victory-to-his-cause," while he himself dies in mid-sentence (or, in a slightly more subtle variant, as soon as he leaves the hall): "Taylor had come there, you must know, from a sick bed. . . . His dark lean face had a growth of shaggy beard round it. He wore a loose neck-cloth and altogether he looked. . . ." We know what is coming, and so does MacHugh. But we only know it consciously when what we expect is denied: "and altogether he looked (though he was not) a dying man." "Aeolus" needs our expectation, and others like it if it is to score its rhetorical points.

Here, as elsewhere in *Ulysses*, the expectation of an original meaning and context becomes a sign of the reader and of the reader's intervention in the text. The particular recognizability of cliché makes this intervention more obvious, but it is not exclusive to it. Rather, it is part of the whole process of confirmation/disconfirmation, of continually reformulated expectations, that characterizes the reader's work. Recognition is an element in our relationship to all language. The kind of double-reading we have experienced with cliché is true more generally as well. But cliché, like the piece of yesterday's paper glued on to a collage, insisting on its tentative relationship to the canvas, makes the contrasts more obvious.

I have defined cliché as a particular organization of language that is recognized as repeated discourse—more specifically, it is a discourse that assumes the reader's recognition and assent, that makes an implicit claim to a shared truth. And yet because of its particular recognizability the reader rejects the claim as empty: sheer repetition having robbed it of meaning. On all these counts cliché has been deemed unworthy—unworthy of inclusion within literary language (except in a clearly satirical context), as of critical interest. Broadly speaking, critics have dealt with it in two ways. One has been to group it with other forms of repeated discourse (quotation, allusion, etc.) and, avoiding judgments about its value in the text, simply to identify the sources. The other has been to show how cliché—in itself an inferior use of language—can be a productive element in a work by constructing (in a satirical or ironic mode) character or point of view. Thus, for example, an analysis of Gerty MacDowell would proceed along the lines suggested above. Either of these approaches would have constituted a full study of its own. In the case of *Ulysses*, however, and to an even greater extent of *Finnegans Wake*, neither would have done justice to the larger themes of originality and repetition in which cliché takes part. My argument has been that in its recognizability and in the reader's response, cliché poses a more general problem of language and of reading. It places us as readers at a self-conscious angle to it, and in a sense, in repeating our own discourse, it mirrors us.

Ulysses does lay bare cliché's claim to complicity, to a shared and self-evident truth, exposing its facile emptiness in the conversation of its Dubliners. And yet it is also used to mediate moments of real feeling in the text—not only as part of Bloom's discourse (normal cliché-ridden man that he is) but within discourses that cannot be assigned to any single character (and, in which, therefore, the character cannot be held responsible for the slip into stereotype). More generally, however, it becomes a meaningful element in the work, not because it has been rid of its emptiness or has been suddenly infused with originality, but because it creates a certain kind of space in which the reader mediates between a point of origins—however diffuse—and a present moment. The fall away from originality into cliché compromises the language of *Ulysses* in a double sense. It may well be an embarrassment to our notions of "high art," but it is also an invitation to mediate a whole series of compromises. They are more often tentative than final, and yet in those negotiations—perhaps because of their precariousness—a complex play of meanings is generated. In an essay on the painter Rousseau and the origins of Cubism John Berger has given a description that, with the substitution of "verbal" for "visual," may well apply to Joyce: "He made an art of verbal wonder out of the verbal scraps sold to and foisted upon the petty bourgeoisie." With a nice irony cliché, as the discourse of the status quo, can be seen in *Ulysses* to expose and illuminate another status quo: that of the reader's relationship to literary language.

DEBORAH POPE

The Misprision of Vision: "A Portrait of the Artist as a Young Man"

Joyce commonly uses the language of spirituality and conventional theology to expand and redirect the nature of the emotional intensity occasioned by a secular epiphany. For example, Stephen's initial encounter with the prostitute and his later trembling submission to communion generate identical feelings of response, the irony of which goes unrecognized by him. In turn, his religious epiphanies are consistently turned to secular uses. Thus, the masochistic series of physical and sensual mortifications he deliberately undergoes in a burst of fervid religiosity only serve to subtilize and extend the very senses they are designed to subdue. Rather than accentuate the ascetic, they further Stephen's apprenticeship as an artist. The interpenetrability of the religious and secular clearly broadens the thematic level and resonance of particular passages thus connected. The two sections detailing Stephen's personal visions of hell—his lurid hallucinations following the retreat sermon—and of heaven—his beatific encounter with the bird-girl—exemplify such a linkage. As the two most dramatically personal, imaginative occasions in A Portrait, these passages significantly correspond in structure, terminology, and portent, to a greater extent than has been previously pointed out. Their alignment bears on the continuing question of the degree of irony intended in Stephen's closing affirmation of the artistic life.

From *James Joyce Quarterly* 3, vol. 17 (Spring 1980). Copyright © 1980 by The University of Tulsa.

Stephen's metaphoric descent into hell, like his ascent into an aesthetic heaven, is private, uniquely vouchsafed him by a higher power. Roused by the retreat sermon to intensities of fear and self-revulsion, he is driven to extravagantly hallucinate out of his surfeited sense of guilt. Escaping to his room, he is reluctant to cross the threshold, dreading what reproach or terror awaits:

> He halted on the landing before the door and then, grasping the porcelain knob, opened the door quickly. He waited in fear, his soul pining within him, praying silently that death might not touch his brow as he passed over the threshold. . . . He waited still at the threshold as at the entrance to some dark cave.

A similar, though muted, sensation of fear comes over Stephen along the seawall: "A faint click of his heart, a faint throb in his throat told him once more of how his flesh dreaded the cold infrahuman odour of the sea: yet he did not strike across the downs on his left but held straight on along the spine of rocks."

An integral part of this fear and disinclination is the auxiliary sense each time of a symbolic crossing being made, a transit between two worlds, marked in the first passage by the threshold of his room; in the second, this is the "thin wooden bridge," "the trembling bridge," over which he must pass. Further inhibiting factors present themselves in the incessant murmuring of voices and the vigilant eyes. As he enters the room, to Stephen's over-charged mind,

> Faces were there; eyes: they waited and watched. —We knew perfectly well of course that although it was bound to come to the light he would find considerable difficulty in endeavouring to try. . . . Murmuring faces waited and watched; murmurous voices filled the dark shell of the cave. . . . He told himself calmly that those words had absolutely no sense which had seemed to rise murmurously from the dark.

The unnerving conviction Stephen has of being scrutinized and smugly commented upon returns in the later passage in the disquieting presence of Ennis, Shuley, and Connolly;

> A voice from beyond the world was calling.—
>   Hello, Stephanos!
>   —Here comes The Dedalus!
>   —Come along, Dedalus! Bous Stephanoumenos! Bous Stepha-neforos!
>   . . . He recognised their speech collectively before he distinguished their faces.
> The mere sight of that medley of wet nakedness chilled him to the bone.

The boys' vaguely threatening, disruptive background of senseless noise and dislocation, like the voices in the room, tends to jargonistic bombast. Both function as an ironic, choric commentary; formal and remote, the voices condescend to Stephen, talking of him rather than to him. They are symptomatic of the insufficiency and casual malevolency of the world outside Stephen: one is like the winding, convoluted prose of the Jesuitical schoolmen; the other, the comic reduction of classical training.

As Stephen strives to maintain some mental order, a wave of soulweariness suffuses his body. This stage—a prerequisite for the regenerative vision to occur—amounts to a state of despair, a spiritual condition connected in each case to the physical sensation of chill and fatigue. Thus, prior to the vision of hell, "His hands were cold and damp and his limbs ached with chill. Bodily unrest and chill and weariness beset him, routing his thoughts." Similarly, upon nearing the place where the bird-girl will appear, though the day had been hitherto pleasant,

> At that instant, as it seemed to him, the air was chilled and looking askance towards the water he saw a flying squall darkening and crisping suddenly the tide. . . . Like a scene on some vague arras, old as man's weariness, the image of the seventh city of christendom was visible to him across the timeless air, no older nor more weary nor less patient of subjection than in the days of the thingmote. Disheartened, he raised his eyes towards the slowdrifting clouds.

In both instances confusion and agitation succeed this numbness, oppressing his consciousness and throwing his thoughts into chaos:

> To be alone with his soul, to examine his conscience, to meet his sins face to face, to recall their times and manners and circumstances, to weep over them. He could not weep. He could not summon them to his memory. He felt only an ache of soul and body, his whole being, memory, will, understanding, flesh, benumbed and weary.

> He heard a confused music within him as of memories and names which he was almost conscious of but could not capture even for an instant; then the music seemed to recede, to recede, to recede. . . .

Operative as well in each privileged circumstance is the proclivity to pride Stephen feels in his secret sensual life. Thus, all the while he is abasing himself for the sordidness of his sexual initiations, there is an unmistakable undercurrent of superiority and personal distinction in the tone of his thoughts:

> Could it be that he, Stephen Dedalus, had done those things? His conscience sighed in answer. Yes, he had done them, secretly, filthily, time after time, and hardened in sinful impenitence, he had dared to wear the

mask of holiness before the tabernacle. . . . How came it that God had not struck him dead?

A corresponding pride deflects the taunts of the clamorous schoolboys:

> It was a pain to see them and a swordlike pain to see the signs of adolescence that made repellent their pitiable nakedness. Perhaps they had taken refuge in number and noise from the secret dread in their souls. But he, apart from them in silence, remembered in what dread he stood of the mystery of his own body. . . . Their banter was not new to him and now it flattered his mild proud sovereignty.

Not the least of the parallels is the surprising resemblance of landscape, first evident in the curious quality of light and foulish air:

> A faint marshlight struggled upwards from all the ordure through the bristling greygreen weeds. An evil smell, faint and foul as the light, curled upwards sluggishly out of the canisters. . . . A rictus of cruel malignity lit up greyly their old bony faces.

> . . . his flesh dreaded the cold infrahuman odour of the sea . . . A veiled sunlight lit up faintly the grey sheet of water where the river was embayed.

> He was alone . . . amid a waste of wild air and brackish waters and the seaharvest of shells and tangle of veiled grey sunlight.

The preponderance of grey throughout (a color Stephen hates in *Ulysses*) qualifies the affirmations he egotistically assumes he has reached by its recurrent suggestion of age, wastage, failure; the tangled weeds and growth, the barrenness of both landscapes, implicate the potential limitation in each plateau.

In both instances, the immediate impetus to Stephen's extreme psychic state—the horrific sermon on the one hand; the decision to reject the priesthood on the other—weighs heavily on his mind, resulting in a strong need for significant compensatory affirmation. Each time he is answered in a mind-shattering vision that draws its transforming intensity from a simultaneous surfeit with the direction of his life to that point. Stephen's hitherto fleshly life is adjured in the first instance, his purely religious life in the second. Just as his orthodox part had earlier been propelled forward with unwonted zeal and conviction, so the aesthetic yearning of his nature is concentrated and sent soaring in a new birth of meaning through his epiphany on the seawall.

Of the principals in these scenes, both the girl and the water and the goats in the field can be regarded as products of Stephen's imagination, the latter explicitly, the former implicitly, heavily endowed as she is with the promptings of his aesthetic and spiritual longing. Both are transformed into peculiarly representative objective correlatives of his consciousness, signaling the apparent end of one mental direction, while suggesting the new. Therefore each has significant dividends for the evolving artistic nature of Stephen. The bird-girl's effect hardly needs elucidation, but the excremental landscape of hell is nonetheless important as part of an accruing pattern of scatological references that serve as impetus to, and comment upon, this developing aesthetic awareness. Additionally, the principals move in a characteristically trance-like manner, circling in upon Stephen's highly suggestible imagination. Their identical, hypnotic pattern of movement is emphatically reinforced by the repetition of the same phrase three times in each passage:

> . . . creatures were moving in the field, hither and thither. . . . they moved hither and thither, trailing their long tails behind them . . . they swished in slow circles round and round in the field, winding hither and thither. . . . They moved in slow circles, circling closer and closer to enclose, to enclose, soft language issuing from their lips. . . .

> . . . she suffered his gaze . . . gently stirring the water with her foot hither and thither. The first faint noise of gently moving water broke the silence, low and faint and whispering, faint as the bells of sleep; hither and thither, hither and thither: and a faint flame trembled on her check.

When Stephen cries out, "Help!" as the goats move, and "Heavenly God!" as the girl stirs, in a sense the cries are reversed. More appropriately speaking, it is a "Heavenly God" whom the hell-vision affirms, while it is a truer "help" that the mortal beauty affords him. The prayer Stephen utters after the goatish hell is, in effect, a plea the wading girl answers. In that early fervent address to the Virgin, she is the figure *"with a creature's comeliness and lustre suited to our state,"* whose *"very face and form, dear mother, speak to us of the Eternal . . . telling of Heaven and infusing peace."* Through this invocation, the figure of Mary is introduced into the vision, offering redemption, as her counterpart on the sea-strand similarly offers Stephen new life. Yet, through the scrupulous repetition of "hither and thither," even to the number of times it occurs, Joyce has undeniably linked the girl with the goats as well. What happens is that the symbolic function of the goats divides: their importance for aesthetic development, and as indicators of natural, ineradicable drives, is taken over by the girl, while their more exaggerated representation of Stephen's still ambivalent sexual maturity is taken over by the scampering boys. The girl on the strand, that marvelous compaction of the promptings of Stephen's ways and days, is beautifully, ironically, in one supreme stroke, both Virgin and goat. She is indeed the reconciling angel of life, the apotheosis of carnal and spiritual, here for the first time in Stephen's mind in graceful balance. Yet just as significantly the balance is not presented here as a final achievement, but only a promise, since the guilty waverings in his mind are still not laid to rest, as evidenced by the other half of the goaty analogues. The affronting aspects of the goats emerge in Stephen's embarrassed, peculiarly offended, reaction to the boys' nakedness and assertive physicality. They discomfit him as reminders of his baser nature; as they clamber about the rocks,

> The mere sight of that medley of wet nakedness chilled him to the bone. Their bodies, corpsewhite or suffused with a pallid golden light or rawly tanned by the suns, gleamed with the wet of the sea. . . . and drenched with cold brine was their matted hair.

"[A] swordlike pain" runs through Stephen "to see the signs of adolescence that made repellent their pitiable nakedness." Like the goats, the boys prompt Stephen's awareness of "in what dread he stood of the mystery of his own body." Even their taunts are reminders of his animal side. While the goats presage a prayer to an orthodox Mary, the boys presage the actual vision of one Mary-like—her aesthetic double. Nor is this to lose sight of the ironic diminution going on in each case; the capering trio undercut Stephen's conceit of voices from another world as, in a curiously similar way, the goats undercut his spiritual groveling by adumbrating the senses, the desires, the tenacious life that will undermine finally his pretense to orthodoxy. The carnality inherent, by implication and detail, in the vision of the wading girl will continue to disconcert Stephen as the sexual contradictions in the passage indicate. That these contradictions go unrecognized by the young artist indicates the presence of Joyce's irony.

Finally each experience culminates in food imagery—the communion which spiritually concludes the return from hell, and the plate of sausages he anticipates with the relish of the reborn; and the loathesome, scatological scraps which follow the sea epiphany:

> He drained his third cup of watery tea to the dregs and set to chewing the crusts of fried bread that were scattered near him, staring into the dark pool of the jar. The yellow dripping had been scooped out like a boghole and the pool under it brought back to his memory the dark turfcolored water of the bath in Clongowes.

How strange that the quintessential excremental hallucination (hell) is resolved by communion, while the extreme of aesthetic revelation is followed with excrement. Surely it is not a coincidence in the early part of

Ulysses when Stephen urinates along the seawall that reminds him of the bird-girl.

In summary, the hell and heaven visions are remarkably parallel. In general this is seen in the mood of fear, disinclination for the unknown, the symbolic crossing, the presence of ominous voices and ambivalent scrutiny, the state of despair and subsequent transformation; explicitly the parallels are there in the grey illumination, the wasteland landscape, the identical phrasings, the hypnotic enclosure, a "communion." Moreover, each is a fundamental watershed, an intensely directive epiphanal moment initiating stages which will have a dominant shaping power over Stephen's emergent consciousness—the life of the Church, the life of the artist. In subsuming and culminating the "old" life, each provides impetus and reassurance towards the new dispensation, the "new" life. Thus, ascending from hell he exults: "Till that moment he had not known how beautiful and peaceful life could be. . . . How simple and beautiful was life after all! And all life lay before him." And in the second passage, with the same serene conviction, "On and on and on and on he strode, far out over the sands, singing wildly to the sea, crying to greet the advent of the life that had cried to him. . . . A wild angel had appeared to him . . . an envoy from the fair courts of life."

Twice a new life, a new purpose, has burst upon Stephen's mind with amazing distinction. Twice the polarities of secular and spiritual, aesthetic and religious, apparently claim his fervent dedication. Yet the distinctions are never clear, the boundaries only tokenly observed in a ceaseless meshing of artistic and orthodox sensibilities that seem finally to be in the service of an incontrovertible irony, causing a persuasive qualification in the assessments given the experiences by Stephen himself. Just as the hell-vision impels him in a direction that proves ultimately false, a kind of religious cul-de-sac cloth, so its linkage with the later scene in the ways described compels us to forecast inevitable revisions in the particular direction Stephen embraces through the girl. It is a glorious promise, but not finally sufficient or complete. Both visions are traps, each something more and something less than Stephen would have them—hell less patently orthodox and more rich in its way for the artistic consciousness; the bird-girl perhaps more the Virgin of the nets he so desperately longs to fly by—setting the stage for the deflected, bedevilled artist of *Ulysses*.

MARY T. REYNOLDS

Paternal Figures and Paternity Themes

At the center of Joyce's and Dante's work, narrative and style come together and are mutually reinforced by conceptions embodied in the construction of dominant images. In the three chapters that follow, three such configurations will be presented in which clear reference to the *Divine Comedy* is found in Joyce's fictions.

Joyce's recovery of Dante resembled Dante's recovery of Virgil in being a combination of devoted attachment and radical difference. Out of all the antique world Dante chose Virgil for comprehensive reincarnation in his fictional journey. He thus entered fully into the genius of ancient art. So also with Joyce who set out to clothe his own new ideas with the formal qualities of Dante's poetry, in a massive effort of what Coleridge called "shaping imagination."

Such a revisiting of the literary past became a reflection of older patterns of the soul's descent, like the journey of Orpheus into the under-world to recover Eurydice. It is a perilous return, for the past encumbers even while it enriches and invigorates. Dante was compared to Orpheus by Benvenuto da Imola, author of the earliest commentary on the *Divine Comedy*. In Benvenuto's Chrisitianizing allegory Orpheus is the man of greatest wisdom and eloquence, and his journey is an effort to recover his soul, poetically embodied as Eurydice, his beloved. Benvenuto saw in Dante a Christian singer who resisted successfully the fatal backward look that had trapped Orpheus. Revelation armed Dante with insight denied to the

From *Joyce and Dante*. Copyright © 1981 by Mary T. Reynolds. Princeton University Press.

pagans. His peril was the loss of salvation and the reality with which he has drawn the antique pantheon is vivid testimony to the depth of his attachment to the pagan world. Joyce, though not so threatened, does show a similarly powerful conflict between two opposing forces that claimed his mind and imagination. Joyce's secular imagination had its origins rooted as firmly as Dante's Catholicism.

In his reshaping of Dante's characters and patterns to fit the Ireland of his day, the clash of antagonistic principles is often apparent. Yet Joyce also presses forward from that recapture of Dante's poetry in which, like Orpheus, he recovered a lost vitality—what John B. Friedman calls the "best voice of the intellect"—and in which the imaginative intellect is reunited with passion as Orpheus with Eurydice. His imitations resisted the backward look. He put Dante's characters and scenes into modern attire and into constructions as novel as Dante's transformations of Virgil. His inventions, particularly in the distortions of some of Dante's paternal fig-ures, indicate the modernist quality of Joyce's reading of Dante. In spite of his denials, Joyce's later work reflects the basic Freudian concept of inevitable ambivalence toward father figures.

Dante uses the idea of fatherhood poetically as a central principle of order. Paternal imagery begins in the *Inferno* and continues through the three divisions of the *Commedia*. By its use Dante expresses the condition of people under civil government as brothers under the rule of their sire. Ultimately the vision extends to the family of Man, as brothers under the rule of God the Father. Within this pattern Dante explores the mystery of generation, the inheritance of intelligence and talent. The negative image also is sharply and subtly drawn; not only the benevolent ruler but the tyrant is shown. The simoniac priest and corrupt pope are an aspect of the configuration, as are also the teacher and the poet who misuse their trust.

Joyce did not need any literary prototype (and there were many from whom he could have chosen) to make the association of family with social order. It is a relation of thought that Joyce, like anyone else, could have made from his own experience and his knowledge of the human heart. But Joyce did read Dante, and did transfer to his own fiction some of Dante's patterns. It is appropriate to remark, as James Atherton has said, the tightly organized and unusually controlled character of Joyce's allusive art, which makes sheer coincidence relatively unlikely as an explanation for the pres-ence of an allusion. His indebtedness to the *Comedy* seems most marked in the consistent association of the poet with the paternal image, in one way or another. Art, for Joyce, is fatherhood. Dante similarly allows Virgil to describe art as in some sense the grandchild of God.

This [essay] will be concerned principally with *Ulysses,* in which the theme of fatherhood serves to identify Leopold Bloom as Homer's hero and Stephen Dedalus as in some sense Telemachus. This theme, in combination with the structure of a journey through a succession of perils, is undoubtedly the most powerful device that Joyce could have used to link his novel with the *Odyssey.* But Joyce's preference for a richly allusive mode of writing, demonstrated in earlier books, was now reinforced by his exploration of the literary tradition. Stanislaus Joyce told W. B. Stanford that his brother had made a comparative study of writers on Ulysses: "Virgil, Ovid, Dante, Shakespeare, Racine, Fenelon, Tennyson, Stephen Phillips, D'Annunzio, and Gerhardt Hauptmann, as well as Samuel Butler's *The Authoress of the Odyssey* and Bérard's *Les Phéniciens et l'Odysée,* and the translations by Butler and Cowper." The *Odyssey* offered a solid basis for Joyce's own intricate weaving of literary cognates. Shakespeare's Hamlet and Dante's two travelers were additional beguiling archtypes for subtle manipulation of the paternal relationship.

Paternal feelings were not, perhaps, the most marked among the characteristics of the first Ulysses. In Homer's story it is the wanderer's aging wife, rather than his son, and his attachment to the general idea of home, that account for his persistence against all odds and dangers. Leopold Bloom fulfills this pattern, but takes on other roles as well. In the terms of Joyce's novel, Bloom cannot be a father to Stephen Dedalus in the Ulyssean sense but he can play the Dantesque fatherly role of Virgil as Stephen's protector and guide. Bloom can also search out his own spiritual inheritance, in the process meeting a remote and unfamiliar ancestor, as does Dante.

In the Eumaeus chapter of *Ulysses,* Stephen Dedalus and Mr. Bloom walk together toward Eccles Street, in the manner of Dante and Virgil.

> As they walked, they at times stopped and walked again, continuing their tête à tête . . . about sirens, enemies of man's reason, mingled with a number of topics of the same category, usurpers, historical cases of the kind. . . .

Their actual association is brief, only 92 pages, or one-eighth of the book, and the Virgilian aspect is overlaid on a context that also gives Bloom the role of Dante as he journeys across Dublin. Bloom's paternal metamorphosis begins part way through the Oxen of the Sun chapter, and continues until Stephen leaves Bloom's house, part way through the Ithaca chapter.

The brevity of Bloom's actual conversation with Stephen is Virgilian, for it points to the fact that Virgil accompanies Dante only part of the way. Virgil himself makes us aware that he knows this, with the re-echoing, "So far as I can go with thee."

Only once does Dante address Virgil by name, at their first meeting in the Dark Wood: "Are you, then, Virgil?" Bloom calls Dedalus by his first name, "Stephen," only on one occasion, at the close of the Circe episode as he tries to wake the young man. Stephen stirs and groans, and murmurs the lines of Yeats:

> Who . . . drive . . . Fergus now.
> And pierce . . . wood's woven shade?

Bloom, recognizing a reference to poetry though he does not know whose, completes the reference to Dante's recognition scene with "In the shady wood." There are other echoes as well. Stephen's fragmentary "black panther vampire" continues the allusive pattern, reflecting Dante's plea for help against "the beast that turned me back." Joyce's authorial inclusion of "A barking dog in the distance" suggests Virgil's statement that the vicious beast who, vampire-like, "after feeding is hungrier than before," will be routed by the mysterious Hound who is yet to come and who will be born "between feltro and feltro."

The final leave-taking of Bloom and Stephen in the Ithaca chapter of *Ulysses* seems to be a reconstruction of a section of *Purgatorio* 30. Here, Virgil silently disappears between one thought and the next. There follows the ringing triple repetition of Virgil's name, combined with the superlative form of the affectionate adjective, "dolcissimo." "Caro," a word frequently applied to Virgil, is never used by Dante in the superlative and only at their parting is the combination, "dolce padre," developed with such poignant music.

> Ma Virgilio n'avea laseiati scemi
> di sé, Virgilio dolcissimo patre,
> Virgilio a cui, per mia salute die'mi.

Dante calls him "father" *"Patre,"* in his own language,

> But Virgil had left us bereft of him,
> Virgil, tender loving father mine,
> Virgil, to whom I gave me for my weal.
> (*Purg.* 30:49–51, trans. Bergin)

The echoing effect of the thrice-uttered name, as Edward Moore noted in an early study of Dante's use of Virgil, is a close reproduction of Virgil's poetic account of Orpheus. Dante has put Virgil's name in exactly the same position that Virgil placed Eurydice's in each line. The poignancy of that last farewell is expressed in a threefold cry:

> . . . Eurydicen vox ipsa et frigida lingua,
> a miseram Eurydicen! anima fugiente vocabat,
> Eurydicen toto referebant flumine ripae.
>
> (Georg. IV. 525–527)

> The bare voice and death-cold tongue, with fleeting breath, called Eurydice—ah, hapless Eurydice! "Eurydice!" the banks re-echoed, all adown the stream.
>
> (trans. Singleton, Purg. II.741)

The Singleton commentary points out that the reiteration of Virgil's name, five times in nine lines, is connected with the dramatic (and unique) naming of Dante by Beatrice. Unquestionably the personal identification marks the moment of Dante's individualization in a journey that is allegorically the journey of Everyman. It is a Christian and a sacramental naming, Dante's personal confession.

But the accumulated echoes of Virgil's poetic fatherhood here give another context as well to the scene of farewell or parting. As Dante is named by Beatrice, Dante names Virgil and quotes his poetry. When Dante turns to Virgil to tell him that he recognizes Beatrice, Virgil's own line is used: "Agnosco veteris vestigia flammae" (Aen. VI.23) becomes "conosco i segni de l'antica fiamma." "I know the tokens of the ancient flame." Still more remarkable is Dante's use of Virgil's line, untranslated, from the parting of Aeneas and Anchises at the close of Aeneid VI. Dante adds one word, "Oh," and brings to life the cry of Anchises in a actual scattering of flowers around and over the chariot of Beatrice: "Manibus, oh, date lilia plenis!" The naming of Dante in such an enclosing design announces the recovered voice of a Christian Orpheus. Dante's "mistranslations" of Virgil are purposeful. Before Petrarch or Spenser or Milton, Dante faced down what Harold Bloom has called "the anguish of attempting to reconcile poetry and religion." Both confrontation and outcome were closely scrutinized by Joyce.

In the Ithaca chapter of Ulysses, Joyce reverses Dante's pattern, for it is Stephen who leaves Bloom. Dante sometimes makes such reversals of Virgil, and it is clear that Joyce has deliberately constructed a parallel to the farewell scene in Purgatorio 30. Joyce was a Latinist—he had made his own study of Virgil as well as of Dante. His copy of the Divine Comedy carried notes to the Aeneid VI allusions described above, and while Joyce was at University College the National Library in Dublin had accessioned the Oxford edition of Dante to which Moore had made such a large contribution. It is possible that Joyce saw Moore's account of Dante's use of classical themes and authors, but he did not really need to go beyond his own reading. We have, in fact, a contemporary account of Joyce's comparison of Dante's poetic devices with Virgil's that indicates his absorption in *Aeneid* VI. . . .

Stephen goes out of the story as completely as Virgil leaves Dante in *Purgatorio* 30. Dante records his own feelings at Virgil's departure, but Joyce records only Bloom's sense of loss.

> Alone, what did Bloom feel? The cold of interstellar space, thousands of degrees below freezing point or the absolute zero of Fahrenheit, Centigrade or Reaumur: the incipient intimations of proximate dawn.

Where, after all, is Virgil at the moment of parting from Dante? On the naturalistic level of the narrative Virgil may be said to be in "interstellar space," above the earth (though attached to it) and below the heavens. He does not go back the way he came. He must leave the Mountaintop and return to Limbo by some magical route, perhaps the route of the Heavenly Messenger of *Inferno* 9:81, and he is certainly not alone. Joyce's antiphonal prose takes account of all this, and also records the emotional response to the leavetaking. Joyce has also reproduced something of the musical quality of Dante's terzina which repeats in the rhyme words and also internally the principal vowels in Virgil's name: Virgilio, Virgilio/ Dolcissimo, Virgilio . . . perdeo. In Joyce's two sentences the "o" is reduplicated like an echo lost in infinity: alone, Bloom, cold, below, or, zero, Reaumur.

In the course of their association, Stephen and Bloom are placed in a Dantean mode by events, topics, and descriptive comment. The narrative voice describes Bloom's Virgilian role in a phrase from the *Aeneid*: "The other, who was acting as his [Stephen's] *fidus Achates.*" Bloom knows no Latin and a misquotation from the *Aeneid* is put into indirect discourse as Stephen's thought: "haud ignarus malorum miseris succurrere disco etcetera, as the Latin poet remarks." Bloom moves around to get on Stephen's right, the narrator commenting, "a habit of his, the right side being, in classical idiom, his tender Achilles."

Their conversation has a number of echoes of the *Divine Comedy*. A showpiece is Bloom's and Stephen's encounter with the redbearded sailor, whose tale of a shipwreck in the southern hemisphere is unmistakably parallel to Dante's account of Ulysses's last voyage in *Inferno* 26. Virgil and Dante in the *Inferno* keep always (with two exceptions that point to the design) to the left; Bloom and Stephen "made tracks to the left." They stop to look at a heap of barren cobblestones, possibly a reminiscence of the shattered rockfall seen by Virgil and Dante in *Inferno* 12 and explained as a result of the earthquake at the time of Christ's crucifixion.

Joyce would have recognized Virgil's earlier trip through hell as one of Dante's inventions, designed, as Mark Musa comments, to emphasize Virgil's competence as a guide. Bloom also is a non-Christian guide, and something of Dante's syncretism may be present as well in Joyce's selection of details. The paragraph describing the stonepile is gratuitously given an atmosphere of fire and gloom, and Stephen begins to "remember that this had happened, or had been mentioned as having happened, before," these words referring to the opening phrase of the paragraph, "Discussing these and kindred topics."

In Eumaeus also Bloom and Stephen talk about the soul. In the *Divine Comedy* it is Statius who explains to Dante the generation of the soul. Stephen's stages are fundamentally the same as the stages in the development of the embryo as set forth by Statius, although described in different terms and in less detail. Mr. Bloom, in the maundering diction of the chapter, seems to agree with the argument, "though the mystical finesse involved was a bit out of his sublunary depth" as Virgil in *Purgatorio* 25 is still below the heaven of the Moon and can go no farther than the Earthly Paradise. Their conversation at this point is an echo of Stephen's earlier exposition of the origin of the soul, which Bloom heard at the maternity hospital in the Oxen of the Sun chapter. Stephen also alludes to Virgil; Dante's Virgil is out of his depth in the discussion with Statius for he can go only so far as the light of natural reason will carry him, while Statius, having been converted to Christianity in Dante's poetic fiction, has the advanage of Divine Revelation as well.

Stephen, in the maternity hospital, spoke of the generation of the embryo from semen, as Statius does in *Purgatorio* 25. Statius, whose argument comes via Scholasticism from Aristotle's *De Anima*, tells Dante that Averroës, "a wiser one than thou." ("che più savio di te," *Purg.* 25:63), had the wrong idea; Stephen also attributes a wrong idea, though a different one to Averroës.

The discourse of Statius, Virgil, and Dante, who are together through five cantos of the *Purgatorio* (Cantos 21 to 25), has been called Dante's most notable portrayal of poetic fatherhood and sonship. Joyce appropriated the substance of the discussion of Statius to support a like effect in the association of Bloom and Stephen. More generally, Joyce has created a mimetic verbal context, partly made up of visual images and partly of rhetorical and substantive connections, that recalls the association of Virgil and Dante in the *Inferno* and *Purgatorio*. He establishes a *paternal quality* in Bloom that makes him a Virgilian guide and protector for Stephen Dedalus.

The figure of Virgil as a paternal image is developed throughout the *Inferno* and the first 27 cantos of the *Purgatorio* by a combination of rhetorical cues with incident and conversational exchange. From their initial meetings in *Inferno* 1, Dante's attitude is consistently respectful; he speaks to Virgil as one does to a teacher and exemplar. Only when encouraged to do so, and even then sparingly, does Dante call Virgil "father." It is Virgil who, by speaking paternally and many times calling him "son," "figliuol," sets the verbal pattern. In Joyce's novel it is Bloom (unsought by Stephen) whose paternal actions set the pattern.

In the *Divine Comedy*, Dante's frugal applications of the word "padre" suggest its importance, particularly in the presence of a very large amount of paternal imagery spread throughout the *Divine Comedy*. The word is used 17 times in the *Inferno*, 20 in the *Purgatoro*, and 29 in the *Paradiso*. Dante applies the word to Guido Guinizelli, addressed as poetic father in *Purgatorio* 26; and he uses it in direct address to his own ancestor Cacciaguida, to Apollo, to St. Peter, and to St. Bernard.

Dante never addresses Virgil as "father" in the *Inferno*, and describes him thus only once. This is in Canto 8, where use of the word emphasizes and makes more real Dante's fear of the demons who are barring them from the gates of Dis. In Purgatory, the word suggests a growing self confidence; Dante addresses Virgil directly as "father" eight times, and he speaks more freely both to Virgil and in general. In Canto 4, as an exhausted Dante says that he can go no farther it is "O dolce padre" and elsewhere it is the simpler "Padre," or "dolce padre mio," or "dolce padre caro" (*Purg.* 13:34; 15:25; 17:82; 23:13). It is not merely the use of the noun that sets the tone of their exchanges, but the addition of the tender "dolce" or "caro." Nine of the eleven occurrences of the word have this form, and in direct address the adjective is only once omitted. Dante's use of "figlio," of course, reinforces the image. With many additional locutions, the associations of "padre" are given to Virgil and other fathers as well, to represent the paternal bond.

Virgil is primarily the teacher and exemplar. He is directly Dante's teacher, as Dante makes clear in *Inferno* 1, but on the journey he becomes something more. He shows himself to be a knowledgeable guide, a powerful protector, and above all an exemplar. These are precisely the qualities that Bloom exhibits as he successfully guides Stephen out of the Circe episode.

His Virgilian role is an indication that Bloom possesses qualities of inner strength that are developed and made apparent as the novel progresses. Joyce told Frank Budgen, "As the day wears on Bloom should overshadow them all," and referred to him as "a battery that is being recharged."

Virgil is a model of behavior for Dante, as well as a poetic figure whose *Aeneid* was, Dante says, his norm of artistic style. The term "padre," as applied to Virgil, seems to have been reserved by Dante to mark the stages in progress toward self-awareness as it develops in his association with Virgil. Dante develops a context, a constellation of atttitudes and actions, that are "paternal" because they are the habitual actions of the natural father with a small helpless child. Virgil becomes a father figure because he acts like a natural father and also, of course, because Dante accepts his guidance. Stephen's acceptance of Bloom's guidance to Number Seven Eccles Street is Joyce's parallel, understated but adequate for the production of a significant echo.

At the beginning of the poem, Dante is fearful and indecisive, the figure of a personality in acute emotional crisis. The evocation of a paternal relationship comes in a dramatic context that is marked by Dante's display of fear. This happens five times, beginning dramatically in the second canto of the poem, when Dante's "fainting courage," is restored by Virgil's vigorous admonition to be bold and free.

> Why then this hesitation and this pause?
> and whence this shameful shrinking in the heart?
> and why should courage now abandon you?
> Three ladies blessed in the court above
> have care for you, and what I have set forth
> is all a pledge and promise of your weal.
>
> Dunque: che è? perché restai?
> perché tanta viltà nel core allette?
> perché ardire e franchezza non hai,
> poscia che tai tre donne benedette
> curan di te ne la corte del cielo,
> e'l mio parlar tanto ben ti promette?
>   (*Inf:* 2:121–126, trans. Bergin)

Aeneas, father of Sylvius, and the meeting of Aeneas with Anchises, appear in Canto 2 as additional paternal images. Dante's fear returns again at the entrance to the city of Dis, when the Furies appear on the walls and Virgil has to summon the Heavenly Messenger to get the pilgrims through; when the Monster Geryon comes to transport the travelers down to the Malebolge; when they are menaced by Malacoda's savage band of demons; and when the giant Antaeus bends down to pick up the two little figures and lift them to the next level. The rare times when Virgil carries Dante, "Come suo figlio, non come compagno" (*Inf.* 23:49–51), are dramatically connected with Dante's fear.

Often, however, the tone of Virgil's remarks to Dante is hortatory or even chiding. Virgil exhorts him to courage, though not harshly, and occasionally reproves his behavior. When Dante is lingering Virgil urges him to quicken his pace; when Dante asks too many questions Virgil suggests that this is an unconscious attempt to hold off from a frightening descent into a dark chasm; when he is depressed at the sad plight of a sinner, Virgil makes him acknowledge the rightness of Divine Justice; when Dante is fearful Virgil bids him be courageous, "forte et ardito."

The appearance of the Virgilian Bloom begins at a specific moment in the chapter called "Oxen of the Sun," when Bloom first looks at Stephen with a paternal vision. Invited to sit down with the roistering medical students, Bloom sits at the head of the table and thinks of his own dead son and of Stephen, "of such gentle courage (for all accounted him of real parts)." Bloom is also sad to see Stephen wasting his talent: "for that he lived riotously with those wastrels."

As these reflections continue, there follows a passage of dreamlike visionary prose, a release from earthly connections, that invokes "parallax" to invite an alteration in the angle of vision, and "metempsychosis" to suggest the reappearance of an individual soul in a different human form, a new embodiment. This passage concludes with "currents of cold inter-stellar wind." This phrase will come again as part of the description of the Virgilian Bloom when the two have parted. It seems a rhetorial connection deliberately announcing the arrival of Virgil to guide a Dantesque Stephen.

Stephen Dedalus says, "There can be no reconciliation without a sundering." The *Divine Comedy* brings Dante on stage when he is already in the full tide of dissociation: "so bitter was it that death is scarcely more." The first appearance of the Dantesque Stephen occurs at the end of the Book's first chapter, with his remark, "Now I eat his salt bread," and it is marked again, and more strongly, by Stephen's silent thought of the opening line of the *Divine Comedy* in the Library chapter. In *Ulysses*, Stephen as an artist shows greater potential than he had in *A Portrait of the Artist*, but he is also more menaced. Joyce's construction reminds us that the physical and material dangers Dante faced in his exile were less than the peril of shattered selfhood. When Stephen is described as "battling against hope-lessness," his predicament resembles Dante's in the Dark Wood of *Inferno* 1. For this reason, Joyce puts the opening line of Dante's poem as a direct quotation, into Stephen's exposition of Shakespeare's *Hamlet*. It is also the reason, in terms of the novel, why his effort to persuade his elders to accept his ideas about *Hamlet* must fail. Bloom and Stephen have not yet met. Before the arrival of the Virgilian Bloom, Joyce puts Stephen into the role of Dante *as he might have been before the appearance of Virgil* at line 63 of *Inferno* 1.

Joyce also give Stephen a theory of artistic creation as a form of fatherhood. "To a son he speaks, the son of his soul, the prince, young Hamlet, and to the son of his body, Hamnet Shakespeare, who has died in Stratford that his namesake may live forever." The presence of the artist in Dante's poem becomes part of the design of the Virgilian Bloom. Assigned by his author to this role, Bloom will follow and watch over Stephen in the pattern of Virgil responding to the call of Beatrice. The writing of Joyce's book thus becomes by analogy an act of filiation. The leavetaking of Stephen and Bloom also holds an analogous design, for it identifies a finality as marked as that which separates Joyce's age from Dante's. The impossibility of Orpheus's keeping Eurydice is a model for Bloom's inability to keep Stephen, as it was for Dante's inevitable parting from Virgil.

Joyce's Virgilian Bloom indicates how completely he had abandoned the nineteenth-century Romantic view of Dante which, in Joyce's youth, dominated English opinion of the poem. (As we shall see, Joyce's teatment of Brunetto is further evidence of a modern rather than Romantic reading of the canto.) Virgil and Beatrice were romantic figures to such nineteenth-centuy critics as John Addington Symonds; he describes them as flawed. His account of the Beatrice of *Purgatorio* 30, indeed, employs the same vocabulary that Joyce gives to Stephen Dedalus for the oblique comment on Dante in Stephen's diary at the end of *A Portrait of the Artist*. Symonds writes: "In the *Vita Nuova* she interests as a beautiful maiden, the 'youngest of the angels.' . . . But when she begins the sermon against Dante's sins (worthy of some Lady Ida before she felt the power of love), or when she is explaining the spots on the moon and smiling in sublime contempt of Dante's mortal grossness, our interest is considerably refrigerated." This attitude, which should not be attributed to Joyce himself, seems to be echoed in Stephen's phrase, "the spiritual-heroic refrigerating apparatus invented and patented in all countries by Dante Alighieri."

Symonds also fails to see Dante's affection for Virgil as a successful poetic element. "Dante dismisses Virgil with a facile tear," he writes, indignant that the poet has left "the good, the trusty Virgil eternally condemned to Limbo." The mixture of symbolism with reality Symonds saw as a flaw in the poetry and he found "both Virgil and Beatrice frigid as persons." His book was enormously popular and may very well have been seen by Joyce.

As Virgil is Dante's paramount image of the father figure, Brunetto Latini is the image equivocally drawn, a failed or fraudulent father whom Dante knew in the world and meets in *Inferno* 15. . . . In *Ulysses*, two father-figures are associated with Brunetto Latini. One is John Eglinton, editor of a Dublin journal; the other is Almidano Artifoni, Stephen's singing teacher. They appear in different chapters and the first reference to Brunetto is by name with a quotation from his book, the *Tresor*. Addressed directly, he is brought back to life in twentieth-century Dublin. The second reference is another concealed imitation of *Inferno* 15. Both the historical and the fictional Brunetto are summoned to a new existence in Joyce's novel.

The first mention of Brunetto is in the Library chapter ("Scylla and Charybdis"), where Stephen is talking to three elders of the Dublin literary establishment. John Eglinton, the editor, has callously announced a forthcoming volume of work by the young poets of Dublin: Stephen is left out. It is in Stephen's private thoughts that John Eglinton is associated with the chief personage of *Inferno* 15, and silently Stephen also has the related thought, "Love that dare not speak its name." Stephen thinks of the editor as a basilisk, using terms borrowed from Brunetto's book, following out the touching request to Dante in *Inferno* 15 that the *Tresor*, "in which I still live," not be forgotten. Stephen recalls Brunetto's line in Italian, "E quando vede l'uomo l'atosca," actually a paraphrase that supplies him with a cruel description of the obtuse editor, "miscreant eyes glinting stern under wrinkled brows," and he says to himself, "Messer Brunetto, I thank thee for the word." Brunetto is recalled from *Inferno* 15 by quotation and by name; Stephen, like Glendower, can call spirits from the vasty deep.

Once again Joyce is paying off old scores. He obviously realized that Wells was too weak a figure to match Dante's Brunetto. The real-life model for John Eglinton was a stronger enemy figure. He is in *Ulysses* under his own status and established pseudonym, the editor of *Dana* who rejected James Joyce's very first version of A *Portrait of the Artist*—an essay with that title written in 1904.

The model for the concealed Brunetto figure in *Ulysses* was also a stronger and more believable father image. Joyce's real-life Italian teacher becomes Stephen's singing teacher, Almidano Artifoni, in the Wandering Rocks chapter. Stephen meets this man very briefly, on the street in front of Trinity College, not far from the Library. Artifoni's name and occupation make it plausible to have the conversation in Italian—not such a simple matter in a novel about Dublin. Italian is carefully used in *Ulysses*, and except for this episode Stephen speaks Italian only in connection with the *Divine Comedy*. Moreover, *only* Stephen Dedalus is allowed to quote the *Divine Comedy* in the original.

Artifoni is a fully sympathetic figure, like Brunetto, recalling the lines from Canto 15, "When in the world, hour by hour, you taught me how man makes himself eternal." This aspect of the character comes from the real-life model. Joyce's Italian teacher at University College was a young Jesuit from Bergamo, Father Charles Ghezzi, with whom Joyce undertook his first serious reading of Dante. Ghezzi is in Joyce's other novels, with the same physical characteristics but with the name or the role changed: in all cases he is a re-creation from life.

In *Ulysses*, Artifoni is a precursor of Leopold Bloom: these are the only two personages in the book who have a sympathetic understanding of Stephen's predicament. Here again Artifoni resembles Brunetto, who is a precursor of a strong and quite unequivocal father figure, Cacciaguida. As a structural element in Joyce's novel, the Artifoni episode shows Joyce's perception of the strategic placement by Dante of his two most important fathers, Brunetto and Cacciaguida, at the structural center of the *Inferno* and the *Paradiso* respectively, both making prophetic comments about Dante's future.

Observe how Joyce ties this little episode to the Eglinton episode in the preceding chapter by the use of "eyes." Stephen has told Artifoni something related to the events in the Library chapter—not what happened, but his reaction to the rejection. This sets up a contrast: the negative father image in John Eglinton, the affirmative image in Artifoni.

The scene opens with Artifoni's exclamation of sympathy: "Ma!" After a few words of conversation, he says again, "Ma, sul serio, eh?" and then the narrator says: "His heavy hand took Stephen's firmly. Human eyes. They gazed curiously an instant." Artifoni's eyes are "human" eyes, in contrast to John Eglinton's "basilisk" eyes. There is also another echo of the *Divine Comedy*. In the Library chapter the narrator's voice describes Stephen as "battling against hopelessness," at the moment when trying to get a hearing from the Dublin literary establishment, a direct quotation from the *Divine Comedy* comes into his mind. This is the only time he says one aloud, and it is the first line of the *Inferno*, "nel mezzo del cammin di nostra vita," recalling the moment of Dante's despair to match Stephen's battle against hopelessness.

The rest of the episode reproduces the naturalistic detail of *Inferno* 15. The conversation is ambiguous. Artifoni reminds Stephen that he has a fine voice, a talent that should not be sacrificed, an echo of

Brunetto's statement that Dante's talents should command good fortune in his future life despite his enemies. Brunetto's advice, "Let the beasts of Fiesole make litter of themselves," ["Faccian le bestie fiesolane strame / di lor medesme . . ." (*Inf.* 15:73–74)], is echoed in Artifoni's comment that in his youth he too felt that the world was beastly: "Eppoi mi sono convinto che il monde è una bestia" (*Inf.* 15:73–74). The Italian word "bestia" ties these passages together. The brief episode ends exactly as *Inferno* 15 ends, and also the 18th chapter of *Stephen Hero*: Artifoni is running, "In vain he trotted, signalling [to a tram] in vain," as Brunetto runs off in *Inferno* 15, and as Wells runs up the driveway of the seminary. Artifoni is the last person seen in the chapter, as a ironic and mockingly obscene gesture to the Lord Lieutenant's parade: "the salute of Almidano Artifoni's sturdy trousers swallowed by a closing door."

Joyce initially wanted to associate Dante's *Inferno* 15 with an attack on the worldly materialism of the Irish clergy, but by the time he came to write *Ulysses*, his perception of the canto's contrasts led him toward a more detached view and a different compositional decision. He apparently concluded that his anticlerical polemic would be stronger if it were not directly given the associations of *Inferno* 15. He kept a strong and attractive clerical personality as his target, however, and kept the association with the *Divine Comedy* by showing this false spiritual father in a telling reference to another canto, *Inferno* 10. The chosen target is Father Conmee, whose story has pride of place as the opening episode of the Wandering Rocks chapter.

Joyce's account of the simoniac Irish clergy in the eighteenth chapter of *Stephen Hero* represents them as false to their spiritual trusteeship. It is an indictment of the failure of the seminaries, preparing young men for the priesthood, to inculcate spiritual values. Wells, the young man at the center of the chapter, is a careerist, a materialist, a pragmatist; Joyce is suggesting that young Irishmen were encouraged to seek the priesthood, for the status and power it offered. There is a good deal of historical reality behind this. For two hundred years and more, under penal laws, the seminary was indeed the only professional education available to Irish boys. William Carleton's stories of the hedge schools, and especially his story of Denis O'Shaughnessy going to Maynooth Seminary, are a vivid portrayal of the long road the Irish Catholic population had to travel to reach the level of an established middle class.

By Joyce's day, this long association of the clergy with the movement upward from helotism had created a solid institutional basis for the Irish Church—large and devoted parish congregations, a disciplined hierarchy, schools, seminaries, and the Catholic branches of the Royal University, including University College in Dublin (Joyce's College), which was taken over by the Jesuits in 1883. The Jesuits of Joyce's day saw their functions, at least in part as the education and social training of a Catholic elite that could be prepared to exercise power on equal terms with the Protestant Anglo-Irish ruling caste, and to take the reins when Irish independence was achieved.

Although this posture had rational basis, with Joyce it was also a temperamental matter. Joyce's attitude is reminiscent, perhaps, of Dante's absolute exclusion from the *Divine Comedy* of any approval, any suggestion that positive values might result from the rise in Florence of the bourgeoisie—the merchants and traders who were making the city prosperous and powerful, but whom Dante despised. Joyce, to the extent that specific political ideas can be found in his writings, can fairly be described as opposing altogether the enlargemet of temporal power in the Church. In this he resembles Dante. In a notebook Joyce kept in 1905, in Pola, while he was preparing to write the book that became *A Portrait*, his jottings included the isolated phrases, "Spiritual and temporal power," "Priests and police in Ireland." Both Dante and Joyce no doubt took a one-sided view of the politics of their time and their city. This strengthened the poetry, whatever one may think of the accuracy of their estimate of historical events. Joyce's charge that the Irish Church was more interested in worldly than in spiritual matters, and even that the clergy were prepared to use their spiritual authority for the temporal goals of power, was an adequate parallel to Dante's indictment of the clerics of his day, an indictment that extended all the way up to the Papacy.

Joyce, by the time he came to write *Ulysses*, was ready for a more subtle portrait of the clerical figure as fraudulent spiritual father. This is the role he assigned to Father Conmee in Wandering Rocks. In the choice of this real life model—a cultivated, gifted, and amiable man—Joyce also took account of the rising currents of liberal humanism, knowing as he did that the Church's strength has always been in its adaptability to change, but he attacked the pragmatic humanism that showed itself willing to exchange spiritual values for political power and social snobbery.

Between the "first draft" and the final version of *A Portrait*, and between his early books and *Ulysses*, Joyce's imitation of Dante became not only more subtle in its literary aspects but more pointed in social criticism and more humane in viewpoint. As his transformations of the *Divine Comedy* submerged into his fiction, Joyce continued to make open references to Dante, but all traces of overt didacticism vanished. By the time Joyce wrote *Ulysses*, his borrowings, although more numerous, were also better concealed. In particular, Joyce redrew and elaborated his portrait of the fraudulent spiritual father and pulled together all the threads of his indictment of the Irish Church.

In the Wandering Rocks chapter of *Ulysses* Joyce gives a full portrayal of false father as a wordly and influential priest, a construction allusively though briefly connected with the *Divine Comedy*. The priest is Father Conmee. The Dantesque allusion is not found in "Wandering Rocks" but much later in the book, in the Circe episode, and it is a precise visual recall of *Inferno* 10:32–33, presented as a hallucination of Stephen's.

Father Conmee and Father Dolan rise from coffin-like structures as the two fathers of *Inferno* 10, Farinata and Cavalcante, rise up from the fiery tombs of the Epicureans. Father Dolan is a comic figure: "Twice loudly a pandybat cracks, the coffin of the pianola flies open, the bald little round jack-in-the-box head of Father Dolan springs up." Father Conmee, on the other hand, "Mild, rectorial, reproving . . . rises from the pianola coffin," very much as the shade of Farinata rises up and with a similar dignity. Father Dolan's plight has nothing to do with Cavalcante but comes from Joyce's opposition to corporal punishment for children. For the fictional Father Conmee there are much more complicated reasons behind the use of Dante's image, for Joyce took Conmee out of his teaching role to make him a figure of unfaithful stewardship.

Dante's two fathers are Cavalcante, father of Dante's friend Guido, and Farinata, the Ghibelline Captain whose forces expelled Dante's ancestors from Florence. Farinata was later condemned as a heretic (the Epicurean heresy), and very likely unjustly condemned by his political enemies. Dante nevertheless selects that official condemnation, out of all the matter of Farinata's earthly life, as the basis for putting him in hell. He is also the father-in-law of Dante's best friend, the poet Guido, whose own father is in the adjoining tomb. The Cavalcanti family were Guelphs: the marriage of Farinata's daughter was an event in the brief policy of armistice between the warring factions when matrimonial alliances were encouraged in an attempt to bring peace to Florence.

Hearing Dante's voice, Cavalcante rises to his knees in the fiery tomb that imprisons him; "piangendo" weeping he asks why his son is not with Dante, as he was in the upper world. Dante's reply uses the past tense: in tones of heightened anguish, Cavalcante rises "subito" instantly erect, and cries, "What are you saying? lives he no longer?" ("non viv' elli ancora?") "do his eyes no longer see the sweet light?" ("non fiere li occhi suoi lo dolce lume?") (*Inf.* 10:68–69). Farinata, however, stands erect and challenges Dante so coldly that his pride "seems to hold even hell in disdain."

The encounter with these two fathers forms a continuous and discrete episode, which was given a classic analysis by Auerbach. Cavalcante interrupts Dante's reply to Farinata; when Cavalcante falls back into his tomb, Farinata continues his sentence without taking notice of the interruption; and when Farinata has finished, Dante asks him to tell Cavalcante that his son Guido is indeed still alive (thus still capable of being saved).

Joyce's attention to the artistry of the little drama is suggested by an entry in his Triestse Notebook. Under the heading, "cavalcanti (Guido)," Joyce wrote, "His father . . . asks Dante where he is (Inf. cant. X) Dante hesitates before he replies." The rest of the entry suggests that Joyce followed up his reading with a little investigation into the life of Guido, for there follows a brief note on Boccaccio's story. Joyce allows Stephen to recall these details in the Proteus chapter of Ulysses, as a silent comparison between Guido's retort to the baiting of his friends, and Stephen's reactions earlier that morning under the attack of the "usurpers" Mulligan and Haines. "The couriers who mocked Guido in Or san Michele were in their own house," Stephen thinks. Mulligan, as one of a brood of mockers, a gay betrayer of Irish Catholicism, is a figure of the Establishment, the Irish ruling class, while Haines is a representative—harmless, to be sure—of the English oppressors; both are interested in Stephen for what they can get out of him. "In their own house" is an intimation of the Martello Tower, for which Stephen has paid the rent, but it carries a larger sense of Catholic Ireland as Stephen's house. The young poet now thinks of himself in Dante's words, "Now I eat his salt bread," as an exile. The reference to Guido in Proteus thus connects Stephen Dedalus indirectly with Dante's Inferno 10, and in "Circe" the connection is made directly with Inferno 10 and with Father Conmee. What warrant has Joyce for this apparent placement of Father Conmee in hell?

In "Wandering Rocks," Father Conmee's itinerary across Dublin is matched by the itinerary of the Viceregal cavalcade. Though their paths seem to cross, because of the complexities of the text, in fact they do not; but each is "saluted" (a term used 17 times) by a carefully selected group of Dubliners, who in theory are showing respectful homage and receiving in return a courteous recognition in feudal fashion. With these reminders of old ceremonials, Joyce comments ironically on the contemporary condition of the institutions of secular and ecclesiastical power in Dublin.

But the opening section of the chapter has another dimension that can only be called a spiritural structure, for the progress of Father Conmee and the people he meets form a running commentary on his personal exercise of the priestly office. The little narrative takes its shape from the Divine Office, to seven canonical "Hours" that every priest is required to recite every day, some lines from which are quoted as the section ends. In doing this, Joyce follows Dante's use of the Office of Complin in another episode, in which the negative image of the father surrogate is shown. In the beautiful valley of *Purgatorio* 8, Virgil and Dante hear the hymn, *Te lucis ante,* which is invariably sung at Complin, the Office recited at sunset. The souls of *Purgatorio* 8, the negligent rulers (who were thus not truly fathers to the people they ruled), are still able to expiate their sins. But Father Conmee will be shown in his last appearance in the book in one of the striking images of the *Inferno,* symbolically condemned.

The Dantesque elements of Joyce's version begin with the narrative aspect, for the story is told by an impersonal voice and by Father Conmee himself through his private thoughts. Like so many of Dante's fictions, it deals with matters the truth of which can be known only to the individual and his Creator. The choice of a strong individual with appealing personal qualities to represent a spiritual father false to his trust goes to the heart of Dante's construction in *Inferno* 15. A lesser figure than Conmee would not be a believable symbol of the authority of the Irish Church. The moral dimensions of Joyce's episode even go some way beyond Dante's *Inferno* 15; for Brunetto's sin no evidence is given, but Joyce's Conmee stands condemned by his own standards and in his own thoughts.

Father Conmee is walking through the northern part of Dublin: "He smiled and nodded and smiled and walked." Motion in the *Commedia* in general is an indication of moral state; the condition of the damned is an absence of motion, which becomes more marked as the pilgrim goes deeper into the realm of evil. Twice, however, the pattern of punishment is one of unremittent motion: in *Inferno* 5, the souls are ceaselessly whirled on the whirlwind of unchecked carnal desire; in *Inferno* 15, the canto of the sodomites, the souls must run unceasingly under a rain of fire. These are the two cantos in which Dante has placed his most ambiguous portraits, Francesca and Brunetto. In Father Conmee's episode the reiterated emphasis on movement may reflect Joyce's observation of Dante's pattern in *Inferno* 15.

Near the end of his walk Father Conmee begins to read his breviary; it is late in the day, and he is reading the "Little Hours," which includes the Psalm "Beati immaculati." The act of walking becomes a reflection of the Divine Office as, in the Psalm, it is a symbol of man's passage through life. The theme of "Beati immaculati" is the path, the way, the Latin "via":

"Blessed are the undefiled in the way, who walk in the law of the Lord."
("Beati immaculati in via qui ambulant in lege Domini.") As Father Conmee proceeds along his walk, it becomes clear that he is not one of those
who "walk in the way of the Lord." It is the breviary that convicts him.

In Joyce's time every religious, whether conventual or one of the
secular clergy, recited the Divine Office every day, from his breviary.
"Father Conmee took his rededged breviary out. An ivory bookmark told
him the page." The exercise amounts to a daily dramatic recital (if the
Office is not chanted communally, it is supposed to be read half-aloud)
that keeps before the mind of the religious the best poetry in the Catholic
liturgy as well as the Church's continuity of tradition in moral theology.
It is a compendium of psalms (so arranged that in the course of a week all
the psalms are recited), hymns, canticles, hagiographic fragments, biblical
texts, homilies and prayers, much of which reflects the historical development of the Catholic liturgy. Reading the breviary is not unlike a continuous re-reading of Dante's poetry, and indeed this comparison has often
been made. But it was emphatically not a literary exercise. Recitation of
the Divine Office was obligatory on all ministers of the Church in major
Orders. Every candidate for the priesthood, particularly in the Irish seminaries, received instruction in the history and moral significance of the
breviary.

Father Conmee would be reminded of his priestly charge every day
of his life, as he read the first psalm with which the daily Office invariably
opens: "Beatus vir qui non abiit in consilio impiorum; et in via peccatorum
non stetit; et in cathedra pestilentiae non sedit." "Blessed is the man that
walketh not in the counsel of the ungodly, nor standeth in the way of
sinners, nor sitteth in the seat of the scornful." The triple negative is a
special charge on the man called to the sacred office of the priesthood for
at his ordination this man receives the unique power to dispense the treasure
of Divine grace.

The meaning of this admonition is avoidance of the habits of worldliness, and the triple negative is followed by a triple exhortation to seek
the higher spiritual aspirations. Thus the devout ecclesiastic in Holy Orders
is required to remind himself daily that he must not busy himself with purely
temporal concerns, secular friendships and diversions; that he must not
consort with those who lack piety; that he must not by example make a
mockery of virtue that will scandalize the weak and corrupt the young.

Father Conmee's progress across Dublin, his encounters and salutations, have been carefully selected and placed to show him in violation
of this crucial admonition. He is a figure of the career priest, shown at a

moment when his efforts have brought him power in the political affairs of city and state, recognition and influence in his Order, and comfort amounting to luxury in his personal life. The position he holds is strategic; he is Father Superior ("The Superior, the Very Reverend John Conmee, S.J.") of the presbytery (that is, the residence of a group of priests), of the Jesuit house in upper Gardiner Street, attached to the parish church of St. Francis Xavier. His power is announced by his introduction under this formal title.

On the 16th of June he is going to Artane, a region in north-east Dublin, where there is an industrial school for boys; his objective is an interview seeking a place in the school for young Patrick Aloysius Dignam, whose father's funeral took place that morning. Thus Father Conmee is emphatically seen as a father figure, assisting an orphan in the traditional role of his church as father of the fatherless. But the priest's private thoughts reveal more complex motivation, foremost in which as a crucial element is the extension of his personal political influence. Martin Cunningham has asked Conmee to secure this place for the Dignam boy, as a personal favor; the good Jesuit will "oblige him" if he can. "Good practical catholic: useful at mission time." Both lay Catholics and clergy are a part of his apparatus of power. Father Conmee's concern for "mission time," for example, indicates his grasp of a complex phenomenon: the way the clergy secure the church's secular power (and incidentally the individual cleric's route to promotion in the hierarchy) by building up their congregations for practical as well as for spiritual reasons. Conmee has made an alliance, which is in effect political, with Martin Cunningham, who is a minor functionary at "The Castle," the seat of British Government. Martin Cunningham is a good "practical" Catholic who will see that his friends turn up to swell the congregation at the three-day "mission" service at which special collections are taken up for the causes sponsored by the bishops and the Pope. Conmee, like any other sensible parish priest, will seek out the most popular preacher he can find for the mission. The one he chooses, Father Bernard Vaughan, is described in "Wandering Rocks" as a mission preacher of "very great success." Father Conmee dislikes his colleague's cockney voice and his vulgarising of the New Testament, but the crowds love Vaughan's preaching.

The larger political objective, establishment of a Catholic ruling elite in Ireland, is quietly indicated by the author's demonstration that Father Conmee meets and converses on equal social terms with the wife of David Sheehy M.P., whose sons are at Belvedere, the Jesuit school in Dublin. The two talk about Conmee's vacation plans, and he is cordially invited to call on the Sheehys.

Some of this is harmless vanity; his action that afternoon is clearly charitable; where is the harm, the evil? Here is found Joyce's imitation of Dante's *Inferno*. In Francesca, Farinata, Ulysses, Brunetto and lesser figures, Dante shows that evil is a complicated matter, not easily recognized, often attractive, and even mingled with good. But Dante's characters in the *Inferno* do not stand each of them alone; they form a pattern. Similarly Father Conmee has a place in a larger pattern, most carefully worked out in *Ulysses* but present in all Joyce's works, which condemns as simoniacal the Irish clerics' use of the instruments of Divine Grace for worldly ends—whether their own personal ends, or some larger institutional purpose. This was Dante's viewpoint also, and it received a far more powerful expression by attachment in a fictional context to a real historical figure. Joyce reduces the Dantean pattern in *Ulysses* to a least common denominator dealing with ward politicians rather than with the thrones and empires of Dante's day.

The cadences of Father Conmee's episode are the rhythms and intonations of the psalter. Sentences are short, and are joined in units of two or three so that an antiphonal effect is produced.

> Near Aldborough house Father Conmee thought of that spendthrift nobelman. And now it was an office or something.

> Father Conmee smelled incense on his right hand as he walked. Saint Joseph's Church, Portland row. For aged and virtuous females. Father Conmee raised his hat to the Blessed Sacrament. Virtuous: but occasionally they were also bad-tempered.

Two quotations from Psalm 118 are made to form part of Conmee's reading. One is verse 160, the other verse 161. Psalm 118 is very long, and thus is divided among the four parts of the "Little Hours," prime, terce, sext and none. It moves in sections of five or six verses, each with a letter of the Hebrew alphabet; verse 160 is the last verse of "Res," and verse 161 is the first verse of "Sin." Joyce puns on this letter, making the last event on Father Conmee's walk the sight of a "flushed young man" and a young woman emerging from a hedge. Father Conmee "blessed both gravely," making the description correspond to verse 158 of the Psalm: "I beheld the transgressors and was grieved; because they kept not thy word." ("Vide praevaericantes, et tabescebam; quia eloquia tua non custodierunt.") The last verse of the psalm is also echoed: "I have gone astay like a lost sheep" in the sight of the "muttoning clouds over Rathcoffey." "The sky showed him a flock of small white clouds going slowly down the wind. *Moutonner*, the French said, a homely and just word."

The combination of soliloquy with antiphonal cadences gives this episode a style quite different from the other episodes in "Wandering Rocks." Joyce laid out a walk for Father Conmee that would make a dramatic scene out of the admonitions of Psalm 118, by the author's selection of Dublin citizens to be met and greeted by Conmee. This urbane and worldly Jesuit is the bad shepherd of *Purgatorio* 16, who knows and professes the letter of the law of God—Conmee reading his breviary—but who disregards the welfare of his flock, his spiritual charges. Joyce has made his construction an extended image of Dante's faithless shepherd; later, he echoes Dante's enigmatic phrase in *Finnegans Wake*, "Who wants to cheat the choker's got to learn to chew the cud."

> Laws there are, but who puts his hand to them? None, because the shepherd that leads may chew the cud but has not the hoofs divided. Wherefore the people, who see their guide snatch only at that good whereof they are greedy, feed upon that, and seek no further.

> Le leggi son, ma chi pon mano ad esse?
> Nullo, però che 'l pastor che procede,
> rugumar può, ma non ha l'unghie fesse;
> per che la gente, che sua guida vede
> pur a quel ben fedire ond' ella è ghiotta,
> di quel si pasce, e più oltre non chiede.
> (*Purg.* 16:97–102, trans. Singleton)

Father Conmee traffics with the mammon of iniquity, which is the sense of the prohibition in Psalm 1, "Beatus Vir," the psalm which opens the musical chant of the Divine Office. The man who accepts the call to the sacred office of priesthood is thereby canonized by the Holy Ghost. Such a man must not become the "secular," the man "qui abiit in consilio impiorum," one of those who run about consorting with worldlings: "that class of restless clerics who are rarely at home, and yet whose wanderings abroad are not after the lost or straying sheep of the flock, but after secular diversions and friendships; for such is the meaning of *impiorum.*"

Joyce's text combines the actions of Psalm 1 with the words of Psalm 118, the first line of which is "Beati immaculati in via: qui ambulant in lege Domini." Blessed are the undefiled in the Way: who walk in the law of the Lord." The words *via* and *ambulant* are a concealed source of the motif that makes Conmee the focus of the Wandering Rocks chapter. As he walks across the city, he is recognizably the spiritual power of Dublin.

But in Joyce's ironic application of *via* and *ambulant*, Father Conmee encounters Dubliners whose occupation is significantly connected with the problem of poverty, and he shows only a bland reaction.

motif that makes Conmee the focus of the Wandering Rocks chapter. As he walks across the city, he is recognizably the spiritual power of Dublin.

But in Joyce's ironic application of *via* and *ambulant,* Father Conmee encounters Dubliners whose occupation is significantly connected with the problem of poverty, and he shows only a bland reaction.

One is the pawnbroker, Mrs. M'Guinness, who bows to him from across the street. Father Conmee's mind makes an adjustment of focus, reflecting the contrast, as he sees it, between her low occupation and her aristocratic appearance. He meets three schoolboys from Belvedere, the sons of a pawnbroker, a bookmaker, and a raffish young journalist. Though these boys may have been at Belvedere on scholarships, as Joyce himself was, it is far more likely that two of them, at least, are there because their fathers have become rich by squeezing pennies from those who have little money to spare. The third boy, as Ellmann discovered, is placed here anachronistically, with a name that attached him to Ignatius Gallaher, Joyce's portrait of the successful but morally callous journalist. Combined with the praise of Mrs. M'Guinness's "queenly mien," Joyce's construction is meant to suggest the Jesuits' extreme practicality where money and power are concerned.

The role of the church in relation to the unfortunate is presented through the thoughts of this humane Jesuit. The Irish peasant's lot in life becomes the subject of a paragraph that carries the antiphonal cadence and also some of the sense of verse 75: "I know O Lord that thy judgments are right and that thou in faithfulness hast afflicted me." Conmee goes along Charleville Mall and sees a turf-barge moored under the trees. "It was idyllic: and Father Conmee reflected on the providence of the Creator who had made turf to be in bogs where men might dig it out and bring it to town and hamlet to make fires in the houses of poor people."

He meets a beggar who asks for alms, a one-legged sailor. Father Conmee has with him only a silver crown—five shillings, about a dollar in 1904. But he intends to walk, not ride, to Artane; why does he not give this relatively small amount to the beggar? We learn some paragraphs later in the chapter that five shillings is the amount that Leopold Bloom contributes to the fund for the Dignam children. Almsgiving by Christian and Jew is contrasted, and Conmee's act of charity toward the Dignam boy is put into a truer perspective. The priest does not ignore the beggar: "he blessed him in the sun." Pauperism, another traditional concern of his church, is in his mind, "but not for long." The pauperized Dignam family, the one-legged beggar, and the other evidences of Catholic poverty in Dublin are less important to Father Conmee than the "mission." It is more bridge to the Howth road stop. The brief ride costs only one penny, we learn as Conmee puts the change back into his purse, but "He disliked to traverse on foot the dingy way past Mud Island." Here is Joyce's ironic translation of the first line of Psalm 118, "Beati immaculati in via." Father Conmee himself lives free from cares and worry: this is learned from his immaculate mode of dress, his silk hat, "plump kid gloves," and smooth watch in an interior pocket. His vow of poverty is not burdensome. For his vacation, he tells Mrs. Sheehy, "he would go to Buxton probably for the waters." These indications of Conmee's refined, sensuous enjoyment of life may be a deliberate dramatization of the ordinary dictionary meaning of "epicurean," the heresy that Dante chose to associate with the two fathers of *Inferno* 10.

In his self-image Father Conmee is an aristocrat and he identifies with aristocratic society. His education is combined with an easy worldliness of manner and intellect; Lady Maxwell comes to see him at the presbytery. He has written a little book, *Old Times in the Barony*, about Jesuit houses that historically were the homes of noble families. In fantasy he sees himself in "Gay Malahide," home of Lord Talbot, as Don John Conmee (the Spanish honorific presumably because of the Spanish origin of the Jesuits), "humane and honoured there. He bore in mind secrets confessed and he smiled at smiling noble faces in a beeswaxed drawingroom, ceiled with full fruit clusters. And the hands of a bride and of a bridegroom, noble to noble, were impalmed by Don John Conmee." He looks like a romantic, sentimentally attached to the medieval past, but this is only the secret of his charm. Joyce has made him a very practical figure, a portrait that goes a long way toward explaining the Jesuits' success in creating a Catholic Irish elite to displace the Protestant monopoly of power.

There is hostility in the Conmee portrait, genuine and deep, but it is not hostility toward the real-life Jesuit for whom Joyce had a great and lasting affection. Joyce's anger is institutional and judgmental, and his decision for the Conmee portrait was a compliment, a guarantee of immortality. He appropriated a personality that would command attention to carry one of his most cherished arguments, and placed the resulting portrait at the very center of his novel. Dante had similarly answered the demands of his poem when he put into hell his beloved old teacher Brunetto, the great savior of Florence, Farinata, and others drawn from life.

If Joyce had really believed there was a hell, he would probably never have written the Conmee episode as he did. But he did believe in the existence of evil, for the depiction of which the old notion of hell is still useful, as it was in Dante's time. Like Dante (and practically every other Christian writer), Joyce insists that man's will is free, that it can be exercised for good or evil, and that the state of the world's affairs will vary with the quality of moral leadership in the world at one time or another. His themes, a social criticism, bear out his statement that, "with me, the thought is always simple." But he also said that his "means" were "quad-rivial." Dante's poet-traveler was able to have his poetic mission ratified at the highest levels of Paradise, but only after his sense of purpose had been refined and strengthened. Poetic fatherhood was Dante's metaphor. Joyce constructed his own literary allegory, with analogous theme and purpose but in a different intellectual climate. This was the writer who, in arguing for the publication of a book (*Dubliners*)that opens with Dante's words for the gate of hell, had said, "I want to write a chapter of the moral history of my country."

When Dante wrote of Virgil, to paraphrase Dorothy Sayers, he taught Joyce how to write of Bloom and Father Conmee. The reader who has followed me this far will see that we are dealing with a fictional design in which a markedly specific literal base—with detail often taken directly from real life, often involving local and private reference—is given multiple symbolic extension. In Joyce's treatment of fatherhood and specifically in his Virgilian Bloom, conceptual imagery is extended into literary allegory by thematic development. The true subject is the fostering of the intellec-tual imagination in the production of art at a particular time and place—Ireland at the turn of the century. Such an allegorical narrative, describing his subject under the guise of another which is suggestively similar, is Joyce's characteristic mode and is most plainly discernible in A *Portrait of the Artist* and *Ulysses*. In the case of the latter work, Joyce actually invited a Dantean reading—fourfold or even more—by the *schema* (his word) that he con-structed and gave to a few friends: Stuart Gilbert, Sylvia Beach, Carlo Linati. The *Schema* was Joyce's equivalent of Dante's *Letter to Can Grande*, a document in which Joyce indicated the complicated patterning of his work, specified some but not all of its connections and extensions, and invited multiple interpretations of the characters and incidents in the book. Joyce's construction of such a *schema* is evidence of a formal principle which attaches his work to Dante's.

It is the business of this study, in this chapter and the two that follow, to discover both the traces and the dimensions of that attachment. Obviously this is not simply a matter of selecting parallel passages for explication, although a degree of parallelism is necessarily involved. As the preceding sections of this chapter have shown, theme, style, and form are intermingled; each contributes some essential part of a design which is explication, although a degree of parallelism is necessarily involved. As the preceding sections of this chapter have shown, theme, style, and form are intermingled; each contributes some essential part of a design which is intricately woven into the fabric of the book as a whole. We are looking beyond thematic equivalence to identify those of the author's compositional decisions that transform theme into structure. Joyce's portrait of Father Conmee is a subtle treatment of a Dantean theme, simony. But some of the force of his portrayal comes also from our observed reminiscence of a specific element of structure. Dante censures the simoniac Pope Boniface VIII, his arch-enemy, in widely separated passages of the *Divine Comedy*, first at *Inferno* 19:52–57 and then definitively at *Paradiso* 30:146–48. Each time the condemnation is made in a passage of the poem that is notable for its quality of subtle indirection. Joyce puts more than three hundred pages between Conmee in the Wandering Rocks chapter and Conmee as he emerges from a Dantesque fiery coffin in the Circe episode. It is the author, Joyce, who draws the portrait of Conmee walking and reading; thus we are made aware of the theme, and we sense intuitively its personal importance to Joyce. It is the apprentice poet, Stephen Dedalus, whose hallucination completes the Dantean pattern. From a general insight that Dante is a presence behind Joyce's writing, we move to a reading of Joyce's work which, in going behind the literal sense of the text, becomes a Dantean reading—"polysemous," as Dante called the method in his *Letter to Can Grande*. In Joyce's complex treatment of fatherhood, the connection of his work with Dante's becomes relatively overt. As Northrop Frye has said, themes as well as plots "have their elements of discovery."

KAREN LAWRENCE

"Eumaeus": The Way of All Language

By the time he reaches "Eumaeus," the reader is prepared for outrageous experiments in *Ulysses;* after "Cyclops," "Oxen of the Sun," and "Circe," he no longer expects the relative tameness of the initial style. The first sentence of the chapter informs him of the book's return to narrative after the expressionistic drama of "Circe." In this first sentence, we recognize the sound of other chapter openings in *Ulysses,* such as "Stately, plump Buck Mulligan came from the stairhead" and "By lorries along Sir John Rogerson's Quay Mr Bloom walked soberly," where the physical action is described in faintly pompous, inaugural tones. But in "Eumaeus," precision is exaggerated into punctiliousness, the literate diction cedes to faded elegance and cliché.

> Preparatory to anything else Mr Bloom brushed off the greater bulk of the shavings and handed Stephen the hat and ashplant and bucked him up generally in orthodox Samaritan fashion, which he very badly needed.

Circumspect, in a succession of phrases, the sentence seeks to modify and amplify its subject. Beginning portentously with the phrase "preparatory to anything else," it betrays its pretensions with slang expressions ("buck him up"). Redundant, idiomatic, it finally collapses into anticlimax. Although the reader no longer expects to find the initial style, he might wonder why this sentence would be produced by a man who could write, "Two shafts of soft daylight fell across the flagged floor from the high barbicans: and at

---

From *The Odyssey of Style in "Ulysses."* Copyright © 1981 by Karen Lawrence. Princeton University Press.

the meeting of their rays a cloud of coalsmoke and fumes of fried grease floated, turning."

As the first sentence indicates, the language of "Eumaeus" is pretentious, verbose, and clichéd. It displays a love of elegant variation, convoluted phrases, and Latinate diction: "Possibly perceiving an expression of dubiosity on their faces, the globetrotter went on adhering to his adventures." Where one word will do, it insists on a phrase ("his expression of features"). But its most salient characteristic is its commonplaces, idioms, proverbs, and clichés.

> . . . on his expressed desire for some beverage to drink Mr Bloom, in view of the hour it was and there being no pumps of Vartry water available for their ablutions, let alone drinking purposes, hit upon an expedient by suggesting, off the reel, the propriety of the cabman's shelter, as it was called, hardly a stonesthrow away near Butt Bridge, where they might hit upon some drinkables in the shape of a milk and soda or a mineral.

As can be seen from the previous examples, the style has pretensions to elegance. Sometimes the writing tries to be coy and cute: "The keeper of the shelter in the middle of this *tête-à-tête* put a boiling swimming cup of a choice concoction labelled coffee on the table and a rather antediluvian specimen of a bun, or so it seemed." It specializes, however, in little verbal twists on clichés ("gone the way of all buttons," "on the tapis," "ventilated the matter thoroughly"), or in coinages ("Sherlockholmsing it") and forced puns ("Telegraphic, Tell a graphic lie") of a type Lenehan would offer in "Aeolus." The style, in fact, is not the "namby-pamby" style of a Gerty MacDowell but a style that exaggerates the qualities of the more educated, garrulous talk of the storytellers, would-be rhetoricians, and resident Dublin wits at their worst moments: "So, as neither of them were particularly pressed for time, as it happened, and the temperature refreshing since it cleared up after the recent visitation of Jupiter Pluvius, they dandered along past by where the empty vehicle was waiting without a fare or a jarvey." The elaborate use of classical allusion to describe rain ("the visit of Jupiter Pluvius"), plus the word "dandered," could originate with a Lenehan but not with a Gerty MacDowell. "Looking back now in a retrospective kind of arrangement," the narrator says and this recalls the pretentious critical vocabulary of Tom Kernan, as mocked by Mr Power: "—Trenchant, Mr Power said laughing. He's [Tom Kernan's] dead nuts on that. And the retrospective arrangement." Stanislaus once described the language of "Eumaeus" as "flabby Dublin journalese, with its weak effort to be witty," and there is something in "Eumaeus" of the headings (both the pomposity of the late Victorian headings and the smart slang of the "modern" headings) and of the conversation in "Aeolus." The common denominator of all these styles, including Gerty MacDowell's, is their pretense to some kind of fine writing.

The elegance is faded and the language misfires—all deliberately, of course, on Joyce's part. For in "Eumaeus," Joyce chooses the "wrong" word as scrupulously as he chooses the right one in the early chapters. Comedy arises from the narrator's misuse of language—"originality" enters through the back door of error. In phrases like "nipped in the bud of premature decay" and "redolent with rotten corn," we see the narrator's reach exceed his grasp. Language in the chapter glances off its object. A succession of phrases is offered, none of which captures meaning fully. In the following example, we see the narrator trying and failing to duplicate subtle novelistic description: "He displayed half solicitude, half curiousity, augmented by friendliness"—the mathematics of the situation (half and half, plus some more) tells us that too many phrases are needed. As in the language of "Cyclops" and "Nausicaa," sentences that begin with fanfare cannot maintain their high tone. In "Eumaeus," however, it is as if the sentences forget where they begin. (See the sentence beginning with the word "Accordingly" and ending with the words "Dan Bergin's" on page 613.) There is something vaguely senescent about this writing, from the wandering sentences to the half-remembered idioms. It is as if all the allusions, clichés, and idioms of a lifetime floated somewhere in the memory and were summoned forth for the sake of the story. The movement of the narrative mind is like the stream-of-consciousness of the early chapters slowed down, its associations grown fuzzy. It is as if the silent monologue of the early chapters had become a rambling and tedious after-dinner speech. The narrative is indeed the "narrative old" that Joyce described to Gilbert.

But the "memory" invoked in the chapter is best regarded not as a personal but a collective one, specifically, a linguistic memory. The cumulative effect of all these clichés is to make "Eumaeus" into a kind of encyclopedia of received phrases. If the language of "Eumaeus" is enervated, it is not merely to reflect the fatigue of the characters or a narrator but to reveal that language is tired and "old," used and reused so many times that it runs in grooves. The language of "Eumaeus" is the public, anonymous "voice of culture" first heard in the headings of "Aeolus," a transpersonal repository of received ideas. Just as the narrative of "Aeolus" offers a compendium of rhetorical figures, the narrative of "Eumaeus" offers a compendium of clichés, from a catchword of popular melodrama ("balderdash"), to bureaucratic jargon ("embark on a policy," "Accordingly, after a few such preliminaries"), to proverbs ("as things always moved with the time"), to the low Dublin idiom of the dun in "Cyclops" ("hang it, the first go-off"). Although one can describe the habit of mind or the tone in the chapter, one's final impression of "Eumaeus" is of a body of language—as Gerald Bruns says, "a world of banal locutions within which both narrator and story struggle into being." Clichés in "Eumaeus" are not relegated through indirect discourse to the mind of a character, as in "Nausicaa," or separated typographically from other writing, like the headings of "Aeolus." In "Eumaeus," all writing has become cliché. Joyce gives us, then, a picture of all language in the debased state of the word "love" in the parody of "Cyclops." More than Flaubert in *Bouvard et Pécuchet* or the *Dictionary of Accepted Ideas*, Joyce focuses on received *locutions*, the ready-made phrases that express the received ideas of society.

Both description and discourse pass through the crucible of cliché. Instead of the narrator's borrowing the language of the characters, as he does in free indirect discourse, in "Eumaeus" the discourse of the characters is assimilated to the language of narration (as it is also in "Oxen of the Sun"). "Mr Bloom, likely to poohpooh the situation as egregious balderdash" is a translation of Bloom's reactions into a language he would never use. Neither the prissy "poohpooh the situation" nor the blustery "egregious balderdash" could possibly originate with Leopold Bloom. Similarly, the following passage of Bloom's thoughts is paraphrased:

> It was a subject of regret and absurd as well on the face of it and no small blame to our vaunted society that the man in the street, when the system really needed toning up, for a matter of a couple of paltry pounds, was debarred from seeing more of the world they lived in instead of being always cooped up since my old stick-in-the-mud took me for a wife. After all, hang it, they had their eleven and more humdrum months of it and merited a radical change of *venue* after the grind of city life in the summertime, for choice, when Dame Nature is at her spectacular best, constituting nothing but a new lease of life.

We recognize this as having elements of Bloom's thought, in its plans for the welfare of society, in its use of the formulae of public wisdom, even in its getting its clichés confused (compare "lease of life" with Bloom's "out of the land of Egypt and into the house of bondage"). But this is not the sound of Bloom's mind—from its beginning in the tones of a newspaper editorial, to its shift to the low Dublin idiom, to its conclusion in the tones of a pretentious advertisement in a travel magazine. (Its anger is also alien to Bloom.) This is a picture of Bloom's mind cheated of all its vitality and curiosity. One has only to compare this passage with a passage of stream-of-consciousness in an earlier chapter to see the distortion:

> The chemist turned back page after page. Sandy shrivelled smell he seems to have. Shrunken skull. And old. Quest for the philosopher's stone. The alchemists. Drugs age you after mental excitement. Lethargy then. Why? Reaction. A lifetime in a night. Gradually changes your character. Living all the day among herbs, ointments, disinfectants. All his alabaster lily-pots. . . . Enough stuff here to chloroform you. Test: turns blue litmus paper red. Chloroform. Overdose of laudanum. . . . Paragoric poppysyrup bad for cough. Clogs the pores or the phlegm. Poisons the only cures. Remedy where you least expect it. Clever of nature.
>
> ("Lotus-Eaters")

The depiction of the act of imagination here is different from the one in "Eumaeus," even though in both passages Bloom relies on the formulae in his memory. In "Lotus-Eaters," his manipulation of these formulae is creative, intelligent, funny. "Eumaeus" gives us a travestied form of Bloom's stream-of-consciousness, a reduction of it to its least common denominator.

What the stream-of-consciousness technique and the third-person narrative norm in the early chapters had in common was that they purported to present "reality" directly, either psychological or material "reality." In "Eumaeus," this pretense of unmediated vision is exposed once more. The chapter marks the climax of the increasing indirection of the narration seen in "Cyclops" and "Oxen of the Sun." The indirection is flagrantly advertised in various aspects of style: rhetorically in the technique of indirect discourse; semantically in the use of elegant variation, euphemism, and cliché; and syntactically in the circumlocutions of the sentence. In "Eumaeus," Joyce shows us language that is patently inadequate to the task of capturing the subtle nuances of behavior or even the quality of physical action—a travesty, that is, of the initial style. Instead of language that is able to fix essences in confident phrases, this is language that casts a net of words in the forlorn hope of capturing meaning. It names rather than presents emotional and psychological behavior: "Mr Bloom, actuated by motives of inherent delicacy, inasmuch as he always believed in minding his own business, moved off but nevertheless remained on the *qui vive* with just a shade of anxiety though not funkyish in the least." The linguistic tools available are impediments to the capturing of the complexity and subtlety of reality: trying to capture nuance with phrases like "inherent delicacy" and "*qui vive*" is like trying to whittle with a sledgehammer. Wolfgang Iser's description of one of the styles in the "Oxen of the Sun" chapter is equally appropriate to "Eumaeus": "As language approached, reality seemed rather to withdraw than to come closer." The twists and turns of the phrases, the elegant variation, the attempt of the writing to wrap itself around its object in "Eumaeus" reveals the essential discrepancy between language and the reality it seeks to describe. If the circumlocution and the modifying phrases of Henry James's style convince us that language is a subtle and pliable enough instrument for capturing the nuances of life, the travestied style of "Eumaeus" reveals Joyce's essential skepticism about language. In "Eumaeus," he demonstrates once again that life is mediated through the abuses of language.

One can say that "Eumaeus" is a version of the writer's struggle to write with a language that is contaminated, a language that is no longer a transparent medium. In the preface to his *Essais critiques*, Roland Barthes discusses the writer's struggle with language, and I quote him at length because I think he describes the view of language Joyce expresses in "Eumaeus." According to Barthes:

> The primary substance of literature is not the unnamable, but on the contrary the named; the man who wants to write must know that he is beginning a long concubinage with a language which is always *previous*. The writer does not "wrest" speech from silence . . . but inversely, and how much more arduously, more cruelly and less gloriously, detaches a secondary language from the slime of primary languages afforded him by the world, history, his existence, in short by an intelligibility which preexists him, for he comes into a world full of language. . . . [T]o be born is nothing but to find this code ready-made and to be obliged to accommodate oneself to it. We often hear it said that it is the task of art to *express the inexpressible*; it is the contrary which must be said (with no intention to paradox): the whole task of art is to *unexpress the expressible*, to kidnap from the world's language, which is the poor and powerful language of the passions, another speech, an exact speech.

"Eumaeus" represents "the world full of language," something that only Flaubert before Joyce had treated so fully in fiction. Through interruption and displacement in the early chapters of *Ulysses*, Joyce dramatized the struggle between writing and rewriting, personal signature and the world's language; in "Eumaeus," he deliberately stages an "accommodation" to writing that is "previous."

There is no particular exponent of language who encroaches on the writer's ego: the "fear" of other writing in "Eumaeus" is generalized beyond individual predecessors (as in "Oxen of the Sun") or even generic models (as in "Cyclops"). Joyce does not display the "anxiety of influence" which Harold Bloom describes, that Freudian battle of Titanic egos; instead, he reveals a more general anxiety about writing as an echo of other writing and language that has been tainted by its prior use. Joyce is quoted as having remarked to a friend: "I'd like a language which is above all languages, a language to which all will do service. I cannot express myself in English without enclosing myself in a tradition." Again, one can see Joyce's desire to transcend the limitations of language and the classifications of reality offered by his predecessors.

The problem posed by this linguistic inheritance, however, is not only that it is a threat to the writer's ego but also that it assaults intelligence and meaning. It is the Flaubertian language of stupidity. The clichés and proverbs, the public wisdom of "Eumaeus," exemplify the premature "conclusions" leading to stupidity. The clichés are a system of classification through which life in all its complexity is forced. This anonymous voice of culture expounds a rigid system of meaning, whether in its old wives' tales or its scientific formulae. It is not that these "conclusions" are always untrue but that they pretend they are the only possible truth. They organize the world in terms of type and generalization that belie the contingency of individual fact.

If in the style of scrupulous meanness Joyce tried to pare away the numerous associations of words, in "Eumaeus" he deliberately decided to let the linguistic memory loose on the page to devour the individual style. If the style of scrupulous meanness was in part a defense against a lapse into the stupidity of language, the style of "Eumaeus" suggests that no one is exempt from this stupidity. For by the time we reach "Eumaeus," we realize that everyone is implicated in it. Wayne Booth's "stable irony" is no longer possible, for no one, no writer or reader, can remain outside the ring of stupidity that Joyce draws. The condescending irony of Flaubert to his characters in *Madame Bovary* and of Joyce to the "submerged population" in *Dubliners* and in "Nausicaa" is obsolete. The narrative of "Eumaeus" embodies, with gross exaggeration, our inescapable stupidities; no one, Joyce seems to be saying, even the most "scrupulous" writer, can prevent the presence of at least some cliché in his writing.

But if he abandoned the defense against stupidity available in the style of scrupulous meanness, Joyce substituted another defense. On one level, the writing of "Eumaeus" functions like the parodies of "Cyclops": it attempts to disarm criticism through self-mockery. There is something redemptive about conceding one's stupidity. Both the writer's and the reader's implicit defense against stupidity is to recognize it. We recognize a cliché as a cliché—a reader who does not would not be the one for whom the book was created (and only someone like Gerty MacDowell or a cliché expert like Joyce could produce such a thorough list of received locutions).

The attempt to outdo a Gerty MacDowell in producing clichés is a strategy that can be used after stable irony is obsolete. But there is a greater sense of defensiveness about the writing in "Eumaeus," for in turning his writing over to cliché, Joyce asserts his own consciousness over the kind of inadvertent slips into cliché displayed by even the best writers. The compulsiveness and comprehensiveness of the catalogue of clichés in "Eumaeus" makes one sense that Joyce felt the worst thing that he could do was to accidentally include a cliché without recognizing it as such. There is a driven quality to the writing, as if by including all possible clichés, Joyce could prove himself their master. Instead of mocking eloquence and emotion by rewriting it in parodic form (as in "Cyclops"), Joyce subjects all writing to "stupidity" right away. In this sense, the writing takes no risks. It is like lying down to prevent a fall.

But on the other hand, the writing of "Eumaeus" is a virtuoso display of what a writer can do once he accepts the inadequacy of language: it is both a demonstration of the problems of language and a linguistic performance. If everybody succumbs to cliché some of the time, no one but Joyce would think of writing in cliché for a whole chapter. By intensifying the use of clichés, by making them come at the reader so thick and so fast at every comma, Joyce exposes their absurdity. He destroys the context in which clichés might appear natural (as in a nineteenth-century sentimental novel, for example, in which some cliché is permissible and indeed, expected). But Joyce also asserts his own ability to tell a story using only this execrable language, to put more of an obstacle in his way than any other writer, and then to proceed to keep our attention by showing us just how wonderfully bad the style is. In fact, what is startling about the clichés in "Eumaeus" is that Joyce deliberately does nothing to revitalize them in the way he does in "Cyclops," for example, or in *Finnegans Wake*. In "Language of/as Gesture in Joyce," David Hayman shows effectively how Joyce often cleverly returns the language of cliché to gesture (for example, by turning the expression "I could eat you up" into "We could ate you, par Buccas, and imbabe through you, reassuranced in the wild lac of gotliness" in *Finnegans Wake*. Conversely, in "Eumaeus," he gives us the narrator's deliberately feeble attempts to revive cliché in expressions like "the horse at the end of his tether," which applies to a literal horse. A phrase like "gone the way of all buttons" is the kind of phrase that would become a pun in *Finnegans Wake* (one can imagine that the substitution of "buttons" for "flesh" in the phrase "gone the way of all flesh" would at least produce "gone the way of all buttoms"). The performance in "Eumaeus" consists of Joyce's *refusal* to revitalize cliché, his insistence on using the worn-out style to tell the story.

The enormous confidence behind the writing and the "risk" that Joyce really does take in "Eumaeus" is most apparent when we realize the chapter's place in the book. In "Eumaeus," what could have been the dramatic and allegorical climax of the plot coincides with the nadir of the writing. "Eumaeus" represents the recognition scene between Stephen (Telemachus) and Bloom (Odysseus), and this has a special place in the plot of the story. The "Eumaeus" chapter is Joyce's deliberate "sabotage" of both style and the dramatic climax. The coming together of Stephen and Bloom is rendered entirely in vacuous clichés and vague phrases: "Side by side," "tête-à-tête," "with a certain analogy," Joyce's Odysseus and Telemachus are united. What other writer would render this climax in the following way?

> The queer suddenly things he popped out with attracted the elder man who was several years the other's senior or like his father. . . . Though they didn't see eye to eye in everything, a certain analogy there somehow was, as if both their minds were travelling, so to speak, in the one train of thought.

and

> —Yes, Stephen said uncertainly, because he thought he felt a strange kind of flesh of a different man approach him, sinewless and wobbly and all that.

Almost everything possible is done to the language here to destroy the emotion and eloquence of the dramatic climax. In the first quotation, for example, the succession of clichés, the vagueness, and the comic literalization of the metaphor "train of thought" all serve to deflate the language and the event. It is possible to imagine certain parts of the second quotation written "straight" in another novel: "He felt a strange kind of flesh . . . sinewless." But characteristically in the chapter, Joyce deliberately overwrites the phrase, making it redundant ("a strange kind of flesh of a different man") and mocking Stephen's important perception and the temporary eloquence of the writing with the sloppy "and all that." Similarly, the phrase "the elder man who was . . . like his father" is conceivable in another novel, but the insertion of the phrase "several years the other's senior" deliberately sabotages the simile (and thus the allegorical unity of Odysseus and Telemachus). The eloquence of the writing and the significance of the drama are deflated: both style and climax are revealed to be clichés—one linguistic, the other dramatic.

And yet, somehow, by "sacrificing" the moment of climax, Joyce gets something back. The clichéd writing is an artistic strategy to allow emotion and inarticulate eloquence to enter the narrative obliquely. In language that deliberately claims very little, he finds a way to suggest emotion while avoiding sentimentality, and significance while avoiding dramatic climax. Somehow the very lameness and incompetence of the writing creates the proper significance of the moment of meeting: displaying neither the solemnity of myth nor the neat doubleness of the "mock-heroic," the moment possesses, to use Joyce's idiom, "a certain sort of significance." By destroying eloquence, he allows emotion to be felt. The climax of the story is transcribed in the language of cliché because there is no other narrative means available that has not been "scorched." The clichés are, in effect, both the sabotage of style and a means of allowing the narrative to continue.

In "Cyclops," the exposure of the book's limitations allows the book to continue and expand. One can view the destruction of "literature" in "Eumaeus" in the same paradoxical way: literature is destroyed as the book expands. I have charted a movement away from "literature" in *Ulysses*, in the introduction of the subliterary text of the newspaper in "Aeolus" and the subliterary clichés of "Cyclops." The inclusion of the subliterary is, however, a part of a larger enterprise of the book, which is to expand its borders to include what is outside of it. The intrusion of the headings in "Aeolus" signifies not only the usurpation of narrative authority and the appearance of the public language of journalism but also the book's incorporation of something it had excluded. If the headings displace the narrative, it is because the narrative, in a sense, displaced journalism in its original narrative contract. It implicitly agreed to exclude it. In *Ulysses*, Joyce progressively incorporates in the novel what has been banished from it previously: other forms (for example, drama, catechism, newspaper) and other styles.

The text, like the self, is a circle that excludes everything outside itself. Through the devices of interruption and displacement, Joyce has dramatized what Stephen learned in "Proteus," that what is outside is "there all the time without you." Now in "Eumaeus," the total displacement of the literate narrative by cliché expands the limits of the book as literature *and* the limits of the self" (both the narrative "self" and the "self" of the characters), for the language is both subliterary and transpersonal (in contrast, allegory, for example, is transpersonal but not subliterary).

"He is a purely literary writer," T. S. Eliot observed of Joyce to Virginia Woolf. "He is founded upon Walter Pater with a dash of Newman." The clichéd style of "Eumaeus" (unlike the pastiche in "Oxen of the Sun") can be regarded as Joyce's deliberate refusal of this kind of mantle. In

"Ithaca," he rejected "literature" in a different way: by pretending to use the "neutral" language of the sciences. By the close of "Eumaeus," he had taken both his indictment of the "anonymous voice of culture" and his use of it as far as it could go in *Ulysses*.

ROLAND McHUGH

The "Finnegans Wake" Experience: Samples

James Joyce is a fashionable writer and his last book, *Finnegans Wake*, is frequently named in awe and reverence by all kinds of literati. There is a great deal of bluff in this naming, for few prospective readers actually sustain their curiosity for more than a page or two. If they want to know more, they usually turn to guidebooks and commentaries, substituting printed doctrines for direct confrontation with Joyce's text. *Finnegans Wake* is seen distantly and from without, like a darkened powerhouse on the skyline.

I suppose I have a natural distrust of gurus. I spent almost three years reading *Finnegans Wake* (abbreviated FW) before looking at any kind of critical account. I contrived to retain this innocence until I had formulated a coherent system of interpretation. I was then able to evaluate the guidebooks from a neutral vantage point and elude indoctrination. Of course, I learned valuable things from them, and had often to discard ill-formed conclusions in consequence. But this seemed a healthy process, although its duration grotesquely exceeded the time any reasonable person would devote to a book. I hardly intend that my present readers should repeat my example, but I feel the experience qualifies me to introduce FW to them in a particularly helpful manner.

Before I describe the stages in a solitary exposure to FW it will be as well to look at a few specimens of the opus. As FW is divided into four

From *The Finnegans Wake Experience*. Copyright © 1981 by The Regents of the University of California. University of California Press.

Books, each having its distinct atmosphere, we will discuss an excerpt from each Book. The excerpts will be reasonably representative of their Books, and our discussion will illustrate generalities important in many other parts of the *Wake*.

The first extract, from Book I, runs from line 1 to line 15 on page 162 (any edition), and is conventionally labelled 162.01–15.

> The older sisars (Tyrants, regicide is too good for you!) become unbeurr-able from age, (the compositor of the farce of dustiny however makes a thunpledrum mistake by letting off this pienofarte effect as his furst act as that is where the juke comes in) having been sort-of-nineknived and chewly removed (this soldier-author-batman for all his commontoryism is just another of those souftsiezed bubbles who never quite got the sandhurst out of his eyes so that the champaign he draws for us is as flop as a plankrieg) the twinfreer types are billed to make their reupprearance as the knew kneck and knife knickknots on the deserted *champ de bouteilles*. (A most cursery reading into the Persic-Uraliens hostery shows us how Fonnumagula picked up that propper numen out of a colluction of prifixes though to the permienting cannasure the Coucousien oafsprung of this sun of a kuk is as sattin as there's a tub in Tobolosk)

A good deal of Book I has this tone—a commentary on some story or letter. Most of the material in parenthesis forms a sort of reconsidered secondary comment on its author and origins. If we ignore this, it should not be too hard to see that the story concerns the assassination of Caesar. The older Caesars become unbearable from age. Having been knifed to death and duly removed, the twin brothers (French, *frères*)—and freers (for they endeavour to free Caesar's people from his tyranny)—are, according to the playbill, to make their reappearance, uprearing, as the new neck-and-neck knick-knacks on the deserted *champ de bouteilles*.

Should the reader at this point glance through the region of FW between pages 161 and 168 he will find the Julius Caesar plot everywhere. Brutus and Cassius, disguised as butter (Burrus) and cheese (Caseous), occur frequently as twin brothers. Take 161.15–19: "Burrus, let us like to imagine, is a genuine prime, the real choice, full of natural greace, the mildest of milkstoffs yet unbeaten as a risicide and, of course, obsoletely unadulterous whereat Caseous is obversely the revise of him and in fact not an ideal choose by any meals." Therefore "unbeurrable from age" can be seen to contain French *beurre* and *fromage*, butter and cheese. And we can quote Brendan O Hehir's gloss on "regicide is too good for you": "among the motives for assassinating Caesar was his apparent desire to become king (*rex*); he was already *tyrannos*, so his murder was *tyrannicide* to forestall the necessity for it to be *regicide*."

Other stories are clearly comprehended besides Caesar's. The "farce of dustiny"—and admittedly everyone's eventual destiny is, like Caesar's, to become dust—echoes Verdi's opera *La Forza del Destino* but is distinguished by its composer's mistake: his first act is to let off a musically unsound triple trumpet kettledrum effect on the pianoforte, a thunder-drum sound like a full (Italian, *pieno*) fart. Now, if we look at the opening page of FW, just such an effect appears in lines 15–17: "The fall (bababadalgharaghtakamminarronnkonnbronntonnerronntuonnthunntrova rrhounawnskawntoohoohoordenenthurnuk!)." This is made out of various foreign equivalents of "thunder," for instance Japanese *kaminari*, Italian *tuono*, Portugese *trovão* and Danish *tordenen*. Its significance has generally been agreed upon since Samuel Beckett's authorised essay on the *Wake* appeared in 1929. It represents the roll of thunder which, according to Giambattista Vico's *The New Science*, characterises the first phase through which all human civilisations must progress. Vico was an astonishingly original thinker of the early eighteenth century, and Joyce, who admired him, stated unambiguously that FW was an expression of Vico's philosophy. Beckett's essay attempts "to condense the thesis of Vico, the scientific historian. In the beginning was the thunder: the thunder set free Religion, in its most objective and unphilosophical form—idolatrous animism: Religion produced Society, and the first social men were the cave-dwellers, taking refuge from a passionate Nature: this primitive family life receives its first impulse towards development from the arrival of terrified vagabonds: admitted, they are the first slaves: growing stronger, they exact agrarian concessions, and a despotism has evolved into a primitive feudalism: the cave becomes a city, and the feudal system a democracy: then an anarchy: this is corrected by a return to monarchy: the last stage is a tendency towards interdestruction: the nations are dispersed, and the Phoenix of Society arises out of their ashes." Caesar's assassination occupies a conspicuous step in the cycle, much of Vico's data deriving from his studies in Roman history.

The "farce of dustiny" then, is partly FW itself, with the "pienofarte effect" in its first act. That's where the joke comes in. The "juke," who also comes in, as the "furst" (German *Furst*, prince), is that "good Dook Umphrey" whose exploits feature at another early stage in the *Wake*, occupying most of its second chapter.

The next parenthesised clause delineates the "compositor." He is soldier and batman as well as author, and we may regard his account of Caesar's fall as a specimen of military history. But for all his commentaries, and for all his political persuasions (it is quite immaterial whether these are "common toryism" or communism) he is, for the narrator of this portion of FW, a mere "South Sea Bubble." This was a short-lived scheme of 1720 to take up the British National Debt by trade with the South Seas. The compositor, then, is an ephemeral wonder. He has never properly woken up ("got the sand out of his eyes"). His strategy was learned at Sandhurst Military Academy rather than directly in the wars, so the campaign he sketches for us is lifeless—as flat as a pancake, a flop as colourless as a plan of the war (German, *Krieg*). He does not stimulate our senses, merely provides glasses of flat (i.e. non-effervescent) champagne.

Brutus and Cassius, the rivals, running neck-and neck, are billed (and built) to reappear on the battlefield, which is also a bottlefield (French, *champ de bouteilles*). It is this italicized phrase to which the next sentence refers, though that might not be immediately apparent to you. One of the commonest difficulties encountered in FW is that of seeing the thread which connects adjacent sentences. If we ignore the qualification ("though . . . Tobolosk") we see it stated that a most cursory (and cursing) reading of this history shows us how the compositor, now called "Fonnumagula," picked up that proper name (Latin, *nomen*) *"champ de bouteilles"* out of a collection of prefaces or prefixes. But says the qualification, to the permitting connoisseur, the Caucasian origin (spring) of the phrase is as certain as there's a tail on a cat. And its offspring, i.e. the phrases deriving from it, are Caucasian.

The longest military parody in FW is Buckley's shooting of the Russian General during the Crimean War (FW 338–355), hence the notion that a *Wake* battlefield should ultimately lie in Russia, in the Caucasus. Tobol'sk is a town in Siberia, and in "Persic-Uraliens" one notices the Urals along with some Persian aliens. But Napoleon's campaigns are also pertinent (as at FW 008–010), hence the inclusion of the phrase "Corsican upstart." Here we may mark a further sub-narrative. We ought to be discussing a "proper name" found in a collection of prefaces, but *"champ de bouteilles"* is not a proper name. The acquisition of a proper name is really another theme from the second chapter of FW, which explains the origin of Duke Humphrey's surname "Earwicker." "Persic-Uraliens" echoes a phrase in that chapter (038.11: "no persicks and armelians") but more dramatically it echoes *Persse O'Reilly*, the name given to Earwicker in the ballad closing the chapter. The ballad is composed by somebody called Hosty, hence "Persic-Uraliens hostery."

By now you are probably finding the personages emerging from the text a problem. Let me presume to simplify things: everyone so far named, except Brutus, Cassius and Hosty, is an aspect of a single composite personality. In his manuscripts Joyce represents Caesar, Earwicker, Persse O'-Reilly (French, *perce-oreille*, earwig), Finnegan, Finn MacCool and many others, by a sign (technically, a *siglum*), **m** .

Tim Finnegan, hero of the Irish-American ballad "Finnegan's Wake," is a builder who falls from his ladder and is assumed dead, but resurrects at his wake. In the first chapter of FW he is conflated with the legendary Irish giant, Finn MacCool, for example at 006.13–15, immediately after the fall: "Macool, Macool, orra whyi deed ye diie? of a trying thirstay mournin? Sobs they sighdid at Fillagain's chrissormiss wake." Finn MacCool is clearly the principal echo in the name of our compositor-author-soldier-batman, "Fonnumagula." We have been told that Finn MacCool picked up a proper name in the Persse O'Reillyan history. In other words, when **m** advanced from the first to the second FW chapter he obtained a significant new name, which in fact helped to prop up his precarious reputation, and was thus a "propper numen."

Before leaving the passage we may note a few subsidiary components. Despite the appearance of Finnish words lower on 162, *sisar*, meaning sister, is probably irrelevant as the tryant is quite unequivocally male. Perhaps he is a "sizar." In *Ulysses*, the fatherly George Russell (AE) is said to have "a sizar's laugh of Trinity," but his use in FW is rather peripheral. **m** is built from numerous avatars some of whom fall for good, but most somehow resurrect. So Caesar is "sort-of-nineknived": he is like a cat of nine lives. He is "chewly removed" by his butter and cheese assassins. Some versions of the death of **m** elsewhere in FW involve ritual cannibalism in parody of Frazer's *The Golden Bough*, and this helps to justify the eating overtone.

Perhaps French *souffler*, to blow, can be discerned within "souftsiezed"—the bubble has, after all, to be blown. It's harder to account for the alliteration in "knew kneck and knife knickknots," though 561.02 does equate the twins with a fork and knife. Obviously some component in "Fonnumagula" remains unidentified, but *numen* is Latin for divine will, so the new name acquired by Humphrey apparently confers some sort of divine authority. This must necessarily proceed from God, that "collector of prepuces," but also from a contest (Latin, *colluctatio*) of prefixes. In fact several other potential names for Humphrey are suggested in the second chapter of FW: "a turn-piker who is by turns a pikebailer no seldomer than an earwigger!" **m** is in one sense a sun-god of a gun," and in the eating context the son of a cook (in "kuk"). Possibly Swift's *Tale of a Tub*, occasionally mentioned in FW, contributes to the "tub in Tobolosk," which has been sat in, but though I can envisage further glosses on "permienting cannasure" I have little faith in them. In fact, in the three remaining excerpts I shall ignore glosses which do not contribute meaningfully to the demonstrable context, so in all cases my explanation will be somewhat incomplete.

FW must always mean many things at once. In the piece just considered there is a battlefield which is also a bottlefield—a table with food and bottles on it. Is the "composition" trying to explain some point of strategy by moving the butter, cheese, etc. about to represent parties in conflict? Only on one level. Unfortunately, the balancing act of keeping one's attention fluid between all the levels defeats most readers, who trust one level and pay lip-service to the others. Perhaps a more extreme example will show the fallacy in that approach.

Joyce is reported to have said "Time and the river and the mountain are the real heroes of my book." It's well known that in FW the concepts of the human female and the river are somehow conflated, although how one takes that appears to be a matter of taste. One may exalt woman by comparison with the majesty of clear flowing water or one may degrade her by depicting the rivermouth as a gargantuan urinogenital orifice. But Joyce treats both attitudes as cliché and instead spotlights fortuitous parallelism with a consequent split image and throwaway humour. In our Book II excerp (327.09–23) the tailor's daughter is described to the Norwegian Captain in such a way that we are continually obliged to construe her in both human and aquatic terms:

> with a grit as hard as the trent of the thimes but a touch as saft as the dee in flooing and never a Hyderow Jenny the like of her lightness at look and you leap, rheadoromanscing long evmans invairn, about little Anny Roners and all the Lavinias of ester yours and pleding for them to herself in the periglus glatsch hangs over her trickle bed, it's a piz of fortune if it never falls from the stuffel, and, when that mallaura's over till next time and all the prim rossies are out dressparading and the tubas tout tout for the glowru of their god, making every Dinny dingle after her down the Dargul dale and (wait awhile, blusterbuss, you're marchadant too forte and don't start furlan your ladins till you've learned the lie of her language!), when it's summwer calding and she can hear the pianutunar beyant the bayondes in Combria sleepytalking to the Wiltsh muntons, titting out through her droemer window for the flyend of a touchman over the wishtas of English Strand

Book II is definitely more complicated than any of the other three and this extract possesses a difficulty whose justification does not concern us right now. To understand what is being said you will need to identify a number of words belonging to an ancient language called Rhaeto-Romanic or Roumansch, which is spoken in certain Swiss cantons. Also, as a Norwegian is being addressed, there are Norwegian words present. Fortunately, lists of the Rhaeto-Romanic and Norwegian elements in FW can be obtained, and with their assistance we can proceed.

On the aquatic plane, the grit of the river-bed is as hard as that found in the river Trent and the river Thames, but the touch of its water is as soft (Norwegian, *saft*, juice) as that of the river Dee in flooding. On the human plane, the anger (Rhaeto-Romanic, *gritta*) of the daughter is as hard as the trend of the times demands, yet she has a touch as imperceptible as the letter *d* which has been removed in the word "flooing." Both the water and the girl are very light, and they are, therefore, compared with hydrogen, the lightest element, impetuously failing to look before they leap. "Look and you leap" sounds like a children's game, at which the girl presumably excels.

The Rhaeto-Romanic (RR) *inviern* means winter, and the first part of our message considers the situation in winter. The girl reads romances all the long evenings in vain: they may be written in Rhaeto-Romanic but they concern persons such as "Little Annie Rooney," the subject of a popular song, and heroines with names like Lavinia and Ester. Swift's friends Esther Johnson (Stella) and Esther Vanhomrigh (Vanessa), who frequently manifest conjointly in FW, may be detected. But the river's preferred reading encompasses geophysical enormities. "Anny . . . Lavinias" reflects the name Anna Liffey, given on old maps of Dublin's principal river, and *lavina* is RR for an avalanche. The river is inspired by thoughts of great waterways and the avalanches of yesteryear, and foreign places (RR *ester*, foreign) towards which it might flow.

Both the girl and the river have a bed. The girl is pleading (RR *pled*, a word) for the heroines as she looks into the pierglass hanging over her truckle bed (a low bed on castors). The stream, undoubtedly young and narrow, looks into the dangerous (RR *prigulus*; Welsh *peryglus*) ice (RR *glatsch*) overhanging its bed. It's a piece of fortune if the mirror never falls from the ladder-rung (German, *Stufe*) supporting it, and a peak (RR *piz*) of fortune if the wind (RR *suffel*) doesn't blow down the ice.

So much for the winter. When that bad weather (RR *malaura*) is over until next year and all the primroses come up on the riverbanks, the rossies (Dublin slang for an impudent girl, a "forward piece") are out parading their spring dresses. The parade boasts tubas tooting for the glory of God, and also (from the non-human platform) the glory of the forest (RR *god*). Both girl and river look attractive in a spring setting and every

Dinny (Irish *duine*, person) feels a tingle as he watches them pass. The river is here the Dargle, tumbling from the Wicklow Mountains; RR *dargun* is a mountain torrent.

The parenthetical admonition warns the girl's admirer that he is marching too loudly (Italian, *forte*) or too quickly (Norwegian, *fort*), with acknowledgements to Margadant, who wrote a study of Rhaeto-Romanic. Courtship by blustering busses (archaic: kisses) is unlikely to succeed. Don't start following the leaders/ladies until you've learned the lie of the land. Don't start furling a flag inscribed in the Ladin dialect of RR until you've learned that language. (Also RR *furlan* means a little rascal.)

The verb "titting" is qualified by the two clauses beginning "when that mallaura's over" and "when it's summwer calding." When summer's calling, or it's somewhere hot (Italian, *caldo*) the girl can hear a piano-tuner in a nearby room (RR *combra*) trying to get to sleep by counting sheep (French, *moutons*). I suppose he might be the (sexually uninteresting) blind piano-tuner of *Ulysses*, although RR *tunêr* (to thunder) evokes the voice of **m**. For the river, he is beyond the beyonds, beyond the waves (Italian, *onde*) of Dublin Bay, in Wales (Cambria), talking to the Welsh Mountains (RR *munt*). The pairing of male mountain and female river is a commonplace in FW, so it is reasonable that the river should yearn for the Welsh Mountains (visible from the Wicklow ones on especially clear days). The girl, however, peeps (Norwegian, *titte*) out of her dormer window, dreaming (Norwegian, *drömmer*, dreams) of her future lover.

This entire speech is part of that made to the Norwegian Captain to encourage his courtship of the tailor's daughter, and he has previously been described by the tailor as a "bugganeering wanderer-ducken" (323.01). Van der Decken is the captain of the *Flying Dutchman*, so the girl is represented as wishing "for the flyend of a touchman." Mention lower on 327 of Kilbarrack, Dollymount and the Blue Lagoon suggest that she is in one of the houses on the Clontarf Road, in North-East Dublin, many of which have dormer windows facing across the strand of Bull Island towards the English and Welsh coasts. The river Dargle, by contrast, is on the South side of Dublin, so there is a transpicuous geographical separation of human and natural modes of interpretation.

Obviously, your appreciation of this kind of thing depends upon your sense of humour. For many people, something intended to make you laugh, whatever else it may do, is intrinsically worthless: a joke is not information. Weirdness fails to appeal to them. FW, however, contrives to be simultaneously ridiculous and sublime, whilst casually reconciling many other apparent contraries. One progresses along its path and unveils wonders, but if one is consciously questing for the secret of the universe failure is inevitable. Our Book III excerpt (478.08–22) intimates as much:

> I am told by our interpreter, Hanner Esellus, that there are fully six hundred and six ragwords in your malherbal Magis landeguage in which wald wand rimes alpman and there is resin in all roots for monarch but yav hace not one pronouncable teerm that blows in all the vallums of tartallaght to signify majestate even provisionally, nor no rheda rhoda or torpentine path or hallucinian via nor aurellian gape nor sunkin rut nor grossgrown trek nor crimeslaved cruxway and no moorhens cry or mooner's plankgang there to lead us to hopenhaven. Is such the *unde derivatur* casematter messio! Frankly. *Magis megis enerretur mynus hoc intelligow.*
> —How? C'est mal prononsable, tartagliano, perfrances. Vous n'avez pas d'o dans vorte boche provenciale, mousoo. Je m'incline mais *Moy jay trouvay la clee dang les champs.* Hay sham nap poddy velour, come on!

The first of these two speeches is delivered by one of a group of four old men seeking to discover **m** in name and person. The reply is made by a composite character called "Yawn," who includes two separate persons prominent elsewhere in FW. One of these is St. Patrick, and Yawn's speech uses a great deal of French on account of Patrick's French origins. The other is a child named Kevin, who in 110.22–111.33 observes a hen digging a valuable letter out of an ancient burial-heap.

As elsewhere in Book III, the old men employ as their interpreter an ass (German, *Esel*; Latin, *asellus*). The ass has told them that in the Magis's language used by Yawn there are six hundred and six words, and of them one word (German, *Wort*) rimes, i.e. celebrates, "alpman," a man as tall as the Alps. Also, he says, in all the roots of these words there is reason for, reason to suppose, "monarch" implicit. But the language has not one pronounceable term in all its volumes to signify **m**, a monarch as tall as the Alps, or as big as a state, "majestate." "All the volumes of Tallaght" suggests the celebrated and lengthy *Martyrology of Tallaght*, compiled at the monastery there.

At the same time that he seeks a name for **m** the questioner desires a manifest sign of **m**. To understand why this is a plant we must sympathise with Yawn/Patrick's standpoint. God is not a man as big as a state: He is the Trinity, and the signature of the Trinity may be read upon the shamrock. From the botanical plane there are 606 ragworts (pronounced "ragwerts") in Yawn's bad herbal, the wood (German, *Wald*) contains meaningful wands (sticks), and all the roots of the monarch-like trees contain resin. But Yawn also subsumes the personality of the finder of treasure in burial mounds,

Kevin. As such he has directed the seekers to the vallums (earthworks, i.e. mounds) of Tallaght. P.W. Joyce's account of the locale explains why:

> The first leader of a colony after the flood was Parthalon, who, with his followers, ultimately took up his residence on the plain anciently called *Sean-mhagh-Ealta-Edair* [Shan-va-alta-edar], the old plain of the flocks of Edar, which stretched along the coast by Dublin from Tallaght to *Edar*, or Howth. The legend —which is given in several very ancient authorities—relates that after the people of this colony had lived there for 300 years, they were destroyed by a plague, which in one week carried off 5,000 men and 4,000 women; and they were buried in a place called, from this circumstance, *Taimhleacht-Mhuintire-Parthaloin* (Four Mast.), the *Tavlaght* or plague-grave of Parthalon's people. This place, which lies about five miles from Dublin, still retains the name *Taimhleacht*, modernized to Tallaght; and on the hill, lying beyond the village, there is to be seen at this day a remarkable collection of ancient sepulchral tumuli, in which cinerary urns are found in great numbers.

Despite their perusal of all this vale of tears the old men have found no one pronounceable tear signifying **m**. Nor any path thence towards him. There is an impressive list of paths, nine of them, that the old men have failed to discover. Besides looking like "red road," "rheda rhoda" suggests to Louis Mink the Rhaetian road, "the main ancient road crossing the Alps in Swiss territory." The "Torpentine path" could be "Tarquintine," i.e. the funeral path between Tarquinia, the chief city of the Etruscans, and its famous necropolis. There is a botanical allusion again, to turpentine trees, and a suggestion of torpor. That is, the path may be a mystical one, to be encountered in a trance, as is the case with its next manifestation, "hallucinian via." It is a hallucination, and the Eleusinia Via, the path followed in the Eleusinian Mysteries. The "aurellian gape" is the Aurelian Gate of Rome, another burial allusion as it led to the Mausoleum of Hadrian. It is also a sensory pathway, a gaping ear. The Sunken Road is harder to justify in its accepted sense as the *Hohle Gasse* near Kussnacht where William Tell ambushed the tyrant Gessler. Then there is a grassgrown track, along which to trek, that has grown gross. The "crimeslaved cruxway" is partly real path, constructed by criminal slaves, and partly a *via crucis*, a mystical way of the Stations of the Cross, which Joyce in fact said was a pattern represented in the form of Book III. It also sounds vaguely like the "Giant's Causeway" in Northern Ireland: **m** is, of course, a giant. None of these potential paths has materialized, or is there any sound (moorhen's cry) or gangplank to bring the investigators closer to "hopehaven." As archaeologists exploring a burial mound in Dublin they might well be reaching towards Copenhagen, for Viking remains abound beneath the pavements. But as mystics in pursuit of a hope of heaven they are confounded by Yawn's French, the language of Malherbe. Is such the whence-(it)-is-derived (Latin, *unde derivatur*) matter of the case, monsieur? Is such the original content of the casemate, the chamber in the mound? Frankly, *(quo) magis enaratur (eo) minus hoc intellego*, the more completely it is explained the less I understand this.

"How?," replies Yawn, translating French *comment*. '*C'est mal prononçable*," it is hard for his questioners to pronounce. They stutter (Italian, *tartagliano*) their French (Spanish, *Francés*). To the one who has just spoken he exclaims, "*Vous n'avez pas d'eau dans votre bouche provinciale, monsieur*," you have no water in your provincial mouth, sir. The mispronounced words sound to him like German (*Boche*) or Provençal. *Je m'incline, mais moi, j'ai trouvé la clef dans les champs*," I acquiesce, but me, I've found the key in the fields. He's found the path there too, not only *la clef* but also German *Klee*, shamrock. *Et ça n'a pas de valure*," and that has no value. "*Comment?*" This contradiction, that the shamrock merely represents the Trinity, and is valueless in itself, completes the bewilderment of Yawn's audience.

We saw in our first example that certain very diverse human beings were incorporated in the character **m**. In the second example he also included inanimate objects, mountains. Now, we must appreciate that FW also employs entirely inanimate conglomerates which are formed in the same way. The story in the first example, the "farce of dustiny," was found to include a drama of Caesar's death, a model of Vico's philosophy, and the text of FW itself. From numerous examples throughout the book, we can state definitively that the burial mound we have just discussed, and the letter which is unearthed from it, are both part of the same complex amalgam, which further includes all Wakean notions of buildings and cities. These things are ultimately containers of **m**, and whether they are real containers of his body or verbal containers of his name they are indifferently represented in Joyce's manuscripts by the siglum □. The language predicament of the four old men—they blame the language and its speaker blames their pronunciation—is often our problem when we attempt to impale **m** in the labyrinth of FW. The more □ is narrated the less we understand. It is this container concept □ which is invoked in our Book IV excerpt (597.04–22):

> Of all the stranger things that ever not even in the hundrund and badst pageans of unthowsent and wonst nice or in eddas an oddes bokes of tomb, dyke and hollow to be have happened! The untireties of livesliving being the one substrance of a streamsbecoming. Totalled in toldteld and teldtold

in tittletell tattle. Why? Because, graced be Gad and all giddy gadgets, in whose words were the beginnings, there are two signs to turn to, the yest and the ist, the wright side and the wronged side, feeling aslip and wauking up, so an, so farth. Why? On the sourdsite we have the Moskiosk Djinpalast with its twin adjacencies, the bathouse and the bazaar, alla-hallahallah, and on the sponthesite it is the alcovan and the rosegarden, boony noughty, all puraputhry. Why? One's apurr apuss a story about brid and breakfedes and parricombating and coushcouch but others is of tholes and oubworn buyings, dolings and chafferings in heat, contest and enmity. Why? Every talk has his stay, vidnis Shavarsanjivana, and all-a-dreams perhapsing under lucksloop at last are through. Why? It is a sot of a swigswag, systomy dystomy, which everabody you ever anywhere at all doze. Why? Such me.

To a degree, FW is supposed to illustrate the activity of the sleeping mind, and Book IV portrays that mind in the process of awakening. At this point the three preceding Books appear in retrospect as the dissolving dream. Of all the strangest things that did not even happen in the hundred and one worst pages of A Thousand and One Nights, or in odds and ends of the Icelandic Eddas or the Egyptian Book of the Dead!

This passage exhibits a common Wakean idiosyncrasy. Its words are often susceptible to two alternative constructions which contradict one another, the so-called "identity of opposites" discussed by the medieval philosopher Giordano Bruno. For instance "badst" ought to mean worst, most bad but it sounds rather like "best." If we view the Arabian Nights as an unholy book, full of pagans and possibly "not sent by thou," the former construction applies. Alternatively we have the hundred best pages of a "nice" book: the night is over and has been won ("wonst"). We should also heed the symmetrical pairing of elements in these sentences: "badst" is opposed to "wonst." The ambivalent syntax, e.g. "to be have happened," widening the connotative spectrum, is also a typical Book IV trademark.

The odd books of "tomb, dyke and hollow" remind us of documents concealed in tumuli, but readers slightly familiar with the rest of FW will probably also perceive the names of Tom, Dick and Harry. This triad relates, for instance, to Brutus, Antony and Cassius in Book I, and both are tech-nically embodiments of the sigla Λ, ⌐ and ⊏.

The dreamer is enthralled to see that all the untiring entities of life's living were made the one substance, in his trance, of a stream of verbalization. To gloss "streamsbecoming" we could notice the subsequent "in whose words were the beginnings" and quote Leo Knuth on another variant of that phrase:

As it says in the book: "In the becoming was the weared" (FW 487.20). The matrix of this sentence is obvious. The opening words of the gospel according to St. John are a recurrent motif. We see that "weared" means "word": the Logos. Phonetically it also suggests "weird"—a suggestion which is semantically supported by the word "becoming," because that is what "weird" originally meant: OE *wyrd,* the power to which everything is subjected, the power that causes everything to become, time (past, present and future) and change (which is merely an aspect of time). Man is born, lives, and dies in time, "dreeing his weird" (FW 199.05). *Wyrd* is cognate with German *werden* (auxiliary of the passive and the future) and with Dutch *worden* (to become).

The "streamsbecoming" totalled life's entireties, and was told in tittle-tattle, in petty gossip. The dreamer questions its purpose and learns that, by the grace of God and of material things (gadgets), it has two sides to turn to, a form literally illustrated in "toldteld and teldtold." There is a West side, falling asleep with the setting sun, and an East side, waking up. The "yest" is yesterday, the past, opposed to the present tense (German *ist,* is). But these definitions are ambivalent, the right side being not only constructed by a rightful God but also by a human wright, and the wrong side also being wronged, i.e. in the right. □, as we generally observed in FW, "has its cardinal points" (114.07), and there are also a South and North side. The South side features the Great Mosque at Mecca prior to Mohammed: it is full of djinns and devils, and incorporates the profane bath-house (and bat-house!) and bazaar. Bloom of course visits "the mosque of the baths" on the South side of Dublin just before "Hades," not hell perhaps but a contrast to the post-Mohammed "sponthesite" with its Koran and rosegarden. However, ambivalence triumphs: the South side is also North, as it includes the Moscow gin palace (German *Palast,* palace), and it is further the energetic bazaar of waking existence, with morning prayers to Allah, as opposed to the paradise of dreams (Italian, *buena notte,* good-night). I do not understand why the South side is deaf (French, *sourd*), but presumably some balancing ingredient exists in "sponthesite." I suppose "puraputhry" and "apurr apuss" might echo "purpose"—the dreamer's current preoccupation—but the cat seems to be here just to match the dog in the next answer.

The "apurr apuss" answer is a sort of inversion of the "sourdsite" one. Again it has two contrasting parts, but now the first is the dream, i.e. the previous three Books of FW, and the second is the hell of reality. "Once upon a time," the opening words of Joyce's *Portrait,* might be taken to represent birth, the characteristic institution of Vico's first age, when man sought shelter in caves (bed and breakfast). Book II contains the parricide of the Russian General and the fighting on equal terms (Italian, *combattere ad armi pari*) of his two sons. Book III is the period of sleep (French, *se coucher*), ocurring after twelve midnight, which chimes at its opening (FW 403).

The future side is less comfortable. We will have to thole, to endure, the hardships of buying, dealing and chaffering the heat, contest and enmity. The English word "chaffer" means to trade or barter, but "chaffering" sounds rather like "suffering." Noticing Humphrey Chimpden Earwicker's initials in the last words we again ask why, but the dream is sliding out of focus. Every dog has his day, witness Shavarsanjivana. If we can trust the late B. P. Misra, this is a book in the Purva Mimamsa school of Indian philosophy. The Purva Mimamsa ("first inquiry") scholars did not accept the existence of God, but thought the Vedas were eternal and uncreated, and devoted themselves to their interpretation. Perhaps there is a parrallel in the recommended approach to the text of FW. Anyway, the stream of the Liffey, now passing Leixlip, or else under the Loop Line railway bridge, nears the sea, into which it will plunge on the closing page of FW. The terminal image of □ is simply that of its antitheses, systole and diastole. Dozing and waking are activities undertaken by everyone you ever saw. Why? Search me. That isn't the sort of question FW is there to answer.

FREDRIC JAMESON

"Ulysses" in History

One does not read Joyce today, let alone write about
him, without remembering the fifteen-year-long struggle
for freedom of the people of Northern Ireland; the
following, then, for whatever it is worth,
must necessarily be dedicated to them.

I had it in mind, in what follows, to say something about the two most boring chapters of *Ulysses*: most people would agree that these are surely the Eumaeus and the Ithaca chapters, the scene in the cabmen's shelter and the catechism. I have found, however, that in order to do that properly one must necessarily speak about the rest in some detail so that finally those parts are greatly reduced. One of the things such a subject leads you to consider, however, is boredom itself and its proper use when we are dealing with literary texts of this kind, and in particular the classical texts of high modernism or even postmodernism. I will still say something about that—I think there is a productive use of such boredom, which tells us something interesting about ourselves as well as about the world in which we live today—but I also mean to use this word in a far less positive sense, so I will do that first and say that if there are boring chapters of *Ulysses*, with which we must somehow learn to live, there are also boring interpretations of *Ulysses*, and those we can really make an effort to do without, sixty years after its publication, and in a social and global situation so radically different from that in which the canonical readings of this text were invented.

From *James Joyce and Modern Literature*. Copyright © 1982 by Routledge and Kegan Paul.

It would be surprising indeed if we were unable to invent newer and fresher ways of reading Joyce; on the other hand, the traditional interpretations I am about to mention have become so sedimented into our text—*Ulysses* being one of those books which is "always-already-read," always seen and interpreted by other people before you begin—that it is hard to see it afresh and impossible to read it as though those interpretations had never existed.

They are, I would say, threefold, and I will call them the mythical, the psychoanalytical, and the ethical readings respectively. These are, in other words, the readings of *Ulysses*, first in terms of the Odyssey parallel; second, in terms of the father-son relationship; and third, in terms of some possible happy end according to which this day, Bloomsday, will have changed everything, and will in particular have modified Mr. Bloom's position in the home and relationship to his wife.

Let me take this last reading first. I will have little to say here about Molly's monologue, and only want now to ask not merely why we are so attached to the project of making something decisive happen during this representative day, transforming it in other words into an Event; but also and above all to ask why we should be committed to this particular kind of event, in which Mr. Bloom is seen as reasserting his authority in what can therefore presumably once again become a vital family unit. (You will recall that he has asked Molly to bring him breakfast in bed the next day—the triumph over the suitors!) In this day and age, in which the whole thrust of a militant feminism has been against the nuclear and the patriarchal family, is it really appropriate to recast *Ulysses* along the lines of marriage counselling and anxiously to interrogate its characters and their destinies with a view towards saving this marriage and restoring this family? Has our whole experience of Mr. Bloom's Dublin reduced itself to this, the quest for a "happy ending" in which the hapless protagonist is to virilise himself and become a more successful realisation of the dominant, patriarchal, authoritarian male?

Still, it will be said that this particular reading is part of the more general attempt to fit "Ulysses" back into the Odyssey parallel. As for the mythical interpretation—the Odyssey parallel undoubtedly underscored for us by the text itself as well as by generations of slavish interpreters—here too it would be desirable to think of something else. We are today, one would hope, well beyond that moment of classical modernism and its ideologies in which, as Sartre said somewhere, there was a "myth of myth," in which the very notion of some mythic unity and reconciliation was used in a mythical, or as I would prefer to say, a fetishised way. The bankruptcy of the ideology of the mythic is only one feature of the bankruptcy of the ideology of modernism in general; yet it is a most interesting one, on which (had we more time) it might have been instructive to dwell. Why is it that, in the depthlessness of consumer society, the essential surface logic of our world of simulacra—why is it that the mythic ideal of some kind of depth integration is no longer attractive and no longer presents itself as a possible or workable solution? There is a kinship here, surely, between this waning of the mythic ideal or mirage and the disappearance of another cherished theme and experience of classical or high modernism, namely that of temporality, *durée*, lived time, the passage of time. But perhaps the easiest way to dramatise the breakdown of myth and myth criticism is simply to suggest that we suddenly, with anthropologists like Lévi-Strauss, discovered that myths were not what we thought they were in the first place: not the place of some deep Jungian integration of the psyche, but quite the opposite, a space preceding the very construction of the psyche or the subject itself, the ego, personality identity and the like: a space of the pre-individualistic, of the collective, which could scarcely be appealed to to offer the consolations that myth criticism had promised us.

On the other hand, as I stated previously, we can scarcely hope to read *Ulysses* as though it were called something else. I would suggest, then, that we displace the act or the operation of interpretation itself. The Odyssey parallel can then be seen as one of the organisational frameworks of the narrative text: but it is not itself the interpretation of that narrative, as the ideologues of myth have thought. Rather it is itself—qua organisational framework—what remains to be interpreted. In itself, the Odyssey parallel—like so much of that tradition of the classical pastiche from Cocteau or even from *La Belle Hélène* all the way to Giraudoux or Sartre or even John Updike—functions as wit: a matching operation is demanded of us as readers, in which the fit of the modern detail to its classical overtext is admired for its elegance and economy, as when, in *Ulysses*, Odysseus' long separation from Penelope is evoked in terms of a ten-year period of coitus interruptus or anal intercourse between the partners of the Bloom household. You will agree, however, that the establishment of the parallel is scarcely a matter of interpretation—that is, no fresh meaning is conferred either on the classical Homeric text, nor on the practices of contemporary birth control, by the matching of these two things.

Genuine interpretation is something other than this, and involves the radical historisation of the form itself: what is to be interpreted is then the historical necessity for this very peculiar and complex textual structure or reading operation in the first place. We can make a beginning on this,

I think, by evoking the philosophical concept, but also the existential experience, called "contingency." Something seems to have happened at a certain point in modern times to the old unproblematic meaning of things, or to what we could call the content of experience; and this particular event is as so often first most tangibly detectable and visible on the aesthetic level. There is something like a crisis of detail, in which we may, in the course of our narrative, need a house for our characters to sleep in, a room in which they may converse, but nothing is there any longer to justify our choice of this particular house rather than that other, or this particular room, furniture, view, and the like. It is a very peculiar dilemma, which Barthes described as well as anyone else, when he accounted for the fundamental experience of the modern or of modernity in terms of something like a dissociation between meaning and existence:

> The pure and simple "representation" of the "real," the naked account of "what is" (or what has been), thus proves to resist meaning; such resistance reconfirms the great mythic opposition between the vécu, [that is, the experiential or what the existentialists called "lived experience"] and the intelligible; we have only to recall how, in the ideology of our time, the obsessional evocation of the de jure exclusion, what lives is structurally incapable of sciences, of literature, of social practices, is always staged as an aggressive arm against meaning, as though, by some de jure exclusion, what lives is structurally incapable of carrying a meaning—and vice versa.

One would only want to correct this account by adding that the living, life, vitalism, is also an ideology, as it is appropriate to observe for Joyce himself more generally; but on the whole Barthes's opposition between what exists and what means allows us to make sense of a whole range of formal strategies within what we call the high modernisms; these range clearly all the way from the dematerialisation of the work of art (Virginia Woolf's attack on naturalism, Gide's omission of the description of people and things, the emergence of an ideal of the "pure" novel, on the order of "pure poetry") to the practice of symbolism itself, which involves the illicit transformation of existing things into so many visible or tangible meanings. I believe that today, whatever our own aesthetic faults or blinkers, we have learned this particular lesson fairly well: and that for us, any art which practices symbolism is already discredited and worthless before the fact. A long experience of the classical modernisms has finally taught us the bankruptcy of the symbolic in literature; we demand something more from artists than this facile affirmation that the existent also means, that things are also symbols. But this is very precisely why I am anxious to rescue Joyce from the exceedingly doubtful merit of being called a symbolic writer.

Yet before I try to describe what is really going on in the text of "Ulysses," let me do something Barthes did not care to do, in the passage I quoted, and designate the historical reasons for that modernist crisis, that dissociation of the existent and the meaningful, that intense experience of contingency in question here. We must explain this experience historically because it is not at all evident, and particularly not in the ideological perspective—existential or Nietzschean—which is that of Roland Barthes, among many others, and for which the discovery of the absurd and of the radical contingency and meaninglessness of our object world is simply the result of the increasing lucidity and self-consciousness of human beings in a post-religious, secular, scientific age.

But in previous societies (or modes of production) it was Nature that was meaningless or anti-human. What is paradoxical about the historical experience of modernism is that it designates very precisely that period in which Nature—or the in- or anti-human—is everywhere in the process of being displaced or destroyed, expunged, eliminated, by the achievements of human praxis and human production. The great modernist literature—from Baudelaire and Flaubert to *Ulysses* and beyond—is a city literature: its object is therefore the anti-natural, the humanised, par excellence, a landscape which is everywhere the result of human labour, in which everything—including the formerly natural, grass, trees, our own bodies—is finally produced by human beings. This is then the historical paradox with which the experience of contingency confronts us (along with its ideologies—existentialism and nihilism—and its aesthetics—modernism): how can the city be meaningless? How can human production be felt to be absurd or contingent, when in another sense one would think it was only human labour which created genuine meaning in the first place?

Yet it is equally obvious that the experience of contingency is a real or "objective" one, and not merely a matter of illusion or false consciousness (although it is that too). The missing step here—the gap between the fact of the human production of reality in modern times and the experience of the results or products of that production as meaningless—this essential mediation is surely to be located in the work process itself, whose organisation does not allow the producers to grasp their relationship to the final product; as well as in the market system, which does not allow the consumer to grasp the product's origins in collective production. I am assuming, rightly or wrongly, that I do not have to insert a general lecture on alienation and reification, on the dynamics of capital and the nature of exchange value, at this point: I do want to dwell at somewhat greater length on one of the basic forms taken by reification as a process, and that is what can be called the analytical fragmentation of older organic or at least indigenous or traditional processes. Such fragmentation can be seen on any number of levels: on that of the labour process first of all, where the older unities of handicraft production are broken up and "taylorised" into the meaningless yet efficient segments of mass industrial production; on that of the psyche or psychological subject, now broken up into a host of radically different mental functions, some of which—those of measurement and rational calculation—are privileged and others—the perceptual senses and aesthetic generally—are marginalised; on that of time, experience, and storytelling, all of which are inexorably atomised and broken down into their most minimal unities, into that well-known "heap of fragments where the sun beats"; the fragmentation, finally, of the older hierarchical communities, neighbourhoods, and organic groups themselves, which, with the penetration of the money and market system, are systemically dissolved into relations of equivalent individuals, "free but equal" monads, isolated subjects equally free to sell their labour power, yet living side by side in a merely additive way within those great agglomerations which are the modern cities. It is incidentally this final form of reification which accounts, be it said in passing, for the inadequacy of that third conventional interpretation of Ulysses mentioned above, namely the fetishisation of the text in terms of "archetypal" patterns of father-son relationships, the quest for the ideal father or for the lost son, and so forth. But surely today, after so much prolonged scrutiny of the nuclear family, it has become apparent that the obsession with these relationships and the privileging of such improverished interpersonal schemas drawn from the nuclear family itself are to be read as break-down products and as defence mechanisms against the loss of the knowable community. The efforts of Edward Said and others to demonstrate the omnipresence of such familial schemes in modern narrative should surely not be taken as an affirmation of the ultimate primacy of such relationships, but rather exactly the reverse, as sociopathology and as diagnosis of the improverishment of human relations which results from the destruction of the older forms of the collective. The father-son relationships in Ulysses are all miserable failures, above all others the mythical ultimate "meeting" between Bloom and Stephen; and if more is wanted on this particular theme, one might read into the record here the diatribes against the very notion of an Oedipus complex developed in Deleuze and Guattari's Anti-Oedipus, which I do not necessarily endorse but which should surely be enough to put an end to this particular interpretive temptation.

But the psychoanalytic or Oedipal interpretation was itself only a subset of the *Odyssey* parallel or mythological temptation, to which, after this digression, I promised to return. What I wanted to suggest about the kind of reading determined by the *Odyssey* parallel in *Ulysses* is that this parallelism, and the kind of matching it encourages between the two levels of written and over-text, functions as something like an empty form. Like the classical unities, it offers a useful but wholly extrinsic set of limits against which the writer works, and which serve as a purely mechanical check on what risks otherwise becoming an infinite proliferation of detail. The point is that, as we suggested a moment ago, the older traditional narrative unities have disappeared, been destroyed in the process of universal fragmentation: the organic unity of the narrative can thus no longer serve as a symbol for the unity of experience, nor as a formal limit on the production of narrative sentences: the single day—that overarching formal unity of *Ulysses*—is a meaningful unit neither in human experience nor in narrative itself. But at that point, if what used to be experience, human destiny and the like, is shattered into such components as taking a walk at lunchtime from your place of business to a restaurant, buying a cake of soap, or having a drink, or visiting a patient in a hospital—each of these components being then in itself infinitely subdivisible—then there is absolutely no guarantee that the transformation of these segments into narrative sentences might not be infinitely extended and indeed last forever. The *Odyssey* parallel helps avoid this unwelcome development and sets just such external limits, which ultimately become those of Joyce's minimal units of composition—the individual chapters themselves.

But what I wanted to show you was that alongside the type of reading encouraged by the mythic parallels—which I have called a matching up— there is a rather different form of reading which resists that one in all kinds of ways, and ends up subverting it. This is a type of reading which interrupts the other, consecutive kind, and moves forward and backwards across the text in a cumulative search for the previous mention or the reference to come: as Kenner and others have pointed out, it is a type of reading, a mental operation, peculiarly inconceivable before printing, before numbered pages, and more particularly before the institutionalisation of those unusual objects called dictionaries or encyclopedias. Now one is tempted to assimilate this kind of reading to the more customary thematic or thematising kind, where we compile lists of recurrent motifs, such as types of imagery, obsessive words or terms, peculiar gestures or emotional reactions; but this is not at all what happens in *Ulysses*, where the object of the cross-referencing activity is always an event: taking old Mrs. Riordan for a walk, the borrowed pair of tight trousers worn by Ben Dollard at a memorable concert, or the assassination in Phoenix Park twenty-two years before. This is to say that these seemingly thematic motifs are here always referential: for they designate content beyond the text, beyond indeed the capacity of any of the given textual variants to express or exhaust them. In such cross-referencing, indeed, one can say that the referent itself is produced, as something which transcends every conceivable textualisation of it. The appropriate analogy might be with the return of characters in Balzac's *Comédie humaine*, where the varying status of a given character—the hero in one novel, a character actor in a second, a mere extra in a third and part of an enumeration of names in a fourth—tends effectively to destabilise each of the narrative forms in question, and to endow them all with a transcendental dimension on which they open so many relative perspectives.

What I want to suggest is that the analogous recurrence of events and characters throughout *Ulysses* can equally be understood as a process whereby the text itself is unsettled and undermined, a process whereby the universal tendency of its terms, narrative tokens, representations, to solidify into an achieved and codified symbolic order as well as a massive narrative surface, is perpetually suspended. I will call this process "dereification," and I first want to describe its operation in terms of the city itself. The classical city is not a collection of buildings, nor even a collection of people living on top of one another; nor is it even mainly or primarily a collection of pathways, of the trajectories of people through those buildings or that urban space, although that gets us a little closer to it. No, the classical city, one would think—it always being understood that we are now talking about something virtually extinct, in the age of the suburb or megalopolis or the private car—the classical city is defined essentially by the nodal points at which all those pathways and trajectories meet, or which they traverse: points of totalisation, we may call them, which make shared experience possible, and also the storage of experience and information, which are in short something like a synthesis of the object (place) and the subject (population), focal points not unlike those possibilities of unifying perspectives and images which Kevin Lynch has identified as the signs and emblems of the successful, the non-alienating city.

But to talk about the city in this way, spatially, by identifying the collective transit points and roundabouts of temple and agora, pub and post office, park and cemetery, is not yet to identify the mediation whereby these spatial forms are at one with collective experience. Unsurprisingly that mediation will have to be linguistic, yet it will have to define a kind of speech which is neither uniquely private nor forbiddingly standardised in an impersonal public form, a type of discourse in which the same, in which repetition, is transmitted again and again through a host of eventful variations, each of which has its own value. That discourse is called gossip: and from the upper limits of city life—the world of patronage, machine politics, and the rise and fall of ward leaders—all the way down to the most minute aberrations of private life, it is by means of gossip and through the form of the anecdote that the dimensions of the city are maintained within humane limits and that the unity of city life is affirmed and celebrated. This is already the case with the ur-form of the city which is the village itself, as John Berger tell us in *Pig Earth*:

> The function of this gossip which, in fact, is close, oral, daily history, is to allow the whole village to define itself. . . . The village . . . is a living portrait of itself: a communal portrait, in that everybody is portrayed and everybody portrays. As with the carvings on the capitals in a Romanesque church, there is an identity of spirit between what is shown and how it is shown—as if the portrayed were also the carvers. Every village's portrait of itself is constructed, however, not out of stone, but out of words, spoken and remembered: out of opinions, stories, eye-witness reports, legends, comments and hearsay. And it is a continuous portrait: work on it never stops. Until very recently the only material available to a village and its peasants for defining themselves was their own spoken words. . . . Without such a portrait—and the gossip which is its raw material—the village would have been forced to doubt its own existence.

So in that great village which is Joyce's Dublin, Parnell is still an anecdote about a hat knocked off, picked up and returned, not yet a television image nor even a name in a newspaper; and by the same token, as in the peasant village itself, the ostensibly private or personal—Molly's infidelities, or Mr. Bloom's urge to discover how far the Greek sculptors went in portraying the female anatomy—all these things are public too, and the material for endless gossip and anecdotal transmission.

Now for a certain conservative thought, and for that heroic fascism of the 1920s for which the so-called "masses" and their standardised city life had become the very symbol of everything degraded about modern life, gossip—Heidegger will call it *"das Gerede"*—is stigmatised as the very language of authenticity, of that empty and stereotypical talking *pour rien dire* to which these ideologues oppose the supremely private and individual speech of the death anxiety or the heroic choice. But Joyce—a radical neither in the left-wing nor the reactionary sense—was at least a populist and a plebeian. "I don't know why the communists don't like me," he complained once, "I've never written about anything but common people."

Indeed, from the class perspective, Joyce had no more talent for or interest in the representation of aristocrats than Dickens; and no more experience with working-class people or with peasants than Balzac (Beckett is indeed a far sounder guide to the Irish countryside or rural slum than the essentially urban Joyce.) In class terms, then, Joyce's characters are all resolutely petty-bourgeois: what gives this apparent limitation its representative value and its strength is the colonial situation itself. Whatever his hostility to Irish cultural nationalism, Joyce's is the epic of the metropolis under imperialism, in which the development of bourgeoisie and proletariat alike is stunted to the benefit of a national petty-bourgeoisie: indeed, precisely these rigid constraints imposed by imperialism on the development of human energies account for the symbolic displacement and flowering of the latter in elo-quence, rhetoric and oratorical language of all kinds; symbolic practices not particularly essential either to businessmen or to working classes, but highly prized in precapitalist societies and preserved, as in a time capsule, in *Ulysses* itself. And this is the moment to rectify our previous account of the city and to observe that if *Ulysses* is also for us the classical, the supreme representation of something like the Platonic idea of city life, this is also partly due to the fact that Dublin is not exactly the full-blown capitalist metropolis, but like the Paris of Flaubert, still regressive, still distantly akin to the village, still un- or under-developed enough to be representable, thanks to the domination of its foreign masters.

Now it is time to say what part gossip plays in the process of what I have called dereification, or indeed in that peculiar network of cross-references which causes us to read *Ulysses* backwards and forwards like a handbook. Gossip is indeed the very element in which reference—or, if you prefer, the "referent" itself—expands and contracts, ceaselessly trans-formed from a mere token, a notation, a short-hand object, back into a full-dress narrative. People as well as things are the reified markers of such potential story-telling: and what for a high realism was the substantiality of character, of the individual ego, is here equally swept away into a flux of anecdotes—proper names on the one hand, an intermittent store of gossip on the other. But the process is to be sure more tangible and more dramatic when we see it at work on physical things: the statues, the com-modities in the shopwindows, the clanking trollylines that link Dublin to its suburbs (which dissolve, by way of Mr. Deasy's anxieties about foot-and-mouth disease, into Mr. Bloom's fantasy projects for tramlines to move cattle to the docks); or the three-master whose silent grace and respectability as an image is at length dissolved into the disreputable reality of its garrulous and yarn-spinning crewman; or, to take a final example, that file of sandwichmen whose letters troop unevenly through the text, seeming to move towards that ultimate visual reification fantasised by Mr. Bloom virtually in analogue to Mallarmé's "livre":

> Of some one sole unique advertisement to cause passers to stop in wonder, a poster novelty, with all extraneous accretions excluded, reduced to its simplest and most efficient terms not exceeding the span of casual vision and congruous with the velocity of modern life.

The visual, the spatially visible, the image, is, as has been observed, the final form of the commodity itself, the ultimate terminus of reification. Yet even so strikingly reified a datum as the sandwichboard ad is once again effortlessly dereified and dissolved when, on his way to the cabman's shelter, Stephen hears a down-and-out friend observe: "I'd carry a sandwichboard only the girl in the office told me they're full up for the next threee weeks, man. God, you've to book ahead!" Suddenly the exotic picture-postcard vision of a tourist Dublin is transformed back into the dreary familiar reality of jobs and contracts and the next meal: yet this is not necessarily a dreary prospect; rather it opens up a perspective in which, at some ideal outside limit, everything seemingly material and solid in Dublin itself can presumably be dissolved back into the underlying reality of human relations and human praxis.

Yet the ambulatory letters of the sandwichmen are also the very emblem of textuality itself, and this is the moment to say the price *Ulysses* must pay for the seemingly limitless power of its play of reification and dereification; the moment, in other words, to come to terms with Joyce's modernism. Stated baldly, that price is radical depersonalisation, or in other words, Joyce's completion of Flaubert's programme of removing the author from the text—a programme which also removes the reader, and finally that unifying and organising mirage or aftermirage of both author and reader which is the "character," or better still, "point of view." What happens at that point can perhaps oversimply be described this way: such essentially idealistic (or ideal, or imaginary) categories formerly served as the supports for the unity of the work or the unity of the process. Now that they have been withdrawn, only a form of material unity is left, namely the printed book itself, and its material unity as a bound set of pages within which the cross-references mentioned above are contained. One of the classic definitions of modernism is of course the increasing sense of the materiality of the medium itself (whether in instrumental timbre or oil painting), the emergent foregrounding of the medium in its materiality. It is paradoxical, of course, to evoke the materiality of language; and as for the materiality of print or script, that particular material medium is surely a good deal less satisfying or gratifying in a sensory, perceptual way than the materials of oil paint or of orchestral coloration; none the less, the role of the book itself is functionally analogous, in Joyce, to the materialist dynamics of the other arts.

Now in one sense textualisation may be seen as a form or subset of reification itself; but if so, it is a unique type of reification, which unbinds fully as much as it fixes or crystallises. They may, indeed, offer the most appropriate contemporary way of dealing with the phenomena Joseph Frank described in his now classical essay as "spatial form." I am thinking, for instance, of the moment in which a remarkable and ingenious method for cabling news of the Phoenix Park murders across the Atlantic is described: the reporter takes an ad (Mr. Bloom's "one sole unique advertisement") and uses its spatial features to convey the trajectory of the killers and the map of the assassination. This is to institute a peculiarly fluid relationship between the visually reified and the historically eventful, since here these categories pass ceaselessly back and forth into one another.

The climax of this development is in many ways reached in the Nighttown section, itself a prolongation of that comparable movement and outer limit reached by Flaubert in *La Tentation de Saint Antoine*. Indeed, had we more time, it would have been pleasant to discuss the peculiar representational space generated by these two "reading plays," these two seeming eruptions and intrusions of a properly theatrical space in that very different space—no matter how experimental—of narrative or novelistic representation. I think we would have been able to show that this new space, with its ostensibly theatrical form (scenic indications, character attributions, printed speeches, notations of expression), has nothing to do with the closure of traditional theatrical representation; far more to do, indeed, with that space of hallucination in terms of which Flaubert often described his own creative processes, and which, in *Saint Antoine*, he represents as follows:

> And suddenly there move across the empty air first a puddle of water, then a prostitute, the edge of a temple, a soldier's face, a chariot drawn by two white horses rearing. These images arrive abruptly, jerkily, detached against the night like scarlet paintings on ebony. Their movement grows more rapid. They follow each other at a dizzying rate. At other times, they come to a halt and gradually waning, melt away; or else they fly off, and others take their place at once.

Hallucinatory experience of this kind can be described, in the language of Gestalt psychology, as the perception of forms without background, forms

or figures sundered from their ground or context, and passing discontin-
uously across the field of vision in a lateral movement, as though somehow
on this side and nearer than the objects of the visible world. The instability
of space or experience of this kind lies in the failure of the discrete or
isolated image to generate any background or depth, any worldness in which
it can take root. On the printed page, this essentially means that the ground,
the anticipatory-retrospective texture, of narrative—what Greimas calls its
isotopies, its ana- and cata-phoric relationships—is ruptured: it therefore
falls to the typographic and material mechanisms of theatrical and scenic
directions to bind (or rebind) these discontinuous images together. Typography thus becomes an event within the text among others. Or, if you
prefer, since it is the reified sense of the visual which has here been solocited
and stimulated, this sense will now begin to function as it were in the void,
taking as its object the material signifiers, the printed words themselves,
and no longer the latter's signifieds or representations or meanings.

At any rate, this peculiar climax of *Ulysses* in the seeming immediacy
of a theatrical representation which is in reality the unmediated experience
of the printed book will now help us to understand two kinds of things:
the peculiarly anticlimactic nature of the chapters that follow it (I'm getting
to them, at last!), and the ground on which the depersonalised textualisation of the narrative of *Ulysses* takes place, what one is tempted to call a
kind of "autistic textualisation," the production of sentences in a void,
moments in which the book begins to elaborate its own text, under its own
momentum, with no further need of characters, point of view, author or
perhaps even reader:

> Mr. Bloom reached Essex bridge. Yes, Mr. Bloom crossed bridge of Yessex.
>
> Love loves to love love. Nurse loves the new chemist. Constable 14A
> loves Mary Kelly. Gerty MacDowell loves the boy that has the bicycle.
> M.B. loves a fair gentleman. Li Chi Han lovey up kissy Cha Pu Chow.
> Jumbo, the elephant, loves Alice, the elephant. Old Mr. Verschoyle with
> the ear trumpet loves old Mrs. Verschoyle with the turnedin eye. . . .
> You love a certain person. And this person loves that other person because
> everybody loves something but God loves everybody.

The point I want to make about passages like these, and they are everywhere
in *Ulysses*, is that "point of view" theory does not take on them, nor any
conceivable notion of the Implied Author, unless the I.A. is an imbecile
or a schizophrenic. No one is speaking these words or thinking them: they
are simply one would want to say, printed sentences.

And this will be my transition to the two most boring chapters of
Ulysses, and thence to a close. Because what happens in the Eumaeus

chapter is that, so to speak, Joyce lapses back into more traditional narrative "point of view": that is, for the first time in *Ulysses* we once again get the "he thought/she thought" form of indirect discourse, what I will call the third person indistinct, and henceforth conventional belief in that central reflective consciousness which is both appropriate and ironic in the chapter in which Bloom and Stephen are finally able to sit down together, two closed or solipsistic monads projecting that most boring theme of our own time, namely "lack of communication." Indeed, I am tempted to say, judging from the sentence structure, the elaborate periphrases, the use of occasional foreign expressions as well as cautiously isolated "colloquial" ones, that this chapter really constitutes Joyce's attempt at a parody or pastiche of a writer he had no particular sympathy or respect for, namely Henry James. (If so, it is not a very good pastiche, and only our supreme belief in Joyce's power of mimicry, in his ability to do anything stylistically, has prevented us from noticing it.) Or better still, this chapter deploys the stylistic mannerisms of Henry James in order to record a social and psychological content characteristic, rather, of James's enemy brother and archetypal rival, H. G. Wells—that is, an essentially petty-bourgeois content whose comfortable fit with the Jamesian narrative apparatus is somehow humiliating for both of them and sends both off back to back, as though their well-known differences on the form and function of the novel were less the taking of incompatible positions than—to use a more contemporary expression—mere variants within a single problematic, the problematic of the centred subject, of the closed monad, of the isolated or privatised subjectivity. The theory and practice of narrative "point of view," as we associate it with Henry James, is not simply the result of a metaphysical option, a personal obsession, nor even a technical development in the history of form (although it is obviously also all those things): point of view is rather the quasi-material expression of a fundamental social development itself, namely the increasing social fragmentation and monadisation of late capitalist society, the intensifying privatisation and isolation of its subjects.

We have already touched on one aspect of this development—reification—which can now be characterised in another way, as the increasing separation, under capitalism, between the private and the public, between the personal and the political, between leisure and work, psychology and science, poetry and prose, or to put it all in a nutshell, between the subject and the object. The centred but psychologised subject and the reified object are indeed the respective orientations of these two concluding chapters, "Eumaeus" and "Ithaca": and it is as though Joyce meant here to force us to work through in detail everything that is intolerable about this opposition. What we have been calling boredom is not Joyce's failure, then, but rather his success, and is the signal whereby we ourselves as organisms register a situation but also forms that are finally stifling for us.

This is perhaps a little easier to show in the Ithaca or catechism sequence: the format—question and answer—is not really, I think, a return to the experimentation—better still, the textualisation—of the earlier chapters. It is rather that quite different thing—the construction of a form of discourse from which the subject—sender or receiver—is radically excluded: a form of discourse, in other words, that would be somehow radically objective, if that were really possible. And if it is observed that even this seemingly sterilised alternation of question and answer turns increasingly, towards the end of the chapter, around Mr. Bloom's private thoughts and fantasies, in other words, around the subjective rather than the objective, then I will reply by noting the degree to which those fantasies, Mr. Bloom's "Bovaryism" (tactfully called "ambition" by Joyce), are henceforth inextricably bound up with objects, in the best consumer society tradition. These are falsely subjective fantasies: here, in reality, commodities are dreaming about themselves through us.

These two final Bloom chapters, then, pose uncomfortable problems, and not least about narrative itself: the subjective or point-of-view chapter, "Eumaeus," asks us why we should be interested in stories about private individuals any longer, given the extraordinary relativisation of all individual experience, and the transformation of its contents into so many purely psychological reactions. Meanwhile, the objective chapter, "Ithaca," completes an infinite subdivision of the objective contents of narrative, breaking "events" into their smallest material components and asking whether, in that form, they still have any interest whatsoever. Two men have a discussion over cocoa, and that may be interesting at a pinch: but what about the act of putting the kettle on to boil—that is a part of the same event, but is it still interesting? The elaborate anatomy of the process of boiling water is boring in three senses of the word: (1) it is essentially non-narrative; (2) it is inauthentic, in the sense in which these mass-produced material instruments (unlike Homer's spears and shields) cannot be said to be organic parts of their users' destinies; finally, (3) these objects are contingent and meaningless in their instrumental form, they are recuperable for literature only at the price of being transformed into symbols. Such passages thus ask three questions:

1. Why do we need narrative anyway? What are stories and what is our existential relation to them? Is a non-narrative relationship to the world and to Being possible?

2. What kind of lives are we leading and what kind of world are we living them in, if the objects that surround us are all somehow external, extrinsic, alienated from us? (It is a question about the simulacra of industrial society, essentially a question about the city, but in this form at least as old as the interrogation of the "wholeness" of Greek culture by German romanticism.)

3. (A question I have already raised but which remains seemingly unanswered, namely) How can the products of human labour have come to be felt as meaningless or contingent?

Yet to this last question at least, Joyce's form has a kind of answer, and it is to be found in that great movement of dereification I have already invoked, in which the whole dead grid of the object world of greater Dublin is, in the catechism chapter, finally, disalienated and by the most subterranean detours traced back—less to its origins in Nature, than to the transformation of Nature by human and collective praxis deconcealed. So to the vitalist ideology of Molly's better-known final affirmation, I tend rather to prefer this one:

> What did Bloom do at the range?
> He removed the saucepan to the left hob, rose and carried the iron kettle to the sink in order to tap the current by turning the faucet to let it flow.
> Did it flow?
> Yes. From Roundwood reservoir in country Wicklow of a cubic capacity of 2,400 million gallons, percolating through a subterranean aqueduct of filter mains of single and double pipeage constructed at an initial plant cost of £5 per linear yard. . . .

RAYMOND WILLIAMS

"Exiles"

The play *Exiles* has usually proved difficult for students of Joyce, and especially for those who are interested in the innovatory fictional methods which are of course his major achievement. I said most of what I thought could be said about the play in an essay written in 1947, though then as now not looking at the marginal and speculative relations between the play and Joyce's life and biography. But there is still one point which I would like to try to take further, and I can begin from a sentence in that earlier essay which I do not now, in terms, agree with. I wrote then:

> The result of the words of the play is not an experience formally different in kind from that of Joyce's more famous work.

Read in context this can be taken as what I still believe to be true, that the theme of *Exiles* is very close to, indeed integral with, the themes of the major fiction. Yet though I then went on to discuss some of the differences between dramatic and fictional writing, which I think ought to be our central concern, I limited this emphasis by running the two points together: on the one hand "the words of the play" and "formally different"; on the other hand "the result of the words of the play" and "an experience formally different." What I now want to move to, in clearer terms, is a consideration of the radical differences in formal composition. At the broadest level of theme the earlier descriptions as "result" and "experience" can still, in general, stand. But the immediate results, as I shall try to show, are more radically different than I then began to indicate. Moreover, the point has some wider importance in the matter of relations between dramatic and fictional writing, and their analysis.

From *James Joyce: New Perspectives.* Copyright © 1982 by The Harvester Press.

The central formal point is that in dramatic composition the writing of speech is a virtually total and explicit mode. Indications of certain actions may also be written, but as instruction for performance rather than words to be performed. Thus, speech is radically separated from anything in the nature of general narrative, analysis or commentary. But while this is necessarily true, at the most general level of dramatic composition, it is also true that the composition of words to be spoken in performance must not be reduced, as it is within the assumptions of naturalist drama, to the simple representation of speech, in the sense of words exchanged between characters in the course of represented behaviour. On the contrary, in conventions as various as the chorus of Greek drama, the messengers narrating other events in Greek and Elizabethan drama, the soliloquy over its range from local and private address to its most developed forms in the speaking of "unspoken" or "indirected" thought, and many other formal methods, the dramatic composition of speech includes functions which in more modern forms have been separated out as, in drama, the representation of direct speech between characters, and, in fiction, the enclosure of such representations within authorial narrative, analysis and commentary. It was of course within these conditions of separation and specialisation that Joyce was beginning to write.

We can then look back for a moment at the beginning of Joyce's idea of "epiphanies," in *Stephen Hero*:

> By an epiphany he meant a sudden spiritual manifestation, whether in the vulgarity of speech or of gesture or in a memorable phase of the mind itself.

"Speech or gesture," but the examples he gives are of speech. Then at once in recording them (and I think we have to say that they must have meant more to him than they now can to us) he starts writing what is in effect a fragment of text of a modern play:

> The Young Lady—(drawling discreetly) . . . O, yes . . . I was . . . at the . . . cha . . . pel. . . .
> The Young Gentleman—(inaudibly) . . . I . . . (again inaudibly) . . . I . . . .
> The Young Lady—(softly) . . . O . . . but you're . . . ve . . . ry wick . . . ed. . . .

The bracketed characterisations of tone are derived from the form of a play-text as this stabilised, under new conditions, in the nineteenth century, with some evident influence from the novel. The bracketed direction can read, there, as an indication to actor or director, though in practice they are more often indications to the *reader*, providing a minimal further characterisation, beyond the spoken words, of a kind now familiar from fiction.

Yet indeed there is already a further problem, not to say confusion, for one of Joyce's characterisations is "inaudibly," which is across the line from any dramatic writing of speech, into the different mode of fictional representation, which can include the inaudible or the fully unspoken.

Now it is a misunderstanding of high naturalist drama, in say Ibsen or early Strindberg or Chekhov, to suppose that they repressed all functions of speech or of dramatic writing other than the representation of probable conversation between persons in everyday behaviour. Indeed one of the basic themes of this major drama is the unresolved tension between what has happened or is happening and what can be spoken about. Rejecting the conventions of theatrical speech, as these had stabilised and ossified in the dominant intrigue drama, the new dramatists entered an area of conscious tension, at one level between what needed to be said and what, within specific social, limitations, could actually be said; at another level between what people wanted to say and the different objectivities of need and limitation. Thus we find the unusual and widely misunderstood phenomenon of a prolonged working within the forms of everyday speech which is at the same time a profound if unfinished critique of the state of being which these at once represent and misrepresent. From *Ghosts* and *Rosmersholm* and *The Wild Duck* to *John Gabriel Borkman* and *Little Eyolf*, Ibsen at once wrought these speech forms, in a newly concentrated intensity, and set them in tension with an only ever partly articulated dimension of otherness—other modes of being and of desire, indicated beyond the dramatic action rather than represented within it. Strindberg, from *Lady Julie* onwards, expressed a comparable tension by including forms of physical action and visual presence which more directly dramatised a destructive interaction, while in the method of "contrapuntal" dialogue—a loosening of speech from simple fixed identity with characters, a composition of speech as both voluntary and involuntary relationship—he began to find ways of presenting rather than simply representing a flow of interactive experience. Chekhov, following Ibsen in the indication of a general dimension of otherness, from *The Seagull* to *The Cherry Orchard*, developed in his later plays what I have called the dialogue of a "negative group": a composition of units of everyday speech into a shared failure of communications. All this is very different from what later became known as "naturalist dialogue," in the drama of the naturalist habit, in which what is represented as said is taken as all that can or needs to be said: an unproblematic medium, through which character and action appear.

Those who are surprised by Joyce's close attention to Ibsen, through so much of his writing life, have been misled by the formulations and practice of the naturalist habit and have failed to see, beyond it, the directly connecting preoccupation with levels of being and communication and with the problems of writing them. Moreover, in Joyce as in Ibsen, there is a conscious relation between these general problems and a pervading sense of a network of illusions, self-deceptions, deceptions of others, and lies. It is in this sense, strengthened by certain structural similarities between situations of the Norwegian and the Irish writer—an autonomy of craft and conviction within the simultaneous rejection of both the local subordinated and the wider dominant cultures—that it is no surprise to find Joyce recording "the spirit of Ibsen" blowing "through him like a keen wind."

But what is then really surprising is that when he came to write his play, Joyce selected a more singular mode. In effect none of the devices of disturbance, dislocation or limitation of speech, none of the indications of unarticulated modes of being and desire beyond its specific and structurally limited forms, is attempted. Of course Joyce does not then rest on the representation of everyday speech as itself. He moves, instead, in a quite different direction, to forms of mutual self-presentation, in a rhetorical and even declamatory mode. Standing right back, we can observe the cold clash of egos which such a mode sustains. We can see, clearly enough, at once the centrality of the drive to an assertion of exiled identity, and the registered consequences of this drive on others who still seek and need relationship while this deliberate distancing occurs. Thematically there is no problem: the need and the loss are very precisely defined. But then the precision of the definition is in its own way an obstacle to recognition of the substance of what is being defined. It is a linguistic mode of enclosure and presentation, not of exploration.

> ROBERT: . . . There was an eternity before we were born: another will come after we are dead. The blinding instant of passion alone—passion, free, unashamed, irresistible—that is the only gate by which we can escape from the misery of what slaves call life. Is not this the language of your own youth that I heard so often from you in this very place where we are sitting now? Have you changed?
>
> RICHARD [Passes his hand across his brow]: Yes. It is the language of my youth.

This is, paradoxically, the language of dramatic declamation which in their different ways Ibsen, Strindberg and Chekhov at once rejected and complicated. It is the language of the predominant actor-manager, "self-exiled in upon his ego." The major naturalist dramatists had profoundly destabilised this kind of assurance. Such declarations were still made, but within a dramatic context which interrogated, indicated or undercut them. It is true that the persons of *Exiles* fail to communicate, though the strict form of this is more local, unfortunately echoing Joyce's misleading definition of drama as "the form wherein [the artist] sets forth his image in immediate relations to others." The assertion of singularity is an inescapably negative form: the immediate relations are cancellations and avoidances. But this persistent and central theme is enclosed, rather than embodied, in the conscious singularity of the language.

This is then the point about formal difference. The play is written as words spoken between persons in a prescribed and limited locality. It excludes virtually all other forms of dramatic action and dramatic speech. Singular characters are isolated, within their own presumed resourcces, in a deliberately limited and locally represented time and space. The disturbing indications of incompleteness, the internal interrogations of these local assurances, which were present in the major naturalist drama and which Joyce explored and embodied in quite new ways in his innovatory fiction, are in *Exiles* overridden by explication, argument and conscious exchange.

In terms of its period, this can be made a contrast between dramatic and fictional modes of writing. It is still an open question whether the necessary processes of interrogation and disturbance can be adequately re-alised by the devices of indication, faults between levels, internal negations and incompletenesses which major naturalist drama relied on, and which have since been erected into whole forms, discarding the more recognisably naturalist ballast and then often, in fact, losing the essential tension. But in fiction these modes were more immediately accessible, in various devices of narrative, analysis and commentary, but just as clearly, in Joyce, in specific transformations of the conventions of speech, place and time. When we come now to analyse dramatic language we can readily observe the differences between this fictional range and what can be made to appear, as in *Exiles*, represented speech which stands alone. In the practices of a specific period this is an adequate working distinction. But more generally it is inadequate. It is not only in the most obvious examples from earlier drama, such as the storm scenes in *Lear* or the soliloquies in *Hamlet*, but also more generally in that writing of actions in which speech is a dominant mode but then speech of many kinds, with operational variations in level, direction and address, that we find, inescapably, different essential forms of the language of drama. These need to be analysed beyond the functions of representation and exchange, setting forth character and action in sin-gular forms, to which both much modern criticism and most modern the-atrical practice have tended to reduce dramatic writing. We should be especially able to go beyond this if we extend formal comparisons beyond the cases of drama and fiction, into the now major evidence of film com-position, which bears very closely on just these problems and solutions.

But we shall not get there from *Exiles*, except negatively. The play effects its exchanges, defines its singularities, at a point of temporary stasis, at once after and before adequate conventions of complexity and mobility. The moment of "epiphany" is not realised but transcribed, and is then not manifestation but exposition. The play achieved its deliberately localised effect, but it is ironic, reading or watching it, to find Joyce in temporary exile from the place he made his home: the area not of representing but of transforming practice.

GABRIELE SCHWAB

Mollyoquy

Molly Bloom has been subjected to
a great deal of psychological criticism; to be more precise, *male* psychological
criticism. As a result, the history of her critical reception has turned out
to be more a documentation of male fears and wishes regarding women
than an analysis of her character limited strictly to textual considerations.

My objective here is to point out not only some of the different
possibilities but also some of the limitations of psychoanalytical criticism.
My main interest does not lie in an analysis of Molly's character as it is
portrayed in the manifest text. Instead I want to show the way one could
speak of the "unconscious" of a literary figure, which is presented in the
textural form of an interior monologue. I will attempt to demonstrate how
one can approach Molly's "unconscious," even though all that is in the
text is her "conscious" utterance.

I would like to examine a short passage in light of the analytical
principles of Freud's *Interpretation of Dreams*. One of the most striking
aesthetic achievements of the Penelope chapter lies in the fact that the
strategies of the manifest text always signal an implicit dimension of "unconscious meaning" comparable to the latent meaning of a dream or of free
association.

Taking place at night just before going to sleep, when the need for
daily censorship is reduced, Molly's monologue is such a highly suggestive
text, so full of condensed intratextual associations and fragmentary allusions
to her past, that the reader reacts unconsciously to Molly's implied "unconscious." This reaction is reinforced by strategies that reveal to him,

From *The Seventh of Joyce*. Copyright © 1982 by Indiana University Press.

sometimes only at an unconscious level, more about Molly than she knows herself. At times, latent negations or internal contradictions in Molly's web of thought become quite obvious. Thus guided, the reader may learn to "see through" Molly.

A psychoanalytical interpretation based on formal textual signals that provide connections to unconscious material differs greatly from a common reader's conscious experience, but may designate textual motivations for his possible unconscious reactions.

ANALYSIS

. . . what was it she told me O yes that sometimes he used to go to bed with his muddy boots on when the maggot takes him just imagine having to get into bed with a thing like that that might murder you any moment what a man well its not the one way everyone goes mad Poldy anyway whatever he does always wipes his feet on the mat when he comes in wet or shine and always blacks his own boots too and he always takes off his hat when he comes up in the street like that and now hes going about in his slippers to look for £10000 for a postcard up up O Sweetheart May wouldnt a thing like that simply bore you stiff to extinction actually too stupid even to take his boots off now what could you make of a man like that Id rather die 20 times over than marry another of their sex of course hed never find another woman like me to put up with him the way I do know me come sleep with me yes and he knows that too at the bottom of his heart take that Mrs. Maybrick that poisoned her husband for what I wonder in love with some other man yet it was found out on her wasnt she the downright villain to go and do a thing like that of course some men can be dreadfully aggravating drive you mad and always the worst word in the world what do they ask us to marry them for if were so bad as all that comes to yes because they cant get on without us white Arsenic she put in his tea off flypaper wasnt it I wonder why they call it that if I asked him hed say its from the Greek leave us as wise as we were before she must have been madly in love with the other fellow to run the chance of being hanged O she didnt care if that was her nature what could she do besides theyre not brutes enough to go and hang a woman surely are they

Molly has slipped into a train of thought revolving around Josie Powell (Mrs. Breen), which reveals jealousy and a need for self-consolation. Abruptly, associations of death and murder emerge—at first on a linguistic level: "a thing like that might *murder* you"; "bore you *stiff to extinction*"; "I'd rather *die* 20 times over than marry another of their sex." The theme of death culminates in Molly's recollection: "take that Mrs Maybrick that poisoned her husband for what I wonder in love with some other man. . . . " The tone of her following reflections on Mrs. Maybrick clearly reveals a secret identification behind her open condemnation of the evil deed. Thus the boat of Molly's consciousness steers clear of the shallows of a death-wish toward her own husband. The wish itself is so near to conscious thought that it becomes fairly obvious to the reader.

Much less accessible is a double unconscious overdetermination of the censored wish. The key to its understanding is Molly's exclamation "O Sweetheart May," which is interspersed in her associations of death. The words come from a song, "Sweetheart May," which Molly has often sung herself. There are two doubly significant lines in that song, not quoted in the text, but presumably known by Molly: "Your dear boy has gone and left you, sweetheart May. . . . Don't you fear for him or cry, sweetheart May, for the boys must win or die, sweetheart May."

From the exclamation "O Sweetheart May" the thread of associations leads on to Mrs. Maybrick—on the surface, because of the occurrence of "May" in both expressions; at a deeper level, because the song's content touches upon material that remains unconscious throughout the associations of death. With its two implicit motifs—a dead son and a lover—the song reaches down to Molly's memory of her dead son (Rudy) and to her fantasy of a son-lover (Stephen). This reading is confirmed by another passage thirty pages later, where, thinking about Simon Dedalus, Molly passes from "dearest goodby *sweet*heart he always sang" to "he was married at the time to *May* Golding" (emphasis mine), then on to Stephen, and from there directly to Rudy: "I was in mourning that's 11 years ago now yes hed be 11. . . ."

From a psychoanalytical perspective, Molly's seemingly arbitrary exclamation "O Sweetheart May" turns out to be the highly condensed vehicle of a whole bundle of unconscious feelings. It reveals the fate of her son Rudy as a hidden motif behind the latent death-wish against Bloom and her fantasies of a young lover.

All this, of course, is not allowed to get through to Molly's conscious. The conflict arising out of all these ideas and wishes is solved in a characteristic manner: she disavows her maternal feelings and her sorrow, which then return in her fantasies of a son-lover. And she disavows her own feeling of guilt concerning Rudy's death, projecting the guilt onto Bloom, and taking her revenge by means of the death-wish and the fantasy of a son-lover.

By analyzing "O Sweetheart May" as a private symbol and bearer of unconscious meaning, I have introduced the two main themes that continually affect Molly's unconscious life. At first glance, the aforementioned critics may feel that their viewpoint has been confirmed. For them Molly is the literary concretization of the archetypal "Great Mother": to some the nourishing and devouring mother, to others the "satanic mistress," if not a "thirty-shilling whore." Indeed, does not Molly's fantasy of a son-lover, together with her latent death-wish toward her husband, correspond to the second interpretation? And do not her mourning, her feeling of guilt, and the tenderness in her thoughts of Stephen express a profound motherly feeling?

Yet the psychoanalytical interpretation demonstrates what is wrong with that controversial split among Molly's critics who conclude that Molly is one or the other. She is both. Behind her death wish, there are mother and lover motifs; behind her son-lover fantasy there is the mother's interest of winning back a son. Molly's text does not dissolve her fundamental ambivalence but thematizes.

A close reading shows that this strategy is constitutive: every feeling expressed in Molly's thoughts and belonging to one side of the ambivalence is counterbalanced by opposite feelings. Even her most famous female "yes" is quite often nothing more than a self-disguised "no." All her manifest utterances are made ambiguous by latent negations, and it is neither in the manifest nor on the latent level but in the interaction of both that one may find the "truth" about Molly. Critics who decide in favor of one or the other version in fact reproduce a common activity of consciousness, which is the reduction of ambivalence. Yet the textual strategy of portraying Molly in terms of her irreducibly ambivalent feelings works against that habitual tendency.

As such, the portrayal of Molly also subverts the presentation of consciousness in previous chapters: it puts an end to the vanity fair celebrated by and for consciousness in Joyce's Ulysses. The permanent doubling and counterbalancing of Molly's utterances by latent negation show that her conscious thoughts very often distort and disavow the feelings from which they derive. This is as true for her motive of revenge and her desire for a son-lover as it is for her death-wish toward Bloom. Thus consciousness is revealed to be a means of self-deception rather than one of self-knowledge. Molly's conscious is always less or other than her self. This self is often hiding or hidden in the stream of her consciousness but is nonetheless latently present and accessible to the reader.

Until now, one important dimension of the text has been neglected: the archetypal pattern of the whole novel. What is the link between "Penelope" and "Molly," if Molly is now considered as part of the whole system of Ulysses as a meta-novel?

The myth of Penelope stresses a reading of "Molly" as a concretization of the archetypal "Great Mother." Yet all the Ulysses references in the Joycean manifestation of the archetypal pattern differ so much from their literary origin that the aesthetic achievement cannot be found in the reference itself. The passage analyzed above shows that archetypal patterns like that of the son-lover or of the nourishing and devouring mother underlie Molly's psychic system. But it becomes quite clear that Molly as a character can never be reduced to or even explained by such a pattern. She is certainly not just a representation of the archetype. It might well designate hidden motives of her behavior or provide a key to the order of her seemingly arbitrary recollections and thoughts. Thus one could work out a whole dynamic system of interacting archetypes that permeates Molly's nocturnal monologue.

But far from giving *the key* to her personality, such a system can only underline the fact that Molly transcends every concrete manifestation of her self. This is quite an unusual way to be confronted with a literary figure. Before Joyce we had been used to getting very specific views of a character. But our view of Molly remains strikingly contingent, for the text abstains from guiding and evaluating the selection of archetypes, which creates a need in the reader to make a selection himself. By doing so he may become aware that the archetypes have undergone a change of function. Their consciousness-forming power, still viable in the mythical foil of Ulysses, has been lost in our civilization. The archetypes underlying Molly's psyche no longer shape her consciousness. In the context of everyday life in Dublin, they melt into the clichés of the pulp novels she reads and become vehicles of unconscious meaning, comforting to a subject who is not allowed consciously to experience the precluded significance. Thus, the archetypes have taken on a new function. They are no longer a means to bring ambivalent feelings to a conscious level but still serve to connect our lived experience with parts of ourselves excluded from consciousness.

Just as Penelope, night after night, secretly unweaves her web in order to hold off her suitors, so Molly's nocturnal web of associations secretly unweaves the diurnal social net in which she is caught. She does this, of course, not in order to avoid suitors, but to fill her imaginary life with them. In thus affirming her own self and its desires, she creates an imaginary order of present and past events, fantasies and fears, which allows her to approach her unconscious. Molly's monologue thus demonstrates how consciousness finds means and ways to live out what it nonetheless refuses to recognize.

FRANCIS WARNER

The Poetry of James Joyce

The wonderful measure and smack of
Joyce's prose is not to be found in his poems; nevertheless, they make a
fascinating study. Echoing his artificer, Stephen Dedalus explains to Cranly
that

> The lyrical form is in fact the simplest verbal vesture of an instant of
> emotion

a "cry or a cadence or a mood."

> He who utters it is more conscious of the instant of emotion than of
> himself as feeling emotion.

When Joyce comes to write prose,

> The narrative is no longer purely personal. The personality of the artist
> passes into the narration itself, flowing round and round the persons and
> the action like a vital sea.

It also fills them out from inside, as Keats knew, and could certainly operate
through narrative verse. Consider John Donne's growing mandrake root:

> His right arme he thrust out towards the East
> Westward his left; th'ends did themselves digest
> Into ten lesser strings, these fingers were:
> And as a slumberer stretching on his bed,
> This way he this, and that way scattered
> His other legge, which feet with toes upbeare.
> Grew on his middle parts, the first day, haire,
> To show, that in love's business hee should still
> A dealer bee. . . .

From *James Joyce: An International Perspective* (*Irish Literary Studies* 10). Copyright © 1982
by Francis Warner. Colin Smythe, and Barnes and Noble Books.

One scarcely goes to Joyce for verse of this kind. However, a glance at "A Memory of the Players in a Mirror at Midnight" shows something of the same gritty delight. The difference is that in Donne's poem we are aware above all of the feelings of the mandrake; in Joyce's of the poet:

> They mouth love's language. Gnash
> The thirteen teeth
> Your lean jaws grin with. Lash
> Your itch and quailing, nude greed of the flesh.
> Love's breath in you is stale, worded or sung,
> As sour as cat's breath,
> Harsh of tongue.
>
> This grey that stares
> Lies not, stark skin and bone.
> Leave greasy lips their kissing. None
> Will choose her what you see to mouth upon.
> Dire hunger holds his hour.
> Pluck forth your heart, saltblood, a fruit of tears.
> Pluck and devour!

Joyce peers at Donne "despoyl'd of fallacies" through Yeat's spectacles. We remember Yeats's letter to Donne's editor, Sir Herbert Grierson, in 1912:

> [I] find that at last I can understand Donne . . . I notice that the more precise and learned the thought, the greater the beauty, the passion.

and letters to Lady Gregory from Yeats about Pound:

> Ezra never shrinks from work . . . A learned companion, and a pleasant one . . . He . . . helps me get back to the definite and the concrete, away from modern abstractions.

By which, presumably, he means the Celtic Twilight. The result was the Yeatsean style already foreshadowed in "The fascination of what's difficult."

> There's something ails our colt
> That must, as if it had not holy blood
> Nor on Olympus leaped from cloud to cloud,
> Shiver under the lash, strain, sweat and jolt
> As though it dragged road metal.

The same "verbigracious bigtimer," having left behind modern abstractions, can now write a marvellous, jaw-breaking line such as

> Where we wrought that shall break the teeth of Time

in that finest of all his poems of friendship, "The New Faces."

Joyce is aware of all this happening between *Chamber Music* (1907) and *Pomes Penyeach* (1927). Hence the difference in style between "Lean out of the window/Goldenhair" and "They mouth love's language. Gnash." During this period Joyce learns to plump out, Hopkinslike but in prose, the human mouth from inside instead of describing it as in the first three lines of "A Memory of the Players" like an irritated dentist. The words now tongue the cheeks, and touch inside the teeth:

> Wine soaked and softened rolled pith of bread mustard a moment mawkish cheese.

In Joyce's poem above (from *Pomes Penyeach*) we know the poet feels betrayed (hence the Judas number thirteen); prefers, like Caesar, a "warm human plumpness" near him, such as Molly's ("Your lean jaws"); and has Lear's lashing beadle (or is it the flagellating God of Francis Thompson's "Hound of Heaven"? "Naked I wait Thy love's uplifted stroke!") on literary mind. Oddly, the rare side of Donne, and more particularly the familiar side of Donne's Elizabethan fellow-singers, whispers from the wings through the second verse; not least of the anonymous author of "I saw my lady weep."

> Leave off in time to grieve

becomes

> Leave greasy lips their kissing

bringing greasy Joan from her pot in *Love's Labour's Lost*. After Yeats, he can now risk a jaw-breaker:

> Will choose her what you see to mouth upon and with a nod to Swinburne (a fruit of tears), end with a flourish playing Prometheus with Dedalus:

> Pluck and devour!

It is not the Donne of the *Satires* that fathers most of Joyce's poems: rather is it Donne and Dowland's

> Stay, O sweet, and do not rise,
> The light that shines comes from thine eyes:
> The day breaks not, it is my heart,
> Because that you and I must part.
> Stay, or else my joys will die,
> And perish in their infancie.

that begets

> Of that so sweet imprisonment
>> My soul, dearest, is fain—
> Soft arms that woo me to relent
>> And woo me to detain.
> Ah, could they ever hold me there,
> Gladly were I a prisoner!
>> (*Chamber Music* XXII)

and we must return to the earlier book of poems. Many critics have drawn attention to the links with "the asphodel fields of Fulke Greville and Sir Philip Sidney" (Horace Reynolds), Rochester (Arthur Symons) Waller and Herrick (*Manchester Guardian*) and noted "a deliberate archaism and a kind of fawning studiousness" (Morton D. Zabel). What strikes us though today in the nineteen-eighties, surely, is the splendidly jarring technique Joyce cultivates of placing an askew word exactly where one might have expected the traditional lyric resolution.

> What counsel has the hooded moon
>> Put in thy heart, my shyly sweet,
> Of Love in ancient *plenilune*,
>> Glory and stars beneath his feet—
> A sage that is but kith and kin
> With the comedian *Capuchin*?
>> (*Chamber Music* XII)

Why should the critic italicize? Let the words speak for themselves, and not only those from *Chamber Music*.

> The sly reeds whisper to the night
> A name—her name—
> And all my soul is a delight
> A swoon of shame.
>> ("Alone")

Back to the earlier volume:

> How sweet to lie there,
>> Sweet to kiss,
> Where the great pine forest
>> Enaisled is!
>> (*Chamber Music* XX)

Many of the words that provide this effect are indeed "antique" but the effect of their use in this way is most modern.

Happy Love is come to woo
   Thee and woo thy girlish ways—
The zone that doth become thee fair,
The snood upon thy yellow hair.
(XI)

  Go seek her out all courteously
    And say I come,
  Wind of spices whose song is ever
    Epithalamium.
(XIII)

and better still, remembering "the more precise and learned the thought, the greater the beauty, the passion,"

  That mood of thine, O timorous,
    Is his, if thou but scan it well,
  Who a mad tale bequeaths to us
    At ghosting hour conjurable—
And all for some strange name he read
In Purchas or in Holinshed.
(XXVI)

Now this is splendid. Far from ruining the delicate lyrics, this is what makes them worth re-reading. We soon forget that the lady's mood was timorous, but happily remember unexpectedly meeting once more the inspirers of Shakespeare and Coleridge. We are astonished to find cherubs like boy scouts using their bugles as loud-speakers:

  When thou hast heard his name upon
    The bugles of the cherubim
  Begin thou softly to unzone
  Thy girlish bosom . . .
(XI)

still more to find this a summons to nuptials. But nuptials they are. For this consummation nothing less than the greatest, the *Song of Songs*, must be versified (XIV). He can crack Yeats's Celtic bells with a grammarian's googly (no, he does not write "innumerable" and follow Keats):

  While sweetly, gently, secretly,
    The flowery bells of morn are stirred
  And the wise choirs of faery
    Begin (innumerous!) to be heard.
(XV)

He can call up Greensleeves from the grave:

> Dear heart, why will you use me so?
> Dear eyes that gently me upbraid
> Still are you beautiful—but O,
> How is your beauty raimented!
> (XXIX)

He can even disturb "The Blessed Damozel" once more:

> His hand is under
> Her smooth round breast.
> (XVIII)

But by the last poem in the book he is doing something different. For Pound, "I hear an army charging" was one of "the few beautiful poems that still ring in my head"—and how well Pound writes on *Chamber Music*! Horace Reynolds listens for Yeats's "Hosting of the Sidhe" as he reads this poem. We should do better to remember Yeats's "Valley of the Black Pig":

> . . . the clash of fallen horsemen and the cries
> Of unknown perishing armies beat about my ears.

when we read

> I hear an army charging upon the land
> And the thunder of horses plunging, foam about their knees.

Morton D. Zabel welcomes "Suckling and the Cavaliers" and "the minor work of Crashaw" to aid our appreciation of the early poems; but the pressure of sensuous thinking in Crashaw is unlike anything in the poems of Joyce, and Joyce is best when he is furthest from the only Suckling he resembles, the coy one.

Joyce may indeed be, in *Chamber Music*, as he confesses, a "sweet sentimentalist" (XII), but the sentimentality is redeemed not only by the overall theme and shape of the book, to which we shall come in a moment, but also by many incidental felicities over and above those mentioned, not least Joyce's ability to capture "a gesture and a pose" or (to exchange Eliot for Pound) a medallion:

> Firmness,
> Not the full smile,
> His art, but an art
> In profile.

If medallion is too strong a word, then Joyce's still moments are at least clear-cut snapshots.

> All softly playing
> With head to music bent,
> And fingers straying
> Upon an instrument.
>   (I)

We hear so much about his musicality, but should also note how visual many of the songs are.

> The old piano plays an air,
> Sedate and slow and gay;
> She bends upon the yellow keys,
> Her head inclines this way.
>   (II)

> My love goes slowly, bending to
> Her shadow on the grass
>   (VII)

(We are in the world of Bonnard rather than the Pre-Raphaelites.)

> The sun is in the willow leaves
> And on the dappled grass
> And still she's combing her long hair
> Before the lookingglass.
>   (XXIV)

This is not to deny his ear. He can fill a line with every open vowel.

> For lo! the trees are full of sighs

"the verse with its black vowels and its opening sound, rich and lutelike," as Dedalus says, misquoting Nashe; and indeed Joyce wrote to Gogarty as early as 1900:

> my idea for July and August is this—to get Dolmetsch to make a lute and to coast the south of England from Falmouth to Margate, singing old English songs.

The musicality, and the visual awareness, the ability to evoke mood with "the cross run of the beat and the word, as of a stiff wind cutting the ripple-tops of bright water" as Pound notes, all draw us back to these poems, but there is a deeper music, of the intellect beyond the senses, that lifts *Chamber Music* above slightness, and to bring this into focus we must go back to Joyce's own words on the book.

On 19th July, 1909, he wrote to G. Molyneux Palmer from Trieste:

I hope you may set all of *Chamber Music* in time. This was indeed partly
my idea in writing it. The book is in fact a suite of songs and if I were a
musician I suppose I should have set them to music myself. The central
song is XIV after which the movement is all downwards until XXXIV
which is vitally the end of the book. XXXV and XXXVI are tailpieces
just as I and II are preludes.

We are now in a position to see the work whole. The central climax of
the suite is the *Song of Songs*, greatest of all love-poems and neatly versified
by Joyce. At the centre of this (thirty-five words before it in a poem of
seventy words) is the upstanding and timeless cedar of Lebanon. The poem
immediately preceding this one urges

> Go seek her out all courteously
>   And say I come,
> Wind of spices whose song is ever
>   Epithalamium.

In other words, as was hinted earlier in this note and in later words of this
poem, a "bridal wind is blowing." *Chamber Music* is a book that presupposes
marriage at its centre. The poem following XIV (the climax) begins

> From dewy dreams, my soul, arise,
>   From love's deep slumber and from death,
> For lo! the trees are full of sighs
>   Whose leaves the morn admonisheth.

We can now see that those poems leading up to the *Song of Songs* are all
of hopeful expectancy. But by XXX

> We were grave lovers. Love is past . . .

"the movement is all downwards" after the cedared celebration, and XXXIV
"which is vitally the end of the book" lays a gentle tombstone on the
memory of the romance:

> Sleep now, O sleep now,
>   O you unquiet heart!
> A voice crying 'Sleep now'
>   Is heard in my heart.

The tailpiece, the final line of the book, simply reads

> My love, my love, my love, why have you left me alone?

So the whole process, from wooing, proposal, eager anticipation of marriage,
fulfilment (either real or imagined), betrayal and desertion by the woman
is complete, and the poet is left alone, rueful, in despair, exchanging

> those treasures I possessed
> Ere that mine eyes had learned to weep
>
> (XXIII)

for a new outward emblem of an inner state, the whirling laughter of a
charging army of horsemen, clanging upon his heart as upon an anvil,
fighting bitterness with an anguished rhetorical question.

The book survives because, over and above the individual qualities
of single poems, the sequence is not only (as many critics have implied)
more than the sum of its parts, but that sum is the archetypal theme of
the depth and intensity of male devotion measured against the playfulness
and "slydynge corage" of a female who is unable to sustain a love involving
those highest stakes we call marriage. Joyce may at times be sentimental
in his book, but we do not feel he is insincere; and in the end we grieve
with him (or his poet in the verse-narrative) and remember the woman as
beautiful, sweet-bosomed, musical, goldenhaired, but girlish and spiritually
inadequate to cope with the poet's intensity and the integrity of a serious
relationship.

Pomes Penyeach does not make this claim on us. "You don't think
they're worth printing at any time?" asked Joyce. "No, I don't," replied
Pound. "Read Ralph Cheever Dunning. They belong in the Bible or the
family album with the portraits." Not so. We have already enjoyed "A
Memory of the Players in a Mirror at Midnight," and the last poem in the
book brings back Hopkin's (and Thompson's)

> I did say yes
> O at lightning and lashed rod

with a vengeance:

> *Come!* I yield. Bend deeper upon me! I am here.
> Subduer, do not leave me! Only joy, only anguish,
> Take me, save me, soothe me, O spare me!

The childhood carol "Star of wonder" is briskly turned insideout in "Bahn-
hofstrasse":

> Ah star of evil! star of pain

(Swinburne's to blame, not Baudelaire), and he can both bring on the
earlier techniques:

> Uplift and sway, O golden vine,
> Your clustered fruits to love's full flood,
> Lambent and vast and ruthless as is thine
> Incertitude!
>
> ("Flood")

and send them up with a straight face in "Simples":

> Be mine, I pray, a waxen ear
> To shield me from her childish croon.

" 'Simples,' " opines Morton D. Zabel, "must rank as one of the purest lyrics of our time."

Joyce has changed since the earlier volume. We have word-coinage that looks forward beyond *Ulysses*:

> And long and loud,
> To night's nave upsoaring,
> A starknell tolls
> As the bleak incense surges, cloud on cloud,
> Voidward from the adoring
> Waste of souls.
>
> ("Nightpiece")

The puns on "tonight" and "(k)nave" scarcely succeed; "voidward" passes; "starknell" is good and the pun on "Waste" excellent. In the first verse of this same poem Francis Thompson's "I fled him down the arches of the years" reappears (perhaps) in

> Ghostfires from heaven's far verges faint illume,
> Arches on soaring arches,
> Night's sindark nave.

but we read this today with added relish recalling Joyce's later pliant girls and knavish priests after dark in Phoenix Park: "bidimetoloves sinduced by what tegotetabsolvers." Richard Ellmann has skilfully unfolded the biographical mystery within "She weeps over Rahoon":

> Still trying to penetrate (Nora's) soul, he wrote a poem to express what he felt to be her thoughts about her dead lover and her living one. He shifted Bodkin's grave from Oughterard, seventeen miles from Galway, to the Galway cemetery at Rahoon with its more sonorous name. . . . The dead sweetheart was brought into a mortuary triangle with the two living lovers. With a sense of sacred coincidence Joyce found a headstone at Rahoon with the name J. Joyce upon it.

Ellmann also explains why the first poem in the book is called "Tilly":

> The word "tilly" means the thirteenth in a baker's dozen; Joyce had thirteen (instead of twelve) poems in *Pomes Penyeach*, which sold for a shilling

and points out that it was written as early as 1904, some months after his mother had died, and James had found and read a packet of love-letters from his father to his mother.

Boor, bond of the herd,
Tonight stretch full by the fire!
I bleed by the black stream
For my torn bough!

None of them are in the same league as that perfect poem *"Ecce Puer,"* written after Helen Joyce's difficult pregnancy and on the day of the birth of Stephen James Joyce, his grandson. The deep joy is set in perspective by the recollection in the last verse that Joyce's own father had died only forty-nine days before. It is superb. As in a different context Samuel Beckett wrote of Jack Yeats's achievement, so here: we will not criticize; "simply bow in wonder."

Of the dark past
A child is born;
With joy and grief
My heart is torn

Calm in his cradle
The living lies.
May love and mercy
Unclose his eyes!

Young life is breathed
On the glass;
The world that was not
Comes to pass.

A child is sleeping:
An old man gone.
O, father forsaken,
Forgive your son!

WILLIAM EMPSON

"Ulysses": Joyce's Intentions

When I was young, literary critics often rejoiced that the hyprocrisy of the Victorians had been discredited, or expressed confidence that the operation would soon be complete. So far from that, it has returned in a peculiarly stifling form to take possession of critics of Eng. Lit.; Mr. Pecksniff has become the patron saint of many of my colleagues. As so often, the deformity is the result of severe pressure between forces in themselves good. The study of English authors of the past is now centered in the universities, where the teachers have a responsibility to the students, and yet there must be no censorship—no work of admitted literary merit may be hidden from the learners. Somehow we must save poor Teacher's face, and protect him from the indignant or jeering students, local authorities or parents. It thus came to be tacitly agreed that a dead author usually hated what he described, hated it as much as we do, even, and wanted his book to shame everybody out of being so nasty ever again. This is often called fearless or unflinching criticism, and one of its ill effects is to make the young people regard all literature as a terrific nag or scold. Independently of this, a strong drive has been going on to recover the children for orthodox or traditional religious beliefs; well, showing them how these beliefs operated in standard authors of their own tradition is of course a good way to do it, providing an actual use for the Eng. Lit. with which the schools have been saddled. The material is processed with confident firmness to suit this intelligible policy; and when you understand all that, you may just be able to understand how they manage to present James Joyce as a man devoted to the God who was satisfied by the crucifixion.

From *Using Biography.* Copyright © 1984 by the Estate of Sir William Empson. Harvard University Press.

The concordat was reached over his dead body. When *Ulysses* first leaked through the censorship, it was almost universally denounced for its cold jeering, its lack of joviality or human sympathy, its unnatural contempt for the world—exactly the qualities which are now praised. It has not got any of these qualities, whether they are good or bad. Clearly, such an extravagant degree of misunderstanding could not happen unless Joyce had laid himself open to it. He was a disciple of Ibsen, who believed that an author should dramatise "problems" and refuse to tell his public the answers; not because he would be in any doubt, but because this was the way to influence his public most strongly. The answers would be sociological and political as well as aesthetic, and the public must hammer them out for itself by debate and turmoil. Joyce would have suffered very much if he had foreseen that his adroit opponents were going to turn the tables on him, taking advantage of the manoeuvre taught him by his Master. I therefore think it important to realise that the massive biography of Richard Ellmann (*James Joyce*, 1959) together with the volumes of letters and occasional criticism, contain enough ammunition to blow sky-high the whole dungeon into which he has been kidnapped.

I am not sure how far Hugh Kenner (*Dublin's Joyce*, 1955) invented the now-established image of Joyce and his work; probably he was riding the crest of an American wave which had already travelled some distance. But no one else has presented it in such a lively, resourceful and energetic manner, so the best name one can find for it is the Kenner Smear. The chief claim of this theory is that Stephen Dedalus is presented not as the author when young (though the book-title pretends he is) but as a possible fatal alternative, a young man who has taken some wrong turning or slipped over the edge of some vast drop, so that he can never grow into the wise old author (intensely Christian, though in a mystically paradoxical way) who writes the book. The author nearly fell but did not quite. I agree that the Stephen of *Ulysses*, though he makes some good jokes, is in a terrible condition, near the edge of madness or of crime; but the title of the earlier book ("the artist when young") should at least encourage us to expect that he will emerge from his throttling situation. On the Kenner view, Stephen is simply deluded when he boasts that he will write a novel ten years later, giving the date when the book actually appeared. Now, Joyce was an extremely self-centred man, fiercely determined to become a great novelist; he is wildly unlikely to have presented himself, without any warning or explanation, as incapable of becoming one.

People arguing this case, I noticed, always make use of the same detail—Joyce in *Finnegans Wake* wrote a parody of a claim made by Stephen in the *Portrait*. Jim the penman, says the joke, was always studying copying:

so as one day to utter an epical forged cheque on the public for his own private profit

whereas Stephen's diary, in the last-but-one sentence of the *Portrait*, says:

Welcome, O life! I go to encounter for the millionth time the reality of experience and to forge in the smithy of my soul the uncreated conscience of my race.

No wonder they use this example, because there is no other where Joyce can be supposed to be giving us a direct hint at the great secret. It is a rather forced joke or pun, likely to have been invented for the second occasion rather than intended to lurk behind the exaltation of the first one, because "to forge in the smithy" is quite another process from forging a cheque. Also, Joyce can be found making this ethical claim in his own person, without using the dubious word. In 1912 he wrote to Nora asking her to join him for Horse Show Week in Dublin:

The Abbey Theatre will be open and they will give plays of Yeats and Synge. You have a right to be there because you are my bride; and I am one of the writers of this generation who are perhaps at last creating a conscience in the soul of this wretched race.

He had recently failed to get *Dubliners* published there, after a long struggle, and no doubt felt particularly keenly that they needed improvement. He had plainly no suspicion that there was anything odd about the claim that his books would help to do it. (He did not mean, of course, that he had recommended Christian virtues such as chastity, which he considered bad.) That he echoed it in a much later book with a jolly bit of self-mockery gives no reason to believe that the title *Portrait of the Artist* was an elaborate lie.

Ellmann, who is not impressed by the moral claim, suggests that Joyce first thought of it in this letter to his wife, and used it soon afterwards in a rewriting of the *Portrait*

Joyce also emphasized, partly as a result of his experiences in 1912, the patriotism of Stephen's effort to hit the conscience of his race and cast his shadow over its imagination.

But the moral claim was deeply built in to Joyce's theoretical position; that (in a way) was the use he was trying to make of Aquinas. To say that he invented it merely as a boast to satisfy his wife is just a way of belittling it. However, I need not quarrel with Ellmann for thinking the claim ridiculous; we agree on a more crucial matter, that Joyce himself did not think the claim ridiculous when he wrote the book. A draft of the *Portrait* certainly existed in 1912, whether or not it already carried this claim; he had thrown it into the fire in 1911, but his sister Eileen had fished it out.

If we consider why he thought of a smithy, for the fine sentence at the end of the book, we find ourselves in another world. At the crisis of *Ulysses*, Stephen bangs his ashplant at the gaslight in the brothel, crying "Nothung," so there is a row, and Bloom helps him away. This was the name of the sword forged by Siegfried in *The Ring* of Wagner, a work recalled fairly often in the course of the book; and surely it is obvious that the reference is meant to be important. We find it being prepared for in the previous novel. Stephen in the last chapter of the *Portrait* leaves a group of students with his friend Cranly, saying, "we can't speak here. Come away," and their conversation is grim and searching, but first:

> They crossed the quadrangle together without speaking. The bird call from Siegfried whistled softly followed them from the steps of the porch.

Dixon is merely arranging to play billiards with Cranly afterwards, but we are reminded that all these young men sing and that Wagner is immensely revered. The birds talked to Siegfried as soon as he entered the forest with the ancestral sword which he had re-forged, but he could not understand them till he had killed the dragon; then they told him he had already won a treasure and need only walk through the fire to win Brünnhilde. The self-importance of Joyce, as many people have felt, is rather unattractive, but at least he is not presenting Stephen as worthless and certain to fall.

Also this part of Wagner was forward-looking and progressive; it meant Socialism. Joyce in a letter to his brother of February 1907, which Ellmann quotes, does indeed say: "The interest I took in socialism and the rest has left me." But this is only to prove that he has been reduced to the hoggish mental condition of his fellow clerks—he has even been left cold by a procession in favour of the Nolan, so he had obviously better leave Rome at once. A critic is free to say that the advanced ideals entertained by authors around the turn of the century were silly; but if he won't even admit that they held such beliefs, what he says about them is sure to be wrong. He might also object that the ideals came in a standard mixed bag and were hard to combine; but, there again, the resulting difficulties are no proof of insincerity. Americans, as is well known, tend to disapprove of socialism unless it is called by some other name; and when Ellmann jeers at the politics of Joyce he feels he is protecting an innocent (because Joyce didn't *know* that a socialist is practically a cannibal). Still, Ellmann gives us an important bit of information here; that Joyce owned Bernard Shaw's book *The Quintessence of Ibsenism* (1891). The book explains that Ibsen is progressive and a liberator, and the article *Ibsen's New Drama* by the young Joyce seems clearly affected by it (recent critics have of course debunked Ibsen, arguing that his final years were anti-democratic; but this, even if true, was not known to Ibsenites at the turn of the century; and it cannot have been oppressively clear to Ibsen himself, when he wrote to Joyce approving his youthful article). Joyce wrote:

> But the naked drama, either the perception of a great truth, or the opening up of a great question, or a great conflict which is almost independent of the conflicting actors, and has been and is of far-reaching importance— this is what primarily rivets our attention.

Such was the generous-minded way to talk about the matter, extremely remote from recent Joyce criticism, and the young man was sure also to have read Shaw's *Perfect Wagnerite* (1898). This description of the theme of *The Ring* as a socialist pamphlet is one of the most splended pieces of writing by Shaw, so lucid, so penetrating, so bare, so full of decisive detail, so rewarding to the imagination. He said in the second edition that he had merely reported what all his friends were saying, and Joyce could not have thought him a "mountebank" here, though it was a fair enough comment on the later plays. The penniless young Joyce was living in a much more expansive world for the imagination than we can afford, and we only look dirty when we try to cut him down to our own mean size. So of course "forging" meant to him the forging by Siegfried, for which even Bernard Shaw could penetrate to such unexpected depths of feeling.

It becomes clear that I must defend every clause of the penultimate sentence of the *Portrait*, as it has been nagged at by a series of critics. We now reach the clause "for the millionth time." Obviously this can't be true, they say, the young man's vanity makes him use inflated language. No, it is a kind of humility; he recognizes that the process has happened a million times before, because he knows he is only an avatar of the needed culture-hero, as it might be of Vishnu or the Buddha. This indeed is the main place where the Victorian "Wisdom of the East" (and for that matter of the Radical Reformers of the sixteenth century, who appear to have held precisely the same opinions), parts company with Christianity, which claims there is no basis for goodness except as derived from the one Atonement. I have to try to put the matter sharply, because for a majority of Eng. Lit. critics, especially in America, it seems to have become a convention to pretend that one has never heard of the opinions of the Enlightenment, and this little elegance of course entails that one's opinions about many past authors are bound to be wrong. The very technique of Joyce in such a case, releasing as it were into the atmosphere an awareness of the status of Stephen as an avatar by little reminders of the socialism of Ibsen, Wagner, Shakespeare and so on, is one which his modern American critics have been "carefully brought up" to be unconscious of, exactly like the rich young ladies in the plays of Oscar Wilde: "Mama, whose ideas on education are remarkably strict, has brought me up to be extremely short-sighted, so . . . . . ." and so too the unfortunate young man, who went into the English Literature business with honest enough intentions, finds that his grant will not be renewed unless he cooperates with the current trend. He is thus forbidden to understand the young Joyce, who is feeling here that to be yet another liberator, another incarnation of the culture-hero, is as high as the artist can hope to go.

Of course, his author might still intend him as a parody-hero, a totally unworking model of Siegfried; I only say that this would be very unlike Joyce, and that all the arguments for thinking so collapse as soon as they are examined.

The beginning of the sentence, "Welcome, O life!", needs also to be considered, as Kenner allots a tremendous scolding to Stephen's ecstasy at the end of the previous chapter; here he has a vision of earthly beauty, and I suspect of progress too (the angel seems to be flying one of the new aeroplanes), so he dedicates himself to the labour of literary creation. Kenner says he is "irresponsible" and not "mature," and that the mean-ingless word *life* "recurs and recurs". Stephen here is just leaving school; only the final chapter shows him at university. If mature he would be incredible. He considers his present condition as a living death, and he is determined to break out of it; naturally he does not know what life will be, only that he has powers within him which demand to be unchained. I find I can believe in this child all right, though he is almost too impressive. To maintain that the author intended to jeer at the whole sequence, and dropped hints so that the reader could join him in this activity, seems to me to betray a degree of mean-mindedness positively incapacitating for a literary critic.

I don't deny, of course, that Joyce is often laughing at Stephen, and at times does it fairly severely ("I haven't let off this young man lightly, have I?" he appealed to Budgen); but to say this is quite different from saying what Kenner does, that the fit reader is intended to enjoy the hopeless fatuity of the thoughts of Bloom and Stephen just as the Blessed in the Christian Heaven (according to Aquinas) enjoy their eternal ringside view of the torments of Hell. Kenner brings out this quaint old bit of tradition with tender amusement; it is just the kind of thing, he feels sure, that

Joyce, with his Irish humour, would find particularly attractive. Joyce would have listened with sickened horror, only gradually realising that his readers are being told to enjoy his book like this *all the way along*. Maybe he would have vomited again. But, later, he would have become keen to explain to Kenner that this smart idea is typical of what is hopelessly wrong with established Christianity, and indeed that, ever since Aquinas proved that this is what really goes on in the Christian Heaven, no decent man has ever been willing to go there. I must say, I find it astonishing that mis-interpretation could reach this wild peak.

Still, I can't deny that, as Joyce deliberately refused to express his reaction to what he described, his reaction is often hard to gauge. Joyce can make a character ridiculous without any loss of sympathy for him, and a modern critic finds this hard to imagine, because he has been taught to be a brass-faced scold; though surely it was familiar to the public of Dickens. Bloom's vision of his dead son at the end of the brothel chapter is intended to make us both laugh and cry, and I gather that the battle over this example has been more or less won. But Ellmann in the biography points out another case, which I do not think anyone could have guessed. Joyce disliked working in Rome so much that he decided he had not given Dublin its due, and he added his best short story "The Dead," to redress the balance. The book had not so far reproduced, he wrote to his brother,

> the ingenuous insularity of Dublin and its hospitality; the latter "virtue"
> so far as I can see does not exist elsewhere in Europe.

Conroy in his conventional speech at the dismal Christmas party says almost exactly the same, and it would be quite reasonable to suppose that the author meant this as a satire on Irish complacency. I must admit then that it is easy to go wrong over what he means. Also, though he was pleased with his skill at the famous Irish bitterness, he felt that he needed to get away from it—whether he "really meant it" might become a question. Bernard Shaw used the admissions of Joyce on this point as the only way he could sincerely praise *Ulysses;* the book exposed, he said, what was fundamentally the matter with Dublin, "the fatal habit of low jeering." And indeed the idea is presented quite firmly in the first pages of the book (the part that Shaw read); for example, Mulligan upbraids Stephen for spoilng a chance to borrow money from the English visitor:

> I blow him up about you, and then you come along with your lousy leer
> and your gloomy Jesuit gibes . . .

After his escape from Dublin, Joyce succeeded in rising above this fault, even if sometimes at the cost of reckless sentimentality. He does not deserve to be forced back, his ghostly protests inaudible behind a barrage of praise, so that everything he wrote must be interpreted as lousy Jesuit jeering.

One or two minor points need fitting in here. It is part of Kenner's argument, to prove that Stephen is already damned, that he is made to expound the wrong aesthetic philosophy. Joyce was letting him get the theory right in *Stephen Hero*, but when he rewrote and concentrated the material as the *Portrait* Stephen was turned into a sentimental neo-Platonist; that is, he considered the artist superior to earthly details, instead of letting the artist deduce realism from Aquinas. If we actually did find this alteration, I agree that the argument would carry some weight, though the evidence would need to be very strong. But, so far as I can see, there is only one definite bit of evidence offered, that Joyce in rewriting left out the technical term "epiphany," invented by himself to describe the moment of insight which sums up a whole situation. I can tell you why he left it out; because he was not always too egotistical to write well. Even he, during revision, could observe that it was tiresome to have Stephen spouting to his young friends about his invented term. But I find no change in doctrine; he still firmly rejects

> Idealism, the supreme quality of beauty being a light from some other world, the idea of which the matter was but the shadow,

and explains that the "claritas" of Aquinas comes when the image

> is apprehended luminously by the mind which has been arrested by its wholeness and fascinated by its harmony.

This is surely the doctrine which Kenner approves, and we next have as clear a pointer from the novelist as he ever allows us:

> Stephen paused and, though his companion did not speak, felt that his words had called up around them a thought enchanted silence.

A critic who can believe that Joyce wrote this whole passage in order to jeer at it has, I submit, himself taken some fatal turning, or slipped unawares over the edge of some vast drop.

It is also argued that the spelling of the legendary name "Daedalus" was changed to *Dedalus* in the *Portrait* so as to warn us that Stephen is now "dead," and that the first syllable should henceforth be so pronounced. One must grant that this would be a romantic name for a doppelgänger; but in the same book "esthetic" is so spelt, and later (for instance) we get "Eschylus" in "The Holy Office." Joyce had merely adopted the Italian way of transliterating Greek, and it involved no change of pronunciation.

I can now say a bit more about the pronunciation of "Dedalus." I asked Professor Ellmann, who kindly wrote and asked Samuel Beckett. He answered that he could not remember any particular incident when Joyce said the word, but if Joyce had said "deddalus" he would remember, because his ear would have been shocked. One might doubt whether he and Joyce were brought up to say "deed" or "dayd" (a new pronunciation of Latin was gradually coming in), but either would count as a long vowel, and this was of great importance for writing Latin verse; the schoolboy would be beaten for a "false quantity," so no wonder the ear of Beckett would be shocked. This short vowel has become universal in America for the work, and was used by Kenner to argue that Stephen was already "dead."

One might think it is the only natural way for an English speaker to pronounce the word so spelled, but the effect is uncertain (compare "lethal," "penal"), only "dedd" would be decisive. The young Stephen in the *Portrait* is well aware that his family name comes from "the fabulous artificer," and draws encouragement from it, though Joyce had already established his new spelling for the name. Maybe the unfortunate tradesmen who dealt with the house often pronounced the name wrong, and old Dedalus gladly snubbed them for it. It does not appear that Kenner believes young Stephen to have gone fatally wrong till he has started drinking. Also, for anyone fairly well-read, this spelling would not be unfamiliar. During the seventeenth century the English sometimes accepted the Italian way of spelling Latin names; and at all other times would pay respect to it by printing "AE" in its curious combined form. Various derivatives were made from "Daedalus," for example "dedale" which is listed as having no other pronunciation than "deedal." This would be irrelevant if Joyce had not insisted upon it himself. He introduces the word among the imitations of period styles in the Hospital chapter, and actually in verse, as if to make sure of the intonation. The medical student Costello is sardonic and appears to be malignant, as was expected of hunchbacks, but when Stephen expresses a resentful despair he tells him to rejoice in the wonder and richness of the world; then the thunder comes, terrifying Stephen but ending the drought.

> Behold the mansion reared by dedale Jack,
> See the malt stored in many a refluent sack,
> In the proud cirque of Jackjohn's bivouac.

Stresses are heaped up at the end of each line, and I do not understand how anybody could want to pronounce the word as "deddle" here. After I had realised that the young man has missed catching his Nora, I was forced to admit that Kenner was right on an essential point; Stephen will never get round to writing the novel. But Stephen as we see him on Bloomsday has only just started to go wrong; he is not less than archangel ruined, or else, indeed, his author could not describe him from within. To say that he is already dead, even as a sectarian dig, is off the target; a dreadful wriggling life as a Dublin bar-fly, all acrackle with scandal and artistic pretension, just enough by his concert-singing to scrape by, extends far before him. In the novel, he is a disagreeable young man, but not more so than the young Joyce, judging from the few records, actually was. Except in his refusal to wash; someone reports that, during that summer, he was greatly enjoying the swimming. But Joyce might easily have talked so, to annoy an English patron.

One can see how the idea arose, of a change in Stephen; Joyce does narrow the portrait as he concentrates it, though probably by degrees and not on any principle. Actually, when at college, his mind had been greedily accepting the latest thoughts and news, but he came to present himself as an underprivileged recluse, a kind of rock-plant, nurturing his aestheticism upon the stones of Aquinas only. It was to show himself in this prickly aspect, refusing service on yet another front, that he is made to reject a socialist manifesto which all the other students were signing—a great help to his later admirers in America. He must have been converted to Socialism a year or two later, so the incident can hardly be made a central pillar of the belief that Joyce intends to denounce and bemoan every development of human culture since the start of the Renaissance. And besides, if this is what the young man is up to, he cannot also be gloated over as the invincibly fatuous modern man. I suppose that Kenner, quite early in his study of this author, glimpsed a truth which would be painful to him— that the mind of Joyce was at a number of points very like that of H. G. Wells. A brilliant recovery was made, and he found two routes of escape from the oppressive conclusion; but the trouble is, he tries to use both at once.

The basic purpose of all the "interpreting" (I take it no one would be eager to deny this) has been to prove that Joyce was not really opposed to Christianity—for example, we are often told that he attacks bad priests but not the priesthood. This is just credible about his published works, where he is struggling to be "detached," though one ought to be able to see through it fairly easily. From the evidence of the letters and the Ellmann biography, his critics would be more sensible to blame him for an obsessional hatred of the religion, strong as ever when he died. I will report a brief sequence, enough to be representative; a full list would be tiresome. One should first realise that he did not quarrel with his Christian friends about religion, as his brother Stanislaus did; sometimes he would talk rather insincerely about it, to avoid ill feeling—as when he told some visitor that the only reason why he didn't become a priest was that he couldn't stand celibacy. And the effect of the anti-intellectual aesthetic movement is that the novels never give any reason why Stephen abandons his religion; the change appears as a kind of wasting mental disease, though really of course the young Aloysius and Stanislaus were arguing about Christianity all the time. But there is very little to be discounted.

In 1908, when he was twenty-six, Nora and Stanislaus became active because he was drinking more than his health or his family could afford, and on one occasion Nora cried out: "Yes, go now and get drunk . . . Faith, I tell you I'll have the children baptised tomorrow." This threat was so appalling to him that he took the pledge; he kept it till the British Fleet paid a visit to Trieste, a time when he became unconscious on a battleship. His immense capacity for making friends, indeed, is one of the surprises of the biography. In 1909, he wrote to Nora from Dublin upset by doubts of her loyalty—she had done a suspicious thing shortly before he left Trieste.

> A priest passed us and I said to you 'Do you not feel a kind of repulsion or disgust at the sight of one of those men?' You answered a little shortly and drily 'No, I don't' . . . Your reply hurt and silenced me . . . Are you with me, Nora, or are you secretly against me?

He sometimes told his South-European friends that the religion was only harmful in Ireland, not elsewhere, but this letter proves he only said it to spare their feelings. (And he was sometimes patriotic enough to assume that Catholics are better than Protestants, but this did not interfere with his conviction that both are very bad.) In 1913, a young woman he was flirting with, Amelia Popper, had appendicitis, and he wrote: 'The surgeon's knife has probed in her entrails and withdrawn, leaving the raw, ragged gash of its passage on her belly . . . Libidinous God!' The operation had been successful, but any reminder that God has a sexual craving to inflict torture on all his creatures is enough to set Joyce off, never mind whether God has been frustrated on this occasion. Realising this settled frame of mind, one can see the force in the novel *Ulysses* of calling God "chewer of corpses" whenever Stephen remembers the slow death of his mother and more elegantly "*dio boia*, hangman god" while sympathising with the troubles of Shakespeare. A superstitious horror, one might also deduce, and not any residual attachment to the religion, was what made the lad Stephen in the *Portrait* say that he dare not go to mass unbelieving, because:

I imagine there is a malevolent reality behind these things I say I fear.

The Christian God cannot be the supreme God—one may feel safe so far; but his doctrines are quite wicked enough to do black magic.

The later references are much less highly strung, but do not mark any softening in theory. In 1917 Joyce is writing gay limericks, with the *Portrait* at last coming out and *Ulysses* nearly finished; one of them describes the bounce of Lloyd George, laughing at it but praising him for it—the populist side of Lloyd George was what Joyce liked in a politician, and it ends: "Bully God made this world, but I'll save it." A bad line, likely to make one guess that *bully* is some kind of jovial American slang; but no, it is just our familiar schoolboy word. The Creator is a cad, but L. G. can outwit him. Joyce sent another one to Pound about himself, the "lounging Stephen"

> Whose youth was most odd and uneven.
> He throve on the smell
> Of a horible Hell
> Which a Hottentot wouldn't believe in.

I have often had essays written for me by students who believed, as they had been brought up to do, that the author Joyce entirely approved of the terrorist sermon, and felt glad it had made young Stephen vomit as he deserved.

Between the wars, he may be found complaining mildly that he is supposed to be in the same political and literary movement as Pound, Eliot and Wyndham Lewis (almost the last friends left for poor Hitler in Europe), but he did not have to complain of being thought a Christian, which nobody dared pretend till he was dead. He seems, in a grim tacit way, to have arrived at a working arrangement about the matter which remained firm for the rest of his life. For example, the elaborate bit of prose which he wrote around 1930 to help the tenor Sullivan only comes to life in the evocation of the bells of the churches of Paris gloating over their hopes of murder on the Eve of St. Bartholomew:

> Have you got your knife handy? asks the
> bellman St Andy. Here he is and brand new,
> answers Bartholomew. Get ready, get ready,
> scream the bells of Our lady. And make sure
> they're not quite killed, adds the gentle Clotilde.
> Your attention, sirs, please, bawls Big Brother Supplice . . .

The church is St. Sulpice, but the tortures were what secured public attention. In 1932 we find him at a party in Zurich where a priest praises the Creation while exhibiting the stars from a terrace, and Joyce grumbles (in German): "the whole thing depends on mutual destruction." Animals eat each other, but hardly stars; it seems an automatic reaction to any thought of the Father. By this time he was fairly advanced upon *Finnegans Wake*, which uses a good deal of Christian symbolism, but it had not affected his basic resistance. His grandson was born in 1932, and "a year or two later" his old friend Byrne paid a visit. During a chat about the grandchild he said something implying that it had been baptised. Joyce was appalled, and Byrne managed to pass his remark off as some flat joke about the child, its leakiness presumably. The baptism would have counted as a personal betrayal. In 1938 he was still inscribing a text of *Ulysses* for a young admirer: "Veille de la fête de Madame Bloom," and this, reports Ellmann, still perturbed Nora, because the day was also the eve of the nativity of the Virgin Mary. This seems to have been the last spurt of lava from the old volcano, but there is good authority for thinking that he did not change at the end. After his death in 1941:

> A Catholic priest approached Nora and George to offer a religious service, but Nora said, "I couldn't do that to him."

She would say it with humour but he really would have considered it a betrayal, and he regarded betrayal with great horror. He would regard it as an enormous betrayal that, since his death, everything he wrote has been twisted into propaganda for the worship of the torture-monster. It is pitiful to think of his ghost for ever dancing in fury.

DANIEL FERRER

"Circe," Regret and Regression

Listen then. There are two things. The first is I dreamed I was killing
her. The second is when I killed her I wasn't dreaming.
                    —MARGUERITE DURAS, *L'Amante anglaise*

Moreover, if the name of the dead man happens to be the same as that
of an animal or common object, some tribes think it necessary to give
these animals or objects new names, so that the use of the former
names shall not recall the dead man to memory. This usage leads to a
perpetual change of vocabulary, which causes much difficulty to the
missionaries . . .
                    —SIGMUND FREUD, *Totem and Taboo*

What are we entering as we enter
"Circe," the fifteenth chapter of *Ulysses?* We are entering, or rather re-
entering, a world which is strange and yet familiar . . . The word *"Un-*
heimliche" springs to mind, and we immediately make ready to list the
abundant archaic contents which present themselves. But this will not do;
it is not quite sufficient to account for everything that is at stake in this
chapter, for all the things which set it apart from all the other chapters
while it remains part of the book. Our recognition that the uncanny lies

Translated by Gilly Lehmann. From *Post-Structuralist Joyce: Essays from the French.* Copyright
© 1984 by Cambridge University Press.

at the heart of "Circe," and that "Circe" is acted out at the heart of the uncanny, can be only a first step. But it is precisely the first step which is a problem here: can any step in "Circe" ever be a *first* step?

As we enter the chapter—"*(The Mabbot street entrance of night-town . . .)*"—we are coming, through the entrance, into "nighttown," the town of the night, the red light district. (But the entry occurs inside a parenthesis.) At the opening of the chapter a topographical opening is inscribed, and the gaping doors of the flimsy houses immediately multiply the opening. The first words of the chapter, the first parenthesis, initiate an entirely different typographical system (from now on, the descriptive passages, printed in italics and set in brackets—the stage directions—will be strictly segregated from speeches, printed in lower-case letters and always preceded by a name printed in capital letters—the dialogue); this system, characteristic of the drama, dramatically establishes an incongruous stage, set, after four hundred pages, in the way of the novel's sweeping movement. We soon realize that this break in the form is representative of a radical change. The laws that obtain on this stage are no longer the same as those which governed the daytime of *Ulysses* in which we have spent the earlier chapters.

From this point only a short step is required to decide that this opening marks a break in the novel, that this strange chapter is indeed a stranger to the novel and may therefore be physically separated from it, or at least should be read as a mere dream-parenthesis within a realistic whole. The red light district thus becomes a restricted scene, or the Other Scene. Critics have often said as much: "nighttown" is quite simply dreamtown.

But, were we to take this step, we would be missing "Circe." For "Circe" is literally inseparable from *Ulysses*. Not merely because it is impossible to study it apart, since the chapter is inevitably part of the continuum of *Ulysses*, just as "nighttown," the brothel area, is part of the geographical and social fabric of Dublin, just as the enchantments of the witch Circe are part of the series of adventures which make up the *Odyssey*. But mainly because it is impossible in practice to effect such a separation, since there is no place where a cut could be made. Despite all appearances to the contrary, the initial parenthesis does not create such an opportunity; the opposite is in fact true. For, while the chapter opens with a passage between brackets (and closes in the same way), it is not, itself, contained within one greater parenthesis. "*(The Mabbot street entrance . . .)*": it is the entrance which is thus bracketed; it is the opening which is shut in. The threshold is inscribed only to be spirited away.

SPECULATIONS

Think of a mirror: one can never enter it—not because its surface is an impenetrable obstacle, but because one cannot approach it without realizing that one is *already* in it. In the same way the reader of *Ulysses* has, without realizing it, been in "Circe" for a long time when he reaches chapter 15. The setting, the characters, the situations, even the vocabulary, are already familiar to him, and he cannot resist an inexorable sense of *déjà vu*. And it is important that he should *not* resist. For, just as the only way of going deeper into a mirror (or rather, of seeing one's reflection going deeper) is to back away from it, the ony way of advancing into "Circe" is by constantly retracing one's steps.

Exploring "Circe" (and any other woman) is always a homecoming to familiar territory. But, inevitably, the homecoming seems uncanny. We meet familiar objects and characters, phrases and scenes, and at the same time we notice that they all undergo very strange metamorphoses. For example, hardly have we recognized the figure of Leopold Bloom than he suddenly takes on the sinister aspect of "lovelorn longlost lugubru Booloohoom," and then at once changes into "Jollypoldy the rixdix doldy." How is this possible? Mr. Bloom has, quite simply, just walked past Gillen's hairdresser's shop, and the concave and convex mirrors set up in the window have reflected him for a brief moment.

It is tempting to see in this episode a model of "Circe," placed by Joyce at the opening of the chapter, a kind of variation on the model of Irish art suggested by Stephen in the first pages of the novel ("The cracked lookingglass of a servant"). According to this model, "Circe" is indeed a mirror, but a distorting mirror, one of those disquieting contraptions which introduce difference in the very place where one is seeking confirmation of one's identity. Such an explanation would account for the systematic repetition of elements found earlier in the novel, and for the constant process of transformation which they undergo; it would account for the fusion, within each image, of the strange and the familiar. And yet we must not forget that the distortions created by a mirror of this type, while they seem to be random, are, in fact, always predictable, because they are based on a determined law of optics; and the knowledge of these laws enables one at any given moment to reconstitute a faithful picture of the lost reality. There is no exception to the rule that an accustomed eye can make the necessary adjustments, and therefore any sense of strangeness is rapidly dissipated. But the disquiet produced by "Circe" cannot be so easily dismissed. The strangeness will persist.

The first model is thus only an introduction, simplified and, indeed, oversimplified if one were to stop at this point. But we shall not stop here; we can do better than that without leaving the field of catoptrics. If we look for mirrors, there are far more diabolical reflections to be found. At the heart of "Circe" is a trick which both anticipates and surpasses certain "experiments in recreational physics." It is a mirror, placed in such a way that it shows the spectator a coat-stand made of antlers in the next room and, simultaneously, one of the spectators, thus apparently wearing an imposing pair of horns (general laughter).

The artefact has a further characteristic: the head thus seeming to be framed by this pair of horns springing from nowhere—like a real bunch of flowers in an imaginary vase—is transformed in the eye of some of the spectators, is so deformed that they see Shakespeare himself, a Shakespeare with horns, in the mirror. If we take into account that this Shakespeare is "beardless" and suffers from facial paralysis—which does not prevent him from speaking, albeit after the manner of ventriloquists, and laughing with a capon-laugh—it will be clear that only Joyce himself (or perhaps Raymond Roussel) could give us a complete diagram of the apparatus.

Some elements of its workings will become clearer, however, if we remember that the spectators are not abstract roles but definite characters. The dramatis personae are as follows: those who see only the comic vision of a horned cuckold are Lynch (Stephen Dedalus's companion) and the prostitutes who are laughing with him; those who see Shakespeare (or rather, who see themselves as Shakespeare) in the mirror are Stephen and Bloom—but also ourselves, spectators/readers. How can we explain this contrast? How can we explain this resemblance? What can there possibly be in common between Bloom, Stephen and ourselves?

Perhaps we should entertain the hypothesis that the same image may be produced by factors which are different for each spectator, or, more exactly, by the combination of one stable, common factor and a series of variable factors proper to each individual spectator. The stable element here is the reflection of a man crowned with horns; the variable element being each spectator's individual past, projected on to this reflection. This time there is no need to go very far back into the past. Bloom's wife has just been unfaithful to him. He has been thinking of this all day. He has even thought of the chance of being contaminated by venereal disease as a result of his wife's infidelity. Moreover, he has talked about Shakespeare several times. Stephen too has thought of Shakespeare in the course of the day. He has even talked about Shakespeare at length. For many reasons, the idea of Shakespeare is linked, for him, with the idea of his father.

Because Shakespeare is the Great Begetter ("When all is said Dumas *fils* (or is it Dumas *père?*) is right. After God Shakespeare has created most"). Because Shakespeare is the father of all poets. Because he played the Ghost of Hamlet's father. Perhaps also (or mostly) because Stephen believes he can demonstrate that Shakespeare was cuckolded.

This leads to the following results: Bloom, as a cuckold, replaced in his wife's bed by a more manly man, symbolically castrated and soon, perhaps, syphilitic, sees himself as Shakespeare, a horned, paralysed Shakespeare, capon-voiced and beardless; Stephen, in so far as he resembles Shakespeare (i.e. his father), sees himself as cuckolded, castrated and syphilitic. Bloom is consoling himself by identification with a great man (in France the great man might be Napoleon, but Shakespeare offers the added advantage of being "all in all"). Stephen, on the contrary, is attacking his own image, and simultaneously, his father with whom he has identified. But, in attacking his father, he is digging at the roots of his own identity, for he is trying—in vain—to deny his own filiation (If my father has been cuckolded, he is not my father. But how, in that case, can I possibly look like him? I don't look like him, I look like Shakespeare. But if I don't look like him, it isn't my father who wears the horns, it's Shakespeare—or me. So my father is not a cuckold and he must be my father . . ."). Every reader must continue to unfold for himself the picture of Shakespeare with horns. His own discoveries will take him closer either to Stephen or to Bloom. Their contrasted reactions are representative of two aspects of this chapter. "Circe" is both a magic lantern, producing phantasies whose function is to consolidate the Self, by concealing reality or filling in its flaws, without ever mingling with it, and an infernal machine which destroys identities and shatters reality.

At this point, we must check our hypothesis by applying it to a more substantial extract (more substantial because longer and more obviously important) than the minor episode of the mirrored Shakespeare. A good choice for this test is the scene in which the ghost of Stephen's mother appears, for this scene is a turning-point in the chapter and, perhaps, in the novel.

Her appearance is infinitely more dramatic than that of Shakespeare (although she is not seen by everyone, any more than was Shakespeare— we shall return to this point later). The scene is given in imposingly macabre detail, worthy of a Gothic novel in the grand manner:

(*Stephen's mother, emaciated, rises stark through the floor in leper grey with a wreath of faded orange blossoms and a torn bridal veil, her face worn and noseless, green with grave mould. Her air is scant and lank. She fixes her*

bluecircled hollow eyesockets on Stephen and opens her toothless mouth uttering
a silent word. A choir of virgins and confessors sing voicelessly.)
THE CHOIR: *Liliata rutilantium te confessorum . . .*
        Iubilantium te virginum . . .

This time we are dealing with a real ghost, who fully deserves the name of revenant, for this is not the first time that it has returned. As is always the case in "Circe," the event, here the appearance of the ghost, is nullified as such. An appearance can never be more than a re-appearance.

Very early in the novel, we saw Stephen remembering: "Silently, in a dream she had come to him after her death, her wasted body within its loose brown graveclothes giving off an odour of wax and rosewood, her breath, that had bent upon him, mute, reproachful, a faint odour of wetted ashes." And later, the same words, with minor variations, are repeated:

In a dream, silently, she had come to him, her wasted body within its loose graveclothes giving off an odour of wax and rosewood, her breath bent over him with mute secret words, a faint odour of wetted ashes.
Her glazing eyes, staring out of death, to shake and bend my soul. On me alone. The ghostcandle to light her agony. Ghostly light on the tortured face. Her hoarse loud breath rattling in horror, while all prayed on their knees. Her eyes on me to strike me down. Liliata rutilantium te confessorum turma circumdet: iubilantium te virginum chorus excipiat.

But is it indeed the same thing which re-appears on each of these three occasions, presented in similar terms? Or, more exactly, does it re-appear in the same way? The two passages from the beginning of the novel describe the memory of a dream. It is, first and foremost, a dream (the two passages are introduced by the signpost words, "in a dream"). Nothing but a dream. A dream, moreover, which, while it retains considerable emotional significance, is not experienced directly, but seen from the vantage-point of the daytime world by being experienced as a memory. It is noticeable that the second passage suddenly changes (in the second paragraph of the quotation) into a description of the "real" agony of the mother. The ease of the transition from dream to reality proves that the use of the past distances both experiences to the point where the remembered dream and the remembered reality merge, and the different formulations in the two passages appear as mere stylistic variations, created in the quest after a formal perfection which would fix these traumatic memories in an epiphany belonging neither to life nor to dreams, but to Art.

In contrast to these two passages, the apparition in "Circe" is presented in an entirely different way. Whereas the dream was described in the past tense (even in the pluperfect), the apparition is experienced in the present tense. We do not find here the hesitation between conventional narrative and interior monologue which is characteristic of the first chapter. Here we are no longer faced with subjectivity hidden behind a facade of objectivity or objectivity revealing subjectivity. From the start we are submerged in extreme subjectivity—hallucination—and in absolute objectivity—the stage directions.

These are objective since they are not interpretative, or even descriptive, but prescriptive. There is no difference of level between *Enter a ghost and hobgoblins* and *Enter the milkman*. It is left to the director (but who is the director of "Circe"?) to *produce* these directions and make them real. In the same way, there is no difference here between the apparition of the mother and the actions of Stephen and the other characters in Circe: they are all set on the same level of reality—or unreality. There is nothing which could make distinctions between them legitimate. On Circe's stage, the memory-narrative becomes a concrete presence. Paradoxically, the ghost makes its first appearance by re-appearing yet again.

Is the hallucination subjective? Yes, but whose subjectivity is implied? Who is having the hallucination? Should we call it Stephen's hallucination, since Bloom, Lynch and the prostitutes see nothing? But we see it too, in every detail . . . Should we therefore speak of a negative hallucination, common to all the characters except Stephen? Or is it a hallucination shared by Stephen and ourselves? When we compare this with the Shakespeare episode, we realize that the dividing line has shifted, but we, readers, are always included in the division, whichever interpretation we accept. The reader is directly concerned by the hallucination, and he cannot escape by explaining it in terms of physiology; Stephen, drunk with liquor and music, is perhaps, subjectively, dizzy, but for the spectator/reader of "Circe" the whole scene is whirling dizzily, and this is objective: "*Stephen whirls giddily. Room whirls back. Eyes closed, he totters. Red rails fly spacewards, Stars all around suns turn roundabout. Bright midges dance on wall.*" Our involvement is not accidental, it is programmed in the very form of the text. We should not forget that, in the well-known schema given by Joyce to Stuart Gilbert, this hallucination is assigned to "Circe" not as a theme but as a literary technique, as narration to "Telemachus" or monologue to "Proteus." It takes a time to accustom ourselves to the idea that the hallucination is not being represented: it is a mode of representation. It is not a question of content, but of writing—and of reading.

Let us say, for the sake of the argument, that the ghost of Stephen's mother is indeed (as verisimilitude seems to require) a hallucination. How can we actually share this hallucination? If the hallucination is, in fact, as was suggested in the case of the horned Shakespeare, the result of the past being projected into the frame created by the present, what form of the past can we, readers, project at this point? The answer is, as a matter of fact, included in the question: it is our own past as readers of the first fourteen chapters, since the systematic regurgitation of earlier elements which forms the very basis of "Circe" constantly appeals to this past experience. These elements, torn from their original context, still function within the logical framework of that context; this logic is totally foreign to the new text in which they are now set, and the conflict between two contrasted systems is what gives their second appearance its hallucinatory quality. It is thus necessary to have met earlier the ghost of Stephen's mother, in the shape of a dream or a phantasy produced by Stephen's feelings of remorse, in order to appreciate the full impact of the ghost's materialization in "Circe," as simultaneously absent and present.

. . . A PERPETUAL CHANGE OF VOCABULARY

But we should not forget that every word in "Circe" has its own past and must be considered, individually, as a kind of ghost, haunting the text, returning with a whole network of associations, woven during its previous occurrences in *Ulysses*. Each sentence recalls a host of other sentences which are superimposed upon it, and which, in turn, recall yet more sentences. The ghost we are studying is, therefore, not created merely by the few lines of "Circe" that we have been examining. It is impossible to have any clear idea of the ghost's volume or its outlines, and, more important, it is impossible to discover the forces at work behind it and which raised it, if we do not allow the associations surrounding every word to come up freely. Let us therefore try to draw towards us, almost at random, some of the threads which make up this network.

Stephen's mother, emaciated . . .

The ghost of Stephen's mother is a concrete presence in "Circe," but its appearance seems to betray a dearth of being. It clearly lacks flesh. This emaciation may, of course, be explained by the cancer which was the clinical cause of death. But, if we return to an earlier sentence used by Stephen, and recalled by the word "emaciated," we shall see things from a different angle. In the earlier passage we are shown an "omnivorous being which can masticate, deglute, digest and apparently pass through the ordinary channel with pluterperfect imperturbability such multifarious aliments as *cancrenous females emaciated by parturition*, corpulent professional

gentlemen, not to speak of jaundiced politicians and chlorotic nuns. . . ."
Thus, for Stephen, females (but the plural hides a singular) are emaciated
by parturition (and they probably suffer from cancer for the same reason).
Because she has given birth, the mother has beeen emptied of her substance,
devoured from inside. But we should note that she too has been swallowed
by the great omnivorous being; swallowed, digested and "apparently" ex-
creted—that is, brought into the world, re-born (and this explains her
return as a ghost). The question remains: what happens, in this tale, to
the omnivorous being? Does he, too, become emaciated by parturition?
Final question: did the mother begin by devouring the children she brings
into the world? Might she not devour them again at any moment? (Stephen
certainly seems convinced of this: he calls his mother a ghoul and a corpse-
chewer.)

> Stephen's mother, emaciated, rises stark . . .

"Stark" suggests the stiffness of rigor mortis, a contagious mortification
which invades Stephen's own body ("his head and arms thrown back stark")
just as he thinks he has got rid of the ghost. This stiffness recalls the
drowned corpse described in "Proteus": "Hauled stark over the gunwale he
breathes upward the stench of his green grave, his leprous nosehold snoring
to the sun."

> Stephen's mother . . . rises stark through the floor in leper grey . . . her face
> worn and noseless, green with grave mould.

Here we have the same leper grey, the same noseless face, the same green
of the grave mould. The description of the drowned man suggests that these
hideous mutilations are not confined to the face. We have a hint of what
is taking place beneath the leper grey drapery: "A quiver of minnows, fat
of a spongy titbit, flash through the slits of his buttoned trousers." In this
peculiar birth, the internal devouring is clearly a form of castration. Is the
noseless ghost of Stephen's mother also castrated by her offspring?

But what is a drowned man? A man who has been engulfed (devoured) by the sea, and who, after having suffered a sea-change (digestion),
is thrown up by the sea.

> Our great sweet mother! Epi oinopa ponton.

The assimilation of sea and mother, referred to by Buck Mulligan in the
very first pages of Ulysses, reappears in this passage. The mother is thus
identified both with the sea and with the drowned man; she is devourer
and devoured, container and contained. This sea/dead mother is also an

instrument of death, but it is a pleasurable death: "Seadeath mildest of all deaths," because it means a return to the womb. And yet . . .

And yet Stephen fears water. He hardly ever washes himself, he never bathes in the sea and he drinks no water. But, immediately after his praise of the delights of drowning, he thinks of "Old Father Ocean." And the father appears too, a few lines earlier, identified with the drowned corpse, through the words of Father Shakespeare, "Full fathom five thy father lies."

The same ambiguities—the ambiguity of the feeling of attraction/repulsion inspired by drowning, the sexual ambiguity created by the abrupt transition from masculine to feminine—occur a little earlier: "A drowning man. His human eyes scream to me out of horror of his death. I . . . With him together down . . . I could not save her. Waters: bitter death: lost." It seems that Stephen would gladly go down to the bottom with him. With *her* would be another matter. The sweetness of death suddenly turns bitter.

These ambiguities recur in another passage, to which we are led by the words "*oinopa ponton*," "Omnis caro ad te veniet," "death" and "ghost": "Tides, myriadislanded, within her, blood not mine, *oinopa ponton*, a winedark sea." . . . Bridebed, childbed, bed of death, ghostcandled. *Omnis caro ad te veniet.* He comes, pale vampire, through storm his eyes, his batsails bloodying the sea, mouth to her mouth's kiss." The sea, with its winedark tides, is identified with the mother, bleeding periodically from a secret wound. But the mother evokes the image of Death, and Death leads us back to the great omnivorous being.

If the mother's colour is that of wine, or of black blood, this is because she is indeed wounded in the depths of her being, eaten up by a mysterious illness. She is like the rubies, "leprous and winedark," which Stephen sees in a jeweller's window, where, under the craftsman's "dust darkened . . . toiling fingers with their vulture nails," they are assimilated to the unclean female genitalia: "She dances in a foul gloom where gum burns with garlic. A sailorman, rustbearded, sips from a beaker rum and eyes her. A long and seafed silent rut. She dances, capers, wagging her sowish haunches and her hips, on her gross belly flapping a ruby egg," offered up to the covetousness of the great omnivorous being in a new maritime guise. The rubies conjure up an image of the interior of the mother's body, defiled and terrifying: "Born all in the dark wormy earth, cold specks of fire, evil lights shining in the darkness. Where fallen archangels flung the stars of their brows. Muddy swinesnouts, hands, root and root, gripe and wrest them."

But soon another shop-window attracts Stephen's gaze away from the maternal rubies. Another frame is provided for his phantasizing, this frame being the literal frame of a faded print. The two people engaged with each other in the centre of this picture, under the interested gaze of a large number of spectators seen from behind, are two *men*. They are boxers, whose exchange is both hostile and affectionate: "The heavyweights in light loincloths proposed gently each to other his bulbous fists."

But, at some point, we must call an arbitrary halt to this flood of words and images which come forward at each fragment of the text. So we might as well confine ourselves to this small sample, and try to draw the outlines of an analysis of the ghost of Stephen's mother, based on this tangled mass of contradictory images.

CHERCHEZ L'HOMME

It is necessary to distinguish between at least two levels of interpretation, which are related to the two contrasting aspects of "Circe" mentioned earlier. On one level, the mother is seen here as a malevolent and dangerous being, because she represents Woman.

Certainly, in *Ulysses* as a whole—setting aside the final chapter—women are presented as nuisances who spoil the friendly or even amorous brotherhood of men. We can detect, especially in "Circe," an attempt to transfer to women a masculine, repressive attitude, thus putting all responsibility onto them. Bloom's masochistic phantasy paradoxically takes the form of a kind of breaking-in of Bella/Bello: the masculinization of the dominating woman is quite as important as the pseudo-feminization of the victim. The game is double-edged: on the one hand the woman is eliminated by making her adopt a masculine role; on the other hand, when the make-believe stops, she can be humiliated as a fitting punishment for the cruelty she has just displayed towards her victim (whether at his demand or simply in his imagination):

> BLOOM: . . . Mutton dressed as lamb. Long in the tooth and superfluous hairs. A raw onion the last thing at night would benefit your complexion. And take some double chin drill. Your eyes are as vapid as the glass eyes of your stuffed fox. They have the dimensions of your other features, that's all. . . . Clean your nailless middle finger, . . . the cold spunk of your belly is dripping from your cockscomb. Take a handful of hay and wipe yourself.

Therefore, the most militantly anti-feminist sentiments may be expressed with a clear conscience:

> As if you didn't get it on the double yourselves. No jerks and multiple mucosities all over you. I tried it. Your strength our weakness. What's

our studfee? What will you pay on the nail? You fee men dancers on the Riviera, I read. . . . Eh! I have sixteen years of black slave labour behind me. And would a jury give me five shillings alimony tomorrow, eh?

Could Bloom's odyssey not be summed up by this single detail: before leaving, he gives his wife breakfast in bed; when he comes home, returning to the natural order of things, he demands that Molly serve him in bed (at least, that is what she understands . . .)?

This gives us an insight into the dual aspect of the mother-figure, the archetype of Woman, in "Circe": now a figure of fun like a music-hall clown—Bloom's mother; now a terrifying bogey ("Rawhead and bloody bones")—Stephen's mother, in the passage we have been studying. The mother is the intruder in the father and son relationship which the heroes are trying to build up. She is responsible for the prohibition which hangs over incest between father and son, a taboo whose exceptional force Stephen recalls in tones of regret.

The persecuting ghost of the mother stands between the union of father and son, taking over the function of prohibiting incest which normally belongs to the father. But the ghost also represents the father, whose forbidden love hides itself as persecution, just as Stephen's love hides itself as hate. This could explain all the sexual ambiguities we have noticed, as well as the phallic nature of the spectre, which "rises stark" like an erect penis, which is a ghost like the Holy Ghost—who, we are re-minded several times, got the Virgin pregnant—and which is like that other "ghost" which appears a few pages further on as a violent emission of semen: "*He gives up the ghost. A violent erection of the hanged sends gouts of sperm spouting through his death clothes on to the cobblestones.*"

The counterpart of the masculinization of the mother, and of Woman in general, is not the assumption by the males of a truly feminine position, but the adoption of a mere disguise. The taste for female clothes found in Bloom and in Stephen ("But you were delighted when Esther Osvalt's shoe went on you: girl I knew in Paris. *Tiens, quel petit pied!* Staunch friend, a brother soul: Wilde's love that dare not speak its name") belongs to a fetishistic tendency: it is a denial of female castration. This form of homosexuality is a rejection of the Other, a narcissistic love of the Self. Its purpose is to reinforce identity.

Unfortunately, this reinforcement does not hold for long, as is shown here by the cataclysm on a cosmic scale which ends the ghost scene, or, throughout "Circe," by the degradation suffered by characters and objects. This incestuous homosexuality is only a phase (perhaps reactional); it is not even sufficient to account for all the characteristics of the parental ghost, phallic, but castrated (lacking nose, eyes and teeth), castrating (it plunges its crab's claws into Stephen's heart, and its toothless mouth suggests its counterpart, a toothed vagina) and bisexual ("dogsbody bitchbody")— not to mention other aspects we have demonstrated to be present: cannibalism, double function as container and contents . . . To cover all these aspects we must go further, beyond the Oedipus complex, negative or positive, and look at highly archaic images, such as that of the "combined parent-figure" or, more precisely, the mother as universal receptacle of good and bad objects.

MULTITUDINOUS MOTHER

This return of so distant a past is less surprising when we realize that the ghost is related to much more than just the recent death of Stephen's mother. We know that the work of mourning (and this is what the theatre of "Circe" is all about) brings us back to a very early phase of the individual's development, forgotten, but still active. The actual loss of the beloved is never more than a repetition of a loss already suffered. As Melanie Klein has shown, "the child goes through states of mind comparable to the mourning of the adult, or rather . . . this early mourning is revived whenever grief is experienced in later life." As a result of this, the adult normally reacts by setting to work the same defence mechanism which he has already used:

> While it is true that the characteristic feature of normal mourning is the individual's setting up the lost object inside himself, he is not doing so for the first time but, through the work of mourning, is reinstating that object as well as all his loved *internal* objects which he feels he has lost. He is therefore *recovering* what he had already attained in childhood.

Mourning is always re-gret, leading to regression. It reactivates what Melanie Klein calls the "manic–depressive position," with its images of the mother as a complete but ambivalent object, concentrating the good and bad elements of partial objects, and carrying its weight of anxieties linked to the damage inflicted on this object by the sadism of the subject.

This is in keeping with the changing nature of the ghost, sometimes protective:

> Who saved you the night you jumped into the train at Dalkey with Paddy Lee? Who had pity for you when you were sad among the strangers? . . . I pray for you in my other world. Get Dilly to make you that boiled rice every night after your brain work. Years and years I loved you, O my son, my firstborn, when you lay in my womb;

sometimes threatening: "Repent! O, the fire of hell! . . . Beware! God's hand!"; it is also consonant with its mutilated appearance.

During the depressive phases, the subject needs constantly to compare the mother he has interiorized and the external, real mother, in order to reassure himself that she has not been wounded, that she has not been destroyed by his uncontrollable sadism, that she has not become an avenging figure. The absence of the mother (in our case by death) removes this opportunity to reassure himself by checking his phantasy against reality, and the subject is left with his interior representation of his mother; he has, in fact, made this figure suffer all kinds of cruel attacks because of his own ambivalence, and he fears its vengeance.

At this level, the hallucination may be explained as an attempt to expel into the outer world the persecutor who is threatening the subject from inside. This is a symptom of mourning which is not being carried through satisfactorily: reality-testing, which is an essential element of the normal mechanism of mourning, is by-passed here by hallucination.

But this does not mean that there is here an attempt to deny the painful reality or to achieve a magic reparation of the damaged object, attitudes characteristic of the manic side of the depressive position. For the dead mother returns, but returns as a *dead* mother. There can be no question of healing her wounds. On the contrary, the hallucination leads to a new aggression, acted out by Stephen who attacks the ghost with his ashplant.

We can now see a fresh difference between the hallucinatory staging of the mother in "Circe" and the dreamed–narrated apparition which we met in the first chapter. The narrative neutralized the terrifying image of the dead mother, enshrining her in a well-wrought dream, trying to heal her by the use of words, of stylistic devices (the perfect or the pluperfect) of increasing perfection at each re-appearance. In "Circe," by contrast, the aim is no longer perfection but destruction.

Here there is no healing of objects which would allow them to be reincorporated, thus ensuring stable identification and structuring of the Self. We find the exact opposite: a simultaneous dislocation of the objects and of the Self—that Self which had created itself by identification with those objects (as is shown by the fact that some terms, such as "toothless" and "dogsbody," associated here with the ghost of the mother, are used elsewhere by Stephen to describe himself).

It would be true to say that here, beyond the mirror stage, we have a return to the original state of fragmentation, or, to continue to use Kleinian terminology, regression beyond the depressive position to the paranoid position, in which the subject, whose Self is scarcely integrated at all, is constantly being overwhelmed by his anxiety, by his fear of the persecuting "bad object," by his own aggressive impulses, and is incapable of conceiving a "complete" object with which he could identify.

Our ghost comes directly from this archaic phase. But it is far more than a phantasy from the past, re-appearing in isolation; it is the central core of the general regression which makes up "Circe." The mother, as fundamental object, returns in an emphatic manner, but she returns as a corpse, and, worse still, in a state of decomposition. This unendurable return sets off the decomposition of the entire Universe: *"Time's livid final flame leaps and, in the following darkness, ruin of all space, shattered glass and toppling masonry."* All things revert to primeval chaos, that is, back to the womb, considered this time as the receptacle for all partial objects, a field in which drives, and more particularly destructive drives, are freely released.

This field is the stage upon which "Circe" is enacted, the background against which the various figures (including that of the mother—container and contained) stand out for a moment before disintegrating, coalescing or vanishing under the impact of the destructive forces. As we have seen with the ghost, these figures do not appear in order to disguise the absence of lost objects, in an obsessive or fetishistic way, but to repeat their very absence, just as the young child repeats his mother's absence by the game of Fort-Da, in which Freud found evidence of a principle contrary to the pleasure principle.

While this analogy affords us a glimpse of the workings of "Circe," in turn "Circe" suggests two ideas about the Fort-Da game. Might it not be that the "o-o-o-o"s and "Da"s of the little boy correspond to *stage directions* which, rather than describing, give rise to the gesticulative part of the game (throwing the reel)? Also, even if, as Freud suggests, the "o-o-o-o" is "not a mere interjection but represents the German word *'fort',*" might we not conclude that this inter-jection is, however, a form of in-terjection, that is, a direct expression (not channelled through the rudi-mentary system of symbols set up by the two contrasting sounds) of pulsive energy, a kind of gestic speech?

The notions of gestic speech, of gestures generated by speech, are the keys to understanding the theatricality of "Circe." It was stated earlier that the stage directions which form the basis of this theatricality must be seen as totally distinct from the narrative to be found in the other chapters of *Ulysses* or in other novels. While these stage directions direct us towards external reality, the mode of direction is not descriptive but prescriptive.

The words used are not substitutes for pre-existing objects, but have the potential to generate images and actions which cannot thereafter be reduced to these words, or others, without loss.

Through the verbal language, another and much older language manages to intrude, a language charged with libidinal intensities, a language of gestures, in which energies are released. Stephen announced this at his first appearance in "Circe": "Gesture . . . would be a universal language, the gift of tongues rendering visible not the lay sense but the first entelechy, the structural rhythm." However, although he has known it from the beginning, he has to ask his mother's ghost for the key to this language "known to all men," but which they have forgotten.

Each sentence should be read as a formula, which is both the verbal consequence of a system of drives lying at its source, and a reservoir from which flows a series of bodily movements through channels which are those of hallucination.

. . . I WASN'T DREAMING

But what is a hallucination? It is a perception which comes not from the external world, but from the internal world. Freud has shown that hallucinations, like dreams, produce perception of a "regressive" character. The cathexes from the Ucs system (Unconscious) proceed backwards to the sensory end of the psychic apparatus. This *topical* regression (the transition from a system of the psychic apparatus to an anterior system) results in a predominance of visual images (see the theatrical form of "Circe"), which correspond to the "ideas of things" characteristic of the Ucs system which is the source of the hallucinatory cathexis.

Some "verbal ideas," stored in the Pcs system (Preconscious), may, however, also be re-activated by unconscious cathexes and reach the conscious perception, but to do so they must go through the Ucs system by means of a topical regression and conform to the rules of the Ucs system, that is, they must undergo *formal* regresion, being treated as "ideas of things" and subjected to the primary processes. Thus, in "Circe," each sentence is the consequence of other sentences which occurred earlier in the novel, and which are subjected to the mechanisms of condensation and displacement, to such an extent that the reader sometimes finds it difficult to recognize the originals. In the same way, many of the numerous tableaux, vignettes and incongruous situations are nothing more than the materialization of verbal clichés from previous chapters, made absurdly concrete.

Regression, then, in the purely rhetorical sense of the word, the systematic reproduction in mirror-image of elements already present in the novel, which is the basis of the composition of "Circe," is the translation onto a novelistic plane of hallucinatory regression—but only in so far as this regression is inseparable from a progression which goes on at the same time (continuation of the novel, of the odyssean adventures, of the cataloguing of organs, arts, symbols . . .).

For this is the fundamental difference between dream and hallucination. In a hallucination, the "regressive" perceptions are not confined to another, separate, plane; they are projected directly into reality, where they mingle with ordinary perceptions. The external falls victim to the internal and can no longer extricate itself. This is what gives the hallucination its outrageous quality: it mixes what should stay apart. Was it not for this reason that Descartes, for example, in his *Meditations,* could not bring himself to identify with the lunatic who believed his body was made of glass, whereas he found it easy to accept the hypothesis of the dream and even of the deceptive spirit (which is only the hyperbole of dream, not of madness)? Once the world of hallucination has been entered, nothing is certain any longer, there are no clear and distinct ideas, since everything is mixed up.

In the same way, the scene of "Circe" is by no means an Other Scene, a different world. Despite its phantasmagorial appearance, it is not outside reality, since the gestures generated by the words exist potentially in reality. (The theatricality makes real the hallucination, and, reciprocally, hallucinates reality.) Nor is it outside *Ulysses,* from which it is impossible (as we have already seen) to separate it. Indeed, it is this integration into the novel—an exceptional chapter in the centre of an exceptional novel—which ensures the unstable viability of "Circe." It is because *Ulysses* is a world meticulously anchored to the geographical reality of Dublin and to the chronological reality of 16 June 1904, while at the same time offering itself to the reader as a perpetual referral to a host of other texts, so that it is impossible to tell where this dazzling flight of the referent may end; it is because its links with reality are both firmly stated and difficult to find, that the principle of representation is, by degrees, completely subverted by the hallucinatory technique used for "Circe." It is by contrast with the narrative form of the other chapters that the dramatic form acquires its hallucinatory status. Finally, it is the extremely taut structure and the inertia of the imposing mass of *Ulysses* which prevent "Circe" from reaching a state of total fragmentation, and which permit a kind of balance between what we might call, to use an oversimplification, the forces of consolidation

connected with the figure of Bloom, and the forces of disintegration connected with the figure of Stephen.

"Circe" must not be confused with those works which confine themselves to the theatre of dream or phantasy in order to copy an imaginary
world, in the same way as others claim to copy the external world, both
practices supporting each other. "Circe" is closer to those forms of fiction
which Freud, while condemnng them as "not unalloyed" and productive
of mystification, considers as the most efficient sources of the uncanny,
because they play on several conventions, and do not allow us to discover
until the very last minute whether "their world of representation . . .
coincides with the realities we are familiar with or departs from them."
Except that here there is no very last minute. The "world of representation"
remains double. "Or" should be replaced by "and."

Moreover, it is not enough for "Circe," unlike these other fictions,
to play on passing ambiguities in order to provoke in us uncanny feelings
by showing us pictures based on ancient beliefs which we have surmounted
or repressed (ghosts, for example). It is characteristic of "Circe" that the
ghosts in it never seem really frightening as such. Whether they are purely
farcical, like Bloom's grandfather, Virag, or darkly melodramatic, like Stephen's mother, we cannot take them seriously. And it is precisely this lack
of credibility that makes the intrusion of these apparitions into a world
which is also the real world so deeply disturbing. The constantly sustained
duality of "Circe" shatters the stage, destroys the foundations of representation, leaving us face to face with a system of words and intensities,
uncanny in the extreme, because they constantly reveal the relentless sway
of the past over the present.

PATRICK PARRINDER

"*Dubliners*"

In *Stephen Hero* the intensity of Stephen's artistic ambition leads him to try out a whole series of aesthetic positions. He is the vivisectionist, dedicated to uncover the "significance of trivial things" and their embodiment of the pathological condition of social paralysis. He is the unfrocked theologian, reinterpreting St. Thomas Aquinas's requirements for beauty and recording a series of unofficial and unhallowed epiphanies. He is at once an Ibsenite, a classicist, and aesthete, and a poet storing up a treasure-house of words. All these attitudes may be found in *Dubliners* and yet the result is not one of incongruous variety or fluctuating uncertainty but of a subtle and substantial artistic achievement. *Dubliners* is a work of its time which owes much to the established conventions of late nineteenth-century short fiction. Nevertheless, in his youthful work Joyce outstripped his immediate competitors to produce a new type of short story, which was as intricate and carefully crafted as a lyric poem.

He was categorical enough in the statements he made about the book in letters between 1904 and 1906, when the bulk of the stories were completed. To Constantine Curran in 1904 he observed that "I am writing a series of epicleti—ten—for a paper. I call the series 'Dubliners' to betray the soul of that hemiplegia or paralysis which many consider a city." To Grant Richards, his prospective London publisher, he initially wrote that "From time to time I see in publishers' lists announcements of books on Irish subjects, so that I think people might be willing to pay for the special odour of corruption which I hope, floats over my stories." When Richards

From *James Joyce*. Copyright © 1984 by Cambridge University Press.

wrote back to say that the printer had objected to certain passages, Joyce retreated from this *épater-les-bourgeois* stance to a firmly self-righteous position. "My intention was to write a chapter in the moral history of my country and I chose Dublin for the scene because that city seemed to me the centre of paralysis. . . . I have written it for the most part in a style of scrupulous meanness and with the conviction that he is a very bold man who dares to alter in the presentment, still more to deform, whatever he has seen and heard. I cannot do any more than this. I cannot alter what I have written."

Were these stories, then, "epicleti"—invocations, epiphanic structures, scientific diagnoses which also set out to "betray the soul" or reveal the confessional secrets of Dublin life? Or were they fictions, written for the market, stories commissioned by a paper (AE's *The Irish Homestead*) and which the English reading public might be willing to pay for? Numbers of critics have set out to prove that the stories of *Dubliners* are "epiphanies of paralysis," and it is true that the volume begins with a priest who has succumbed to physical paralysis, and with a narrator who lingers feelingly over the word itself ("It had always sounded strangely in my ears, like the word gnomon in the Euclid and the word simony in the Catechism"). The volume ends with a story giving a broad view of Dublin's musical life, past and present, under the title "The Dead." Nevertheless, the final impression left by the book is not of a series of cold-hearted studies in spiritual paralysis, prominent though the motif may be. Neither is it true, as is often assumed, that Joyce refuses all authorial comment on the significance of his Dubliners' lives. The air of impersonality in the narration is itself a mask, and *Dubliners* uses a richly complex technique to convey a set of strongly ambivalent feelings towards Dublin life and people.

In the 1890s—H. G. Wells later recalled—short stories "broke out everywhere." Writers of all kinds responded to the new demand, and "the sixpenny popular magazines had still to deaden down the conception of what a short story might be to the imaginative limitation of the common reader." "Serious" and "popular" writers alike found a market in the newspapers and magazines of the period. Though many of these writers may be loosely described as "neo-romantics," specializing in adventure tales, in marvelllous and uncanny incidents or in crime and detection, others introduced the sobriety, objectivity, and irony of French naturalism into English prose. The naturalist school in France claimed to have brought the scientific spirit into fiction by means of the accurate, carefully-documented and deliberately impartial portrayal of social conditions and psychological states. The naturalistic writers were materialists, holding that humanity was part of the biological kingdom and was subject to the universal laws of heredity and environment. The artist's role was that of a scrupulously accurate recording instrument, or "court stenography." Zola was the ideologist of naturalism, while Flaubert and Maupassant—though standing at some distance from the more doctrinaire "scientific" claims of the movement—were its leading practitioners in the short story. Joyce's most influential early admirers, including Pound and Edmund Wilson, saw *Dubliners* as a work in the naturalist tradition. In Wilson's view it differed from the work of Maupassant mainly by virtue of the graceful musicality of Joyce's prose.

Zola's great novel-series *Les Rougon-Macquart*, following Balzac's less systematic series *La Comédie humaine*, had set out to make a representative sociological and psychological study of modern France. *Dubliners* belongs to a group of short-story collections with topographical titles, published around the turn of the century, which also claim to offer a composite portrait of a particular culture. Yet, by contrast with the massive novel-sequences, the "portrait" they provide can only be a series of sketches or impressions. The popularity of this form and its techniques owes something to the advent of impressionist painting, which had drastically altered the relationship between the visual artist and his subject-matter. The subjects of the impressionists were "found" rather than being elaborately designed and reconstructed in the studio. Established rules of pictorial composition were ignored and the paintings were executed deftly and rapidly, so as to capture the "impression" before it was lost. The literary equivalent of the impressionists' concern with capturing the moment was the so-called "slice of life" story which attempted to create a particular emotional "atmosphere." In France Maupassant was regarded as the master of this form of short fiction; but Joyce, as we shall see, took it further than Maupassant had done.

The genre to which *Dubliners* at first sight belonged was that defined by the urban realism of Arthur Morrison's *Tales of Mean Streets* (1894), Arnold Bennett's *Tales of the Five Towns* (1905) and, a little later, Sherwood Anderson's *Winesburg, Ohio* (1917). In Irish writing Joyce's predecessor and rival was George Moore, whose collection *The Untilled Field*—its title symbolizing an Ireland in which "Nothing thrives . . . but the celibate, the priest, the nun and the ox"—appeared in 1903. Moore's stories are, for the most part, bleak tales of the west of Ireland peasantry. Moore, however, uses the frame-story of a pair of Irish artists to present, in dialogue form, his own attitudes to the national culture. *Dubliners* betrays fewer illusions about Ireland and Joyce's manner is rigorously detached and impartial. He is a naturalist to the extent that he allows the paralysis of Dublin society to "betray" itself, rather than analysing or denouncing it openly. None of his characters strike us as primarily a mouthpiece. Eveline, Maria, Bob Doran, Tom Kernan, Gabriel Conroy and the others must convince us of their reality before we see them as exemplifying a thesis. Joyce took great care, too, that his settings should be utterly authentic. He admired the knowledge of India that Kipling had shown in *Plain Tales from the Hills* 1888) and, amusingly enough, he attacked Moore for showing a suburban lady looking up the times of trains on the Dublin–Bray commuter line—a line with a frequent and regular service. In *Dubliners* "scientific" concern for authenticity is taken further, perhaps, than any previous writer had done.

The specificity of *Dubliners* inevitably conditions the reader's response. "Two Gallants" takes place around St. Stephen's Green; Mrs. Sinico dies at Sydney Parade. Eighty years ago this was felt to be uncomfortably realistic. A more conventional writer would have changed some of the names, as Arthur Morrison changed the names of his haunts in the London slums and Arnold Bennett changed the names and number of the North Staffordshire pottery towns. Joyce's refusal to use invented names was one of the reasons why *Dubliners*, which was completed in 1905 and revised and expanded a year or two later, did not appear until 1914. George Roberts of Manusel & Co., a Dublin publisher, cited the naming of actual shops and pubs as one of his reasons for backing out of his agreement with Joyce. (Another reason was a disrespectful reference by one of the characters to King Edward VII; the English publisher Grant Richards, on the other hand, took these things in his stride but was upset by the word "bloody.") Why, one might ask, was Joyce so obdurate about details such as these? It is as if he had discovered in the physical actuality of Dublin, as well as in its speech, his essential and lasting subject-matter. To the modern reader of Joyce the city delineated in *Dubliners* is frequently enriched and overlaid by later impressions; for example, the Magazine Hill in Phoenix Park from which Mr. Duffy in "A Painful Case" spied on couples lying in the grass, is the "Magicscene" of an act of voyeurism which resounds throughout *Finnegans Wake*. Yet the activity of Joyce's writing is never confined to the single function of evoking a sense of place. Often —disconcertingly—the very phrases in which he evokes the presence of place have the effect of casting radical doubt on that presence. Take, for example, the opening sentence of "A Painful Case": "Mr. James Duffy lived in Chapelizod because he wished to live as far as possible from the city of which he was a citizen and because he found all the other suburbs of Dublin mean, modern and pretentious." Does such a sentence convey useful information or misinformation about Chapelizod? The boorish recluse Mr. Duffy is scarcely someone we can accept on trust as an urban historian. The narrator, characteristically, offers no opinion on this matter, and the reader is left to make his own mind up.

There is another device Joyce uses to suggest that his narrator is an invisible recorder of Dublin itself—not the author of a prepackaged, "fictionalized" view of the city. This is his insertion of what appears to be actual documentary material—shop-signs, canvassing cards and so on—into the narrative. The effect is rather like a Cubist collage. Once represented in fiction, the signs and notices lose their purely instrumental function and can be appreciated simply as items of language. The protagonist of *Stephen Hero* makes a similar discovery, finding "words for his treasure-house . . . at haphazard in the shops, on advertisements, in the mouths of the plodding public. He kept repeating them to himself till they lost all instantaneous meaning for him and became wonderful vocables." Some of these words are on display in the opening story of *Dubliners*, "The Sisters":

> It was an unassuming shop, registered under the vague name of *Drapery*. The drapery consisted mainly of children's bootees and umbrellas; and on ordinary days a notice used to hang in the window, saying: *Umbrellas Recovered.*

The narrator reaches the door, but instead of reading the umbrella notice he reads another, and so do we:

> 1st July, 1895
> The Rev. James Flynn (formerly of S. Catherine's Church,
> Meath Street), aged sixty-five years.
> R.I.P.

The narrator is a child, by whom signs are still taken for wonders. Later, he will be tricked by a cynical and meretricious use of language—the use of the exotic word "Araby," to glamorize a charity bazaar. Shop-signs are also reproduced in "Araby," and in "Two Gallants." Later stories include such cultural source-materials as the verse of "I Dreamt that I Dwelt" that Maria sings twice (in "Clay"), and the canvassing cards and text of Joe Hynes's ode on the death of Parnell (in "Ivy Day in the Committee Room"). Most remarkably, there is the newspaper report of Mrs. Sinico's inquest which takes up about fifteen per cent of the length of "A Painful Case." In all these instances Joyce's documentation goes conspicuously beyond what was usual even in the annals of naturalism. There are several reasons for this: hints towards an interior view of those characters in whose minds the various documents are unforgettably lodged; the "silence" or interruption of authorial disclosure in the text which such documents provide; and, not least, simple authentication of the incidents Joyce describes. Like his use of proper names, the fictive documents assert that it is an actual city and not a mere figment of the artist's imagination that is portrayed in *Dubliners.*

The naturalistic novelists tended to show their characters as helpless victims of the "fate" constituted by the forces of heredity and environment. Where the earlier nineteenth-century novel portrayed processes of moral, social and historical causation, by the end of the century the naturalists had come to understand character-development in increasingly brutal, biological terms. Julien Sorel, in Stendahl's *Le Rouge et le noir* (1831) was an ambitious boy born into a generation in which social advancement could only be bought at the price of hypocrisy. In 1800 he could have found preferment in the army; twenty years later, he must seek it through the church. George Eliot's Lydgate similarly lets himself get entangled in a restricting web of social circumstances not of his own making. In each case the character must take moral responsibility for his actions. When we come to Zola, however, we find characters whose lies are in theory closed to moral judgment since the author does his best to show that they could not do other than what they did. Joyce showed the same reductive impulse in choosing a medical term, paralysis, to sum up the spiritual condition of Dublin. Occasionally we meet with a phrase in his early work which comes straight out of the vocabulary of turn-of-the-century naturalistic clichés. Thus Eveline, unable to respond to her lover's entreaties, "set her white face to him, passive, like a helpless animal." Such a phrase makes a pretence at scientific impassivity but expresses a mixed attitude of authorial pity and disdain. Occasionally—despite the generally impersonal tone—Joyce permits himself a narrative comment wielding irony at the character's expense. Mrs. Mooney, we are told in "The Boarding House," "dealt with moral problems as a cleaver deals with meat." Appropriately enough, she is descended from a family of butchers.

In the "slice of life" story pioneered by Maupassant, character is neither analysed at length (in the way that George Eliot does), nor is it unfolded (as in Zola) through a long-drawn-out action leading to an inevitable fate. Instead, it is sketched or sampled at a particular moment. Nevertheless, a typical Maupassant story revolves around an exceptional event and incorporates, as part of its narrative development, a biographical summary of the past life of the main character. The same is true of many of the *Dubliners* stories—notably "A Painful Case" and "The Dead"—but not all. "Clay," for example, is an impressionist sketch which, adapting the title of a 1960s film by Agnès Varda, we might call "Maria from 5 to 10." Its "plot" involves nothing more startling than the loss of a slice of cake. "Ivy Day in the Committee Room" also lacks any sort of recognizable plot. These are stories of a kind which might have been dismissed as "mere anecdotes." (As Wells recalled, "The short story was Maupassant; the anecdote was damnable.") Yet, in their humble way, they are anticipations of *Ulysses* where the "slice of life" extends across eighteen hours in the lives of three main characters with a huge supporting cast. It is no accident that *Ulysses* began as a project for an additional story in *Dubliners*.

The "slice of life" story replaces extended description with the suggestive evocation of "atmospheres." "Atmosphere" was a favourite book-reviewers' terms of the period, although Joyce himself decidedly preferred the word "odour." He wrote to Grant Richards of the "odour of corruption which, I hope, floats over my stories." In "Eveline" we meet—strategically placed in the opening paragraph, and later repeated—the phrase "odour of dusty cretonne." This gives an impression of Eveline's entanglement in drab and dingy circumstances, stated with an obviousness not found in the later stories in the book. Descriptive repetition, however, features elsewhere in *Dubliners*, and has often been misunderstood by critics unconcerned with the literary context in which Joyce was writing. Magalaner and Kain, for example, detect a "heavily weighted structure of Hell symbolism" in "Ivy Day in the Committee Room":

> It seems inconceivable that so disciplined a writer as Joyce would mention maybe a score of times the fire, smoke, cinders and flames on the hearth of the committee room simply to tell the reader that the room contained a fire.

Joyce, here, is creating an "atmosphere." The fire in "Ivy Day" is a beneficent fire, warming the shabby crew of canvassers, lighting their cigarettes and popping the corks on their bottles of stout. Whatever Dantesque overtones readers may find, this is a vividly-rendered impressionistic background to a story which deserves better than to be reduced to trite Christian allegory.

Still more striking than Joyce's treatment of external atmosphere is his use of the free indirect style to create a narrative coloured by his characters' internal impressions or mental landscapes. "Free indirect style" is a form of third-person narrative which mimics the vocabulary and idioms of a particular character. It aims to convey a mode of thinking and feeling informally and "from the inside," without resorting to the explictness of direct speech, reported speech, or authorial summary. Once again it is a naturalistic technique, working through "impressions" rather than analysis, and pioneered by the French. "Clay"—a boldly experimental story which has had much less than its due—exemplifies Joyce's use of free indirect style. The opening paragraph offers such brazen narrative clichés as "spick and span" and "nice and bright." The second paragraph coyly describes the heroine as "a very, very small person indeed." As the story proceeds the distance between Maria's self-protective version of events and the reality insinuated between the lines is a source of gentle comedy:

> What a nice evening they would have, all the children singing! Only she hoped that Joe wouldn't come in drunk. He was so different when he took any drink.
>
> Often he had wanted her to go and live with them; but she would have felt herself in the way (though Joe's wife was ever so nice with her) and she had become accustomed to the life of the laundry. Joe was a good fellow. She had nursed him and Alphy too; and Joe used to say:
> —Mamma is mamma but Maria is my proper mother.

To Maria this has all come to seem a very natural state of affairs. The narrator appears at first glance to be neutrally recording her views. Yet lurking beneath the surface is not only an awareness of the banality of Maria's idiom ("in the way," "ever so nice") but a realization of the travesty that, in this environment, passes for conventional family life. What caused the absence or dereliction of Maria's mother? We are never told. What is it that drives Irish husbands and fathers to the bottle? Here we are verging on the major theme of *Dubliners*—the tribulations of manhood, womanhood and family life in a society that Joyce knew intimately.

The free indirect style is a stage in Joyce's development towards a fully-fledged "stream-of-consciousness" method such as he employs in the early chapters of *Ulysses*. Its use of colloquialism, cliché and euphemism draws attention to the uncertain distance between narrator and character. The narrator's implicit attitude wavers between sympathy and ironic superiority. If irony separates him from his characters, it links him to his potential readers or addressees. Who are the implied readers of *Dubliners*, and what is involved in Joyce's appeal to them? The "two or three unfortunate wretches," mentioned in discussion with Stanislaus, who "may eventually read" this chapter in the moral history of their country are, in fact, a type of audience whose existence had been attested in other countries by many earlier nineteenth-century writers. Stendhal, for example, addressed himself to the "HAPPY FEW"; Flaubert, to those superior enough to their surroundings to savour a *Dictionnaire des idées reçues*. Such audiences form a self-selected elite which prides itself on an inner detachment, not merely from particular classes of "received ideas," but from the whole mode of discourse in which society at large exchanges ideas. Joyce's ironies in *Dubliners* often imply that sort of negativity. They are unearned, in the sense that they make no attempt to explain or justify the feelings they evoke or the prejudices to which they appeal; the reader is simply given a set of coded instructions, on pain of exclusion from the "happy few" if he cannot interpret them correctly.

To what extent, for example, is Maria a simpleton or Eveline a "helpless animal"? What should we make of the complacent wisdom of Mr. Duffy, who, after a brief contact with an Irish socialist group, concludes that "No social revolution . . . would be likely to strike Dublin for some centuries"? In a sense (and this is what Joyce meant by the "scrupulous meanness" of his writing) such questions are left to the reader. That does not mean that they are unanswerable. The answer is subtle and difficult to be sure of, but it does exist. In general the tone of *Dubliners* is harsher, the author's assumption of superiority over hapless humanity is more palpable, than in his later work. It is the "moral history" of his country as seen by a somewhat embittered young writer. Some of the stories (especially "Eveline," "The Boarding House," "Counterparts" and "A Mother") have crudely cynical touches; none could be described as over-indulgent. It is significant that "The Dead" was composed later than the other stories, and that it was preceded by the following confession in one of Joyce's letters to his brother:

> Sometimes thinking of Ireland it seems to me that I have been unnecessarily harsh. I have reproduced (in *Dubliners* at least) none of the attractions of the city for I have never felt at my ease in any city since I left it except Paris. I have not reproduced its ingenuous insularity and its hospitality. The latter 'virtue' so far as I can see does not exist elsewhere in Europe. . . . And yet I know how useless these reflections are.

Significant, too, is the difficulty we may find in decoding the later part of the *Portrait of the Artist*, where Joyce's irony is turned against his own earlier artistic ambitions.

If a work is difficult the suspicion arises that it is esoteric—that the reader is missing some arcane or hidden level of meaning, which would provide the key to full comprehension. Hence the inscrutability of Joyce's irony in parts of *Dubliners* inevitably leads to the question of symbolism. For many years symbol-hunting of various sorts has made the running in the criticism of Joyce's short stories. Yet it is far from clear that the occult correspondences fetched up by scholars have actually made the book more readable. A technique of retrospective interpretation, in which devices of multiple identification and symbolic association appropriate to *Finnegans Wake* are read back into the earlier Joyce regardless of the difference in fictional conventions, may actually lead to the delusion that *Dubliners* is *more* difficult (because ostensibly more simple) than anything that followed it. Yet, if symbolic interpretations of *Dubliners* have often been very wide of the mark, the dilemma they address is a real one. Joyce's earliest readers, once they had been alerted to the possibility of unseen depths in the stories, found themselves assailed by dark suspicions that all was not as it seemed. The publisher George Roberts (as Joyce recorded in a letter written from Dublin in 1912) "asked me very narrowly was there sodomy also in *The Sisters* and what was 'simony' and if the priest was suspended only for the breaking of the chalice. He asked me also was there more in *The Dead* than appeared."

Symbolism was decribed by Arthur Symons in 1899 as "a form of expression, at the best but approximate, . . . for an unseen reality apprehended by the consciousness." Like naturalism, the symbolist movement in literature was a late nineteenth-century import from France. The theory of epiphanies described in the previous chapter is indebted to both naturalist and symbolist doctrines. Joyce's readers, however, did not encounter this theory until 1944, when *Stephen Hero* was published. The same year saw the publication of a scholarly article offering—I believe for the first time— an esoteric interpretation of *Dubliners*. Richard Levin and Charles Shattuck argued in "First Flight to Ithaca" that *Dubliners* like *Ulysses*, incorporated an elaborate structure of allusions to Homer's *Odyssey*. The Homeric allusions made up a consistent layer of meaning which, they claimed, no earlier reader had spotted. This theory has been received, for the most part, in stunned silence. For one thing, it can neither be proved nor refuted. Seamus Deane, speaking in general terms, has written that "Many of the coincidences that surround Joyce's work seem entirely accidental." But who knows which are and which aren't? A later symbolic interpretation of "Clay," by Marvin Magalaner, drew the fire of no less formidable an enemy than Stanislaus Joyce. "I am in a position to state definitely that my brother had no such subtleties in mind when he wrote the story," Stanislaus pronounced. I cannot resist quoting Magalaner's reply, a little gem of scholarly self-importance:

> This type of personal-acquaintance criticism is understandably dangerous. What family of a deceased writer has not felt that blood relationship and lifelong closeness afforded deeper insight into the writer's work than detached criticism could? This is a natural and healthy family tendency;

... at the same time, one may suspect critical judgments enunciated by such sources as the last word on, say, literary symbolism.

It might equally be asked if here are any known cases of symbolic inter-pretations of literary works being withdrawn as a result of criticism. But nobody in this largely conjectural area will ever have the last word. Even Stanislaus Joyce accepted the presence of parodic allusions to Dante's *Divine Comedy* in "Grace," because his brother told him they were there.

Symbolism was a topical and widely discussed literary technique when Joyce was writing *Dubliners*. Yeats had been acclaimed by Arthur Symons as the leading English symbolist. Baudelaire's famous poem "Cor-respondences," with its evocation of Nature as a temple filled with "forests of symbols," had first appeared fifty years earlier. Baudelaire had been fol-lowed by the *symboliste* school of poets expounded by Symons, and also by a school of symbolist painters. Wilde's statement in the preface to *Dorian Gray*—"All literature is both surface and symbol"—had done much to familiarize the concept. Later historians such as Edmund Wilson would regard symbolism and naturalism as opposing tendencies, thanks to their polemical association with the doctrines of spiritualism and materialism respectively. Yet Flaubert and Zola are inveterately symbolic novelists, and Ibsen's symbolic mode is a crucial presence behind Joyce's story "The Dead" (to be discussed later in this essay).

Symbolic interpretation is an aid to understanding *Dubliners* so long as it is not pursued in isolation from other modes of reading. Just as Stephen Dedalus rested his theory of beauty on the epiphany or spiritual manifes-tation, each of the *Dubliners* stories works towards an intuitive and unpar-aphraseable insight into reality. Sometimes—as in "A Painful Case" and "The Dead"—these are elaborately presented, in a heightened and con-sciously poetic prose. But far more often the story ends on an understated and anticlimactic note. The presentation of Maria's song at the end of the Hallowe'en party in "Clay" is a good example:

She sang *I Dreamt that I Dwelt*, and when she came to the second verse she sang again:

> *I dreamt that I dwelt in marble halls*
> *With vassals and serfs at my side*
> *And of all who assembled within those walls*
> *That I was the hope and pride.*
> *I had riches too great to count, could boast*
> *Of a high ancestral name,*
> *But I also dreamt, which pleased me most,*
> *That you loved me still the same.*

But no one tried to show her her mistake; and when she had ended her song Joe was very much moved. He said that there was no time like the long ago and no music for him like poor old Balfe, whatever other people might say; and his eyes filled up so much with tears that he could not find what he was looking for and in the end he had to ask his wife to tell him where the corkscrew was.

Only a three or fourfold reading will begin to do justice to this passage. Joyce's naturalism enables him to present a wholly convincing picture of a lower-class Dublin family party. The popular song is written out in full as Maria performs it. Joe is all too clearly "given away" by his final words and actions. We might (though Joyce doesn't) draw morals from this about the cultural functions of music and drink in turn-of-the-century Dublin. In fact Joyce distracts our attention from such incipient moralizing by the other layers of his technique. Impressionism dictates that our reaction to the song will be mediated entirely through Joe and that the story will close abruptly, on a ironic note, with the party still in progress though rapidly deteriorating. The irony leaves us hesitating whether to take Joe's nostalgia as a feeling of substance, or whether to dismiss him as a mere sentimentalist, a maudlin drunkard groping for the corkscrew. A symbolic reading, however, must start with Maria's mistake; at a symbolic level (Freudian or otherwise) no mistake is innocent or accidental. The verse that she has left out describes the young heiress as besieged by suitors. This will connect for us with earlier incidents, each of which involves shame and the deliberate suppression of instinctive feelings. There is the unexplained loss of the plumcake; we deduce that Maria was so flustered by her conversation with the elderly gentleman as to have left it on the tram. There is also Maria's choice of the clay and the prayer-book (not the ring) when she is blindfolded in the Hallowe'en game—the clay from the garden has been brought in for a prank by "one of the next-door girls." A detailed knowledge of Irish Hallowe'en customs is the key to these enigmatic incidents. Such knowledge, however, can only bring us back to the poignant human situation which can be appreciated without any special study of folklore. Maria is shown undergoing a painful if minor ordeal, and she nearly cries over her loss of the plumcake. Joe actually does cry at the end, with the result that "he could not find what he was looking for." In one sense he is a buffoon whose miniature farce contrasts with what, for Maria, is a genuine miniature tragedy. (In the Hallowe'en games the rebuffs she has received signify spinsterhood and death.) But Joe also stands for the reader who—not having been told why Maria omitted the second verse, or what happened to the plumcake, or that the stuff in one of the saucers was "Clay"—equally has difficulty in finding what he is looking for. The ending is not only realistic, moving, and ironic, but also delicately self-referential. Joyce's story is very like a bottle for which someone has hidden the corkscrew. The homely metaphor suggests all those feaures of *Dubliners* which have prompted ingenious and learned critics to "hunt the symbol." Yet it should be remembered that in "Ivy Day in the Committee Room" Joyce shows an alternative method of opening a bottle of stout, for which no corkscrew is needed. This method simply requires patience and warmth.

SIGNS OF PARALYSIS

Joyce's "scrupulous meanness" of expression sets up a certain resistance to discussing the themes of his stories. Can we approach them thematically without violating the restraints and ignoring the indirectness which the author has so meticulously imposed upon himself? Joyce himself did so by describing their burden as one of "paralysis." Paralysis, as a metaphor for the doomed and self-defeating life of Dublin, is most starkly seen in the story of Patrick Morkan's horse, as told in "The Dead." The horse, having been employed for years to drive a treadmill, was unable to master any other mode of locomotion. One day Mr. Morkan decided to harness him to a trap and go for an outing in the park. The journey came to an end when the horse reached King Billy's statue, and began to walk round and round it. The horse, a creature of habit going round in circles, was a true Dubliner. Or is it that the story is a true Dublin story?

Central in *Dubliners*, as in all his work, is Joyce's handling of sexual and family relationships. Though the first three stores may have some autobiographical basis, the child in them is an orphan, living with his uncle and aunt. In other stories the family—especially the father—displays all the signs of paralysis. Fathers in *Dubliners* tend to be drunken, quarrelsome, inadequate at work and ineffectual in the home. They are bullies who take out their frustrations on their wives and children. Mothers are less uniformly selfish, but they too fall far short of what is desirable. Eveline thinks of her mother's "life of commonplace sacrifices closing in final craziness." The mother of Joe and Maria was mysteriously absent. Mrs. Sinico takes to the bottle. Little Chandler's baby is caught between a weak-minded father and an over-protective mother. Farrington's wife, and the mother of his five children, is "a little sharp-faced woman who bullied her husband when he was sober and was bullied by him when he was drunk." Beside the squalid families of *Dubliners* the Blooms in *Ulysses* are paragons of mutual consideration and family happiness.

Joyce shows us the unfortunate courtships which lead to marriages like these. Lenehan in "Two Gallants" dreams of having "a warm fire to sit by and a good dinner to sit down to." He could live happily "if he could only come across some good simple-minded girl with a little of the ready." His friend Corley has found such girl, but has no intention of marrying her. In "The Boarding House" marriage is forced on the unwilling Bob Doran by a determined mother-in-law. His bride, Polly Mooney, is nineteen. Bob Doran is around thirty-five. Mrs. Kearney in "A Mother" got married "out of spite." Before marriage "the young men whom she met were ordinary and she gave them no encouragement, trying to console her romantic desires by eating a great deal of Turkish Delight in secret." She also settled in the end for a much older man.

Florence L. Walzl has recently argued that, sordid though it may be, Joyce's portrayal of Dublin family life has an uncomfortable sociological accuracy. It reflects the position of early twentieth-century Ireland as one of the poorest countries in the civilized world, with a population depleted by the Great Famine and by mass emigration. "For over a century following 1841, Ireland had the lowest marriage and birth rates in the civilized world. As a natural concomitant, it also had the highest rate of unmarried men and women in the world." Irish labour brought far more prosperity to London, Liverpool, Belfast, New York, Boston, and Chicago than it did to Dublin. Mr. Henchy in "Ivy Day in the Committee Room" laments the lack of industrial investment in the Irish capital, and other stories reflect the prevalence of arranged marriages, fruitless courtships, and wary bachelors. Gabriel and Gretta are the only married couple represented at the Misses Morkan's annual dance. Lily, the caretaker's daughter, is bitterly resentful of the opposite sex, and Freddy Malins, a middle-aged soak, is represented as an eligible "young man of about forty." Measured by the middle-class norms of more prosperous countries, most of the relationships in *Dubliners* are degenerate.

The opening story, "The Sisters," is explicitly concerned with "paralysis" and links it to the theme of degenerate fatherhood. The priest is addressed as "Father," and embodies some of the moral authority lacking in the actual fathers Joyce portrays; moreover, Father Flynn has taken a paternal interest in the narrator, who is an orphan. Father Flynn has died of paralysis (also known as paresis, a consequence of tertiary syphilis). To the boy the name of the disease is "like the name of some maleficent and sinful being. It filled me with fear, and yet I longed to be nearer to it and look upon its deadly work." The details of the boy's relationship with the priest are left vague, yet he is aware that it is a source of adult disapproval. His curiosity is whetted by his uncle's friend Cotter, who has his own theory about Father Flynn, but won't say what it is. Cotter saw something "un-canny" and "queer" about the priest; something to be kept away from the young boy. The boy dreams that the priest is confessing something to him from beyond the grave. The dream is an "out of the body" experience in which "I felt my soul receding into some pleasant and vicious region"—something that will occur also to Gabriel Conroy in "The Dead." Down-stairs, over a glass of sherry, a few details of the priest's guilt and mental collapse slowly emerge from among the conversational pieties. Earlier he had enthralled the boy with his descriptions of the mysterious rituals of the Church and the secrecy of the confessional. After he broke the chalice he himself was found one night "sitting up by himself in the dark in his confession-box, wide-awake and laughing-like to himself." The priest's sis-ter's account has the effect of confirming what the boy sensed in his dream—that Father Flynn had something on his mind he would have liked to confess. The delicacy of Joyce's telling consists in what is left unspoken as the boy encounters for the first time the world's corrupt and shameful mysteries. He feels liberated by the old priest's death, but it is an open question whether or not that feeling is an illusion. Will he in turn inherit, or discover himself, the guilt and solitude which he still does not fully understand? Will he fall victim to physical or mental paralysis?

"The Sisters" is unusual in *Dubliners* in that it shows a penitent figure—the old priest in his confession-box, his mind unhinged—without making it clear what he has to confess (though a clue is provided by the word *simony*). Many of the other stories end with an act of formal penitence, but their subject-matter is the drama of rebellion or thwarted escape. "An Encounter" and "Araby" explore the schoolboy attractions of the Wild West and the mysterious East respectively. "An Encounter" open racily and describes a day spent wandering the streets and playing truant. Finally the boy attracts the attentions of another degenerate father-figure—a paedophile with sadistic interests. The man's obsession is a form of mental and emotional paralysis, a circuit of feelings from which like Father Flynn, he cannot escape:

> He gave me the impression that he was repeating something which he had learned by heart or that, magnetized by some words of his own speech, his mind was slowly circling round and round in the same orbit. . . . He began to speak on the subject of chastising boys. His mind, as if magnetized again by his speech, seemed to circle slowly round and round its new centre.

Both here and in "The Sisters" Joyce was probing unpleasant (and at that time little written about) aspects of the relationship between adult and child. The stories are deliberately disturbing. The child's imaginative alertness and taste for the unorthodox leads, in the end, to a deeply disillusioning encounter. Both priest and paedophile have an "elaborate mystery" to unfold; the mystery is corrupt and repellent and yet undeniably human. Both men exert a powerful, tacit claim on his sympathies. In the final paragraph, the boy feels ashamed of calling to his companion for help, and "penitent" for having earlier despised him. His shame and penitence strike deeper than the ostensible reasons he gives for them. These emotions suggest that the boy is learning to take on himself the guilt of the adult world, and also the circularity of a system of feeling in which "sin" is forever being chased by "penitence."

"Araby" shows an intimacy with the narrator's experience, and a poetic intensity, such as Joyce perfected in A Portrait of the Artist. The boy has now reached adolescence, but the themes explored are entirely con-sistent with the two preceding stories. In his dream in "The Sisters" he found himself in a strange oriental land, perhaps Persia. Now he is capti-vated by the magic of the name "Araby," which is not only a charity bazaar but a symbol of his infatuation for Mangan's sister. (Her name—not to be defiled as the name "Araby" is by the end of the story—is kept secret even from the reader.) The boy has moved into a house where a priest has just died. In "The Sisters" we left Father Flynn in his coffin, "solemn and truculent in death, an idle chalice on his breast." In "Araby" the narrator is a solemn adolescent who bears his imaginary "chalice" (the worship of Mangan's sister) "safely through a throng of foes." He enters the room where the priest died and prays to Love instead of God. The boy himself has become an idolatrous priest, but his sacramental visit to the bazaar (where he hopes to buy his beloved a gift) turns into a squalid farce. Delayed by his drunken and negligent uncle, he arrives only in time to hear the chink of coins and the banter as the stallholders shut up for the night. He sees himself as a "creature driven and derided by vanity." His "anguish and anger" might have been directed at the adult world which has thwarted his dreams; instead, it is turned inwards, in an act of self-mortifying pen-itence. In worldly terms this is no very disastrous development; it will probably send the narrator back to his schoolwork. Put together with the other stories, however, it shows the operation of a culture which forces both adults and children into an intimate acquaintance with defeat.

The formula of escape leading to penitence occurs in many of the succeeding stories. At the end of "After the Race" Jimmy "knew that he would regret in the morning"; the heroine of "Eveline" no doubt is in the same predicament. Bob Doran in "The Boarding House" is ready to marry Polly Mooney since both he and his future mother-in-law agree that he owes "reparation" for the "sin" of making love to her. Chandler's revolt in "A Little Cloud" ends in "tears of remorse." Mr. Duffy is haunted by his cruelty to Mrs. Sinico. "Grace" ends with Tom Kernan's formal act of penitence, and Gabriel feels shame near the end of "The Dead." These acts of penitence are often morally suspect—most of all that in "Grace," which is sanctioned by the explicit authority of the Church. Tom Kernan's drunkenness is an act of transgression which—like the other miniature escapes and rebellions in *Dubliners*—seems to express both a positive inner need and a self-destructive urge. The Church's role is to represent such actions as sins—sources of guilt, that is, for which reparation must be made. The priest hearing confessions in "Grace" is there to "to wash the pot," a circular process of cleansing and pollution which gives the communicant a fresh start so that he can sin again. Tom Kernan's wife, we are told, "accepted his frequent intemperance as part of the climate." Though Mr. Kernan ends the story in a state of grace, there is no reason to suppose that the climate has changed.

"Grace" satirizes a whole range of Irish absurdities. There are the pompous opinions of Mr. Kernan's gentlemen-friends, who come to his sickbed; the "climate" in which men drink themselves insensible and beat up their wives, only to be nursed as invalids and fed with beef-tea; and, above all, there is the Church which adds social cement with its businessmen's retreat, at which Father Purdon presents himself as a "spiritual accountant" and speaks to his flock "as a man of the world speaking to his fellow-men." A less explicit, though equally potent, anticlericalism is to be found in a much earlier *Dubliners* story, "Eveline."

Eveline Hill, a frustrated and deprived young woman, is a version of the conventional naturalistic heroine pioneered by Flaubert in *Madame Bovary*. She dreams of escaping from her drab and dingy life, but at the crucial moment when escape is within her grasp, she is powerless to act. Eveline is not an inspiring figure, and the condescension that most readers feel towards her is perhaps merited. She is in love with a sailor, a "kind, manly, open-hearted" figure called Frank, who has promised her marriage and a home in Buenos Aires. Eveline's father suggests that Frank is not what he seems, and at least one critic, Hugh Kenner, agrees with him. On the quayside waiting for the steamship, Eveline prays for guidance; the result is that she is pinned to the spot and lets Frank go off without her. The ship, Kenner maintains, would not have been bound directly for Buenos Aires, but for Liverpool. Has Eveline, thanks to divine intervention, just avoided a "fate worse than death"? And if she has, would such a life be worse than the life her own mother was condemned to in Ireland? Her father was a drunkard, a bully and a wife-beater; her mother eventually went mad. Joyce himself had successfully wooed Nora Barnacle with promises which must have seemed no less far-fetched than those Frank makes to Eveline. Indeed, I would suggest that Nora's existence, and her willingness to leave for Europe without a marriage certificate and with a young man she had only known for a few weeks, is the standard against which Eveline's faint-heartedness ought to be measured. Curiously, one of the two or three major English naturalistic novels, Arnold Bennett's *The Old Wives' Tale* (1908), tackles a similar problem through its contrast of two sisters, Constance and Sophia Baines—the one a stay-at-home, the other a runaway. Joyce's impressionistic sketch leaves various questions unanswered; its tone, however, falls well short of Bennett's compassionate fair-mindedness. We leave Eveline seized by physical paralysis, "like a helpless animal."

At her moment of crisis she "prayed to God to direct her, to show her what was her duty." There is more to this than the circularity of escapism followed by penitence. Eveline is a young girl, facing the first great challenge of adulthood. She is trying to defy the will of her father, but her defeat comes, not in a direct confrontation with parental authority, but through an inner struggle resolved by her prayer. What Joyce shows repeatedly in *Dubliners* is not just the direct workings of repression—parental, sexual, religious—but its reproduction and internalization. Eveline is stopped, not by external restraints, but because she has learnt a self-restraint which cuts off her capacity for action and wipes out the adult personality she was struggling to establish.

A simple and, indeed, crude illustration of the reproduction of repression is the story "Counterparts." Here Farrington rebels against the tedious drudgery of his job, and is given the choice of making an abject apology or getting the sack. Humiliated at the office, he has a few drinks after work and goes home to bully his son. Home is the one place where he can exercise power over others. His wife is at the chapel, otherwise she too would (no doubt) have to bear the brunt of his rage. Tom, the son, instinctively relapses into pious whimperings as he is beaten:

—O, pa! he cried. Don't beat me, pa! And I'll . . . I'll say a *Hail Mary* for you. . . . I'll say a *Hail Mary* for you, pa, if you don't beat me. . . . I'll say a *Hail Mary*. . . .

Where there is repression, there too is the Church with its message of mercy and forgiveness. Yet the Church, in Joyce's eyes, represents a humaner and more subtle system of repression. Each character in "Counter-parts"—even poor Tom as he tries to strike a bargain with a "Hail Mary"—resorts to some form of power in a vain attempt to wipe out his subjection to forces not of his own making. The circuit of subjection continues.

The anticlericalism of *Dubliners* is a quality it shares with Moore's *The Untilled Field.* In Moore's collection the opening story ("In the Clay") sets up a schematic opposition between the priest and the artist. Rodney, an Irish sculptor, wants to work from the nude and finds a willing sixteen-year-old model. Her father sends for the priest and, as a result, the girl is forbidden to sit and Rodney finds his studio broken into and his work smashed to pieces. He leaves Dublin in disgust for Paris while Lucy the model (like many other characters in *The Untilled Field*) eventually goes off to settle in America. Moore's allegory here is not difficult to read: the deep bond between the Irish artist and the Irish people, thwarted by the Church, is nevertheless affirmed by their mutual resort to emigration, even though in practice that emigration takes them in different directions. Though Joyce disliked the melodrama and sentimentality of *The Untilled Field*, such a parable was clearly not lost on him. He, too, shows the "paralysis" of Irish life opposed by people of a certain artistic bent. Little Chandler, Mr. Duffy, and Gabriel Conroy in *Dubliners* are internal exiles, semi-alienated from their surroundings, yet, lacking the talent and force of character to make a genuine bid for independence. Their role in the book is to be defeated, though in the case of Gabriel Conroy (and perhaps of Mr. Duffy) there is some glory in defeat. Chandler, in "A Little Cloud," is a would-be minor poet whose pathetic shallowness is evidenced by his admiraton for his friend Ignatius Gallaher—a journalist who has escaped from Dublin only to be-come the vulgarest of cosmopolitans. Mr. Duffy, author (like Joyce) of an unpublished translation of Hauptmann's *Michael Kramer,* is a fastidious recluse who nevertheless find himself implicated in the most commonplace of sentimental tragedies. Gabriel, another lonely and sensitive man with literary tastes, tries to fulfil the social responsibilities thrust upon him by his aunts; but his self-respect is sorely tried by the need to be agreeable to people whose "grade of culture differed from his." In all three cases the artist's relationship with ordinary people—as in Moore—is the underlying burden of the story. But Joyce's way of exploring that relationship is entirely his own. He does so by creating halfway or partially alienated characters, rather than the stock Bohemian representatives of the artistic "type." The awkwardness of their participation in society is highlighted through their suspicion of its language.

The rich and mysterious potential of language has been seen in two of the childhood stories, "The Sisters" and "Araby." In a story like "Two Gallants" the style of narrative description has a confusing richness:

> The grey warm evening of August had descended upon the city and a mild warm air, a memory of summer, circulated in the streets. The streets, shuttered for the repose of Sunday, swarmed with a gaily coloured crowd. Like illumined pearls the lamps shone from the summits of their tall poles upon the living texture below which, changing shape and hue unceasingly, sent up into the warm grey evening air an unchanging unceasing murmur.

"Fine writing," we might think, and pass on, were it not that the three sentences of this opening paragraph come progressively closer to paradox. It is August yet the air is only a "memory of summer." The streets are at once swarming and in repose. The crowd is both unceasingly changing and "unchanging unceasing." Here the narrator is dandyishly trying out his own virtuosity while his two actual dandies, Corley and Lenehan, betray the shallow and mercenary nature of their thought the moment they open their mouths. Lenehan's ponderous expansion of a cliché—"That takes the solitary, unique, and, if I may so call it, *recherché*—biscuit!"—is the nearest they come to vitality of expression. The first sign of paralysis is a paralysed language.

It is language, again, which establishes the essential absurdity of Chandler's admiration for Gallaher. The pub conversation in which Gallaher shows off his worldliness and patronizes his friend is a prize collection of clichés. For Chandler to go home wondering "Was it too late for him to try to live bravely like Gallaher?" exposes his ludicrous self-deception; after this, we might feel, the little solicitor's clerk deserves all he gets. Joyce's satire is rather crude here. Mr. Duffy and Gabriel, by contrast, establish some of their credentials in the reader's view by their fastidiousness about the words they use. Mr. Duffy "had an odd autobiographical habit which led him to compose in his mind from time to time a short sentence about himself containing a subject in the third person and a predicate in the past tense." His friendship with Mrs. Sinico ripens until one night "he heard the strange impersonal voice which he recognized as his own, insisting on the soul's incurable loneliness." Mrs. Sinico seizes hold of his hand and presses it to her cheek—a linguistic error or failure of understanding which destroys their relationship: "Her interpretation of his words disillusioned him."

Mr. Duffy is so alienated that he has no language in which to share his feelings with anyone. Gabriel, however, is anxious to find the right level of language and avoid a "wrong tone." He is faintly embarrassed at the literary phrase he has coined, "a thought-tormented age"; nevertheless he uses it in his after-dinner speech, though omitting the quotation from Browning which he "feared . . . would be above the heads of his hearers." In the event his speech successfully blends personal feeling with the banalities expected on a festive occasion; his success, however, does nothing to appease his consciousness of himself as a "nervous well-meaning sentimentalist, orating to vulgarians and idealizing his own clownish lusts." Like Mr. Duffy, he experiences his alienation from other people as a gulf between his private language, and public language.

Frequently in *Dubliners* Joyce turns a half-ironic, half-approving scrutiny on the public language of festive and social occasions. We hear Gabriel's speech, Maria's song and Joe Hynes's ode on the death of Parnell. Though irony is present, such moments do much to redeem the impression of drabness, degeneration, and failure that is otherwise so prevalent in the book. In his 1906 letter to Stanislaus (quoted above) Joyce wondered whether he had done justice to Irish hospitality. The book, as it happens, is full of hospitable and festive occasions. Where in later works he shows the comradeship of pubs and bars, *Dubliners* coveys the sense of community through a succession of private parties. Even in "The Sisters" the boy's visit to the house of mourning is an occasion for cream and crackers and the glass of sherry which is perhaps what gets the sisters talking. "After the Race," one of the slightest stories in the book, is the story of an evening's high living among a group of cosmopolitan young men. They drink "Ireland, England, France, Hungary, the United States of America," and then settle down to play cards. The story is a political and economic allegory in which the game of cards stands for the "great game" of European diplomacy and high finance. The American foots the bill, and the outcome lies between the French and the English. Jimmy Doyle, the Irishman, gets cleaned out. Jimmy's doomed but sporting attempt to engage on level terms with the representatives of the great powers is Joyce's comment on Irish aspirations to nationhood. The Hungarian finally announces the new day, however, because Arthur Griffith, the founder of Sinn Fein, had taken Hungary's resistance to Austrian domination as an emblem of Ireland's struggle.

Jimmy Doyle's night of folly is succeeded by the Hallowe'en party in "Clay," the political anniversary of "Ivy Day in the Committee Room," and the bedside gathering in "Grace." All three are thoroughly Irish occasions, with bottles of stout well in evidence. Even while remaining detached from them the Joyceian narrator shows them as occasions for jokes and sentiment, for poetry and song. These festivities bring out an underlying tension between local attachments and Irish pride, and the international culture of the modern bourgeois world. On the one side are the Hallowe'en customs, the Parnellite tradition and respect for the Irish priesthood, which is said in "Grace" to be "honoured all the world over." On the other side are the "two masters," London and Rome—not to mention the plutocracy of wealth and the internationalism of culture. Politics in "Ivy Day in the Committee Room" are dominated by material interests; Parnell's memory has no place in a Nationalist party that is happy to accept Conservative support in the municipal elections to secure the defeat of Labour. Will the Nationalists endorse an address of welcome to be presented to the English King on his visit to Dublin? The signs are that they will. Mr. Henchy's belief in enticing capital to Ireland seems to be carrying the day. Militant patriotism, which in 1904 was not yet a political force to be reckoned with, can be dismissed as a matter for "hillsiders and fenians." If political rule comes from London, religious authority, as we see in "Grace," is invested in the Vatican and the doctine of papal infallibility. Leo XIII, Mr. Power says in reverential tones, was "one of the most intellectual men in Europe, . . . I mean apart from his being Pope." These political and cultural tensions are dramatically heightened in "The Dead." On one level, the dance held on the Feast of Epiphany is almost disrupted by the intransigence of Miss Ivors, representing the resurgence of cultural nationalism, who accuses Gabriel of being a "West Briton" and then walks out. At another level, however, a true cosmopolitanism is affirmed through the medium of musical culture. The good feeling at the Morkans's is in clear contrast to the acrimony of the Irish Language Society's concert, which Joyce satirizes in "A Mother." At the Morkans's Italian opera, the waltz, Mary Jane's Academy piece, and at the last moment an Irish folk-song "The Lass of Aughrim" all contribute to the festivity. In a minor key the same cosmopolitanism is present in earlier stories. For example, the music of Balfe—a Dublin-born composer who began his career with the Italian Opera before settling and making his fortune in England—is present in "Eveline" and "Clay." The much-travelled Frank takes Eveline to see *The Bohemian Girl*, and—after the Irish Hallowe'en rituals—Joe and Maria become sentimental over "I Dreamt that I Dwelt." Much later in his life Joyce was to rebuke his friend Arthur Power, who said that he was "tired of nationality" and that he wished to write like the French, not the Irish, since "all great writers were international." Joyce's reply was "Yes—but they were national first—if you are sufficiently national you will be international." Music in *Dubliners* seems to bear out this paradox. It is a positive expression of the bourgeois culture that, in other ways, Joyce was condemning for its "paralysis." Where there is music—with the dreadful exception of the semi-professional, semi-amateur concerts portrayed in "A Mother"—there is also spontaneity, joy, and animation. It is here that we glimpse such zest and resilience as Joyce's Dubliners possess.

VISIONS OF THE OUTCAST: "A PAINFUL CASE" AND "THE DEAD"

Mr. Duffy in "A Painful Case" comes to feel that he is "outcast from life's feast." He too has been a music-lover, whose "only dissipations" resulted from his liking for Mozart. He is an utterly solitary man whose abortive friendship with the middle-aged Mrs. Sinico could well have been the material of melodrama. A lesser novelist might have been tempted to show Mr. Duffy coming across the dead body of his jilted lady on the railway line, or at least catching sight of her under the influence of drink. Joyce, however, conveys her degeneration only through the flat-footed prose of a newspaper report. He shows Mr. Duffy rejecting all voluntary bonds of relationship both with an individual ("every bond . . . is a bond of sorrow," he tells Mrs. Sinico) and with society at large. He lives far from the city and soon loses interest in the socialist party whose meetings he once attended. In fact, he languishes in the state of inert and purposeless disconnection which the French sociologist Emile Durkheim diagnosed as *anomie*. *Anomie*, a state of mind in which the individual feels no solidarity with his fellow-men and is free of all social restraints, is both a typical modern urban phenomenon and a contributing cause of suicide. Mr. Duffy lacks the self-destructive impulse of Mrs. Sinico and at the end, when he feels his "moral nature falling to pieces" we cannot say for certain that he is a suicidal figure. What he does experience, at a level of visionary intensity, is an awareness of the life he has missed by standing aloof.

His first impression after reading the report of Mrs. Sinico's inquest (described by the Coroner as a "most painful case") is one of revulsion: "He saw the squalid tract of her vice, miserable and malodorous. His soul's companion!" Her death is an illustration of the struggle for existence and it seems to justify his own ruthless instinct of self-preservation: "Evidently she had been unfit to live, without any strength of purpose, an easy prey to habits, one of the wrecks on which civilisation has been reared." Mr. Duffy here sees civilization in Darwinian terms as a competitive, predatory struggle in which he at least does not intend to be among the victims. When the evening draws on and he walks out into the park, however, his repressed feelings and emotions seem to rebel against him. He is haunted by the sense of Mrs. Sinico's presence. In his hallucinatory state "he seemed to feel her voice touch his ear, her hand touch his": she has risen from the grave, as it were, like the priest in the narrator's dream in "The Sisters." He finds himself envying the "venal and furtive" sexual transactions taking place under the park wall. Finally the vision dies away:

> He turned his eyes to the grey gleaming river, winding along towards Dublin. Beyond the river he saw a goods train winding out of Kingsbridge Station, like a worm with a fiery head winding through the darkness, obstinately and laboriously. It passed slowly out of sight; but still he heard in his ears the laborious drone of the engine, reiterating the syllables of her name.
> He turned back the way he had come, the rhythm of the engine pounding in his ears. He began to doubt the reality of what memory told him. He halted under a tree and allowed the rhythm to die away. He could not feel her near him in the darkness nor her voice touch his ear. He waited for some minutes listening. He could hear nothing: the night was perfectly silent. He listened again: perfectly silent. He felt that he was alone.

The goods train, like a "worm with a fiery head," is a powerfully suggestive piece of symbolism. The passage both describes the rhythm of the engine and perfectly conveys the rhythm of Mr. Duffy's feeling. It describes an uncanny experience, a hallucination—the engine reiterating "Emily Sinico, Emily Sinico" picks up the earlier suggestion that she is somehow present and haunting the landscape—but the realistic control never falters and we are not inclined to view this as more than a momentary mental aberration. Joyce's achievement here was to create a prose style capable of fully rendering the private despair of a lonely, sensitive man. Earlier we heard that Mr. Duffy was in the habit of composing short sentences about himself, with a subject in the third person and a predicate in the past tense. He is Joyce's creation and these are his sentences.

In "A Painful Case"—for the first time in *Dubliners* since the opening stories of childhood—we sense a close identification (though the identification is balanced by revulsion) between Joyce and his protagonist. (His brother Stanislaus, as it happens, was an acknowledged model for Mr. Duffy.) A still greater sense of sympathy and identification is felt towards Gabriel Conroy in "The Dead." Gabriel, who like Joyce has fallen in love with a country girl from Galway, is probably a fantasy-projection of the novelist as he might have been had his talent failed him and had he lived on to become a man of settled habits in his native city. The story is the longest and most substantial in *Dubliners*, and the last to be written. In it, however, Joyce abandons some of the technical innovations he had introduced in earlier, more impressionistic stories.

"The Dead," unlike "Ivy Day in the Committee R
Both its dramatic structure and its symbolism testify to a r
part of his undergraduate passion for Ibsen. Ibsen's favourit
one in which the complacent, accommodating surface of b
shattered by a long-delayed revelation of decisive events in th
the same thing happens in "The Dead," where Gabriel's self-complacency
is destroyed by the discovery that his wife once loved another man whose
name, Michael Furey, signifies the passionate nature that Gabriel lacks.
The title of the story not only implies haunting but echoes Ibsen's *Ghosts*
and *When We Dead Awaken*. The deathly appearance of some of Joyce's
characters, such as Aunt Julia, and the spiritual deadness of others recall
Mrs. Alving's famous outburst which is responsible for the title of the former
play:

> I am half inclined to think we are all ghosts, Mr. Manders. It is not only
> what we have inherited from our fathers and mothers that exists again in
> us, but all sorts of old dead ideas and all kinds of old dead beliefs and
> things of that kind. They are not actually alive in us; but there they are
> dormant, all the same, and we can never be rid of them. Whenever I
> take up a newspaper and read it, I fancy I see ghosts creeping between
> the lines.

If *Ghosts* is an attack on the deadness of bourgeois society, *When We Dead
Awaken* holds out the promise of a new life of self-liberation. Rubek, the
hero, is a sculptor whose masterpiece was a tableau of the Resurrection.
Years later, at a health resort in the mountains, he meets the woman who
had served as a model for the central figure in his sculpture. Neither has
remained faithful to the vision that sustained them in that earlier time,
but now they resolve to break with the bourgeois world and "resurrect"
their lives. They disappear into the snowfield, and the play ends with the
sound of the avalanche that engulfs them.

Joyce had written an attentive précis of *When We Dead Awaken*,
published as "Ibsen's New Drama" in the *Fortnightly Review* in 1900. Thirty-
four years later he has to write a burlesque of *Ghosts*, in the form of a verse
epilogue spoken by the ghost of the dissolute husband of Mrs. Alving. The
general theme of paralysis in *Dubliners* is an extention of Ibsen's diagnosis
of social death or *rigor mortis*. In "The Dead" Gabriel, as we have seen, is
not a great artist but a less exceptional and only partially alienated figure.
He is not the man to make a grand gesture of self-immolation like that of
Rubek and Irene. Yet, in the visionary passage at the end of the story, he
has an "out of the body" experience in which he travels in spirit to the
region of the dead, and then westward across the snow-covered Irish land-

scape. Finally his soul "swooned slowly" amid the snowfall. This experience—which may be no more than the wanderings of a mind falling asleep—is Joyce's way of rehandling the material of Ibsen's dramatic catastrophe.

Ibsen's dramatic symbolism serves to evoke an "unseen reality" determining the action and yet excluded by the four walls of the bourgeois drawing-rooms in which his middle-period naturalistic plays are set. This excluded world may be evoked through verbal imagery, as in *Ghosts,* or by a physical representation on stage as in *The Wild Duck.* The snow-landscape which symbolizes Gabriel's fantasies of escape from the social world is presented in a similarly tentative, yet insistent way; at no point do we see Gabriel actually lost in a snowy wilderness. His preoccupation with snow is opposed to the fire-symbolism associated with the "boy in the gasworks," Michael Furey. There have been endless explications of the symbolism of the story, thanks to the complexity of Joyce's interweaving of themes and his use of stories within stories. There is a strong subsidiary geopolitical theme, which opposes Dublin (the centre of English influence where Gabriel's visit to the glassworks, of the old Italian opera companies and of Patrick Morkan's horse. Yet throughout "The Dead" Joyce's symbolism, like that of Ibsen's naturalistic plays, is in the service of a realistic dramatization of social life and individual emotional dilemmas. In it Joyce demonstrates his mastery not just of "visionary" writing but of a rich and crowded social scene.

"The Dead" shows his intimate knowledge of the musical culture of Dublin, and it also relies tacitly on our awarenes of another art, which appropriately is that of theatre and "stage-management." Theatricality and "putting on an act" play a prominent part in several earlier stories: the boys of "An Encounter" adopting false names and mimmicking a Wild West adventure, the self-dramatization of Corley and Gallaher, the backstage manoeuvrings of "A Mother" and (for that matter) of Polly's betrothal in "The Boarding House." In "The Dead" the Misses Morkans's dance is a well-rehearsed affair in which Gabriel is a key figure both as behind-the-scenes manager (Freddy Malins in particular needs to be "managed") and as a principal actor with a carefully scripted speech who nevertheless suffers badly from stage-fright. From the moment of his arrival his over-hearty salutations betray him as acting a role. One of his last actions at the party—pacing around the hall in his goloshes in imitation of Patrick Morkan's horse—is still more unmistakably theatrical. Yet it is immediately after that, when he catches sight of his wife listening to Bartell D'Arcy's singing—a prospect which at first makes him think of a third art, that of symbolist or impressionist painting—that the theatrical continuity is shattered. There is nothing staged about Gretta's emotion. Back at the hotel, listening to her story and seeing himself as a "pitiable fatuous fellow" in the mirror, Gabriel is like an actor with his greasepaint off.

A remarkable feature of "The Dead" is the new understanding which Joyce brings to his central woman character. In several of the earlier stories the women are unsympathetic and shadowy figures. ("Clay" and "Eveline" do not suffice to correct the prevailing impression.) In the last section of "The Boarding House" we find Joyce trying, but not wholly succeeding, to show Polly Mooney's thoughts as she waits upstairs for the outcome of the interview between her mother and the lodger. Though her marital fate hangs on this she is neither frightened (once she has recovered from a bout of tears), nor calculating, nor penitent. Unlike her lover she feels no shame about her situation. Instead she becomes lost in reverie, achieving a momment of mental freedom which is precarious and measurable, almost, against the clock. When her mother calls her there is a split second before she remembers that she is in the middle of a crisis. All this is admirable, yet beyond references to her "hopes and visions" and "secret amiable memories" Joyce gives very little idea of what might be going on in her mind. He shows that she is not, like so many of his other characters, overburdened by a conviction of sin; but he cannot make her interesting.

Gretta Conroy in "The Dead" has suddenly recalled an old lover, of whom she has never spoken and who moved her passions more deeply than her husband has done. After the dance she confesses as much to Gabriel, yet she too is remarkably free of shame, penitence, or the desire to apologize. Her love for Michael Furey, in fact, stands alone in *Dubliners* for its mutual passion (though we should remember that Gretta observed the social conventions and allowed herself to be sent away to a convent). At their last meeting Furey stood outside her bedroom window on a wet winter night and told her he "did not want to live." He died a week later, presumably of consumption. Gretta re-lives the agony of her loss but there is no sign that she blames herself for the course her life has taken. Has her immature passion for Michael Furey been succeeded by a mature love for Gabriel? Joyce does not say so openly, but we do sense that the humiliation Gabriel feels as a result of her confession is an exaggerated, over-dramatized first response. Later he calmly accepts the situation and this is what leads to the visionary state evoked at the end of the story.

Like the boy in "The Sisters" and "An Encounter," Gabriel is the involuntary recipient of a confession. Unlike the boy, however, he is able to hear the confession out and to receive it with full and generous sympathy. Though he fails to achieve the sexual intimacy with Gretta for which he had been hoping, he overcomes his purely selfish disappointment and achieves, in the last lines, a curiously passive liberation of the spirit:

> Generous tears filled Gabriel's eyes. He had never felt like that himself towards any woman but he knew that such a feeling must be love. The tears gathered more thickly in his eyes and in the partial darkness he imagined he saw the form of a young man standing under a dripping tree. Other forms were near. His soul had approached that region where dwell the vast hosts of the dead. He was conscious of, but could not apprehend, their wayward and flickering existence. His own identity was fading out into a grey impalpable world: the solid world itself which these dead had one time reared and lived in was dissolving and dwindling.
>
> A few light taps upon the pane made him turn to the window. It had begun to snow again. He watched sleepily the flakes, silver and dark, falling obliquely against the lamplight. The time had come for him to set out on his journey westward. Yes, the newspapers were right: snow was general all over Ireland. It was falling on every part of the dark central plain, on the treeless hills, falling softly upon the Bog of Allen and, farther westward, softly falling into the dark mutinous Shannon waves. It was falling, too, upon every part of the lonely churchyard on the hill where Michael Furey lay buried. It lay thickly drifted on the crooked crosses and headstones, on the spears of the little gate, on the barren thorns. His soul swooned slowly as he heard the snow falling faintly through the universe and faintly falling, like the descent of their last end, upon all the living and the dead.

For all its undoubted beauty this passage has a little the air of an exercise—the conscious perfection of Joyce's "epiphanic" technique. The epiphany ends with a dying fall. "Falling" is echoed seven times, with one "descent." "Their last end" picks up an earlier reference to the monks of Mount Melleray who sleep in their coffins. As in "A Painful Case," the passage describes a vision or hallucination which is nevertheless easily believable; the mind is drifting between waking and sleep. Gabriel's deathly "swoon," like Rubek's last gesture in *When We Dead Awaken*, suggests both death as the end of everything (which is one meaning of "his journey westward"), and death as a release from the false animation around him into a genuine spiritual life. Gabriel's soul, however, is not that of a Christian but of a would-be artist, a man of sensitivity and compassion who stands at a certain distance both from the festivities of ordinary life and from the "feast" of passionate love. What he lacks compared with other men of a different "grade of culture" makes up for his capacity for vision. While the first story of *Dubliners* shows the death and "paralysis" of a priest, the conclusion to the volume thus points towards the transcendence of death through the artistic imagination. Yet if Gabriel, his soul swooning slowly, seems to have given up the struggle of life in this world, there is a remarkable emotional dissonance between this ending and the tone of Joyce's later works. A ribald defiance of death would take over, in *Ulysses*, from this reverent intensity of feeling. Its intensity and deliberate beauty help to account for the ease with which we may find ourselves detaching the ending of "The Dead" from the rest of *Dubliners*. To do so, however, is to upset the balance of attraction and repulsion towards the common life of Dublin which makes Joyce's stories, for all their impressionism and "scrupulous meanness," a "chapter in the moral history of my country."

Chronology

1882   James Augustine Aloysius Joyce born in Dublin on February 2 to John Stanislaus Joyce, tax-collector, and Mary Jane (May) Murray Joyce. He is the eldest of ten children who survive infancy, of whom the closest to him is his next brother Stanislaus (born 1884).

1888–91   Attends Clongowes Wood College, a Jesuit boarding school. He eventually is forced to leave because of his father's financial troubles. During Joyce's childhood and early adulthood, the family moves many times, from respectable suburbs of Dublin to poorer districts, as its size grows and its finances dwindle. Charles Stewart Parnell dies on October 6, the young Joyce writes an elegy, "Et tu, Healy." His father, a staunch Parnellite, has the poem printed, but no copies survive.

1892–98   Briefly attends the less intellectually prestigious Christian Brothers School, then attends Belvedere College, another Jesuit school.

1898–1902   Attends University College (another Jesuit institution); turns away from Catholicism and Irish nationalist politics. Writes a play, *A Brilliant Career*, (which he later destroys) and essays, several of which are published. Graduates in 1902 with a degree in modern languages, having learned French, Italian, German, Norwegian and Latin. Leaves Dublin to go to Paris and study medicine.

1903   Joyce works primarily on writing poems (which will be published in 1907 as *Chamber Music*) and reading Jonson at the Bibliothèque Ste. Geneviève. Receives a telegram from his father ("Mother dying come home Father"). Returns to Dublin, where May Joyce dies of cancer on August 13, four months after her son's return.

1904   An essay-narrative, "A Portrait of the Artist," is rejected for publication; several poems are published in various magazines, and a few stories, which eventually appear in *Dub-*

liners, are published. Stays for a time in the Martello Tower with Oliver St. John Gogarty (Malachi Mulligan in *Ulysses*). Joyce takes his first walk with Nora Barnacle on June 16 ("Bloomsday" in *Ulysses*). The daughter of a Galway baker, she is working in a Dublin boarding house. In October, Joyce and Nora leave for the continent, where they will live the remainder of their lives. Joyce finds work at a Berlitz school in Pola (now in Yugoslavia).

1905   The Joyces (as they are known, although they do not marry until 1931, for "testamentary" reasons) move to Trieste, where Joyce teaches at the Berlitz school. Birth of son Giorgio on July 27. Joyce submits manuscript of *Chamber Music* and *Dubliners* to Dublin publisher Grant Richards. Joyce's brother Stanislaus joins them in Trieste.

1907   After a year in Rome, where Joyce worked in a bank, the Joyces return to Trieste, where Joyce does private tutoring in English. *Chamber Music* published in London (not by Grant Richards). Birth of a daughter, Lucia Anna, on July 26. Writes "The Dead," the last of the stories that will become *Dubliners*. Works on revision of *Stephen Hero*, an adaptation of the essay "A Portrait of the Artist," later to be *A Portrait of the Artist as a Young Man*. Begins writing articles for an Italian newspaper.

1908   Abandons work on *Portrait* after completing three of five projected chapters.

1909   Joyce pays two visits to Dublin: in August, to sign a contract for the publication of *Dubliners* (not with Grant Richards), and in September as representative for a group who wish to set up the first cinema in Dublin. Returns to Trieste with sister Eva, who will now live with the Joyces.

1910   Cinema venture fails; publication of *Dubliners* delayed.

1911   Publication of *Dubliners* is held up, mainly because of what are feared to be offensive references to Edward VII in "Ivy Day in the Committee Room." Joyce writes to George V to ask if he finds the story objectionable; a secretary replies that His Majesty does not express opinions on such matters.

1912   Final visit to Dublin with his family. Printer destroys the manuscript of *Dubliners*, deciding the book's aims are anti-Irish. Joyce takes the proofs of which he has gotten a copy from his equally unsympathetic publisher, to London but cannot find a publisher for them there, either.

1913   Joyce's original publisher, Grant Richards, asks to see the manuscript of *Dubliners* again. Ezra Pound, at the urging of William Butler Yeats, writes Joyce asking to see some of his work, since Pound has connections with various magazines, and might be able to help get Joyce published.

1914   Grant Richards publishes *Dubliners*. At Pound's urging, *A Portrait of the Artist as a Young Man* is published serially by the London magazine *The Egoist*. Joyce begins work on *Ulysses*. World War I begins on August 4.

1915   Joyce completes his play, *Exiles*. After Joyce pledges neutrality to the Austrian authorities in Trieste who threatened to intern him, the family moves to Zürich, with the exception of Stanislaus, who is interned. Joyce awarded a British Royal Literary Fund grant, the first of several grants he will receive.

1916   Publishes *A Portrait of the Artist as a Young Man* in book form in New York.

1917   Undergoes the first of numerous eye operations.

1918   Grant Richards publishes *Exiles* in London; it is also published in the United States. The American magazine *The Little Review* begins serializing *Ulysses*, which is not yet complete. Armistice Day, November 11.

1919   Joyce refuses to be analyzed by Carl Jung. *The Egoist* also begins serializing *Ulysses*. The U.S. Post Office confiscates issues of *The Little Review* containing the "Lestrygonians" and the "Scylla and Charybdis" chapters.

1920–21 More issues of *The Little Review* confiscated. In September, John S. Sumner, the secretary of the New York Society for the Prevention of Vice, lodges a protest against the "Nausicaa" issue. The case comes to trial, and the *Review* loses, in February 1921. Publication ceases in the United States. Joyce and family move to Paris. Joyce finishes *Ulysses*. Sylvia Beach agrees to publish it in Paris.

1922   Shakespeare and Company, Sylvia Beach's press, publishes *Ulysses* in Paris on February 2, Joyce's birthday. Nora takes children to Galway for a visit, over Joyce's protests, and their train is fired upon by Irish Civil War combatants.

1923   Joyce begins *Finnegans Wake*, known until its publication as *Work in Progress*.

1924   Part of the *Work* appears in the Paris magazine, *transatlantic review*.

1926   Pirated edition of *Ulysses* (incomplete) serialized in New York by *Two Worlds Monthly.*

1927   Shakespeare and Company publish *Pomes Penyeach.* Parts of *Work* published in Eugene Jolas's *transition,* in Paris.

1928   Joyce publishes parts of *Work* in New York to protect the copyright.

1929   Joyce assists at a French translation of *Ulysses,* which appears in February. Lucia Joyce operated on unsuccessfully to remove a squint. She gives up her sporadic career as a dancer; her mental stability seems precarious. To his father's delight, Giorgio Joyce makes his debut as a singer, with some success.

1930   At Joyce's instigation, Herbert Gorman begins a biography of Joyce. Joyce supervises a French translation of *Anna Livia Plurabelle,* part of the *Work,* by Samuel Beckett and friends, which appears in the *Nouvelle Revue Française* in 1931. Marriage of son Giorgio to Helen Kastor Fleischman.

1931   Joyce marries Nora Barnacle at a registry office in London. Death of Joyce's father.

1932   Helen Joyce gives birth to a son, Stephen James, on February 15; Giorgio and Helen have the baby secretly baptized so as not to upset Joyce. Joyce writes "Ecce Puer," a poem celebrating the birth of his grandson. Daughter Lucia suffers first mental breakdown; she is diagnosed as hebephrenic (a form of schizophrenia). Bennett Cerf of Random House contracts for the American publication of *Ulysses.*

1933   On December 6, Judge John M. Woolsey admits *Ulysses* into the United States, declaring that "whilst in many places the effect . . . on the reader undoubtedly is somewhat emetic, nowhere does it tend to be an aphrodisiac." Lucia Joyce hospitalized, as she will often be until her permanent hospitalization.

1934   Random House publishes *Ulysses.*

1934   Publishes *Collected Poems* in New York, and *A Chaucer A.B.C.* with illuminations by Lucia.

1939   *Finnegans Wake* published in London and New York. War declared. The Joyces move to Vichy, France, to be near Lucia's mental hospital.

1940   Herbert Gorman's authorized biography of Joyce appears. After the fall of France, the Joyces manage once more to get to Zürich.

1941   Joyce dies following surgery on a perforated ulcer on January 13. He is buried in Fluntern Cemetery, in Zürich, with no religious ceremony, at Nora's request.

1951   Nora Barnacle Joyce dies in Zürich on April 10. She is buried in Flutern as well, but not next to Joyce, since that space has been taken. In 1966, the two bodies are reburied together.

Contributors

HAROLD BLOOM, Sterling Professor of the Humanities at Yale University, is the author of *The Anxiety of Influence, Poetry and Repression* and many other volumes of literary criticism. His forthcoming study, *Freud: Transference and Authority*, attempts a full-scale reading of all Freud's major writings. A MacArthur Prize Fellow, he is the general editor of *The Chelsea House Library of Literary Criticism*.

SAMUEL BECKETT is perhaps the most eminent of living Western authors. His major works include *Endgame, Waiting for Godot*, the trilogy *Molloy, Malone Dies* and *The Unnameable*. His superb first novel, *Murphy*, remains unsurpassed.

S. L. GOLDBERG was Professor of English at the University of Melbourne. He has published two books on Joyce.

RICHARD ELLMANN is Goldsmiths Professor of English at Oxford University. Besides his many works on Yeats and Joyce, he is preparing the definitive biography of Oscar Wilde.

ANTHONY BURGESS, celebrated novelist and man of letters, is the author of *A Clockwork Orange, Honey for the Bears, Nothing Like the Sun* and the *Enderby* saga.

HARRY LEVIN is Irving Babbitt Professor Emeritus of Comparative Literature at Harvard University. His books include studies of Shakespeare, Marlowe and Joyce.

HUGH KENNER is Professor of English at Johns Hopkins University and the author of *The Pound Era* and studies of Wyndham Lewis, T. S. Eliot and Joyce.

JENNIFER SCHIFFER LEVINE teaches English at the University of Toronto.

DEBORAH POPE is Assistant Professor of English at Duke University.

MARY T. REYNOLDS is Lecturer in English at Yale University and the author of *Joyce and Dante: The Shaping Imagination*.

KAREN LAWRENCE is Professor of English at the University of Utah, and the author of *The Odyssey of Style in "Ulysses."*

ROLAND McHUGH, an entomologist living in Dublin, is author of *The Sigla of "Finnegans Wake"* and *Annotations to "Finnegans Wake."*

FREDRIC JAMESON is Professor of Humanities at Duke University. His books include *The Prison House of Language* and *The Political Unconscious.*

RAYMOND WILLIAMS is Professor of Drama at Cambridge University. His books include *The Country and the City* and *Keywords.*

GABRIELE SCHWAB teaches literature at the University of Konstanz.

FRANCIS WARNER is Tutor in English Literature at St. Peter's College, Oxford. A poet and playwright, his works include *Poetry of Francis Warner* and the play *Moving Reflections.*

WILLIAM EMPSON was Professor of English at Sheffield University. His books include *Collected Poems, Some Versions of Pastoral* and *The Structure of Complex Words.*

DANIEL FERRER is Maître-Assistant in English at the University of Besançon. He has published articles on Joyce, Virginia Woolf, William Faulkner and literary theory.

PATRICK PARRINDER is Reader in English at the University of Reading.

Bibliography

Adams, Robert M. *Surface and Symbol: The Consistency of James Joyce's "Ulysses."* New York: Oxford University Press, 1962.

———. *James Joyce: Common Sense and Beyond.* New York: Random House, 1967.

Attridge, Derek, and Ferrer, Daniel, eds. *Post-Structuralist Joyce: Essays from the French.* Cambridge: Cambridge University Press, 1984.

Beck, Warren. *Joyce's "Dubliners": Substance, Vision, and Art.* Durham, N.C.: Duke University Press, 1969.

Beckett, Samuel et al. *James Joyce/Finnegans Wake: A Symposium: Our Exagimination Round His Factification for Incamination of Work in Progress.* Norfolk, Conn.: New Directions, 1962.

Benstock, Bernard. *James Joyce.* New York: Frederick Ungar Publishing Co., 1985.

———, ed. *The Seventh of Joyce.* Bloomington: Indiana University Press, 1982.

Ben-Zvi, Linda. "Exiles, The Great God Brown, and the Specter of Nietzsche." *Modern Drama* 3, vol. 24 (1981):251–69.

Blamires, Harry. *The Bloomsday Book: A Guide Through Joyce's "Ulysses."* London: Methuen & Co., Ltd., 1966.

Bowen, Zack. *Musical Allusions in the Works of James Joyce.* Albany: State University of New York Press, 1974.

Budgen, Frank. *James Joyce and the Making of "Ulysses."* Bloomington: Indiana University Press, 1960.

Burgess, Anthony. *Re Joyce.* New York: W. W. Norton & Co., Inc., 1965.

———. *Joysprick: An Introduction to the Language of James Joyce.* London: André Deutsch Ltd., 1973.

Bushrui, Suheil Badi, and Benstock, Bernard, eds. *James Joyce: An International Perspective.* Totowa, N.J.: Barnes & Noble Books, 1982.

Chace, William R., ed. *Joyce: A Collection of Critical Essays.* Englewood Cliffs, N.J.: Prentice-Hall, Inc., 1974.

Deming, Robert H. *A Bibliography of James Joyce Studies.* Lawrence, Kan.: University of Kansas Libraries, 1964.

———, ed. *James Joyce: The Critical Heritage.* 2 vols. New York: Barnes & Noble, 1970.

Ellmann, Richard. *Eminent Domain: Yeats Among Wilde, Joyce, Pound, Eliot, and Auden.* New York: Oxford University Press, 1967.

———. *Ulysses on the Liffey.* New York: Oxford University Press, 1972.

———. *The Consciousness of Joyce.* New York: Oxford University Press, 1977.

———. *James Joyce.* New York: Oxford University Press, 1982.

Foshay, Toby. "The Desire of Writing and the Writing of Desire in *Ulysses.*" *The Dalhousie Review* 1, vol. 62 (1982):87–104.

Foster, Thomas C. "Joyce's Grammar of Experience." *Eire-Ireland* 4, vol. 17 (1982):19–40.

Frank, Joseph. *The Widening Gyre: Crisis and Mastery in Modern Literature.* Bloomington: Indiana University Press, 1963.

French, Marilyn. *The Book as World: James Joyce's "Ulysses."* Cambridge, Mass.: Harvard University Press, 1976.

Friedman, Melvin. *Stream of Consciousness: A Study in Literary Method.* New Haven: Yale University Press, 1956.

Garrett, Peter K. *Scene and Symbol from George Eliot to James Joyce: Studies in Changing Fictional Mode.* New Haven: Yale University Press, 1969.

Gifford, Don, and Seidman, Robert J. *Notes for Joyce: An Annotation of James Joyce's "Ulysses."* New York: E. P. Dutton Co., Inc., 1974.

Gilbert, Stuart. *James Joyce's "Ulysses": A Study.* New York: Vintage Books, 1952.

Givens, Seon, ed. *James Joyce: Two Decades of Criticism.* New York: Vanguard Press, 1948.

Goldberg, S. L. *The Classical Temper: A Study of James Joyce's "Ulysses."* London: Chatto & Windus, 1961.

Goldman, Arnold. *The Joyce Paradox: Form and Freedom in his Fiction.* London: Routledge & Kegan Paul, 1966.

Gottfried, Roy K. *The Art of Joyce's Syntax in "Ulysses."* Athens: University of Georgia Press, 1980.

Gould, Eric. "Condemned to Speak Excessively: Mythic Form in James Joyce's *Ulysses.*" *Sub-Stance* 22 (1979):67–83.

Groden, Michael. *Ulysses in Progress.* Princeton: Princeton University Press, 1977.

Gross, John. *James Joyce.* New York: The Viking Press, 1970.

Handwerk, Gary. "What Really Goes Before the Fall?: Narrative Dynamics in *Finnegans Wake* III.4." *James Joyce Quarterly* 3, vol. 20 (1983):307–24.

Hanley, Miles L. *A Word Index to James Joyce's "Ulysses."* Madison: University of Wisconsin Press, 1951.

Hart, Clive. *James Joyce's "Ulysses."* Sydney: Sydney University Press, 1968.

Hart, Clive, and Hayman, David, eds. *James Joyce's "Ulysses."* Berkeley: University of California Press, 1974.

Hayman, David. *"Ulysses": The Mechanics of Meaning.* Englewood Cliffs, N.J.: Prentice-Hall, Inc., 1970.

Iser, Wolfgang. *The Implied Reader: Patterns of Communication in Prose Fiction from Bunyan to Beckett.* Baltimore: The Johns Hopkins University Press, 1974.

James Joyce Quarterly, 1963–.

James Joyce Review, 1957–59.

Kenner, Hugh. *Dublin's Joyce.* Boston: Beacon Press, 1962.

———. *Joyce's Voices.* Berkeley: University of California Press, 1978.

———. *Ulysses.* London: George Allen & Unwin Ltd., 1980.

Kimpel, Ben D. "The Voices of *Ulysses.*" *Style* 9 (Summer 1975):283–319.

Lawrence, Karen. *The Odyssey of Style in "Ulysses."* Princeton: Princeton University Press, 1981.

Levin, Harry. *James Joyce: A Critical Introduction.* New York: New Directions, 1960.

Litz, A. Walton. *The Art of James Joyce: Method and Design in "Ulysses" and "Finnegans Wake."* New York: Oxford University Press, 1964.

————. *James Joyce.* Boston: Twayne Publishers, 1972.

Maddox, James H., Jr. *Joyce's "Ulysses" and the Assault Upon Character.* New Brunswick, N.J.: Rutgers University Press, 1978.

MacCabe, Colin, ed. *James Joyce: New Perspectives.* Bloomington: Indiana University Press, 1982.

McBride, Margaret. "Watchwords in *Ulysses*: The Stylistics of Suppression." *The Journal of English and Germanic Philology* 77 (July 1978):356–66.

McCormack, W. J., and Stead, Alistair, eds. *James Joyce and Modern Literature.* London: Routledge & Kegan Paul, 1982.

McHugh, Roland. *The "Finnegans Wake" Experience.* Berkeley and Los Angeles: University of California Press, 1981.

Modern Fiction Studies 15 (Spring 1969). James Joyce issue.

Murillo, L. A. *The Cyclical Night: Irony in James Joyce and Jorge Luis Borges.* Cambridge, Mass.: Harvard University Press, 1968.

Norris, Margot. *The Decentered Universe of "Finnegans Wake": A Structuralist Analysis.* Baltimore: The Johns Hopkins University Press, 1974.

Oates, Joyce Carol. "Jocoserious Joyce." *Critical Inquiry* 2 (Summer 1976):677–88.

Parrinder, Patrick. *James Joyce.* Cambridge: Cambridge University Press, 1984.

Peake, C. H. *James Joyce: The Citizen and the Artist.* Stanford: Stanford University Press, 1977.

Peterson, Richard F.; Cohn, Alan M.; and Epstein, Edmund L., eds. *Work in Progress: Joyce Centenary Essays.* Carbondale and Edwardsville: Southern Illinois University Press, 1983.

Prescott, Joseph. *Exploring James Joyce.* Carbondale: Southern Illinois University Press, 1964.

Reynolds, Mary T. *Joyce and Dante: The Shaping Imagination.* Princeton: Princeton University Press, 1981.

San Juan, Epifanio, Jr. *James Joyce and the Craft of Fiction: An Interpretation of "Dubliners."* Rutherford, N.J.: Fairleigh Dickinson University Press, 1972.

Schechner, Mark. *Joyce in Nighttown: A Psychoanalytic Inquiry into "Ulysses."* Berkeley: University of California Press, 1974.

Seidel, Michael. *Epic Geography: James Joyce's "Ulysses."* Princeton: Princeton University Press, 1976.

Senn, Fritz, ed. *New Light on Joyce from the Dublin Symposium.* Bloomington: University of Indiana Press, 1972.

Shurgot, Michael W. "Windows of Escape and the Death Wish in Man: Joyce's 'The Dead'." *Eire-Ireland* 4, vol. 17 (1982):58–71.

Staley, Thomas F., ed. *"Ulysses": Fifty Years.* Bloomington: University of Indiana Press, 1974.

Staley, Thomas F., and Benstock, Bernard, eds. *Approaches to Joyce's "Portrait": Ten Essays.* Pittsburgh: University of Pittsburgh Press, 1976.

————, eds. *Approaches to "Ulysses": Ten Essays.* Pittsburgh: University of Pittsburgh Press, 1970.

Steinberg, Erwin R. *The Stream of Consciousness and Beyond in "Ulysses."* Pittsburgh: University of Pittsburgh Press, 1973.

Thornton, Weldon. *Allusions in "Ulysses": A Line-by-Line Reference to Joyce's Complex Symbolism.* New York: Simon & Schuster, 1973.

A Wake Newslitter, 1962–.

Wilds, Nancy G. "Style and Auctorial Presence in *A Portrait of the Artist as a Young Man.*" *Style* 7 (Winter 1973):39–55.

Acknowledgments

"Dante. . .Bruno. Vico. . Joyce" by Samuel Beckett from *James Joyce/Finnegans Wake: A Symposium: Our Exagimination Round His Factification for Incamination of Work in Progress* by Samuel Beckett et al., copyright © 1929 by Sylvia Beach. Reprinted by permission.

"Homer and the Nightmare of History" by S. L. Goldberg from *The Classical Temper: A Study of James Joyce's "Ulysses"* by S. L. Goldberg, copyright © 1961 by S. L. Goldberg. Reprinted by permission.

"Bloom Unbound" by Richard Ellmann from *Ulysses on the Liffey* by Richard Ellmann, copyright © 1972 by Richard Ellmann. Reprinted by permission.

"The Dublin Sound" by Anthony Burgess from *Joysprick: An Introduction to the Language of James Joyce* by Anthony Burgess, copyright © 1973 by Anthony Burgess. Reprinted by permission.

"*Ulysses* in Manuscript" by Harry Levin from *Memories of the Moderns* by Harry Levin, copyright © 1975 by Harry Levin. Reprinted by permission.

"The Consciousness of Joyce" by Richard Ellmann from *The Consciousness of Joyce* by Richard Ellmann, copyright © 1977 by Richard Ellmann. Reprinted by permission.

"Joyce's Voices" by Hugh Kenner from *Joyce's Voices* by Hugh Kenner, copyright © 1978 by The Regents of the University of California. Reprinted by permission.

"Originality and Repetition in *Finnegans Wake* and *Ulysses*" by Jennifer Schiffer Levine from *PMLA* 1, vol. 94 (January 1979), copyright © 1979 by The Modern Language Association of America. Reprinted by permission.

"The Misprision of Vision: *A Portrait of the Artist as a Young Man*" by Deborah Pope from *James Joyce Quarterly* 3, vol. 17 (Spring 1980), copyright © 1980 by The University of Tulsa. Reprinted by permission.

"Paternal Figures and Paternity Themes" by Mary T. Reynolds from *Joyce and Dante* by Mary T. Reynolds, copyright © 1981 by Mary T. Reynolds. Reprinted by permission.

" 'Eumaeus': The Way of All Language" by Karen Lawrence from *The Odyssey of Style in "Ulysses"* by Karen Lawrence, copyright © 1981 by Princeton University Press. Reprinted by permission.

"The *Finnegans Wake* Experience: Samples" by Roland McHugh from *The Finnegans Wake Experience* by Roland McHugh, copyright © 1981 by The Regents of the University of California. Reprinted by permission.

"*Ulysses* in History" by Fredric Jameson from *James Joyce and Modern Literature* edited by W. J. McCormack and Alistair Stead, copyright © 1982 by Routledge and Kegan Paul. Reprinted by permission.

"*Exiles*" by Raymond Williams from *James Joyce: New Perspectives* edited by Colin MacCabe, copyright © 1982 by The Harvester Press. Reprinted by permission.

"Mollyloquy" by Gabriele Schwab from *The Seventh of Joyce* edited by Bernard Benstock, copyright © 1982 by Indiana University Press. Reprinted by permission.

"The Poetry of James Joyce" by Francis Warner from *James Joyce: An International Perspective (Irish Literary Studies 10)* edited by Suheil Badi Bushrui and Bernard Benstock, copyright © 1982 by Francis Warner. Reprinted by permission.

"*Ulysses*: Joyce's Intentions" by William Empson from *Using Biography* by William Empson, copyright © 1984 by the Estate of Sir William Empson. Reprinted by permission.

" 'Circe', Regret and Regression" by Daniel Ferrer, translated by Gilly Lehmann, from *Post-Structuralist Joyce: Essays from the French* edited by Derek Attridge and Daniel Ferrer, copyright © 1984 by Cambridge University Press. Reprinted by permission.

"*Dubliners*" by Patrick Parrinder from *James Joyce* by Patrick Parrinder, copyright © 1984 by Cambridge University Press. Reprinted by permission.

Index